ENCYCLOPEDIA OF
GARDEN
DESIGN

ENCYCLOPEDIA OF
GARDEN
DESIGN

FOG CITY PRESS

Published by Fog City Press
814 Montgomery Street
San Francisco, CA 94133 USA

Copyright © 2004 Weldon Owen Pty Ltd

Chief Executive Officer: John Owen
President: Terry Newell
Publisher: Lynn Humphries
Managing Editor: Janine Flew
Design Manager: Helen Perks
Editorial Coordinator: Jennifer Losco
Production Manager: Caroline Webber
Production Coordinator: Monique Layt
Sales Manager: Emily Jahn
Vice President International Sales: Stuart Laurence

Project Editor: Ariana Klepac
Project Designers: Stephen Smedley, Tonto Design; Kylie Mulquin
Consultant: Jennifer Stackhouse
Contributors: Bonnie Lee Appleton, Peter Brownlee, C. Colston Burrell,
Denise Greig, Lewis and Nancy Hill, Erin Hynes, Cheryl Long, Susan McClure,
Patricia S. Michalak, Judy Moore, Nancy J. Ondra, Cass Peterson, Rob Proctor,
Lee Reich, Alfred F. Scheider, Jennifer Stackhouse, Elizabeth Stell

ISBN 978 1 87701 993 7

Color reproduction by Bright Arts Graphics (S) Pte Ltd
Printed by Kyodo Nation Printing Services Co., Ltd.
Printed in Thailand

A Weldon Owen Production

Contents

How to Use This Book

The *Encyclopedia of Garden Design* will be an inspiration to gardeners, both novice and experienced. It is packed with information about creating a garden, choosing a style, assessing and preparing your site, selecting plants, working with color and gardening for the senses. The book is easy to read and each page has colorful photographs showing how beautiful your garden can be. Section Nine of the book is an encyclopedia of plants to help you choose and identify them.

Each section is color-coded for easy reference.

Section heading

The beginning of a new chapter within one of the nine major sections in the book. The line above is the section heading.

Detailed garden plans are provided, with clear instructions and labels, for a variety of styles to suit every site and taste.

Colorful photographs give you guidance and inspiration in planning and designing your garden.

---

164 GARDEN FEATURES

Juniperus 'Sky Rocket'

Roso 'Iceberg'

Alyssum maritima

Buxus 'Suffruticosa'

Gardenia augusta

FORMAL GARDEN WITH WATER FEATURE The above garden
Behind this wall are hidden a shed (which contains the e
conifers. From the fountain, the water overflows and run
underground pipes. In the pool is a containerized water
hedge. White roses feature in the beds and are surroun
area. However, this plan shows only the curved step

---

50 COLOR BY DESIGN

Pink

Pink flowers are charming, sprightly and vibrant. They are the flowers of romance, from the early-flowering cherry blossom and pink camellias to the later-flowering roses, peonies, lilies and nerines.

Pink Effects

Pink can be a warm color, when in the coral and salmon-pink range, or cool, when in the mauve-pink range. The cool pinks, that are linked with blue pigments, blend well with blue and purple flowers. When mixing different pinks, make sure you keep the tones closely related and use appropriate foliage to either heighten the effect, or to calm things down.

The glossy-leaved acanthus is a good foil to all pink flowers and bears its own flower spikes of pinkish purple. Peonies of all types have interesting divided leaves and are complemented by nearby plantings of green-leaved hostas.

Gray foliage, such as that of lamb's ears *Stachys byzantina*, anthemis or lavender cotton, will highlight most pink flowers particularly well.

You can deepen mauve-pink flowers with purplish sage, feathery purple fennel or the plum-colored leaves of *Weigela florida* 'Follis Purpureis'.

Hydrangeas that turn pink in alkaline soil, as well as frothy pink rhododendrons, are both excellent for brightening up partly shady areas of the garden.

An Enchanted Garden

An all-pink garden walk has an almost fairy-tale charm. Be adventurous with pink and grow old-fashioned roses extravagantly over arches and to curtain

TOP LEFT: Lilies add height and color to any flower bed or border. Combine them with mounding annuals, perennials or groundcovers that can shade the soil and keep the bulbs cool.
TOP RIGHT: Besides being a great garden accent, globe amaranth Gomphrena globosa dries well for dried flower arrangements.
LEFT: Old-fashioned pink roses are perfect for a romantic, scented, pink-themed garden.

walls. Create a flowering backdrop of pink clematis, which can also be grown over large shrubs or small trees.

Include many of the irresistible pink flowers, such as camellias, peonies, carnations and pinks themselves (*Dianthus* spp.), but also include some perennials with architectural qualities. Show-stoppers such as the giant of the lily family *Eremurus robustus*, with its tall flower-spikes of pale pink, and clumps of pink Russell lupins are great accent plants for full sun. Other plants of distinction are the striking, plumelike, summer flowers of pink astilbes and *Sedum spectabile* with

Favorite Pink Flowers

Argyranthemum 'Bridesmaid',
'Mary Wootton', 'Vancouver'
(Marguerite daisy)
Amaryllis belladonna
(belladonna lily)
Armeria maritima (sea pink)
Camellia spp. (camellias)
Clematis 'Nelly Moser'
Daphne cneorum (rose daphne)
Deutzia x elegantissima 'Rosealind'
(deutzia)
Dianthus spp. (carnations and pinks)
Dierama pulcherrimum (fairy's
fishing rod)
Kalmia latifolia (mountain laurel)
Kolkwitzia amabilis 'Pink Cloud'
(beauty bush)
Lavatera 'Barnsley' (mallow)
Magnolia liliiflora (lily magnolia)
Nerine bowdenii (pink spider lily)
Paeonia lactiflora (peony)
Prunus x subhirtella (flowering
cherry)
Rhododendron spp.
(rhododendrons and azaleas)
Rosa spp. (roses)
Syringa meyeri 'Superba'
(lilac)
Weigela florida (old-
fashioned weigela)

Mountain laurel

ABOVE: Astilbes are perfect for moist shade gardens. Their airy plumes add grace and motion to the garden. Plant masses beside a pond where their blooms can be reflected in the water.

scalloped leaves and dusky pink flowers. Good background bedding plants include pink cosmos, poppies and the spider flower *Cleome hassleriana*. The showy pink turtlehead *Chelone obliqua* and some of the alliums are good for late summer, while pink cultivars of dahlia and *Aster novi-belgii* will carry their late summer flowers well into autumn.

In the Shade

Pink flowers will brighten up a shady spot beneath deciduous trees and here you could add a few treasures such as the delightful *Cyclamen hederifolium*, with its heavily marbled, ivy-like leaves and sometimes scented, autumn flowers in shades of rose pink. The autumn crocus *Colchicum autumnale* also has flowers in shades of pink. The highly desirable pink trout lily *Erythronium revolutum*, with strongly mottled leaves and lilac-pink early summer flowers, multiplies easily when planted in partial shade around shrubs and trees.

ABOVE: Use fast-growing, butterfly-like cosmos Cosmos bipinnatus to fill the spaces left by early-blooming annuals and perennials.

WATER FEATURES 165

water plants. Koi, also popular in ponds, need sophisticated filters to keep their water clean and healthy.

If you have created a good pond ecosystem, your fish colony may expand at a dizzying rate. If not, and you want to introduce more fish, do so a few at a time to make sure everything is working well.

To add new fish, float the unopened bag they came in on the surface of your pond to equalize water temperatures. Let the bag sit in the water for an hour or so before opening it slowly, letting the water mix and your new fish gradually to swim out into their new home.

You can feed the fish with commercial goldfish food, but do not over-feed.

A Container Water Garden

A small water garden adds a special sparkle to any collection of container plants. As a bonus, the open water will attract birds, insects, frogs and toads. You can use any large container—an old bathtub or sink, a half barrel or glazed pot (properly sealed), or a special plastic tub sold complete with a filter and small fountain.

Most garden centers and some chain stores now stock a selection of small (and not so small) water garden kits, fountains and the plants to put in them. These kits are available in a range of styles.

This garden is separated from the swimming pool by a wall.

Set the container on your patio or deck, or sink it into the ground for a natural pool effect. A filter usually isn't necessary for a small water garden if you include a few oxygenating plants, such as *Elodea canadensis*, to help keep the water clear.

Swimming Pools in the Landscape

Unless you have a very large garden, it will be difficult to make any swimming pool look relatively unobtrusive or "natural" in your landscape. Choosing dark waterline tiles instead of the usual electric blue pool interiors can make a pool seem more like a natural pond. While a pool can be made to fade into the landscape, it is far easier to keep the pool at the center of your landscape plan.

Moss pink

In many localities, there are regulations governing swimming pool fencing, so you should check on these.

Swimming pool landscaping is all too often something of an afterthought. You need to consider such things as types of plants, potential maintenance, sunlight patterns and shading from trees before you start planting. You should also consider your lifestyle and activity level. If you really want a garden around the pool, you need to recognize that plants will always shed leaves and bark, and this means more maintenance.

Avoid plants with thorns and prickles and trees with invasive root systems. Make sure runoff water from flower beds does not drain into the pool and consider using gravel (rather than bark) to mulch beds close to the pool. Do not plant anything that will actually grow over the perimeter of the pool and, wherever possible, use groundcovers and grasses as alternatives to larger plants.

Most plants will tolerate occasional splashes of properly maintained pool water. However, heavily chlorinated water will take its toll over time and can raise the soil salt content. Periodic flooding and flushing with regular tap water avoids salt build-up. Use container plants or raised beds with retaining walls to protect plants from chlorinated or otherwise chemically rich pool water.

You might like to play up the essentially formal shape of most swimming pools with complementary plantings. Low-growing plants, groundcovers and lawns can ring the pool site in a neat border, leading to taller plantings further from the pool itself.

Many gardeners like tropical plants near swimming pools. While many of these plants are not hardy everywhere, you can still use a few for their strong effects. If you live in a cool-climate Zone, you may be able to grow these plants in containers, protecting them indoors through the winter.

Water features can incorporate sculptural elements, such as this water spout head.

Iris pseudacorus
Iris pseudacorus
Gardenia augusta

…is a garden with a screening wall at the far end on which is mounted a water fountain. …connection for the fountain) and a utility area. Also behind this screening wall is a row of … rill (small stream) that ends in a small pool, and this is carried back to the fountain via … either side of the rill are two symmetrical, formal beds. These are edged with a low, clipped … groundcover of sweet Alice. At the near end of the garden is a pergola-covered entertaining … paved area. On either side of the curved step is a row of fragrant gardenias.

Chapter heading indicates the subject being discussed within a main section.

Helpful illustrations feature throughout the book.

Detailed information about all aspects of garden design, from planning to plant selection.

Photograph of individual plants, showing what they look like when grown in the right conditions.

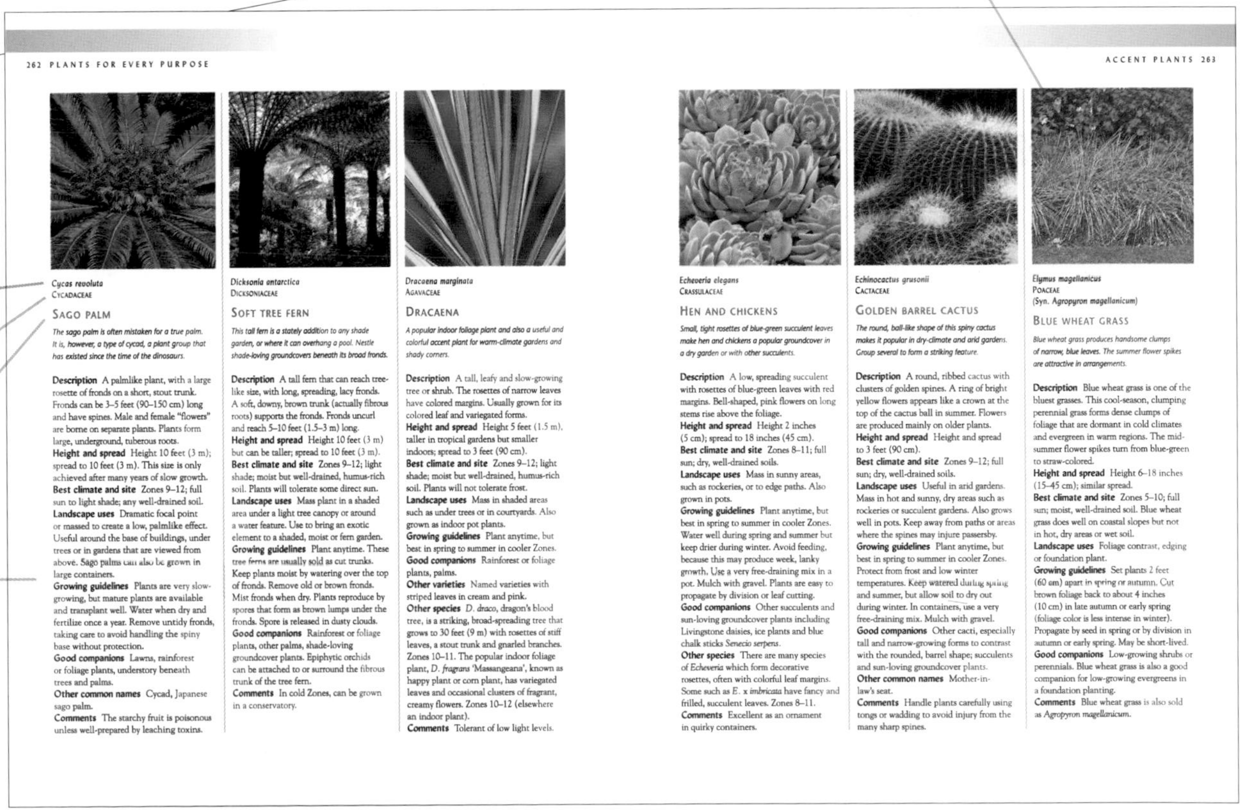
262 PLANTS FOR EVERY PURPOSE

Cycas revoluta
CYCADACEAE
SAGO PALM

The sago palm is often mistaken for a true palm. It is, however, a type of cycad, a plant group that has existed since the time of the dinosaurs.

Description A palmlike plant, with a large rosette of fronds on a short, stout trunk. Fronds can be 3–5 feet (90–150 cm) long and have spines. Male and female "flowers" are borne on separate plants. Plants form large, underground, tuberous roots.
Height and spread Height 10 feet (3 m); spread to 10 feet (3 m). This size is only achieved after many years of slow growth.
Best climate and site Zones 9–12; full sun to light shade; any well-drained soil.
Landscape uses Dramatic focal point or massed to create a low, palmlike effect. Useful around the base of buildings, under trees or in gardens that are viewed from above. Sago palms can also be grown in large containers.
Growing guidelines Plants are very slow-growing, but mature plants are available and transplant well. Water when dry and fertilize once a year. Remove untidy fronds, taking care to avoid handling the spiny base without protection.
Good companions Lawns, rainforest or foliage plants, understory beneath trees and palms.
Other common names Cycad, Japanese sago palm.
Comments The starchy fruit is poisonous unless well-prepared by leaching toxins.

Dicksonia antarctica
DICKSONIACEAE
SOFT TREE FERN

This tall fern is a stately addition to any shade garden, or where it can overhang a pool. Nestle shade-loving groundcovers beneath its broad fronds.

Description A tall fern that can reach tree-like size, with long, spreading, lacy fronds. A soft, downy, brown trunk (actually fibrous roots) supports the fronds. Fronds uncurl and reach 5–10 feet (1.5–3 m) long.
Height and spread Height 10 feet (3 m) but can be taller; spread to 10 feet (3 m).
Best climate and site Zones 9–12; light shade; moist but well-drained, humus-rich soil. Plants will tolerate some direct sun.
Landscape uses Mass plant in a shaded area under a light tree canopy or around a water feature. Use to bring an exotic element to a shaded, moist or fern garden.
Growing guidelines Plant anytime. These tree ferns are usually sold as cut trunks. Keep plants moist by watering over the top of fronds. Remove old or brown fronds. Mist fronds when dry. Plants reproduce by spores that form as brown lumps under the fronds. Spore is released in dusty clouds.
Good companions Rainforest or foliage plants, other palms, shade-loving groundcover plants. Epiphytic orchids can be attached to or surround the fibrous trunk of the tree fern.
Comments In cold Zones, can be grown in a conservatory.

Dracaena marginata
AGAVACEAE
DRACAENA

A popular indoor foliage plant and also a useful and colorful accent plant for warm-climate gardens and shady corners.

Description A tall, leafy and slow-growing tree or shrub. The rosettes of narrow leaves have colored margins. Usually grown for its colored leaf and variegated forms.
Height and spread Height 5 feet (1.5 m), taller in tropical gardens but smaller indoors; spread to 3 feet (90 cm).
Best climate and site Zones 9–12; light shade; moist but well-drained, humus-rich soil. Plants will not tolerate frost.
Landscape uses Mass in shaded areas such as under trees or in courtyards. Also grown as indoor pot plants.
Growing guidelines Plant anytime, but best in spring to summer in cooler Zones.
Good companions Rainforest or foliage plants, palms.
Other varieties Named varieties with striped leaves in cream and pink.
Other species *D. draco*, dragon's blood tree, is a striking, broad-spreading tree that grows to 30 feet (9 m) with rosettes of stiff leaves, a stout trunk and gnarled branches. Zones 10–11. The popular indoor foliage plant, *D. fragrans* 'Massangeana', known as happy plant or corn plant, has variegated leaves and occasional clusters of fragrant, creamy flowers. Zones 10–12 (elsewhere an indoor plant).
Comments Tolerant of low light levels.

ACCENT PLANTS 263

Echeveria elegans
CRASSULACEAE
HEN AND CHICKENS

Small, tight rosettes of blue-green succulent leaves make hen and chickens a popular groundcover in a dry garden or with other succulents.

Description A low, spreading succulent with rosettes of blue-green leaves with red margins. Bell-shaped, pink flowers on long stems rise above the foliage.
Height and spread Height 2 inches (5 cm); spread to 18 inches (45 cm).
Best climate and site Zones 8–11; full sun; dry, well-drained soils.
Landscape uses Mass in sunny areas, such as rockeries, or to edge paths. Also grown in pots.
Growing guidelines Plant anytime, but best in spring to summer in cooler Zones. Water well during spring and summer but keep drier during winter. Avoid feeding, because this may produce week, lanky growth. Use a very free-draining mix in a pot. Mulch with gravel. Plants are easy to propagate by division or leaf cutting.
Good companions Other succulents and sun-loving groundcover plants including Livingstone daisies, ice plants and blue chalk sticks *Senecio serpens*.
Other species There are many species of *Echeveria* which form decorative rosettes, often with colorful leaf margins. Some such as *E. x imbricata* have fancy and frilled, succulent leaves. Zones 8–11.
Comments Excellent as an ornament in quirky containers.

Echinocactus grusonii
CACTACEAE
GOLDEN BARREL CACTUS

The round, ball-like shape of this spiny cactus makes it popular in dry-climate and arid gardens. Group several to form a striking feature.

Description A round, ribbed cactus with clusters of golden spines. A ring of bright yellow flowers appears like a crown at the top of the cactus ball in summer. Flowers are produced mainly on older plants.
Height and spread Height and spread to 3 feet (90 cm).
Best climate and site Zones 9–12; full sun; dry, well-drained soils.
Landscape uses Useful in arid gardens. Mass in hot and sunny, dry areas such as rockeries or succulent gardens. Also grows well in pots. Keep away from paths or areas where the spines may injure passersby.
Growing guidelines Plant anytime, but best in spring to summer in cooler Zones. Protect from frost and low winter temperatures. Keep watered during spring and summer, but allow soil to dry out during winter. In containers, use a very free-draining mix. Mulch with gravel.
Good companions Other cacti, especially tall and narrow-growing forms to contrast with the rounded, barrel shape; succulents and sun-loving groundcover plants.
Other common names Mother-in-law's seat.
Comments Handle plants carefully using tongs or wadding to avoid injury from the many sharp spines.

Elymus magellanicus
POACEAE
(Syn. *Agropyron magellanicum*)
BLUE WHEAT GRASS

Blue wheat grass produces handsome clumps of narrow, blue leaves. The summer flower spikes are attractive in arrangements.

Description Blue wheat grass is one of the bluest grasses. This cool-season, clumping perennial grass forms dense clumps of foliage that are dormant in cold climates and evergreen in warm regions. The mid-summer flower spikes turn from blue-green to straw-colored.
Height and spread Height 6–18 inches (15–45 cm); similar spread.
Best climate and site Zones 5–10; full sun; moist, well-drained soil. Blue wheat grass does well on coastal slopes but not in hot, dry areas or wet soil.
Landscape uses Foliage contrast, edging or foundation plant.
Growing guidelines Set plants 2 feet (60 cm) apart in spring or autumn. Cut brown foliage back to about 4 inches (10 cm) in late autumn or early spring (foliage color is less intense in winter). Propagate by seed in spring or by division in autumn or early spring. May be short-lived.
Good companions Low-growing shrubs or perennials. Blue wheat grass is also a good companion for low-growing evergreens in a foundation planting.
Comments Blue wheat grass is also sold as *Agropyron magellanicum*.

Botanical name

Family name

Common name

Information about plant

A Well-planned Garden

A garden that looks good and works well comes with good planning. Whether it is a garden that is being started from scratch, or an existing garden that is being remodelled, it is important to understand both the site and the needs of those using the garden. The key to a well-planned landscape is to work out what you want from your garden, but also to identify the features that make your little bit of the world special.

Creating a Garden

In classical times, enclosed parks, or "pleasance gardens," existed in Egypt and Persia, from where they spread to conquered lands around the Mediterranean. We know the ancient Greeks appreciated the value of shaded walks, because there is evidence of plane trees planted in a market place in Athens in the fifth century BC. Later, aristocratic Roman landowners adopted many of the elements used in these vast parks, as they began to surround themselves with decorative villa gardens, as opposed to purely kitchen, or "hortus," gardens.

We can learn many relevant garden design lessons from the classical Romans. They perfected the interplay between indoors and the garden, and used focal or pivotal points as well as symmetrical layouts. In addition, they considered the relevance of the surrounding landscape, not only regarding orientation for climate control, but to take advantage of views.

These initial concepts have been adapted by garden designers ever since. Later Italians built on these elements and adapted them to varying geographical and climatic conditions, as did the French and English. You'll find these basic principles are as relevant today as they ever were, regardless of the prevailing fashion.

Ongoing Trends

Gardens were once designed for gracious living by prosperous families and a great gulf existed between the owners and the gardeners who worked in them. Gradually, with the advent of technological advances that transformed society from rural to urban, this changed as a middle class sought to emulate the classical garden estates—be it on a much reduced scale. Over the years, a declining work force has combined with many other factors to result in the smaller, suburban gardens of cities around the world.

Parallel to the above changes taking place, an increasing array of plants from exotic lands began to be introduced and hybridized to meet the ever-growing demand by gardening aficionados. People were fascinated by all these wonderful new plants and were keen to have as many of them as possible.

Then, early in the twentieth century, people began to question the way in which we gardened. In California, for instance, designers decided to take full advantage of the sunny climate by adding swimming pools. This was a logical extension of earlier, sparsely planted gardens in that area which took full regard of the climate. These gardens had their

This traditional, formal garden has clipped, low box hedges. These are an attractive garden feature, but take into account that the clipping and shaping will be quite time-consuming.

origins in the gardens of Spain, where cloistered walkways opened out to sunny courtyards. This trend was quickly incorporated into the garden design of countries all over the world—even in areas where the climate made such design elements as swimming pools undesirable, it became popular to link the indoors to a pleasant, sunny or shady outdoor area. In addition to this idea, which today we take for granted, designers in both The Netherlands and North America began to address problems of ubanization by turning to more natural landscapes in both form and plant material.

If you are lucky enough to have a view from your garden, ensure that you use trees to frame, rather than obscure the view.

Designing Your Own Garden

Above all, creating a garden is about creating pictures—building up an overall pleasing design, combining plants and architectural features, or what's usually referred to as the "hard" landscaping features. You'll often hear terms such as "framework" or "bare bones" used when people discuss a particular garden. When this framework is in harmony, in terms of both proportion and scale, a garden is said to have good "bones." Make this your first aim, then the garden will be ready for you to complete the picture with creative plantings to complemet whatever type or style of garden you choose to create. On the following pages we walk you through all the joys of creating a garden that you'll never want to leave. But first, the most important issue is to work out what you envisage your garden to be.

Defining Your Goals

Regardless of whether yours is a bare-earth garden or one that's ripe for renewal, this is grand vision time. Write down everything you ever wanted from a garden, no matter how grand—don't worry, it's only on paper; there's time for costing and other practicalities later.

Do you envisage a swimming pool, barbecue and large outdoor paved living area, or a secluded nook for intimate

The plain brickwork color around the swimming pool area provides a great foil for the surrounding lush plantings of lawn, groundcovers, trees and shrubs in a red, white and blue color scheme.

dining under the stars? Do you want an arbor to witness the ever-changing seasons? Is the approach to the house of major importance to you? Have you a hobby, such as bonsai, that needs specialized requirements?

Ask housemates, or family members—whatever their age—what they see as the most important needs of the yard. Perhaps a teenager needs space to tinker with her bicycle. Or maybe a budding ecologist wants a pond to lure frogs into the garden. Do you want to accommodate an energy-saving, traditional clothes-drying area in a full-sun portion of the garden, or are you prepared to sacrifice this, if space is limited, for a scented rose garden?

This is the time to think of the big picture—what you see as your goal. Long term you may envissage a water feature that can be overlooked from the patio; short term, though, a sandpit may be what's needed for youngsters.

A garden is an ongoing creation, evolving as our needs change and the garden matures, but the main structure of a garden begins with a list.

When you have completed your appraisal, you'll find there are a number

of ways in which all these ingredients of a garden can be blended together. If you haven't already begun, start a scrapbook by slotting in photos and illustrations from magazines. Make a note of page numbers in your gardening books that show styles that have caught your eye. This record, together with the guidelines given below, will soon give you a true feeling for the type of garden you are inclined toward.

While your children are young, you might want to set aside part of the garden as a play area.

Grow fragrant lavender along paths where you can enjoy the delightful scent as you pass by.

This typical classically inspired garden features clipped hedges in a circular pattern, surrounding a formal stone ornament.

What Kind of Garden Suits You?

There are many different styles of garden, all equally beautiful. However, there are probably one or two styles that you find particularly appealing. Some designs, especially the classical or formal designs, have their roots in ancient times.

The Classical Garden

Classical or formal gardens rely very much on a framework, which is especially evident in winter, when many of the plants have shed their leaves and the layout and structural features of the garden are highlighted.

Formal landscaping uses straight lines, sharp angles, and symmetry both in form and plantings, with usually a limited number of different plants. These structured kinds of landscapes often include features such as clipped hedges or brick walls to define different spaces in the garden.

Plants such as the traditional small-leafed, deep green, common box *Buxus sempervirens* and English yew *Taxus baccata*, which are amenable to clipping,

are classical favorites. However, you'll find, too, there's an ever-increasing number of flowering plants, such as sasanqua camellias *Camellia sasanqua* and star jasmine *Trachelospermum jasminoides*, that can be used in imaginative espalier designs against walls.

Containers also play an important role in this type of garden—usually, even numbers are used to emphasize the symmetry. Occasionally a single potted specimen is used as a focal point at the end of a vista or to emphasize an axial point.

When you install a water feature, it needs to be in keeping with these guidelines—purely classical, geometric shapes are best.

Formal designs tend to have an ordered, yet restful feel. But they may not be as restful for the gardener, since you'll need to clip, stake and weed frequently to keep the plants looking perfect.

Variations on a Theme

Within the definition of formal or classical, you'll find variations to consider before you start to dig. The accepted definition of a formal garden has changed from one suitable for a grand estate and

based on classical principles, and now encompasses a new, minimalistic look. This is ideal for those who have a busy lifestyle and just a small garden or plot. This style of garden relies on very symmetrical or even lines with a modern, almost abstract interpretation. This may seem totally different from formal designs of the past, but it is not. Think of the gardens of the Moors, where courtyards have a cooling water feature and not much else to distract from this focal point.

These minimalist gardens are ideally suited to easy-care plantings of slow-growing plants, such as agave *Agave attenuata* and the popular, burgundy-bronze aeonium *Aeonium arboreum* 'Schwartzkopf', which not only look magnificent against bagged, masonry walls of urban court-yards, but relish in the reflected heat that such walls generate.

Cottage Gardens

The opposite to the highly structured, formal garden is the rampant cottage garden, where plants blend haphazardly with each other. This type of garden is well suited to full sun and a gardener who likes to potter in an informal mix of

A spectacular blossoming tree is reflected in the lake at one of the world's most famous designed gardens—the Impressionist artist Claude Monet's garden in Giverny, France.

The amount of sun and shade your garden receives varies throughout the day. You should consider these factors as you plan your plantings. The above garden is designed to flourish in partial shade.

sweet-scented, old-fashioned roses and annuals, such as tall hollyhocks *Alcea rosea*, cleome *Cleome hasslerana* and cosmos *Cosmos bipinnatus*, as well as the more permanent perennial mainstays, such as euphorbia species, agapanthus *Agapanthus praecox* and torch lily *Kniphofia uvaria*.

Romantic Gardens

As shrubs and trees mature, they cast shade and their roots invade areas of the garden once devoted to a harlequin quilt of colorful plants. As a result, the older garden often achieves a sense of over-gown, enchanted romance and seclusion that newly planted gardens rarely have. Some people see these gardens as wild and overrun and immediately pick up their chainsaw. Others, more astute, see these gardens as ripe for renewal and build on this atmosphere by creating winding paths, rustic seats, arbors or grottoes cut from the tangle of roses or bushes.

Gardening with Nature

The converse of the sophisticated garden is the naturalistic approach—gardening with nature. With an ever-increasing awareness of the importance of protecting the environment, you could choose to create a native or wild garden. In 1597, Francis Bacon defined a garden as "an escape from nature" because at that time nature still posed a threat to humans. Today, however, we appreciate that the reverse is true. By choosing a naturalistic type of garden to surround your house, you may well find that native species use less water, return humus to the soil in the form of falling leaves, or cover the ground with a carpet of wildflowers to encourage native insects and small animals to return to your area.

The Sustainable, Organic Garden

If you are interested in sustainable, natural gardening, you might consider the idea of a permaculture garden, which incorporates principles and design ideas from bygone eras. Here, practicality rules. Plants are positioned to benefit one another, harmful chemicals are not used, and small farmyard animals are kept in a natural environment. Gardeners enjoy using their plot of land to feed themselves and their family rather than using it for purely decorative purposes.

Whatever type of garden you choose, remember that a garden is your own private space. Enjoy it during the changing seasons, watch it evolve over the years as the plants mature, and continue to embrace the joy of creating your own garden.

Plan for multi-season color in the garden. After these prunus trees finish blooming in spring, the stunning, mass underplanting of red valerian *Centranthus ruber* will take over.

Planning by Design

Building or buying a house can be a stressful process, but once you've finally moved in, take time out to be enthralled—this is the time to dream about and plan the garden. Although it's tempting to give in to the impulse to start working on the garden right away, it will be easier in the long run if you hold off a while and plan first.

Reclaiming and Renewing

In a garden that was established by previous owners, it's best not to be in a hurry. When you live with an inherited garden for a little while, you may find that unexpected treasures—such as spring or autumn bulbs, herbaceous perennials, or scented plants from a bygone period—are waiting to be discovered. These may be hiding in the weedy undergrowth or camouflaged by shrubs that need pruning.

Look up into the taller shrubs and trees. At first glance, it may seem that a judicious cut to a particular branch will allow more light and air into that section. But a second look may reveal that the branch shields your garden from the view of neighbors or protects fragile plants

A self-sown flower garden keeps weeds and work down. Here, a wide variety of trees, shrubs and flowers grow together in a happy disorder, and lawn size is kept to a minimum.

when it is in full summer leaf. Or you may find that the lower branches of an overgrown shrub could be underpruned to open up an inviting vista. It is definitely not quite yet the time to slash and burn— rather, to ponder and consider.

Recycle Materials

Established gardens often also provide a wealth of paving materials. Sometimes, these may have been lifted by the root systems of established shrubs and trees and will need to be dug up and re-laid. Others may look mossy and unkempt, but a sweep with a stiff broom may reveal a well-laid path under the moss. Likewise, retaining walls or garden edging may be hidden. If you work methodically and gently, you won't need to keep buying new materials, and you will also be in the enviable position of renewing the heritage of your garden.

Getting Started

There is work to be done. Take photos, take measurements, check the compass points to position your summer outdoor seating areas. Assess the health of any established trees or shrubs in the garden. Maybe all that's required is a cleanup. But if on closer inspection there seems to be trouble lurking in the form of broken branches, or old or rotten wood, don't

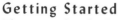

Architectural features, such as patios and benches, add year-round interest to a shady site.

Creating Space by Design

The confining visual effect of a long, rectangular yard can be lessened by adding strong cross-features. A vine-covered trellis, hedge or outdoor setting placed across the site rather than lengthwise will provide a more expansive feel.

In a small garden, think outside the square when paving. By laying bricks or pavers in concentric circles or a spiral pattern, you'll make a greater visual impact.

Strong colors in the foreground graduating to pale colors beyond gives a sense of distance and depth. Or you can gain a similar effect by planting large, bold-leaved plants, receding to smaller-leaved ones.

hesitate to call in an arborist. Many a tree can be saved by these tree experts, who will know your local government regulations as to what can and can't be done to the surrounding greenery. A call to an arborist to rectify a perceived problem can have you sitting in the shade years before a tree that you plant yourself will be of sufficient size to form a shady canopy.

Creating Anew

When you're starting from scratch, you can design a garden by making a detailed plan on paper (for more information on this, see "Putting It on Paper" on page 26). But as a preliminary step, walk around the garden and carefully appraise it from all angles. Take a notebook and jot down what comes to mind, because thoughts can easily vanish once you're inside again. It's also important to go inside and stand at all the windows. While you view the garden from this position, you'll get a feel for where best to position eye-catching features or focal points.

A row of topiarized shrubs creates a kind of wall along the edge of a garden terrace.

Focal points are not only well-placed plants, though. They can be all manner of things, from classical urns, a sculpture you've fashioned from "junk", or a summer house built at an axial point. Their placement can give a marvelous illusion of length as well as adding extra interest to a garden whatever its size. Indeed, the French perfected this idea with trompe l'oeil, or painted murals, which can be reflected by placing a mirror in front of the design to make even the smallest garden appear quite grand.

Costing Your Goals

Once you've decided on the type of garden that appeals to you, work out whether it suits your site. On relatively level ground, your options are wide open. Any style of garden can be created on such a site. But if the site slopes, it may be very costly to cut and fill areas to form the classical terraces and long avenues of a formal garden, for example. A meadow or cottage garden might be a more practical choice for such

a site. Assess what is economically feasible if you are planning to have construction work done. Or, if you're doing the work yourself, make sure you have enough time.

It's good practice to itemize your goals in terms of needs and wants. Obviously the interaction between the garden and indoors has to be at the top of the list, but what comes next?

Set Priorities

As you install your new landscape, it's wise to start on the "hard" elements—such as walls, fences and paths—first. This is also a good time to plan and install garden lighting and an automatic irrigation system if you need one.

Once the permanent elements are in place, then you can start planting. Whenever possible, begin with slow-growers, such as trees and shrubs, then the groundcovers. You may choose to plant a few beds of annuals for quick color during the first few seasons, or to just wait for the permanent plantings to develop.

Plan for Easy-care Features

You can plan for low maintenance right from the start. After all, who wants to spend all their spare time shaping hedges, trimming edges or weeding? These are tasks that can, with a little forethought, be discarded. Unsightly views can be blocked with vine-covered fences or trellises, while groundcovers can make weeding a thing of the past.

Also, make sure that you leave plenty of room within the garden design so you can move wheelbarrows and lawn mowers in and out without running over and damaging plants. A wide path allows for plants to tumble over its edges and give a softening effect while reducing the irksome task of clipping the edges.

Pick Plants Carefully

As you choose plants for your new landscape, be sure to consider their growth rates and mature sizes. You can find this information on nursery labels or in this book (see "Plants for Every Purpose," starting on page 176). If you allow plants

Lavender cotton *Santolina chamaecyparissus* and other low-growers, in a muted color scheme of mauve and gray-green, are a low-maintenance solution for this sloping site in a warm-climate garden.

enough room to develop without crowding the house or each other, you'll have healthier plants that harbor fewer pests and diseases and also need minimal pruning. If you're using foundation plantings, look for dwarf species and cultivars that won't grow up and block your view in a few years.

Scale, too, is important. As house blocks become smaller and therefore closer together, your neighbors will remain friendly if your trees don't overwhelm their yard as well as yours. Some trees you may like to consider are *Acer palmatum* cultivars, bauhinia, camellias, *Cornus* species or crape myrtle *Lagerstroemia indica*. The last two species in particular are great-value trees for your garden plan, since they

Consider steps and paving to be part of the overall garden design, rather than just being purely functional elements. These stone steps are perfect in the cottage garden setting.

have both flower and foliage interest at various seasons, thereby giving you bonus points every year.

Remember, the plants will look small when you put them in, but they'll grow surprisingly fast. If they look too awkward and sparse, plant annuals or perennials to fill in until the shrubs spread a bit.

Priority Planning Checklist

- Placement of outdoor living areas with regard to aspect and privacy as well as interaction with indoors
- The need for utility areas, such as a garden shed for storage of furniture/tools/toys, greenhouse, clothes drying area
- Underground irrigation/lighting installations
- Underground drainage requirements
- Taking existing trees and shrubs into account
- Placement of compost and garbage bins for ease of use

Mix and Match

If you're like most gardeners, you'll probably delight in impulse buying at the local nursery or garden center. Or, if you're lucky, friends and neighbors may inundate you with plants. Suddenly you may find that your garden is becoming a hodgepodge—not at all what you had intended when you began. This is perhaps the most difficult lesson a gardener has to learn—to plant by design. Unless you like the cottage garden look, which can become a little chaotic by the end of the season, it pays to consider such things as combining shape, texture, height of individual plants within a grouping, as well as pleasing foliage and flower color combinations. Plenty of helpful hints are given later in this book, but first things first.

Tried and True Trio

Before you turn to the pages on the principles of design, there are three vital ingredients you'll need to consider when creating a well-planned garden—climate, aspect (sun and shade) and soil. If you do not take these into consideration in initial planning, all the know-how in the world won't allow plants—the mainstay of a garden—to triumph.

Climate affects plants just as it affects our well-being. It has a huge bearing, not only on how we use our gardens, but also on what we plant in them. With plants, it's not just whether they prefer full sun

With careful planning, you can have a colorful garden during the winter months. Pictured here are the bare branches of golden willow *Salix alba* var. *vitellina* surrounded by rhododendrons and heath.

or shade, but the actual year-round temperatures, which have been classified into Zones. You'll find these listed in "Plants for Every Purpose," starting on page 176, to help you in your decision making. You may be charmed by a pretty cherry tree, for example, but if you live in a hot, humid Zone you may never see it bloom. Conversely, a heat-loving croton *Codiaeum variegatum*, common allamanda *Allamanda cathartica* or chilean jasmine *Mandevilla suaveolens* will not perform in a cold-climate garden.

Aspect is another factor that affects plants. Some plants get by with a little morning sun, others relish a full-sun position, while others insist on full shade— a bonus to gardeners once

Use complementary colors, such as purple and yellow combinations, for eye-catching effect in your garden design.

your trees mature, since shade-loving plants are usually easy-care, too.

Another critical factor is soil. Again, there are many plants that grow successfully almost anywhere, but there are also many that require soil of either an acidic or alkaline nature. The importance of soil pH, texture and structure is discussed in detail in the following section. You need to keep in mind, too, that there's also moisture tied up in soil—too much moisture, and plants such as succulents, cacti and many that have silver or gray leaves will not thank you. When excessive soil moisture is a problem, turn it into an asset by creating a feature. Make a statement by choosing such plants as water iris *Iris pseudacorus*, the magnificent ornamental rhubarb *Gunnera manicata* or papyrus *Cyperus papyrus*, which actually thrive in moist, boggy soils.

Working toward a practical solution that also creates beauty is really the essence of designing a garden that will continue to delight well after the initial work has been completed.

Garden Design Basics

Before even lifting up a spade to start planting, it is essential to assess what a site has to offer. Clever design and planting ideas can turn negative features into positive attributes, and show what is there to best advantage. Think beyond the square to get the most from any views, the garden's aspect and its interesting and appealing features. Also take into account the reality of the climate, the lay of the land and seasonal patterns of sun and shade.

Design Considerations

Every garden is unique. This simple fact means that books that prescribe how to landscape your garden miss the point—no single set of rules or plans suits all types of houses, sites and people.

Each garden design should reflect the uniqueness of the site and the people who live there. To be truly effective, it will take into account the style and lines of the home and its structural materials and colors, and the way the garden will be used by the homeowners—as well as a host of other factors unique to that site.

In starting with either a new or existing home landscape project, the planning procedure is the same. It includes an orderly and logical inventory of the conditions and facts about the building and site, plus the needs of the homeowners.

Thinking in Time

Designing a new garden from scratch, or a major makeover of an existing garden, can seem such a daunting task that it is hard to know where to begin. One useful first step is to consider time. While garden design plans usually concentrate on the physical dimensions of your site, the climate, soil type and other important factors, time is frequently overlooked.

Assess how long you will be living with the garden and how much of your own time, effort and money you want, or are able, to invest in the garden. Is it something you want to create, nurture and pass on to future generations? Or are you unlikely to be there in 10, or even 5, years' time? Circumstances can obviously change, but setting your design plans within a workable, realistic timetable will help you to choose which tasks have priority and what can wait or cannot be realistically attempted in the timeframe you have.

Time also can affect some of the existing elements in your garden that you may want to keep. Do you have an old summer house or pergola that you would like to renovate? Are there traces of paths

The vivid colors of autumn foliage take on jewel-like splendor when lit by the sun.

that might be useful to restore? Mature trees can add stature, even grandeur, to your new design but they may also need rejuvenating by judicious pruning and other care. They may also be reaching the end of their lives; if so, you will need to consider replacement and removal.

Getting to Know Your Site

The most useful and efficient landscape design is one that overcomes or modifies the restrictions of the site (such as ugly views or treeless, flat ground), or enhances and protects the good points (such as views, mature trees or running water).

Successful landscape design deals with
- Climate
- Soil type
- Topography
- House, garage and other buildings
- Paths, steps, wall, fences, drives, patios, courtyards, decks
- Swimming pool, other outdoor activity areas
- Plant materials
- Neighborhood.

Formal gardens, with their sculptural shapes and symmetrical designs, look superb year-round, even when covered with frost and snow.

Getting to know each of these factors, and the ways in which they interact, helps us to understand what the site has to offer and its potential for a home landscaping project.

One way to get an objective view of your site is simply by photographing it in its existing state. The camera will capture things that your eye, subconsciously, fails to see—especially if you have been living in that location for some time. Take shots of the hidden corners in the garden, and also photograph the garden at different times of day, so you can see how the sun will move across your new landscape.

Consider Sun and Shade

The principal rooms of a house should benefit from winter sun and summer breeze. Sunlight and shade can be controlled by the location of buildings, fences and trees. You should also consider possible shade from trees and houses on neighboring sites.

Plan future shade from tree plantings with great care, in order to keep sunny areas for the garden, and summer shade for the house and terrace.

Deciduous trees (those that shed their leaves during winter) shade the house in summer and admit the sun in winter. Place trees at the corners rather than the sides of the house where they will accent the house and not block views and air circulation from windows. Remember that too many trees tend to shut out sunlight and air.

Consider Maintenance

When creating your garden design, you need to decide on maintenance standards. For the person who enjoys puttering about the yard, your landscape design may be elaborate. However, a low-maintenance plan is the goal of most homeowners. In general, the simpler the site, the less there is to maintain. You can achieve a low-maintenance garden by adopting one or more of the following:

- Keep the design simple.
- Pave heavy traffic areas.
- Use fences or walls instead of clipped formal hedges for screening.
- Keep lawn areas small—or eliminate them completely.
- Use groundcovers in place of lawns.
- Design raised flower beds for easy access and to help control weeds.
- Keep flower beds small—or eliminate them completely.
- Use flowering and autumn-coloring trees and shrubs for color.
- Choose plants that require little or no care.
- Use native plants and plants you know do well in your area.
- Use mulches for weed and moisture control wherever possible.
- Install an underground irrigation system in areas of low rainfall.

Choosing the Style

Unless you have a very large site that is divided into distinct areas or "garden rooms," it is difficult to accommodate several different garden styles attractively and effectively in one garden.

Begin by thinking about whether you want your garden to have a formal

An informal, blue-themed, summer garden with winding path, featuring delphinium, campanula, petunia, salvia and clematis.

appearance (straight lines, near-perfect symmetry, usually high maintenance) or something more informal (gentle curves, less rigid or no balance, less maintenance).

As well as formal and informal garden styles, there are many others—cottage gardens, woodland gardens, meadow gardens, native gardens, courtyard gardens, Mediterranean gardens, Japanese gardens, tropical gardens and more.

Although you don't have to be too rigorous about striving for a consistent style, you'll want to avoid the confused look of a jumble of unrelated elements.

Formal garden

Informal garden

The Art of Design

When you first approach design theory, the subject can seem very abstract with a lot of familiar words used in new and special ways that may not be altogether clear to you. Some designers can also be rather inflexible about what is "good" design (mostly theirs) and "bad" design (everyone else's). However, if you apply basic design principles to what you know about your landscape site, and about gardening in general, you can make up your own mind about what "good" design means for you.

The Principles and Elements of Design

A lot about garden design is personal opinion. A landscape design could follow all the theoretical design principles but still not feel right to you. Nevertheless, the following principles can provide a kind of map for your new landscaping scheme and enable you to understand why some gardens attract you while others don't.

The basic principles of any design are:
- Balance
- Contrast
- Emphasis
- Harmony
- Movement
- Unity
- Variety.

You may see other terms used, but these will generally be another way of saying exactly the same thing. These largely theoretical principles are used

to guide our use of the more concrete basic elements of design, which are:
- Color
- Line
- Shape
- Size
- Space
- Texture.

If you consider these different factors, and use plant material and structures in ways consistent with these ideas, you will achieve design unity.

Other Aspects of Design

You might also like to consider a few further aspects of design, such as light and shade, scent, sound, time, climate and season, motion, transition and layering.

Light and shade are forever changing, altering the appearance of your landscape and affecting the health and growth of plants in varying degrees.

Scent and sound appeal to some of our most fundamental senses. The gurgling of a waterfall, flowers or seeds that attract birds, and scented plants all enhance your experience and enjoyment of the landscape you have created.

ABOVE: The sounds made by running water are delightful, and can muffle outside noise, too.
LEFT: This arrangement of shrubs leads the viewer's eye to the mountain scene in the distance.

Time, climate and season Over time, and the course of the year, many plants grow and appear very different. Plants change shape and color with age, so many landscapes need revision about every 5 to 7 years as plants grow. The needs of those who use the garden may also change, making other alterations necessary.

Motion Though your landscape should provide a variety of views and features, landscapes are often designed for only one view, so you should consider what you will see as you walk through the garden.

Transition is gradual change. Transition in color can be illustrated by the sequence of colors in the spectrum— red to orange to yellow to green to blue. Transition can also be achieved by the arrangement of objects with varying textures, forms or sizes in a logical, sequential order.

Layering reflects the fact that, in nature, plants grow at different levels. Using taller shrubs in the background, with lower shrubs in front, creates a pleasing, naturalistic effect. Layering plants at different heights is also an effective way to add depth and character to a garden bed or border.

Developing a Landscape Plan

By now you probably have lots of thoughts and ideas swirling around in your head. You know where and how big you want your garden to be and which plants you

The Principles of Design

Balance is equilibrium or equality of visual impact. Used carefully, perfect symmetry can be a powerfully appealing design technique, but, when overused, balance can become stiff and boring. The natural landscape is not governed by symmetry. In nature, something more subtle is at work; something artists and designers refer to as "asymmetrical balance." For example, a group of small, bright plants can be used to balance the appearance of a single, large shrub of muted coloring. Another form of balance is radial balance. This is used in formal gardens where design elements radiate from a single point.

Contrast is the degree of difference in the treatment of different elements. The bold contrast of a curve with a straight line, for example, can be interesting if you design it carefully. To achieve contrast with plant material, mix fine foliage with something coarser, rounded outlines with vertical or spiky plants, blend flower and foliage color, or use the vivid contrast of white flowers against red or yellow.

Emphasis (or accent or focalization) is the quality of a design which requires the viewer to focus on a given point or points. Without emphasis, a design may be dull, static or uninteresting but, when skillfully organized, various parts of the landscape lead the eye toward a focal point. This may be a garden accessory, a splendid view, a plant specimen, a pond or some other special feature. Dramatic emphasis can also be obtained by using contrasting textures, colors or forms, or even by highlighting a plant arrangement with garden lights.

Harmony is a pleasing relationship between all the different parts of a design, and can be achieved by following a strong theme, or using similar design elements. Repetition in the landscape is not the same as monotony. Repetition is more subtle; for example, in the use of curves in the landscape design. Curves may begin in bed lines in the front garden, continue along the sides of the house and the side yard, and be picked up once more in the back garden.

Movement (or rhythm) refers to the direction in which the viewer's eye moves naturally when studying a design. You can use different color schemes, line and form to create a sense of movement in landscape design, and this can help bring order to different design elements.

Unity is the bonding together of all elements by organization and balance. A sense of unity is the goal in virtually all landscape design and this is achieved when individually attractive components of the landscape mesh to form an equally attractive whole. This stems from the rhythm of natural landforms, a variety of plant types and buildings and human uses that are harmonious with their surroundings. The simplest landscapes are often the most attractive.

Variety is the quality of a composition that provides interest because of difference. This is a critical element in design since too little variety is monotonous, while too much is chaotic. It is best to strive for a balance between the two extremes.

Sweet peas

Don't forget to appeal to the sense of smell, and include swathes of fragrant flowers, such as roses.

want to grow. However, before you start digging up the lawn or heading off to the garden center, it's smart to take a few minutes to jot down your ideas on paper.

There are great benefits in having an organized system in developing a landscape design. One useful method of proceeding is to:

1. Develop a site plan.
2. Conduct a site analysis.
3. Match needs and desires to the site.
4. Locate activity areas.
5. Design activity areas.
6. Select and position plants.

Putting It on Paper

It is difficult to visualize some aspects of design without drawing them to scale on paper. You, or the designer, should think with drawings or sketches. That way, you can make the mistakes on paper and not on the landscape site.

The site plan is built on:

- Accurate building positioning
- Accurate site and building dimensions, including window and door placement
- Accurate positioning of existing driveways, walks and other access points
- Precise indications of sloping ground or changing ground levels.

You will need an accurate plan of your site in order to draw up an accurate design plan. You may already have a survey plan—especially if you have purchased your home recently—and surveyed site plans may be included in your property documents.

It is useful to have a rough outline to work to, so sketch out the garden first and then write the distance down as shown. For more detailed areas, draw an "inset"-style sketch on another page, making sure that you have the measurements that will enable you to relate this to the whole later.

Start from the house and measure the boundaries. Measure the diagonal distances as well as the length of each fence, because these will enable you to pinpoint corners

and, later, major features. Measure the position of windows and doors in the house so that, later, you have an accurate idea of how house and garden relate. Mark and measure electricity and other utility connections so you do not plant anything big in the ground that may interfere with such services. Measure and mark trees, driveways, swimming pools, steps and stairs—anything that is large or likely to stay put in your scheme needs to be noted.

The Elements of Design

Color gives the physical landscape a life, definition and interest, and many books have been written about using color in the design process. You can approach color as a technician, using the color wheel to create harmonious combinations, or you can use your own eyes and emotions to guide you in creating the look and feel you want. (For more information about using color, see Color by Design, starting on page 34.)

Line is related to eye movement or flow. In the overall landscape, line can be seen in the arrangement of garden beds, in paths, steps and structures of all kinds, as well as the ways in which these elements fit or flow together. Line is also created vertically by changes in plant height and the height of tree and shrub canopies. Straight lines tend to give the impression of solidity and stability, and can direct the observer's eye to a point faster than curved lines do. Curved or free-flowing lines are smooth and graceful. They create a relaxing, natural feeling, gently lead observers to focal points, and seem to invite visitors to wander through the garden.

Shape (or form) in plants includes upright, oval, columnar, spreading, broad spreading, weeping, prostrate and so on. Structures also have shape and should be considered when designing the area around them. A variety of different shapes makes a garden interesting, but too much diversity can create visual confusion.

Size is related to proportion or scale. You can create a pleasing relationship among the three dimensions of length, breadth and depth or height. Size refers to definite measurements, while scale describes the size relationship between adjacent objects. The size of plantings and buildings compared to the human scale must be considered. Most size or scale problems are due to skimpiness—such as beds and paths that are too narrow, or plantings that are too small and tentative. If in any doubt, err on the side of boldness and generosity. Knowing the eventual or mature size of a plant is critical when locating it near a building.

Space, and the ways in which it is handled, is as much a part of garden design as dealing with the plants and structures that will form a physical presence (mass) in your garden. Space is air or volume defined by physical elements. Landscape spaces are defined by earth, trees, plants, buildings and other structures.

Texture is the surface quality of an object that can be seen or felt. Important landscape surfaces include buildings, walks and steps, patios and other structures; mulches, soil and exposed rock and water; and plant materials—lawns, groundcovers, trees, shrubs and all manner of plants.

Amaryllis

garden will have just the right blend of colors, heights and textures and you'll know exactly what you need to buy. (Of course, you don't have to go to the trouble of drawing up an accurate site plan. Your plan may simply be the outline of the bed with scrawled notes as to roughly where the plants will go.)

Draw rough outlines on your base plan to show where each plant or type of plant will go. Check heights to make sure you don't have tall plants blocking short ones, unless the short plants bloom before the tall plants fill out.

If you have room, allow space for three or five plants of each type—odd numbers of grouped plants tend to look best together—and a few different plants in large masses can have a more dramatic effect than many single plants.

Garden Zones

One idea that can be useful is to divide your site into zones—even very small gardens can usually accommodate at least three zones, such as:

- A public area, which everyone sees from the street
- A service area, where you put the clothesline, woodpile, storage sheds and anything else that may be unsightly but necessary
- A private area, which includes entertaining and recreation areas.

Larger gardens may include spaces for different garden rooms according to your interests.

The Advantages of Making a Plan

Sketching garden designs allows you to try out many different ideas, however unrealistic, without the hassle of physically digging up and moving existing plants.

If you invest the time in drawing up a formal scale plan, you can make sure the

ABOVE: This contemporary design shows how striking even a small garden space can look.
RIGHT: An effective design for a small courtyard, with brick paving, fountain and foliage plants.

Assessing and Preparing Your Site

It is sometimes hard to convince new gardeners of the need for patience. They are so eager to begin buying plants and planting them that nothing can stop them. More experienced gardeners, however, know that such bursts of enthusiasm can lead to badly planned, even chaotic landscapes that do not work and may be doomed to failure. A much better approach is to find out precisely what will grow in your new garden. To do this, you will need to understand the conditions in which your new plants will have to grow.

Climate

Climate is the way temperature, moisture and wind interact in a particular region to produce weather. Before making your garden plan and selecting the plants, you should consider the normal weather patterns of your climate.

All plants have a certain range of temperatures and moisture levels in which they grow best. If you know what your garden has to offer, you can look for plants that are adapted to those conditions and be fairly confident that they will grow well with a minimum of fuss on your part.

The typically lush, dense growth of ferns, evergreen shrubs and trees suits a temperate to tropical climate.

Microclimate

Another influence on your garden's temperature is its microclimate—the specific, localized conditions. For instance, the microclimate beneath a large, old oak tree is significantly cooler (as well as much shadier) than a sunny patch of ground on the other side of the same garden. Sunken areas can collect water that has drained from higher parts of the garden, allowing you to grow moisture-loving perennials, such as astilbes and primroses, without extra watering.

Prevailing Winds

As you spend time in your garden, observe which direction the wind usually comes from. Strong winds may quickly dry out plants and erode bare soil. When it's cold, winds can draw water out of exposed plant tops and roots faster than it can be replaced, leading to damage or death.

Wind can, however, be an asset in very humid climates, where good air circulation becomes more important to prevent the development of plant diseases.

Over time, winds deform plants— think of sideways-growing trees in coastal areas. Sudden gales can snap branches and

stems and an unexpected cold wind may scorch tender new growth. Even gentle winds can scorch plants that naturally live in sheltered woodlands or humid regions.

Where winds are strong or frequent, protect your gardens by locating them on

Plants that have adapted to dry climates, such as cacti, are the perfect choice for the desert garden.

Snow-covered grasses and shrubs create a magical scene in a cold-climate, winter garden.

Sandy   Clay   Loamy

Main Soil Types

Clay soil
- Drains poorly
- Lumpy and sticky when very wet; rock-hard when dry
- Has few air spaces
- Warms slowly in spring
- Is heavy to cultivate
- With improved drainage, plants can grow well, as clay holds more nutrients than many other soils

Sandy soil
- Free-draining
- Gritty
- Warms up quickly in spring
- Easy to cultivate
- Dries out rapidly
- May lack nutrients, which are easily washed away

Chalky soil
- Free-draining
- Alkaline, with a pH of 7.5 or more
- Usually stony
- Often overlays chalk or limestone
- Some minerals, such as manganese and iron, become unavailable to plants, causing poor growth and yellowing of the leaves

Loamy soil
- Good structure
- Drains well
- Retains moisture
- Full of nutrients
- Easy to cultivate
- Warms up quickly in spring yet does not dry out in summer

Soil may look the same to you, but your plants can tell the difference. Understanding the properties of your soil helps you pick the best plants and give them the right growing conditions, resulting in thriving specimens, such as these lupines.

the sheltered side of walls, solid fences or hedges. You can limit wind damage by using stakes or canes to support plants. In exposed locations, evergreen hedges provide year-round shelter.

Moisture

Plants are dependent on water. They cannot absorb nutrients and maintain essential processes unless they receive adequate moisture. Rain is the best source of moisture during the growing season, but you will need to supplement this by irrigation or hand-watering if rains fail.

In some climates, snow contributes a great part of the annual water supply. Even though snow usually falls when most plants are dormant, it still contributes to the water reserves held in the soil below the surface.

Moisture Problems

Consistently inadequate moisture levels may cause irreparable damage to plants. An obvious sign is wilting foliage. Drought-sensitive plants grow slowly, become dormant, or die under dry conditions.

At the other extreme, too much water may flood the root system and prevent the plant from absorbing the oxygen and nutrients it requires. Plants susceptible to flooding may also wilt, drop their leaves, and die if the excess water is not quickly drained away.

Your plants will require more water under windy conditions, as wind draws away moisture released through pores faster than normal. Wind shelter is important for your more sensitive plants.

Soil

A good soil is the gardener's key to success, influencing the health and vigor of all your plants. Soil texture can have a great effect on the growth of your plants. Roots will spread easily in open, sandy soil, but water will drain away quickly, so your plants may need more frequent watering. In a dense, clay soil roots will not penetrate so readily or widely and the soil will tend to become waterlogged.

There are six main soil types: clay, sandy, silty, peaty, chalky and loamy. The ideal garden soil is a loam, composed of about 40 percent sand, 40 percent silt and 20 percent clay. The ideal soil also has a crumbly, granular structure that allows water to drain and oxygen and carbon

Groundcovers can act as a living mulch in ornamental plantings, protecting and cooling the soil.

soil-testing agencies will conduct tests on soil samples and provide you with a statement of the relative amounts of essential plant nutrients, namely nitrogen, phosphorus and potassium.

It is also helpful to know how acid or alkaline your soil is. If you have the soil tested, the results will include pH, which is the measure of acidity or alkalinity. Soil pH is important because it influences soil chemistry. Plants can absorb most nutrients from the soil when the soil pH is in the neutral range. Plants cannot absorb nitrogen and sulfur, for example, if the soil pH drops far below 5, while iron and magnesium are less available as the pH moves above 8.

Soil Depth

Soil depth also has an impact on root growth and affects what plants thrive on the site. If you can dig 2 feet (60 cm) without hitting a sheet of rock or a band of dense, tightly compacted soil, you'll be able to grow a wide range of perennials, vegetables, herbs and other shallow-rooted plants with little trouble. Larger plants, such as shrubs and trees, generally need soil that's at least 3 feet (90 cm) deep (above rock or a dense, compacted layer) for healthy, vigorous growth.

Soils that are shallower than 2 feet (60 cm) above some limiting layer are less hospitable to good root growth; they may be prone to waterlogging, and they often have fewer nutrients than deeper soils. If your soil is shallow, you may decide to build raised beds and fill them with a good-quality soil to provide more area for root growth.

Light and Shade

The intensity and duration of sunlight are critical factors in your garden. Without adequate sunlight, growth and flowering would cease. Light is your plants' energy source for making food. Most plants prefer sun, but others do

dioxide to move freely from the air into the pore spaces. A soil with a light, loose structure is said to be "friable." A good garden soil will also hold enough water for plant growth while letting excess water drain down to deeper layers.

Soil Nutrients

The availability of soil nutrients depends on the interaction of many factors, including soil texture, soil structure, moisture, organic matter and pH. Fine texture, loose structure, ample moisture, high organic matter content and near-neutral pH are all conditions that make the most nutrients available to your plants.

One of the most important plant nutrients is nitrogen. Keeping an adequate supply of nitrogen in the soil can be a challenge, since nitrogen is used up quickly by plants. Soil micro-organisms are also important for maintaining healthy soil. They help to decay organic matter and turn it into nutrients.

pH test

To check the nutrient content of your soil, it may be worthwhile to have a lab test your soil before you begin serious gardening. Even soils known to be highly fertile often lack specific nutrients or essential minerals. Private

better in shade. Light affects plants' size and form, as well as growth rate and yield.

In climates with frequent cloud cover, the light is said to be less intense than in areas with clear skies. Light intensity influences photosynthesis, which is the plant's internal mechanism for turning light energy into carbohydrates for food, with the help of carbon dioxide and water.

Many plants require full sun. This means they need an uninterrupted 8- to 12-hour period of unfiltered sunlight. Plants that require partial sun usually need about 5 to 6 hours of direct sunlight, with shade or filtered sun the rest of the day. Plants that require partial shade must have either filtered, indirect light, or some

Low-growing, spreading perennials are attractive and help to prevent erosion on gentle slopes.

A Hands-on Test for Soil Texture

This quick test will give you a good indication of whether your soil is sandy, silty or clay.

1. Start by taking a chunk of soil about the size of your thumb.
2. Moisten it enough so that you can roll it into a ball.
3. Flatten the ball between the pad of your thumb and the side of your bent index finger.
4. Push your thumb forward repeatedly, pressing the soil outward to form a ribbon. The longer the ribbon, the more clay is in the soil. A heavy clay will make a ribbon 1 inch (2.5 cm) long; a sandy soil might not make a ribbon at all.
5. To confirm your findings, put the ribbon in your palm and add enough water to make a runny paste.
6. Rub the index finger of your other hand around in the slop in your palm. If it feels gritty, the soil is sandy. If it's smooth, the soil is silty. If it's on the sticky side, you've got clay.

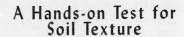

direct light for less than half of the day and full shade the rest of the time. Plants that require full shade need just that: a solid and dense shade away from light.

Topography

Topography refers to the lie of the land. While a level plot is the ideal gardening site, you will most likely be forced to make do with whatever nature and time have sculpted.

For low-maintenance landscaping, level sites are ideal. On a completely level property, topography need not be an issue as you lay out your landscape—but orientation will be. Orientation refers to the direction the garden faces, relative to prevailing winds and the shade cast by buildings and trees. If your garden is on an east-facing slope you will have a different microclimate than if you face west.

Hills and valleys create slight differences in climate, or "microclimates," within the average climate of your region. The air temperature in a valley tends to be cooler than that of the flat land above. Cool air is heavier than warm air and settles on lower ground. For this reason, gardens located at the bottom of valleys suffer the latest frosts in the spring and

the earliest frosts in autumn. The absence of wind in valleys exaggerates this susceptibility to frost.

Soil tends to be wetter in a valley, because water flows down from the surrounding slopes. The water forms puddles, leaving spongy wet areas of ground where drainage is poor. Fungal diseases are a greater threat in valleys, since air circulation is poor and moisture levels are high. You may, however, find the best topsoil at the bottom of a valley. As the water flows downhill, it erodes the slope above and carries loosened topsoil and organic matter down to the valley.

Hilltop gardeners will have greater protection from frost and plant diseases, because of increased air circulation. Excessive winds, however, can damage plants, increase soil erosion, and speed up the loss of moisture from the soil. Because water drains from high to low ground, soil at the top of a hill is drier than on the flat land below. On hilltops, soil is thinner due to erosion, and loses more nutrients due to excessive water drainage.

Drainage and Irrigation

Drainage problems can wreak havoc in your garden and around your home. Damage can include rotting timberwork, weakened foundations, structural damage

When clearing the rubble and weeds from a site, keep a look out for plants that are worth saving.

and poor (or lethal) growing conditions for landscape plantings.

All parts of your drainage system should lead away from the house, as should solid surface areas such as driveways, patios and paths. As a minimum, the slope should be not less than 1 inch (2.5 cm) per 10 feet (3 m) of linear length. A higher ratio may be necessary in heavy rainfall areas or areas where runoff can occur from surrounding terrain.

In some areas, irrigation systems are necessary to maintain your landscape during periods of extended drought or hot summer weather.

Irrigation spray heads should not be directed at fencing, structures or the home's exterior walls, especially if they are wood siding or brick. In flower beds, spray heads should be on risers appropriate for the size of the shrubs they are irrigating.

Surveys, Access and Utilities

Before you start planning your garden design, you should be absolutely certain of the boundaries of your land. Are all buildings and the fence located within the property lines? If you live in a regular house in a normal street it is likely that the boundaries of your garden are shared with one or more of your neighbors. You may need a survey of the property to determine this. With established homes, however, a previous survey should show this information.

Knowing the exact location of utility lines—water supply, sewerage, stormwater drains, telephone and data cables, gas and electricity lines—will help avoid disasters, especially if you plan some deep digging.

To avoid damaging utility lines while digging, have the utility companies locate all underground services—they will often do this free of charge. Above-ground power and telephone lines should also be noted, because you will want to avoid planting large trees near them.

Getting Permission

Planning rules and regulations vary from region to region. Before proceeding with any plans to build garden structures—such as walls, garages, gazebos or summer houses—it is best to telephone your local authority planning office to check if you need permission or not.

Tree preservation orders are just one example of local authorities having a policy that may affect you—if you want to remove an established tree, you may need to get permission to do so.

If you live in a conservation area, there may be restrictions on what landscaping and other changes you can make.

Clearing the Site

To give plants a good start in life, it's essential to provide well-prepared, fertile soil. The amount of soil preparation will depend on what you're faced with. You may have a garden that just needs lots of weeding, your completely new garden may have a layer of topsoil hiding piles of builders' rubble or you may want to remove areas of lawn to make space for

more plants. Time spent doing the ground work will repay you many times over in lower maintenance once your new garden is established.

The first step is to get rid of the rubbish and dig out tired old shrubs and weeds, especially perennial weeds such as thistle, nettle, bindweed, ground elder and couch grass. Remove all parts of the roots. (Keep

LEFT: A garden shown before clearing, during digging and replanting, and in its finished state.

an eye out for surviving plants. This is especially important in winter when they may be dormant below ground.)

Attacking weeds is one of the least appealing aspects of putting in a new garden, but doing a thorough job is the only way to prevent your new garden from being overrun with grass, weeds, suckers and re-growing shrubs before the end of the first season.

Adding an organic soil amendment, such as compost, well-rotted manure or peat moss, will loosen up clay soil and improve drainage. Most people want shade and ornamental trees, shrubs, a little lawn and a few perennials, all of which will benefit from soil amendments.

Improper soil preparation will cost much more through subsequent maintenance costs than the cost of originally doing it correctly. Know the existing soil condition in terms of how easily water percolates into it (that is, know how quickly or slowly it will absorb water before the water starts running off).

Never water past the runoff point. Often, water is applied to a surface until it runs off, and the assumption is made that the soil is sufficiently wet. However, the water may actually have soaked in only a few inches and the ground may be as dry as before by the middle of the next day.

The only sure way to tell is to occasionally dig down into the soil to check the level of the soil moisture. If the existing soil cannot take ¾–1 inch (2–2.5 cm) of water with 6–8 inches (15–20 cm) penetration at one application, soil conditioning will be necessary.

This may be no more than tilling and loosening the soil—compaction of the soil surface during building construction and daily use can hinder water absorption.

The effect of a soil's inability to easily take in water is the same as if the soil was

Bindweed

not being given enough water or was receiving shallow watering. Plants will not be able to maintain good, healthy growth and will be susceptible to stress during any dry period, and will need watering much more frequently than is usually necessary as a result. Also, good soil aeration is essential to good water percolation into the soil and its availability to plants.

Getting Help from Professionals

Try not to be over-optimistic as to what you can achieve. Do not attempt to remove large trees or carry out large-scale earthworks if you have limited or no experience in these tasks. Don't hesitate to get help from a professional.

The Internet allows you to compare specialists in your area. Other sources of information include local newspapers and magazines, nurseries and garden centers, agricultural extension services or your local landscape association.

In some cases a consultation fee may be charged, but this could save you thousands of dollars in repair costs as well as the risk of serious injury.

You may be able to manage minor structural work yourself, such as building paths.

Color by Design

*Garden color comes from plants—from their flowers,
fruit and foliage—and from other elements in the landscape,
such as paths, paving and even the house. Color can be used
with restraint or exuberance, and may vary from season to season.
In the following pages, we examine the major plant colors, then
look at how they can be combined successfully in a garden.*

Green

Few monochromatic garden schemes work as well as peaceful green. Green hues are the most restful to look at and are the kindest of all colors, visually.

The Italians were the first to make decorative use of the all-green garden, notably in the symmetrical, Renaissance gardens where carefully pruned trees were used to create formal avenues and vistas. Clipped hedges were used to link the villa and garden structurally and to divide the garden into compartments. Classical ornaments were some of the decorative features used in these gardens. Only a limited variety of plants was used and you can imitate this inventiveness on a smaller domestic scale.

Hedges can serve as screens, windbreaks or walls dividing the garden into separate areas. Low-growing, shrubby plants, such as dwarf box and small-leaved hollies, can be used to make tightly clipped, low hedging. Conifers are excellent for taller hedges.

Foliage for Food

In Medieval monastic gardens, plants were grown both for their beauty and for use as kitchen crops or herbs. The modern garden, with its often restricted space, is ideal for reviving this style of mixed gardening. Vegetables and herbs can be

as decorative as flowering plants, and look particularly effective when planted in an all-green garden. Here you can experiment with different plant combinations and really enjoy (as well as feed) yourself. With its dramatic sculptural shape, angelica *Angelica archangelica* is an herb to be used boldly. Group three or four together for height at the back of a border. Make use of the aromatic bay *Laurus nobilis* with its dense, rich green foliage that will

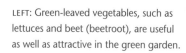
Grape vine

LEFT: Green-leaved vegetables, such as lettuces and beet (beetroot), are useful as well as attractive in the green garden.

tolerate close clipping—the bay has always been popular for hedges and topiary.

Leafy perennials, such as rhubarb, cabbages, spinach and chard, can be fitted in between existing plantings, while ornamental, edible foliage plants, such as fennel and lovage, can be used as features. Paths can be edged with small, frilly lettuces and parsley. Thyme has always been a popular foliage plant and taller types can be clipped as very dwarf hedges. Marjoram and oregano are good edging plants that will quickly spill over the edges of paths or fill bare patches between paving and steps. Perhaps tuck in some variegated mint for a change of texture. And don't forget a grape vine, which can be grown against a wall or over a pergola, creating a ceiling of greenery and dangling clusters of decorative green fruit.

ABOVE: Green herb garden with lemon balm *Melissa officinalis*, thyme *Thymus* spp. and rosemary *Rosmarinus officinalis*.
LEFT: Garden alcove with standard *Robinia pseudoacacia* 'Mop Top' and Monterey cypress *Cupressus macrocarpa* hedge.

Go Tropical

If a lush, green tropical look is for you, then an abundance of carefully chosen evergreens planted at different levels will help create the mood of a tropical garden—even in a temperate climate. Rich, verdant greens, bold foliage forms and textures become all-important, as do the movement and form of shadows. Retain any existing trees to provide structure to the landscape and shelter for any large-leaved plants that may become damaged by wind. Beneath them you can grow a colony of shade-loving ferns, clumps of aspidistras or bold masses of hostas. Both the windmill palm *Trachycarpus fortunei* and the Japanese banana *Musa basjoo* are reasonably hardy, tropical-looking specimens for warm, sheltered spots. Groves of *Cordyline australis* and tree ferns such as *Dicksonia antarctica* will definitely add a touch of class, especially when viewed against the light. For a pool-side setting, plant the arum lily *Zantedeschia aethiopica* 'Green Goddess' for its large, glossy leaves and exotic, green-tinged flowers. However, for enhancing a water feature it is hard to beat *Gunnera manicata* with its fabulous, giant leaves. Last but not least, don't forget to include some climbers.

BELOW: Subtropical green garden featuring cabbage trees *Cordyline* spp., bromeliads, mondo grass *Ophiopogon* spp. and crotons *Codiaeum* spp.

Foliage Plants for a Tropical Retreat

Adiantum pedatum (American maidenhair)
Cordyline australis (New Zealand cabbage tree)
Dicksonia antarctica (soft tree fern)
Dryopteris filix-mas (male fern)
Fatsia japonica (Japanese aralia)
Hosta spp. (hostas)
Matteuccia struthiopteris (ostrich fern)
Musa basjoo (Japanese banana)
Phormium tenax (New Zealand flax)
Phyllostachys spp. (medium-sized bamboos)
Polystichum setiferum (soft shield fern)
Tetrapanax papyrifer (rice-paper plant)
Trachycarpus fortunei (windmill palm, chusan palm)

Variedated

Variety creates interest in the garden and this can be highlighted with the decorative use of foliage with contrasting, variegated leaf color. With evergreen or prolonged display, variegated leaves are invaluable when more fleeting seasonal flowers have disappeared, especially toward the end of summer.

Using Variegated Plants

Hostas are among the most beautiful and useful foliage plants and many have variegated leaves—they are even lovelier when grown in dappled shade and are ideal for moist, woodland-type areas. Use them in masses as an edging to highlight a winding pathway, or plant them together with waterside plants.

Don't overlook the endless possibilities of the variegated ivies that will lighten a dark corner even through the bleaker months. They can also be used as groundcovers in places where grass won't

survive and may be trained over fences, archways or sheltered walls as well as unsightly sheds. Ivies can also be trained on wire frames to produce topiary features. Smaller-leaved cultivars of *Hedera helix* produce a wide range of attractive variegations in gold, cream and silver. These can be trained horizontally along the front of a border or rock garden to form a dainty hedge.

It's hard to beat the variegated phormiums for sheer design, strong visual impact and individuality. They form large clumps of long, leathery, swordlike leaves and the eye is naturally drawn to them. Use them as focal points to entryways, pools, courtyards and rock gardens, as well as set among perennials.

ABOVE: A sea of variegated ivy among acanthus.
BELOW LEFT: Choose giant hostas for creating drama in a mixed planting, or alone as an accent.

Create positions in your garden to suit your favorite variegated plants. If you like arum lilies, tuck in a few clumps among your shrubs. Lush, broad-leaved plants can be set off against the striped spear-like leaves of *Iris pallida* 'Variegata'. For flower arrangers, the intricately patterned leaves of *Arum italicum* and the white-splashed leaves of *Zantedeschia elliottiana* can be picked for indoor arrangements.

Variegated Grasses

Although you don't want to overdo the use of variegated leaves in your garden

ABOVE: Caladiums are invaluable for summer color in shady beds and borders, especially in warm- and hot-summer areas.

RIGHT: Coleus are great for all-season color. Groups of mixed leaf plantings can look too busy, so grow them alone in masses.

design, as the effect can be very busy, you may want to experiment with some of the less invasive of the ornamental grasses. Often the most interesting forms have striking variations, especially cultivars of *Miscanthus sinensis*, such as 'Morning Light' and 'Variegatus.' 'Zebrinus' is a tall variety with horizontal bands of gold across the leaf blade, giving it the common name of zebra grass. It is a real eye-catcher and looks good in cottage gardens. All the above grasses are moderately frost-hardy and may also be used for waterside plantings.

Placing Variegated Plants

Variegated leaves are rarely as vigorous as their plain green counterparts, so it's often best to keep the plants out of direct sunlight. White-patterned plants, especially, are apt to be scorched in full sun. Use them to bring light and artistry to shaded places. Also, variegated plants tend to revert to plain green: If you see a green shoot, remove it straight away or it will eventually crowd out the variegated ones.

LEFT: Variegated ornamental grasses make wonderful garden accents, especially when used creatively in sculptural containers.

Variegated Foliage Plants

Arum italicum 'Marmoratum' (Italian arum)
Aspidistra elatior 'Variegata' (cast-iron plant)
Glechoma hederacea 'Variegata' (variegated ground ivy)
Hedera colchica 'Sulphur Heart' (Persian ivy)
Hedera helix varieties and cultivars (English ivy)
Hosta crispula
Hosta fortunei 'Albopicta'
Hosta fortunei 'Aureamarginata'
Hosta 'Moonlight'
Hosta 'Shade Fanfare'
Hosta undulata var. *univittata*
Iris pallida 'Variegata' (Dalmation iris)
Lamium maculatum (dead nettle)
Liriope muscari 'Variegata' (lily turf)
Melissa officinalis 'Aurea' (lemon balm)
Mentha suaveolens 'Variegata' (variegated apple mint)
Miscanthus sinensis 'Morning Light' (Japanese silver grass)
Miscanthus sinensis 'Variegatus'
Miscanthus sinensis 'Zebrinus' (zebra grass)
Phalaris arundinacea var. *picta* (gardener's garters)
Phormium tenax 'Variegatum' (flax)
Pleioblastus variegatus (bamboo)
Vinca major 'Variegata' (periwinkle)

Dead nettle

White

Many beautiful garden effects are achieved by using white flowers alone. Because they reflect so much light, white flowers appear almost luminous as dusk falls and seem to glow through the night. Make good use of this feature by growing white flowers to highlight paths, driveways and entrances, to create an impression of light. For quick results, advanced annual seedlings, such as candytuft, violas, petunias, primulas and lobelias, all come in white and are excellent for edging.

An all-white garden looks cool in the hottest weather. However, in masses, white can be a little overwhelming. Include some soft gray-leaved plants, such as some of the artemisias, lavender cotton *Santolina* spp. and mats of lamb's ears *Stachys byzantina*, to soften the impact of the bright whites. The occasional pale pastel-colored flowers, such as ivory tulips or creamy white roses, together with the occasional white-variegated foliage, add a complementary and subtle contrast.

Studying Form

Planning a white garden often involves choosing a framework of key plants.

Favorite White Flowers

Azaleas
Camellias
Clematis
Gardenias
Moonflower (right)
Jasmine
Japanese anemones
Lilies

Lily-of-the-valley
Petunias
Roses
Tobacco flowers
Tulips
Viburnum
Wisteria sinensis 'Alba'

Climbers

Clothe walls and fences with *Clematis armandii* or *C. montana*. Climbing, white roses are another choice, perfect for adorning arches, pergolas and arbors. Against a warm, sunny wall Confederate jasmine gives you neat, evergreen foliage all year, and clusters of dainty, white, jasmine-like flowers in summer. It can also be used as a groundcover. Climbing hydrangea *Hydrangea petiolaris* is good for shady walls and fences.

Among the most magnificent of climbers is the white Chinese wisteria *Wisteria sinensis* 'Alba' with its long, vertical festoons of perfumed flowers. It does not always have to grow against a wall or support—it can be planted in the open as a standard and with careful pruning, will become more beautiful and shapely over time.

Flower Beds and Borders

Most gardeners find it easiest to grow their white flowers within a border. When planting herbaceous beds and borders, consider the height of the plants. By all means position the taller plants behind low-growers, but make sure that they are well displayed at their flowering

ABOVE: White annuals and perennials look stunning when planted with white-variegated foliage plants, such as hosta.
RIGHT: White poppies, white cosmos and sweet alyssum *Lobularia maritima*.

times. A border might include daisies, aquilegias, lilies, baby's breath, dahlias, carnations and some annuals. Clump-forming perennials, such as white campanulas, foxgloves and columbines, with their tall, elegant spires of flowers, look great when backlit by morning sun.

Designing with Shrubs

A number of shrubs of the same species planted in a row as a hedge or in groups provides good structural form to the garden. For instance 'Iceberg' roses, camellias, azaleas, viburnums and the double form of the gracefully arching *Spiraea cantoniensis* all make stunning white-flowering hedges.

A White, Scented Garden

Many white flowers are perfumed. You can create a romantic, white, scented garden within a "secret," or private, area

of your garden surrounded or defined by hedges. Plan for a succession of scented, white bulbs from early spring with the honey-scented snowdrop and *Crocus chrysanthus*, then the exquisite lily-of-the-valley, freesias and hyacinths, followed by the glorious summer lilies *Lilium candidum* and *L. regale*. *Galtonia candicans* will fill the garden with delicious fragrance from midsummer to early autumn. In warmer areas plant a border of heady gardenias and provide a comfortable garden seat to prolong the pleasure.

Night Scents

Famed for its evening fragrance, the tobacco plant *Nicotiana elata* can be placed at the back of the border. As soon as the sun goes down, it sends its rich sweet scent into the night air. Dame's rocket *Hesperis matronalis* var. *albiflora* is another favorite night-scented plant.

TOP: Black and white paved courtyard featuring standard white 'Iceberg' roses.

ABOVE: A silver and white garden looks crisp and clean during the day and also stands out at night.

Silver and Gray

Silver and Gray Plants

Agave parryi (agave)
Artemisia absinthium 'Lambrook Silver' (common wormwood)
Artemisia ludoviciana 'Silver Queen' and 'Valerie Finnis' (silver king artemisia)
Artemisia 'Powis Castle'
Artemisia stelleriana 'Broughton Silver' (beach wormwood)
Buddleia alternifolia (fountain butterfly bush)
Cynara cardunculus (cardoon)
Echeveria spp. (echeveria)
Festuca glauca (blue fescue)
Lavandula angustifolia 'Hidcote' (English lavender)
Ruta graveolens 'Jackman's Blue' (rue)
Salvia officinalis (sage)
Santolina chamaecyparissus (lavender cotton)
Senecio cineraria (dusty miller)
Senecio viravira
Stachys byzantina (lamb's ears)
Verbascum olympicum (mullein)
Yucca rigida (yucca)
Yucca whipplei (our Lord's candle)

Some of the most outstanding foliage plants have silver or gray leaves. The silvery color of certain plants' leaves is caused by the reflection of light from millions of tiny hairs. And a gray leaf color is due to small beads of wax in leaves, which protect the plants from dehydration. Silver and gray plants harmonize beautifully with other colors, but a silver and gray theme by itself can look delicate and magical.

Silver and Gray Stunners

For a breathtaking sight, you can't beat the magnificent Colorado spruce *Picea pungens* 'Glauca', long regarded as one of the most highly desirable, silvery blue conifers. If you lack space, the smaller-growing 'Koster' will form a neat, conical shape with the same coloring and can be used for specimen and group planting. The slower-growing dwarf 'Montgomery' could become the star of your rock garden,

especially through the long winter months. If you want something truly unusual, you could train the cascading *Cedrus atlantica* 'Glauca Pendula' over a timber support to display its fantastic curtains of silvery gray foliage.

One of the most statuesque of gray-leaved plants is the cardoon *Cynara cardunculus*—a close relative of the artichoke. It reaches 7 feet (2.1 m) and has large, silvery gray, deeply divided leaves. To be seen at its best it needs plenty of space, and it makes an outstanding addition to any silver garden scheme.

You could also include some of the aromatic lavenders, especially the silvery gray *Lavandula angustifolia* 'Hidcote'. This lavender has a neat, compact habit and is very popular in herb garden designs.

TOP: Cardoon, dusty miller, wormwood and ballota create a stunning silver-gray grouping.
RIGHT: Colorado spruce *Picea pungens* 'Glauca'.

Artemisias have some outstanding gray and silver leaves—*Artemisia ludoviciana* and its cultivars 'Silver Queen' and 'Valerie Finnis' and *Artemisia absinthium* 'Lambrook Silver' are all great assets in a mixed, silver border. For a fine foliage contrast, tuck in some blue fescue *Festuca glauca*.

A beautiful specimen plant is the silvery green form of *Buddleia alternifolia*—a tall, deciduous shrub that can be trained as a standard to give a graceful, weeping effect that is further enhanced in summer with fragrant, lilac flowers.

Silver Succulents

Many succulent perennials with interesting, architectural qualities have silver or gray foliage. They are valuable in emphasizing structure in the garden and make dramatic focal points. *Agave parryi* is a good accent plant, forming rosettes of gray-blue, succulent leaves. When planted in rows, it makes a pleasing low hedge and looks beautiful against a softly colored sandstone wall.

Yucca rigida has 3-foot (90-cm) long, powdery blue leaves that form a rosette from the top of a trunk that grows to 6 feet (1.8 m) tall. It makes a dramatic landscape feature, especially near pools, and looks good planted with a small group of stemless *Y. whipplei*, which form a dense, almost globular clump of rigid, gray-green leaves. Both species bear spectacular, straight spikes of creamy white, waxy flowers in summer.

Small and Silver

Smaller plants can also be important accents, providing emphasis at ground level. They are best planted in groups of three or more to give the whole arrangement form.

Lavender cotton *Santolina chamaecyparissus*, with its lacy, silvery, aromatic foliage, makes an excellent low hedge. Because it is trouble-free and withstands close trimming, it is extremely popular for setting off the

more solid greens of formal, clipped gardens and old-fashioned, herbal knot gardens.

Another well-loved border plant is lamb's ears *Stachys byzantina*, which creates a lovely mat of silvery, velvet-textured leaves and in summer bears spikes of small, pinkish or mauve flowers. The non-flowering form, *S. byzantina* 'Silver Carpet', is also popular.

For a dry, sunny spot, make use of the echeverias—striking silver-leaved succulents that can be used as ground-covers or rockery edging, or allowed to spill over urns or walls.

RIGHT: Silver-gray succulents make an eye-catching feature.

Red

If you like bursts of brilliance and visual drama in your garden, red flowers are for you. Red cannot help but make an impression and it is the easiest color to use for impact.

Mum

Begonia

Gerbera

Pansy

Daylily

Up Close and Personal

Red flowers seem to come forward. This can be put to good use to help create a feeling of intimacy in a small garden, or even to lead the eye to the front door or a particular garden feature. Hot, vibrant reds often look better close to the house or in areas associated with various kinds of activity, such as the swimming pool or a private terrace used for dining.

Watch the Tones

Scarlet reds with an orange undertone, and crimson reds with a blue pigment may clash violently, so try to keep the two colors apart in a flowering border.

Scarlet dahlias, verbenas, begonias, *Crocosmia* 'Lucifer', *Zinnia elegans* Dreamland Series and the firecracker plant *Russelia equisetiformis* all have tomato-red tones that work well together, particularly when they are used against plain green foliage.

Crimson red flowers, such as some of the darker red roses, tulips, dianthus and fuchsias, blend together. The plum-colored foliage of purple sage *Salvia*

officinalis 'Purpurascens', varieties of *Heuchera* and the strappy leaves of the purple New Zealand flax will pick up the blue pigment of crimson red flowers and will enrich their setting.

Non-flowering Plants with Red Features

In all gardens, plants look more arresting if placed next to others with very different textures. Here are some fabulous plants with red features that will provide you with an interesting balance of texture and shape throughout the year.

Berberis thunbergii 'Red Pillar' is a small upright shrub to 4½ feet (1.35 m) with small, neatly rounded, reddish-purple leaves and glossy, red fruit. Although deciduous, this is a charming background shrub for a red flower border.

Dwarf capsicums or chilies *Capsicum* spp., with their bright, dangling red fruits, can be grown as ornamentals and add texture and variety in a group of red-flowering plants.

LEFT: Red maple *Acer rubrum*.
BELOW: The striking red stems of ruby chard.

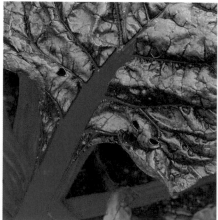

ABOVE: Joseph's coat *Amaranthus tricolor*.
TOP RIGHT: The stone path is a great foil to the massed planting of red flowers which includes petunias, geraniums, lobelias and begonias.
BOTTOM RIGHT: If you are looking for can't-miss color, then an all-red border may be the perfect accent for your garden.

Cornus alba 'Sibirica' is a deciduous shrub with dark green leaves that turn red in autumn. But its outstanding feature is its bare, shiny, red branches that provide stunning color during the winter months.

Many of the cotoneasters will provide you with an abundance of small, glossy, red fruit in late autumn that may persist through winter.

Imperata cylindrica 'Red Baron' (syn. 'Rubra') is the Red Baron blood grass that provides great foliage contrast and should be sited where the sun can highlight its rich, vibrant color.

Nandina domestica 'Nana' is an excellent edging plant. Its leaves are red-tinged when young, and develop red tones when the cold weather arrives. It also has red berries in autumn and winter. 'Fire-power' has bright red leaves.

New Zealand flax *Phormium tenax* 'Dazzler' is an outstanding feature, waterside or border plant with red, strap-like leaves edged with plum-purple.

Rheum palmatum 'Atrosanguineum' is an ornamental rhubarb with burgundy-

red, emerging leaves that fade to dark green, but retain their reddish color underneath. Tall panicles of small, cherry-red flowers appear early in summer. This is especially beautiful as a waterside plant.

Ricinus communis 'Gibsonii' is a compact variety of the castor-oil plant. It has bronze foliage with red veins and

striking red stems. An outstanding background plant for the red flower border, it also looks good framing billowing grasses.

Rosa rugosa has many fragrant, carmine-red flowers, but it is the large, tomato-shaped, red to orange-red hips that are its most stunning feature.

Blue and Purple

Blue is both brilliant and pure. It is one of the most intense colors, even when it is clouded into more purple and mauve tones. Blue flowers encompass a wide variety of tones and shades and are as infinite as the sky in their ability to reflect light in different ways. They are seldom one-colored and there are also many variations on blue within a single group, for example the delphiniums and hydrangeas, which come in every shade of blue and purple.

Open Up Your Space

Optically, blue is a receding color. It appears to move back, away from the viewer. You can exploit this effect by placing blue or mauve-blue flowers at a distance from the house or at the bottom of your garden to increase the sense of space. A beautiful backdrop to a fence or wall could be a curtain of blue trumpet vine *Thunbergia grandiflora* or the frost-hardy, mauve *Wisteria sinensis*. Blue-flowering climbers are also good for concealing swimming pool enclosures. They add a sense of calm, harmonize with most colors, and blend in with the

distance. Pale blue or mauve flowers edging a garden walk will increase the feeling of length.

Create a Blue and Purple Garden Theme

If all the blue tones from gray to purple are included in your color scheme, as well as all the delightful blue-purple herbs, such as hyssop, borage and lavender, there are enough blues to fill an entire garden, or at least a whole section of your garden.

ABOVE LEFT: Blues and purples are perfect for a cool-color border. Plant blue and purple flowers and blue-green leaves together for best effect.
ABOVE: Columbines (*Aquilegia* spp.).

Favorite Blue Flowers

Anchusa azurea (Italian bugloss)
Borago officinalis (borage)
Campanula persicifolia (peach-leaved bellflower)
Centaurea cyanus (cornflower)
Cynoglossum amabile (Chinese forget-me-not)
Delphinium cultivars
Felicia amelloides (blue Marguerite)
Gentiana spp. (gentian)
Hydrangea macrophylla (hydrangea)
Iris cultivars
Myosotis spp. (forget-me-nots)
Nigella damascena (love-in-a-mist)
Polemonium caeruleum (Jacob's ladder)
Salvia farinacea (mealy cup sage)
Teucrium fruticans (bush germander)
Thunbergia grandiflora (sky flower)
Veronica prostrata (prostrate speedwell)
Veronica spicata (spike speedwell)
LEFT: *Felicia amelloides* with *Ajuga reptans*

RIGHT: Pathway bordered by catmint *Nepeta* spp.
BOTTOM: Purple-blue 'Damson' plums.

For starters, there are the innumerable violets and irises, columbines, cornflowers, verbenas and more.

Purple and lavender colors create stunning accents. They can be found in lilacs, lupins, asters, Canterbury bells, delphiniums and many of the sages.

Blue-green or gray leaves can be used to balance blue flowers and create a gentle drift of changing hues, like a misty seascape. For example, try the decorative leaves and bracts of Miss Willmott's ghost *Eryngium giganteum*, set among agapanthus and the spiky blue flowers of *Allium caeruleum*. The grayish green foliage of catmint, borage and cornflowers all work beautifully together. Mauve flowers can be emphasized by placing them against the silvery leaves of lavender cotton *Santolina* spp. or the leaves of cardoon *Cynara cardunculus*.

On the Wild Side

Use forget-me-nots to create a marvelous spring carpet effect below deciduous shrubs. Their soft blues will link different areas and, once established, they will self-sow for years to come.

For cooler climates, a favorite meadow plant is the perennial Jacob's ladder *Polemonium caeruleum*, which displays its erect, lavender-blue flowers in early summer. This is a beautiful old-fashioned plant that self-sows successfully in a wild garden.

The best location for naturalizing bulbs, such as bluebells, is beneath deciduous trees and, here, a romantic woodland glade can be created on either a small or large scale.

Bulbs usually have the most impact when planted in masses of just one color. But if you want variety, you could plant together drifts of bulbs such as irises, bluebells and hyacinths, of varying hues from the palest blue to the deepest purple, for a wonderful, and often fragrant, effect.

ABOVE: Forget-me-nots *Myosotis* spp. are ideal for naturalizing under deciduous trees. They reseed prolifically, so if you don't want to deal with seedlings, shear off the developing seed heads.

Yellow and Orange

LEFT: Sneezeweed cultivar *Helenium* 'Waldtraut'.
BELOW: Marigolds come in a range of oranges and yellows with either single or double flowers.

BELOW: Cottage garden with sunflowers, sweet peas, busy Lizzie and hollyhocks.

Yellow is the color of sunshine and orange the dazzler. While yellow flowers seem to give the garden a feeling of airy lightness, orange flowers optically foreshorten distance, so that the color appears to leap out from its surroundings. Both yellow and orange are attention-seekers in the garden and create a bright and cheerful atmosphere.

Take a Tip from Nature

Nature provides us with a profusion of yellow-to-orange flowers, both cultivated and growing wild. For example, wonderfully scented wallflowers grow in a rich harmony of yellow, tawny gold, russet and orange. Daffodils and jonquils *Narcissus* spp. combine many shades of yellow, while the flowers of the pot marigold come in pale yellow to deep orange in both single and double varieties. Both the Californian poppy *Eschscholzia californica* and the Iceland poppy *Papaver nudicaule* come in a range of these tones from yellow and gold to orange. For later in the season, there is a wide variety of yellow and orange daylilies *Hemerocallis* hybrids and *Lilium* spp., including the flecked tiger lilies. The trailing annual, garden nasturtium *Tropaeoleum majus*, gives us various shades of yellow, gold, orange and orange-red flowers—gorgeous colors that can be picked up in nearby plantings.

Cream and Yellow

If you want to tone down your orange and yellow setting, add some creamy colored flowers. Cream flowers make great companions to most flower colors, but are particularly valuable in softening any harsh effects created by bright yellow and orange flowers. Here you could choose the lighter tones of orange and yellow plants, or add a few creamy or pale yellow roses. False Solomon's seal *Smilacina racemosa*, with its lemon-scented, creamy white, feathery plumes, is good in partial shade, grown between shrubs. For a bright, sunny position, silver- and gray-foliaged plants will blend well as background color.

At the Water's Edge

If you have a damp, low-lying area beside a pond or water garden, you could provide a congenial home for those plants that like to grow in permanently wet soil. Some of the best waterside plants have yellow flowers and clearly reflect their blooms in the calm water's surface. Plants such as *Ranunculus lingua*, yellow flag iris *Iris pseudocorus*, Japanese iris *Iris ensata*, candelabra primulas, ligularias and yellow loosestrife *Lysimachia punctata* are just the plants to cheer up a difficult wet area.

At the very edge of the water you could grow a bold, single clump of *Acorus calamus* 'Variegatus', a pretty grass with aromatic, bright green leaves to 4 feet

TOP: The gentle, pale yellow flowers of fern-leaved yarrow *Achillea filipendulina*. Plant at the front or middle of perennial borders, or with grasses in wildflower meadows.
LEFT: Water lily *Nymphaea* 'Pygmaea Helvola'.

A Yellow and Orange Cut Flower Garden

Many yellow and orange flowers are used for indoor flower arrangement. Traditionally a small portion of the country garden was set aside for cutting flowers. You may lack the space for such an area in your garden, but cut-flower plants can be grown in the flower border or, in the best tradition of a cottage-style garden, set among your vegetables. If you have the space, don't forget the fabulous sunflower for impact both in the garden and indoors.

Achillea spp. (yarrows)
Antirrhinum majus (snapdragon)
Calendula officinalis (pot marigold)
Dahlia cultivars (dahlias)
Erysimum cultivars (wallflowers)
Helenium cultivars (sneezeweed, Helen's flower)
Helianthus annuus (sunflower)
Hemerocallis spp. (daylilies)
Iris spp. bearded varieties
Kniphofia cultivars (red hot pokers)
Narcissus spp. (daffodils/jonquils)
Papaver nudicaule (Iceland poppy)
Ranunculus spp. (buttercups)
Tulipa spp. (tulips)

(1.2 m) long with cream and white stripes. *A. gramineus* 'Ogon' is a smaller version with pale green and deep cream variegated leaves to 10 inches (25 cm) long.

Aquatic plants, such as water lilies, will further enhance the setting. Some of the *Nymphaea* cultivars come in clear, bright yellows and pale creamy yellows. The yellow floating heart *Nymphoides peltata*, best for frost-prone areas, has fringed, bright golden-yellow flowers that resemble miniature water lilies.

Pink

Pink flowers are charming, sprightly and vibrant. They are the flowers of romance, from the early-flowering cherry blossom and pink camellias to the later-flowering roses, peonies, lilies and nerines.

Pink Effects

Pink can be a warm color, when in the coral and salmon-pink range, or cool, when in the mauve-pink range. The cool pinks, that are linked with blue pigments, blend well with blue and purple flowers. When mixing different pinks, make sure you keep the tones closely related and use appropriate foliage to either heighten the effect, or to calm things down.

The glossy-leaved acanthus is a good foil to all pink flowers and bears its own

flower spikes of pinkish purple. Peonies of all types have interesting divided leaves and are complemented by nearby plantings of green-leaved hostas.

Gray foliage, such as that of lamb's ears *Stachys byzantina*, anthemis or lavender cotton, will highlight most pink flowers particularly well.

You can deepen mauve-pink flowers with purplish sage, feathery purple fennel or the plum-colored leaves of *Weigela florida* 'Foliis Purpureis'.

Hydrangeas that turn pink in alkaline soil, as well as frothy pink rhododendrons, are both excellent for brightening up partly shady areas of the garden.

An Enchanted Garden

An all-pink garden walk has an almost fairy-tale charm. Be adventurous with pink and grow old-fashioned roses extravagantly over arches and to curtain

TOP LEFT: Lilies add height and color to any flower bed or border. Combine them with mounding annuals, perennials or groundcovers that can shade the soil and keep the bulbs cool.
TOP RIGHT: Besides being a great garden accent, globe amaranth *Gomphrena globosa* dries well for dried flower arrangements.
LEFT: Old-fashioned pink roses are perfect for a romantic, scented, pink-themed garden.

Favorite Pink Flowers

Argyranthemum 'Bridesmaid',
    'Mary Wootton', 'Vancouver'
    (Marguerite daisy)
Amaryllis belladonna
    (belladonna lily)
Armeria maritima (sea pink)
Camellia spp. (camellias)
Clematis 'Nelly Moser'
Daphne cneorum (rose daphne)
Deutzia x *elegantissima* 'Rosealind'
    (deutzia)
Dianthus spp. (carnations and pinks)
Dierama pulcherrimum (fairy's
    fishing rod)
Kalmia latifolia (mountain laurel)
Kolkwitzia amabilis 'Pink Cloud'
    (beauty bush)
Lavatera 'Barnsley' (mallow)
Magnolia liliiflora (lily magnolia)
Nerine bowdenii (pink spider lily)
Paeonia lactiflora (peony)
Prunus x *subhirtella* (flowering
    cherry)
Rhododendron spp.
    (rhododendrons and azaleas)
Rosa spp. (roses)
Syringa meyeri 'Superba'
    (lilac)
Weigela florida (old-
    fashioned weigela)

ABOVE: Astilbes are perfect for moist shade gardens. Their airy plumes add grace and motion to the garden. Plant masses beside a pond where their blooms can be reflected in the water.

ABOVE: Use fast-growing, butterfly-like cosmos *Cosmos bipinnatus* to fill the spaces left by early-blooming annuals and perennials.

Mountain laurel

walls. Create a flowering backdrop of pink clematis, which can also be grown over large shrubs or small trees.

Include many of the irresistible pink flowers, such as camellias, peonies, carnations and pinks themselves (*Dianthus* spp.), but also include some perennials with architectural qualities. Show-stoppers such as the giant of the lily family *Eremurus robustus*, with its tall flower-spikes of pale pink, and clumps of pink Russell lupins are great accent plants for full sun. Other plants of distinction are the striking, plumelike, summer flowers of pink astilbes and *Sedum spectabile* with scalloped leaves and dusky pink flowers. Good background bedding plants include pink cosmos, poppies and the spider flower *Cleome hassleriana*. The showy pink turtlehead *Chelone obliqua* and some of the alliums are good for late summer, while pink cultivars of dahlia and *Aster novi-belgii* will carry their late summer flowers well into autumn.

In the Shade

Pink flowers will brighten up a shady spot beneath deciduous trees and here you could add a few treasures such as the delightful *Cyclamen hederifolium*, with its heavily marbled, ivy-like leaves and sometimes scented, autumn flowers in shades of rose pink. The autumn crocus *Colchicum autumnale* also has flowers in shades of pink. The highly desirable pink trout lily *Erythronium revolutum*, with strongly mottled leaves and lilac-pink early summer flowers, multiplies easily when planted in partial shade around shrubs and trees.

Combining Colors

Color is one of the principal contributors to a great-looking garden, but the best gardens aren't based on flower color alone. By using plants of different sizes, forms, colors and textures we achieve variety and interest when building up a complete garden picture.

Color in the Garden

The basic, ever-present and most important color in the landscape is green. There are many diverse and subtle shades of green—from the palest lime to vibrant emerald. Some greens are dark, others more grayish, silvery or olive in tone. Consider also the color of your house, fence, walls, paving or other features when choosing your plant colors. Many trees and shrubs produce flowers in their season and although fleeting, these colors should also be taken into account.

Shrubs, especially the evergreens, are likely to be permanent parts of the landscape and will largely act as a long-

Irises and daylilies

term, leafy background to a garden setting. As a general rule, best results are achieved if strongly contrasting shrubs are not placed in close proximity, or the effect is jarring. A descending scale of leaf size or subtle variations of closely related colors are harmonious.

Bright-leaved or golden-foliaged plants give a garden vitality and can be used in shadowy areas of a garden to brighten and lighten them. For example *Sambucus racemosa* 'Plumosa Aurea' in a dull corner can bring a splash of light. *Robinia pseudoacacia* 'Frisia', with its rich yellow, pinnate leaves that turn orange-yellow in autumn, is also a valuable brightener.

For breathtaking autumn color there are some rich reds provided by deciduous plants, such as the Japanese maples and *Nyssa sylvatica*—both make outstanding specimen plants, and are best sited where they will catch the weak autumn light. The pretty, slow-growing *Acer palmatum*

'Sango-kaku' will provide a contrasting delicate tracery of amber-gold in autumn.

Use a variety of other forms to draw attention to a particular location or add a little light relief. You could introduce some good architectural plants such as the cordylines, palms, variegated phormiums and low-growing, symmetrical conifers to draw the eye to an entrance or a particular garden feature. Tall, vertical accent plants and stately conifers, no matter what color, are best grown as specimens to create eye-catching interludes in a garden plan or to attract attention to a vista.

A Palette of Flowers

Most gardeners find it easiest to grow flowers within a flower border. The border may include annuals, but mostly it is made up of perennials. Here you can truly paint with color, form, texture and line.

On the true color wheel, where red, blue and yellow are the primary colors, the colors that are opposite each other make the strongest contrast—green with red, or blue with yellow for example.

LEFT: A blue wall creates an appropriate backdrop for a grouping of blue-leaved cabbages and citrus-yellow blooms.
ABOVE: The yellow, nodding flowers of 'February Gold' daffodils look stunning paired with plants with yellow-variegated leaves.

Purple and yellow are complementary colors on the color wheel, and therefore making an exciting, yet harmonious combination. Here low-growing purple hyacinths and velvety pansies are mixed with taller-growing yellow tulips.

Compare the same garden design but with two different color schemes—cool blue and purple on the left and hot yellow and orange on the right.

When colors share some of the same pigment—such as blue combined with its near-relative purple—the result is harmonious. But pair blue with lemon—its opposite on the color wheel—and the impact is more eye-catching.

Color combinations are personal. Some gardeners enjoy the result of mixing orange and yellow with purple or blue; others prefer crisp whites or the restful feel of pale yellows, soft pinks and silvers.

Combining similar flower colors with dark and light tones, quite close to each other, creates a pleasing effect. Try grouping reds with oranges and yellows; citrus-yellows with greens and blues; or blues with purple and reds. Colors sharing the same degree of lightness or darkness also work well; for instance, several different pastels, such as pale blues, pale yellows and pale pinks, blend more effectively than several pure hues.

White and gray don't appear on the color wheel, but they play an important role in the garden. White has a split personality: It can be exciting or soothing. Bright white is surprisingly bold; it stands out among both bright and dark colors, even in a group of soft pastels. A dash of pure white in a spread of harmonious colors is as dramatic as a dash of a bright complementary color. Cream and muted whites are softer; they tend to blend well with everything.

Gray is the great unifier. Silver or gray foliage works even more effectively than green to soften the transition between two complementary or bold colors. Gray adds a certain drama of its own by contrasting with neighboring green foliage. Gray-foliaged plants look particularly lovely with flowers of a pastel shade and those that are evergreen will hold the fort in winter.

Get Some Rhythm

Take a tip from garden designers and grow foliage plants in repeated groupings. Lush, green plants such as *Euphorbia characias* subsp. *wulfenii* and the architectural *Acanthus* spp. look good through all seasons and provide a link between different types of flowering plants. With its foamy, lime-green flowers, clumps of *Alchemilla mollis* are a charming, long-season companion to all neighboring plants.

ABOVE: Green agave nestling among a riot of beefsteak plant *Iresine* spp.
RIGHT: Cottage garden with a mix of colorful annuals in the pink, blue and purple range, including delphinium, poppies, foxgloves and violets.

You could also include some spiky leaves, such as those of the irises and some of the variegated grasses, to provide definition and contrast.

Some Super Combinations

Color associations offer scope for creating very different and interesting effects. Don't be too timid, as you can easily move most perennials at almost any time of the year. After all, that's what gardening is all about—retaining our interest and enthusiasm by changing things about to suit our individual style and moods. Here are some color combinations you might like to try, bearing in mind that foliage color is just as important as flower color.

Combine crimson and pink flowers, but tone down the planting with plum-colored foliage, such as that of *Berberis thunbergii* 'Red Pillar'.

Create a theatrical, tropical effect with the coppery red *Ricinus communis* 'Gibsonii', underplanted with canna lilies with bold bronze or rich purple leaves, or the striking green and yellow 'Striata'. The flamboyant red, orange and apricot flowers look stunning.

White flowers and white-variegated leaves make excellent companions. Grow dozens of *Hosta undulata* var. *univittata* with their bold, white streaks with white violas and tulips to lighten a shady garden walk.

Plant out masses of blackish green *Ophiopogon planiscapus* 'Nigrescens' as a bold border to several prostrate junipers with silvery blue leaves, to create a beautiful carpet of contrasting foliage.

LEFT: Combine similar-colored plants with different leaf shapes for an eye-catching effect.
BELOW: Variegated hostas and orange tulips.

For architectural contrast, but with harmonious color, grow the purple-leaved *Phormium tenax* 'Purpureum' with the slate-gray *Hosta sieboldiana* 'Elegans' around its base.

Imitate Claude Monet's planting at Giverny, France, and grow orange nasturtiums in front of violet-blue asters. And if you're lucky enough to have a red footbridge, drape it with purple wisteria.

For a charming, gray picture, use the glaucous foliage of some of the shrubby eucalypts with the silvery green, pinnate leaves of *Melianthus major*. Set this off with the bold, bronze-leaved *Rogersia podophylla* and some of the blue-leaved hostas, together with a substantial clump of *Ajuga reptans* 'Catlin's Giant' for a frilly, informal carpet.

For a late-season burst of fiery color, plant rudbeckias, sunflowers, heleniums, Turk's cap lilies, yellow and red dahlias, celosias, red hot pokers and *Monarda* 'Cambridge Scarlet'. These flowers all have complementary colors from the hot side of the spectrum, and they can all be picked for arrangements to warm up the house as the days get cooler.

ABOVE: A soft, gentle, pastel effect created by white daisies, mauve irises and yellow wallflowers.

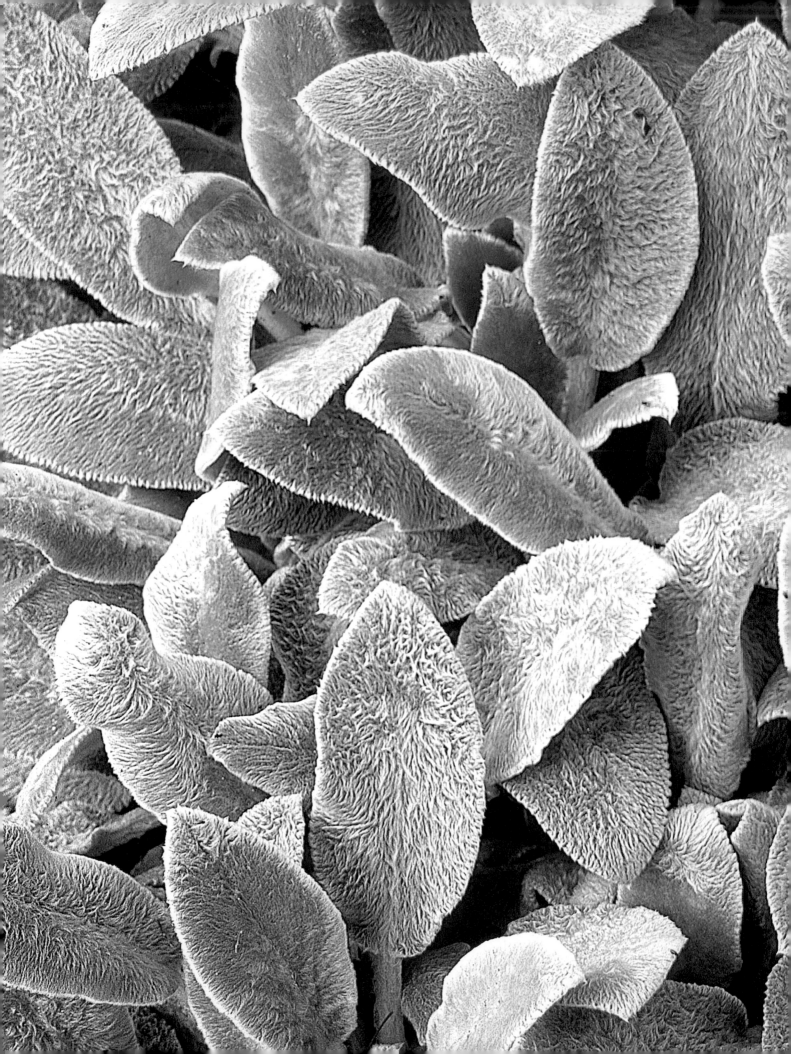

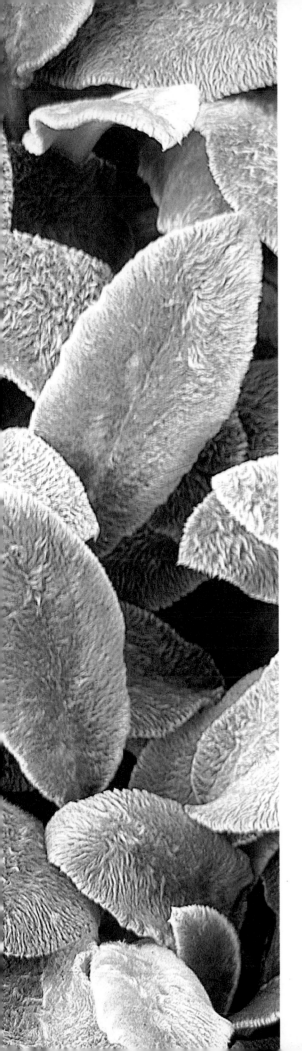

A Garden for the Senses

A well-designed garden will appeal to all the five senses. With clever planning and an eye for detail, it is possible to create a garden that looks, smells, tastes, sounds and feels good. Making a garden that is appealing to all the senses comes with the right choice of design elements, decorative features and, of course, plant selection.

Sight

Gardens are visually stimulating places. Much but not all of the feast for our eyes comes from colorful plants. Plants contribute color from flowers, leaves and even bark. Each plant also affects the look of other plants nearby, contrasting or complementing its surroundings. Of course, the picture never stands still for long, as patterns of light and dark, along with the season cycles, mean that plants and gardens are constantly changing.

Hard landscaping features, such as walls, paths and even the choice of mulches, further enrich the visual impact of a garden. And, with some carefully placed potted, topiarized or clipped plants you can also introduce some visual "jokes" to bring an element of fun or perhaps mystery to even the simplest garden.

Even individual flowers can be visually stimulating due to their patterning, shape or size. Consider the amazingly detailed checkerboard pattern of a checkered lily, the perfectly circular shape of a drumstick primula flower head or the odd shape and bright colors of a calceolaria (sometimes called a lady's purse).

Decide the Mood

It is possible to control the degree of visual stimulation a garden design provides by the way plants are selected and combined. Gardens with many

The nodding flowers of checkered lilies *Fritillaria meleagris* add a charming touch to spring gardens. Naturalize them in wild areas.

different colored plants and surfaces can seem busy and complex. On the other hand, limiting the choice of plants, and therefore the number of color combinations, can subdue a garden, making it more peaceful and restful. By taking advantage of the seasonal changes plants undergo, you can have a garden that takes on different moods at different times of the year. For example, a garden that's full of color and contrast in spring may become a quiet, leafy, green oasis in summer.

Floral Pictures

Flowers provide immense visual variety and excitement. You can think of flowers as a living paint. They can provide a wash of color that enlivens a large area, or be daubs of color that create visual highlights. Unlike paint on a wall, however, flowers are usually seasonal. In addition, they vary in the length of their display. Flowers can last for just a day or for many months. Some even change color through the day, like the miraculous four o'clock *Mirabalis jalapa*, which opens a brilliant pink and then fades to yellow, or the rose of Sharon *Hibiscus mutabilis*, which opens rosy red and fades through pink and then to white.

It's hard to match hybrid tulips for pure color power; here they team with forget-me-nots.

To get the most from plants when they flower, be aware of their flower color, the normal flowering season and how long it may last. Remember too that masses of a single color will have more visual impact than many different colors mixed together. If you are using annuals for colors, look for plants that offer single color selections so you can mix and match the color you want in your garden.

Visual Tricks

As soon as two colors—whether they are on cushions on a sofa or flowers in a garden—are placed beside one another, they affect our perception. Dark colors, for example, will recede, while lighter colors will seem to stand out. In a garden, combining plants so that colors recede and others leap forward adds a sense of depth, even in a small space.

Other visual tricks in a garden are done to make a space seem larger or more

A stunning and classical effect can be achieved with a trompe l'oeil framed by a living vine.

varied than it really is. A long path, for example, can seem even longer if its sides are not parallel but are angled (so they would eventually converge). Our eyes perceive a path that appears longer than it actually is.

Garden mirrors or even ponds can also be used to fool the eye as they reflect parts of the garden, thereby making it appear larger. A mirror disguised as a gate will appear to lead to an as yet unexplored section of garden.

Painting a small panel or even an entire wall with an imaginary scene is a device known as trompe l'oeil, and it has been used in gardens for thousands of years. The painting may be a landscape that doesn't exist, such as a glimpse to an imagined view, or an ornament for which there isn't room, such as a fountain or statue.

To make the trompe l'oeil seem realistic, frame it with real plants. A painting that evokes a Tuscan landscape scene, for example, can be flanked by a pair of columnar cypress or junipers such as *Juniperus virginiana* 'Skyrocket'.

LEFT: Include some exotic and unusual flowers in your garden, such as this delightful Queen's tears *Billbergia nutans*.
RIGHT: The colorful patterns of peeling bark can be an attractive feature.

Touch

We "see" a garden through our hands and our feet, as well as with our eyes. We can even lie or sit in, on or among plants, to enjoy the texture of their leaves, or to soak up the warmth from sun-soaked paving.

Designing a garden to stimulate the sense of touch can bring a lot of pleasure, yet the way a garden feels is not often considered when it is being designed. To cater to your sense of touch in a garden, use a mix of plants and surfaces that will stimulate and excite.

Planting for Comfort

One of the most important issues of touch is for something to feel good. Plants may feel pleasant to touch, or they can be a pain—quite literally. Those with sharp thorns or prickles can be touched in painful rather than pleasurable ways. Avoid using plants with prickles or sharp spines in places where you are likely to come in contact with them. Agaves beside the swimming pool or roses crowding next to the driveway are not going to feel good. However, thorny

If you're looking for something a little different to grow, with an unusual texture, try growing Turkestan onion *Allium karataviense*, with its bulbous flower heads. It looks great with silvery-leaved plants.

The velvety-soft leaves of lamb's ears *Stachys byzantina* are popular with children.

plants do have a place—they make excellent deterrents along boundaries.

In areas where you want to encourage people to touch and feel plants or where they may be brushed against accidentally, concentrate on selecting plants that feel good. When something feels comfortable, it also feels safe.

The concept of touch in a garden goes beyond plants to the other elements of the landscape. Burning hot paving under bare feet isn't a good feeling, neither are vast expanses of prickle-infested lawns or damp, slippery, mossed-over paths. Much cooler and more pleasant to touch are soft lawns or groundcovers.

Touchy-Feely Plants

Some plants just cry out to be touched, felt or patted. Plants with a rounded, cushiony shape or felty leaves ask to be stroked. Lamb's ears, such as the large-leaved *Stachys byzantina* 'Big Ears', has soft, gray leaves that feel felty to the touch. Baby's tears *Soleirolia soleirolii* (also called helxine) has tiny, green leaves that look and feel soft. This is a lovely soft groundcover for a shaded spot.

The curry plant *Helichrysum italicum*, with its small, soft, rounded leaves, feels good to touch. And, when you do brush or touch the leaves of the curry plant, they release a strong curry scent, therefore stimulating both your sense of smell and taste. Heighten the sense of touch by clipping the curry plant into a rounded shape that echoes the rounded shape of the aromatic leaves.

Other plants that lend themselves to the soft cushiony look and feel include

Feel-good Plants

Ferns (e.g. maidenhair fern
   Adiantum aethiopicum)
Lamb's ears *Stachys byzantina*
Lawn grasses (especially cool-
   season grasses)
Mondo grass *Ophiopogon japonicus*
Mosses
Sedums
Selaginella
Snow-in-summer *Cerastium
   tomentosum*
Spanish moss *Tillandsia usneoides*

lavenders, hebes, boxwood, some dwarf conifers and many small succulents. But plants aren't always as they seem. They can look soft and inviting, yet conceal a spiky nature, as do cleomes, which have small spines under their leaves.

It's not just leaves that feel good to touch. Many flowers are tempting to touch, too. The foaming flower heads of hydrangeas, for instance, seem to ask to be ruffled. The crape-like flowers of the crape myrtle *Lagerstroemia indica* need to be touched to see if they feel as well as look like crape.

Some plants that feel good to touch aren't usually considered as garden plants. Moss, for example, when it's growing on rocks, steps or under a woodland canopy, looks soft and inviting. If you have a moist, shaded area, think about using moss as a groundcover and turning the area into a moss garden—a traditional form of garden in Japan. Moss can be transplanted or encouraged to grow naturally. Painting bare rocks with plain yogurt or milk helps encourage mosses and algae to develop on the damp surfaces.

Walk Through

Plants that are good to feel aren't just encountered at ground level. Plants that

A pathway of stepping stones, among soft groundcovers, is a delight to walk over in bare feet.

The spines of the golden barrel cactus *Echinocactus grusonii*, which has the alternative common name of mother-in-law's seat.

trail over paths or cascade over archways are felt as they are brushed past. The effect is much like walking through a beaded curtain in a doorway—or perhaps a dense, tropical rainforest.

Evoke a feeling of a lush, tropical paradise by planting vines so they have to be pushed aside as you move through a garden or along a path.

The same effect can also be achieved with tall-growing plants that have cascading leaves or branches, such as tree ferns and dwarf palms, which have arching fronds, or weeping standards such as weeping elms and mulberries, that form a curtain of green branches.

Make a Point

Plants that are sharp and prickly also have a place in a garden to appeal to the senses—even if they are outside our normal comfort zone. The golden barrel cactus *Echinocactus grusonii* has a round shape that looks a bit like a squat stool. The sight of its armory of long, sharp spines, however, quickly puts any ideas of sitting on the barrel-shaped cactus seat well out of mind.

Smell

In recent years, the way flowers or foliage smell has become an important element in plant choice in landscape design. Fragrant plants, whether they are herbs or sweetly scented flowers, are much in demand to delight our sense of smell.

Finding Fragrance

Always use your nose when you are selecting plants—after all, if there is a fragrant variety that fits the design brief, you may as well select it over a plant without scent. Roses, for example, may vary in their fragrance. Some have gorgeous heads of flowers but no scent. Rose growers list the choicest scented roses in their catalogs. If you are buying roses in winter or early spring while they are dormant, be guided by the catalog description to find a strongly scented rose.

Fragrant Foliage

When choosing plants for fragrance, smell leaves as well as flowers. Fragrant foliage provides months of scent. Herbs are an excellent source of fragrance and can be used in many garden situations. Thyme, for example, can be grown in cracks in paving, while chamomile is a fragrant alternative to lawn in cool to mild areas.

Foliage plants can even imitate floral fragrances. One of the most wonderful rose scents in the garden comes not from roses, but from the leaves of the shrubby rose geranium *Pelargonium graveolens*. There are also other scented geraniums, such as lemon and tutti frutti.

Other plants with fragrant, if slightly acrid, scents in their leaves include artemisias, lavenders, Marguerite daisies, marigolds and tomatoes.

Harvest aromatic herbs lightly and often to release their fragrance and to keep the plants producing fresh, new growth.

Catching the Scent

Selecting a fragrant plant is only part of the task of introducing fragrance to your garden. Getting the most benefit from your perfumed plants means considering the position they are to grow in. There's no point in growing a perfumed plant in a part of the garden you rarely visit.

Instead, make sure that you plant perfumed plants near windows and doors that are often open. If there's no space in a garden bed, you can plant a perfumed plant in a container positioned near an entranceway. A row of scented shrubs along the front fence or near the gate is a delightful way to welcome visitors and

Heady-scented roses are a classic part of a scented garden. Plant them over an archway or gate.

Fragrant Selections

A selection of the following shrubs in your garden ensures the air is filled with wonderful perfume throughout the year.

Winter sweet *Chimonanthus praecox*
Daphnes *Daphne* spp.
Mexican orange blossom
    Choisya ternata
Gardenias *Gardenia* spp.
Witch hazels *Hamamelis* spp.
Luculia *Luculia gratissima*
Port wine magnolia *Michelia figo*
Murraya *Murraya paniculata*
Osmanthus *Osmanthus fragrans*
Plumeria *Plumeria rubra*

will also be much appreciated by people walking by your home.

Enjoy the fragrance of plants inside, too, by picking a few sprigs of whatever's smelling great outside and bringing it indoors to scent the house. For long-term fragrance from the garden, turn fragrant plants into homemade potpourri by drying their leaves and petals.

Another smart place to grow fragrant plants is in a courtyard, so the scent is captured and held. If your garden design doesn't include a courtyard, position the fragrant plant against a wall, as this helps to confine the perfume.

Often, pungent or fragrant leaves have to be rubbed, crushed or brushed against before they will release a noticeable scent. It is important to position plants with fragrant foliage where they will be touched. Good locations include the edge of paths, gates or steps.

As well as growing perfumed shrubs or vines in the garden, use smaller, fragrant

Position a garden bench in a favorite part of the garden and surround it with fragrant lavender.

plants in pots as seasonal highlights so you can get close-up and take in their fragrance. Hyacinths grow well in pots and are decorative and fragrant. Also great for potted fragrance are dwarf sweet peas *Lathyrus odoratus*, dwarf wallflowers, narcissus and freesias.

Night Fragrance

Some plants vary in the way they smell depending on the time of day. There is a group of plants that are more strongly scented in the evening than they are in the daytime. These plants intensify their scent at night in order to attract nocturnal insects, such as moths, as pollinators. These are plants to select to grow outside your outdoor dining area or under a bedroom window. They add an extra dimension to your garden by making it a place to visit and experience by night as well as by day.

Some interesting night-scented plants include nicotiana, many of the cestrums (some of which are so strongly scented as to be quite overwhelming) and the so-called queen of the night *Selenicereus grandiflorus*, a climbing cactus with large, white, fragrant flowers at night.

Catmints *Nepeta* spp. have gray-green leaves with a pungent, minty scent that cats love. They look wonderful with other perennials and shrubs.

Sound

Some people talk to their plants, but few gardeners listen to the sounds of plants when deciding what to grow. The sounds of plants are usually highlighted by the wind stirring their leaves or branches, but some plants explode and crackle as the heat triggers seedpods to burst open. Even the sound of dropping fruit on a path or the garage roof adds a different dimension to the garden. Falling walnuts, for example, can really crash down on a metal roof.

Sound in gardens is used to create an atmosphere or highlight a mood or a theme. Gentle sounds bring an air of calm and tranquillity, while more boisterous or unusual sounds can make a garden seem alive and exciting.

Pleasant sounds, such as the wind rustling through leaves, or splashing water, are also used to mask unwanted sounds of traffic, neighbors or passersby. It is impossible to use plants or even water features to completely block out unwanted noise (especially from nearby roads) but garden sounds can offer a welcome distraction.

Plant painted bamboo *Bambusa vulgaris* 'Vittata', to hear the wind rustle through its leaves.

The crackling, dry, silvery seedpods of honesty *Lunaria annua* are great for dried arrangements.

The Sounds of the Wind

One of the best plant choices to bring sound to your garden is bamboo. The rustle of its leaves in even the slightest breeze brings an added dimension to any garden with an oriental theme. Select a clumping bamboo or grow bamboo in a large container. Some ideal choices are buddha's belly bamboo *Bambusa ventricosa*, painted bamboo *B. vulgaris* 'Vittata', with its beautifully marked golden stems, or hedging bamboo *B. multiplex* 'Alphonse Karr'.

If a running form of bamboo is planted, keep it confined with root barriers sunk at least 3 feet (1 m) into the ground to prevent its underground spread.

In a large garden, or for an avenue planting, enjoy the sighing, rushing sounds wind makes blowing through pine needles by growing a windbreak of pines. Some of the best sounds come from trees that are far too large for the average garden, such as Monterey pine *Pinus radiata* or the beautiful Mexican weeping pine *P. patula*, with its cascades of needles that also ripple in the wind.

You can also use the wind to set chimes or bells ringing that will add yet another layer of sounds to your garden.

Water Music

One of the best ways to introduce sound into a garden is with moving water. It can bubble, gurgle, splash, trickle or cascade, depending on the type of water feature. Create more varied sounds by lining the cascade or pool with pebbles. Add an oriental touch with the clunk of a *shishi odoshi*, a Japanese water feature made from bamboo, which rhythmically spills water into a small pond.

A water feature at the front gate can be used to set the scene and mark the transition from the street to the private space of your garden. People will feel a sense of arrival as soon as they open the garden gate and hear the sound of water.

Alternatively, use water in a courtyard where the noise will be magnified by the surrounding walls. Install a wall fountain or a pond with a fountain.

Water can also be used to transform part of a larger garden into an oasis or as a focal point for a small space. It is even possible to have a small, self-contained water feature on a deck or balcony.

Attracting Wildlife

Another source of garden sounds comes from birds and insects, attracted to gardens by plants, a birdbath or a feed table. As native habitat is reduced to isolated pockets or removed altogether from urban areas, the plants in gardens

ABOVE: The sound of crunching gravel underfoot is always satisfying and appealing.

LEFT: A water feature, such as a fountain or trickling water spout, is one of the most popular additions to a Japanese-style garden.

have become vital for the survival of native animals and insects.

To make your garden wildlife-friendly, make sure that you plant groups of dense shrubs that will offer homes and shelter to small birds. Prickly evergreen shrubs make an excellent safe haven. Also ensure you select plants with their flowering or fruiting time in mind so that there is a succession of nectar-rich flowers in bloom during the year. Additional food also comes from seeds and fruit, so don't always prune away fruits and seeds that may offer food to native wildlife.

Don't overlook the sounds of frogs and toads, which can be attracted to live and breed in garden ponds or bog gardens.

Selecting Surfaces

As you or others move around a garden, there is interaction with surfaces. Loose surfaces, such as gravel, shingle and even cobblestones, bring a very different sound to your garden. The scrunch of gravel underfoot on a path or driveway can be a welcoming sound, or even alert you that visitors are approaching.

Taste

The earliest gardens were about growing food plants for survival rather than esthetic reasons, but today's gardens can combine edible plants in ways that are attractive to look at.

Herbs, vegetables and fruit trees are the most obvious choices for a garden to appeal to your sense of taste. They can be grown in a part of the garden that's specially set aside for productive plants (a vegetable patch, herb garden or orchard), or intermingled within a garden of ornamental flowers and shrubs.

Not every tasty-sounding plant is actually edible. There are plants that smell good enough to eat but don't produce edible fruit or leaves. Tempt your mental taste buds with chocolate cosmos in your flower garden or a hedge of peppermint geranium, without the work that productive plants can entail.

Designer Vegetables

The potager is a vegetable garden designed and planted to use edible plants in an ornamental way. Potagers are usually laid out in a decorative pattern, such as with beds formed as segments of a circle. Select vegetables and herbs and a sprinkling of flowers with an eye to both taste and appearance.

Pears bear fruit on long-lived spurs, so they are perfect for training in espalier patterns against walls.

Edible plants that look good grown in a potager garden include lettuce, Asian greens, cabbages (including ornamental cabbage), chili peppers and herbs of all sorts. You can also introduce color with flowers such as nasturtiums and calendulas, or marigolds.

Vegetables and fruit trees can also be used decoratively in small spaces by being grown in large containers. Citrus trees, for example, make excellent pot plants. Herbs and small varieties of popular vegetables can also be grown in pots, window boxes or even large hanging baskets.

Grazing the Garden

If you want to appeal to your sense of taste but don't want a separate vegetable patch or orchard, simply mingle productive and ornamental plants. Whenever you select a plant, consider using an edible variety.

Grapevines are great climbers to grow over a pergola. They provide shade in summer and sunlight in winter. There are ornamental grapevines, such as the magnificent crimson glory vine *Vitis coignetiae*, grown for its autumn color, or select a fruiting variety of *Vitis vinifera*, which will have bunches of edible grapes in late summer and autumn.

Also useful and productive for an arch or a strongly built pergola is the kiwifruit or Chinese gooseberry *Actinidia deliciosa*. This deciduous climber needs a strong support and full sun. Male and female vines are needed for fruit production.

Create a colorful, edible planting with herbs, and annuals such as pot marigold *Calendula officinalis*.

Beans, too, can be used as productive ornamentals. Train the scarlet runner bean *Phaseolus coccineus* over an arch or on a trellis, enjoy its attractive flowers and then harvest the beans. Gourds, pumpkins and peas can also be used to be both decorative and productive.

Herbs can also be used for their ornamental as well as edible qualities. The deep green of parsley can be grown as a low border to a flower garden. Chives, garlic or ornamental onions can be grown with or among roses. As well, select tall-growing herbs or vegetables, such as dill or artichokes, to use in clumps in a herbaceous border.

There are many fruiting trees that can be used as shade and shelter plants. Apples, crab apples, cherries, almonds and other nut trees and, in a Mediterranean climate, olives, are just some of the fruiting trees that can be grown for their ornamental qualities as well as their fruit.

The native American serviceberry *Amelanchier laevis*, a valuable and highly decorative ornamental tree, will produce a crop of edible berries after its fragrant white flowers.

Some flowers are edible, such as nasturtiums *Tropaeolum magus*, pictured here, as well as daylilies and zucchini (courgette) flowers. They can be used to garnish foods or can be mixed into a salad.

Even in a small garden there are dwarf fruiting trees that can be used in containers or dwarf hedges. One of the best of the new dwarf fruiting trees for ornamental use is the Ballerina Series of apples and crab apples. These narrow, columnar trees are an excellent choice for a narrow screen or to grow as a focal point in a small garden, in the ground or in a pot.

Also useful for hedges are many of the edible berry plants, such as raspberries, thornless blackberries or blueberries.

If you've only tasted store-bought figs, you're in for a real taste treat if you grow your own.

The fruits of yellow currant tomatoes *Lycopersicon pimpinellifolium* are tiny but are produced in abundance. Both red and yellow variants are available. Use them whole in salads.

Landscaping with Plants

Plants are growing things to be put to work in the garden. Train plants into living walls, floors and ceilings of the garden, or call on them to solve garden problems. Because plants respond to varying environmental factors, the right plant choice will transform a problem area into a showpiece. However bad or varied the growing conditions, such as poor soil, a sloping site, a drainage disaster, an area that needs winter sun but summer shade, or a utility area that needs to be screened—there will be a plant to fit the bill. The key is good plant selection and appropriate growing conditions.

Living Walls, Floors and Ceilings

Most of us have some experience in applying design principles to completely human-made structures, usually the exteriors and interiors of buildings. Unless something goes wrong with the stability of the structure on which we are working, everything is under control and the materials we are working with more or less stay put.

However, when designing a landscape, we are working with materials that quite literally have lives of their own. As with decorating a room, however, understanding and, where necessary, enhancing the basic structure of the landscape is essential, since this is the foundation upon which all other garden work is built.

When starting a garden from scratch, beginners in landscape design can feel intimidated by the magnitude of the task in front of them, but whether you are designing the structure of a large garden, or putting together a group of plants in, say, a window box or trough, similar design considerations can apply—even if you are not always aware of them.

Whether in a container or the open garden, each design is literally unique. A design may be tall and dramatic, or low and rounded. It may be fan-shaped or triangular, circular, curving or completely asymmetrical and random looking. It may closely follow the boundaries of the space within which you're working, or meander, or cut diagonally across the space.

A mass planting of intensely blue-purple, upright-growing delphiniums makes an eye-catching display.

And you are not limited to exploring the space within side boundaries: The floor and ceiling of your garden—or the "garden rooms"—can also be modified.

You can change the ground levels of your site and try different surfaces, textures and colors. Ceilings can be represented by garden structures and the developing canopies of maturing trees as well as by the wilder-growing climbers, such as some roses, that will send their long canes shooting skyward.

Lilies

twining, upright-growing, pyramidal, rounded, vase-shaped, spreading, spiky or otherwise. While you can prune or train many plants to direct the shape they take, it will mean a lot less work for you if you select plants that naturally take the shape you want.

One useful approach may be to think of plants as performing one of three basic design roles: as vertical accents, as fillers for bulk and color, or as climbers and creepers, twining through other plants or cascading over retaining walls.

Blooms, fruits, variegated or unusually colored leaves and interesting growth habits can also contribute to these effects

Working with Plant Form

When you consider plant forms, you are exploring and experimenting with the ways they can contribute to the overall structure of your landscape design.

Form refers to a plant's shape and growth habit—

LEFT: A garden path is framed by a wisteria-covered pergola.
RIGHT: Virginia creeper *Parthenocissus tricuspidata*.

RIGHT: The attention-grabbing, red stems of *Cornus sericea* can grow to 7 feet (2 m) tall.

by attracting the eye and emphasizing the plant's structural roles.

Vertical accents include trees and shrubs, vines on trellises and tall, flowering plants (such as hollyhocks, delphiniums, irises and lilies), as well as the dramatic shapes of ornamental grasses, New Zealand flax and palms, and some tall cacti and other succulents.

Fillers are low-growing or mounding plants, and can range from small annuals, such as primulas and dwarf French marigolds, and perennials, including the various sages and Mexican daisies, to naturally mounding shrubs, such as some rhododendrons, aucuba, flowering quinces and many more.

Everybody has their own favorite vines and creepers, such as wisteria, some roses, ivies (choose docile cultivars), vinca, jasmine, nasturtiums, spider plant and others. A wall, a fence, the side of your house or an old tree can be suitable for growing beautiful climbing plants on. In small gardens, you may find that there is actually more vertical surface space than the total ground area.

With all forms of plants, the objective is to make optimum use of the resources available to you.

As with a conventional plant border, you will need to base your selection of wall plants and climbers not only on the colors and varieties that most please you but also on a range that will provide interest through the year.

Deciduous or Evergreen

Whether your trees and shrubs hold their leaves throughout the year, or shed them as the colder months approach, will determine an important part of the seasonal structure of your landscape.

Trees and shrubs that lose their leaves in autumn and produce new foliage in

RIGHT: Include feature plants with stunning autumn foliage, such as this vibrant *Acer*.

spring are called deciduous. They lose their leaves as they become dormant during winter with the result that, except for limited root growth, the plants' biological processes are suspended.

Deciduous trees and shrubs are popular and many have leaves that turn brilliant

colors before they fall. They include oaks, maples, elms, liquidambars, dogwoods, ashes, viburnums and hydrangeas.

Camellia

Evergreen trees and shrubs hold most of their leaves throughout the year, but do not make the mistake of believing that they do not shed—they do lose some leaves all year round.

Popular evergreen trees include conifers, such as pines, cypresses, spruces and firs, as well as eucalypts, boxwood, most types of holly, and most rhododendrons, camellias and azaleas.

Complexities do arise, however, even within the same family of plants. For instance, although most hollies are evergreen, there are deciduous hollies. There are also deciduous and evergreen azaleas. In some cases, whether a tree or shrub loses its leaves will depend on just how cold it gets in winter where you live.

It has been common design practice to mark outer boundaries of the landscape with evergreen trees and shrubs, while positioning deciduous specimens in front

of the evergreen background. This means that the center of the garden is sunnier during the coolest time of the year.

In larger gardens, there is a trend to mark internal divisions and screens in the garden as strongly as the outer boundaries.

Surprises and a sense of going on a journey are valuable elements in designing a garden, and planning for paths to turn corners and go through archways is a delightful way of guiding visitors through your garden. Plan paths so that they lead to a concealed feature such as a gazebo, water garden or simply a pleasant bench on which to sit.

Mature height is an important factor to consider when planning whether you will choose evergreen or deciduous trees and shrubs—the higher your maturing plant grows, the greater the shade it will cast. The amount of privacy you want or whether you need to screen an ugly view will also be factors in determining if you want evergreen cover or not.

A Framework of Plants

True plant lovers always delight in the possibilities involved in creating a new garden, but before beginning, it is wise to look at the garden's existing structure and surroundings.

Because of their size, any existing large trees will be important elements in your landscape design. If any plant has to be removed for any reason, usually the sooner this is done the better. Assess the visual impact of all existing plantings but pay particular attention to the mature

This wooden archway frames a winding path that leads through to a hidden area of the garden.

trees and shrubs you want to keep. Try to imagine what other plants might be added for balance or to strengthen the visual framework of the site. If you are trying to move away from a rather bitsy mixture of plantings, you might consider planting additional specimens of plants that you like that are already doing well in your garden.

An existing row of mature trees or shrubs might provide enclosure along a busy street, but you might prefer to thin the row to create vistas from the street and openings to entice visitors to enjoy your garden—even from a distance.

Since the house is usually, but not always, the dominant design element around which you will be working, examine it closely for inspiration. Try to define the architectural style of the house. Also, because many homes combine elements of more than one style, look for the most prominent features, and the ones that you like most.

A row of blossoming trees in spring creates a superb, colorful garden "wall" or screen.

If there is a favorite bay window or a terrace that catches the sun in the morning, you may want to design vistas that extend these features into the garden, enhancing the view or highlighting a favorite tree or some other feature.

Larger, spreading trees along the borders provide screening yet avoid casting too much shade on the inner garden. Walls, arbors and columnar trees will give vertical structure to the garden, leaving more space for flower beds and other features in the garden's heart.

Feature Plants and Gap-fillers

For your initial planting, focus on landmark plants—the trees and shrubs that will grow to be the mature framework of your garden, or form the special features upon which the design of the landscape as a whole will focus. These will help give your garden a sense of structure. If you

Ivy

like roses and your garden offers the right conditions, they can provide a lovely theme for your garden, because they have so many different forms—bushes, small trees, climbers, ramblers—and grow quickly in suitable conditions. Other options include the wide range of hedging plants as well as evergreen and deciduous shrubs and trees.

One rule to remember is to have taller plants toward the back of your viewing area, so that you create a sense of balance and flow as well as preventing smaller plants from being smothered and killed.

Foundation Planting

One area that is sometimes overlooked is the foundation planting—the parts of the garden that anchor the house and other structures to the landscape and create a sense of transition between the two.

When choosing foundation plants, consider how their forms can reinforce the

LEFT: Sealing-wax palm *Cyrtostachys renda* makes a stunning feature plant in a warm-climate or tropical garden.
RIGHT: Japanese kerria *Kerria japonica*.

lines of your architecture. Columnar trees or tall grasses accentuate the height of the house and mirror vertical elements such as tall chimney stacks.

The horizontal lines of contemporary and ranch-style homes can be reinforced by spreading and weeping trees or low-growing shrubs; aim to complement rather than compete with the architecture.

Spreading trees and low shrub masses can balance strong vertical lines and make any building appear a part of the landscape, but it is important not to plant shrubs that cover the bottom of the house. This can create a boring, dense horizontal mass as well as problems with damp inside the house.

When planting shrubs beneath windows, and working with informal or semiformal design styles, look for plants with horizontal growth habits so that you do not have to hack upright-growing shrubs into flat-topped travesties of their natural selves.

You could create a low-maintenance foundation planting by planting a straight row of dwarf evergreens and surrounding them with a layer of mulch. With a little extra effort, you can combine a variety of plants for an interesting, dynamic planting scheme that is a pleasure to stroll by on your way in and out the door.

Foundation plantings have traditionally contained mostly evergreen conifers, such as yew and juniper, or broad-leaved evergreens, such as azaleas and boxwood. Evergreens do add color and hide the foundation all year, but deciduous shrubs have their place, too. Many species, including dwarf fothergilla *Fothergilla gardenii* and Japanese kerria *Kerria*

japonica, offer year-round interest with brightly colored flowers, autumn leaf color or attractive stems.

Although there is an enormous range of plants from which you might choose, try to limit your design to just a few different plant types, and plant multiple specimens of each. Not only will the design look better but you'll have fewer kinds of plant to maintain.

If you choose interesting species, you don't have to worry that the lack of diversity will be monotonous. Look for plants with attractive textures or growth habits or with interesting fruit, flowers, or bark—and remember to include groundcovers, trailing plants, climbers and vines to help fill in empty spaces and bind the different elements together.

Because climbing plants usually grow quickly, they can fill spaces while slower-growing plants mature. Some are very rapid growers and benefit from enriched soil at planting and feeding occasionally until well established.

When your main plantings have matured, you can thin out the temporary climbers and vines, using the clippings as cuttings to start them anew elsewhere.

When choosing foundation plants, look for flower colors to complement the colors of your house.

Solving Landscaping Problems with Plants

There may be a landscape somewhere that has never had any substantial problems, but such perfection is not very likely. Every garden is the result of someone dealing with a range of problems in an intelligent and creative way.

Because home gardeners can now choose from a very wide range of plants and, in nature, plants have adapted to the most unlikely and extreme environments, careful plant selection can help you make a beautiful garden from what might seem a very difficult site.

Also, the chances are good that at least some of your problems are shared by your neighbors—you are unlikely to be alone. Local garden centers and plant stores will be only too familiar with the tales of woe you bring them. They will also stock plants that suit your site and be able to suggest remedies when things do go wrong. You may also find that local agricultural organizations, universities or colleges provide a horticultural advice service—perhaps available on the Internet.

Astilbe

One useful approach is to work with, not against, what you have. What seem to be hurdles in your garden can be overcome, especially if you are prepared to amend your plans so that you are working with

Add color to a shady area with beautiful flowering plants such as hellebores *Helleborus* spp.

natural conditions. This may also point your landscape in directions that you might not have considered otherwise.

Take time to identify your garden's biggest drawbacks and observe what effect these are having. In a new garden, try not to make really major changes for the first year so that you can identify the pluses and minuses through every season.

If you have a few problems, try to prioritize them and do not attempt to solve all problems at once. Some will inevitably take several seasons to fix, while others may involve high costs. Professional advice and reconstruction or soil amendment may be needed in more extreme cases.

Going With the Wind

Very windy landscapes can have a rather unearthly appearance. Trees can be stunted or bent over, or even nonexistent, plants of any kind are difficult to establish and soil dries out quickly. In summer, plants can get blown down and in winter, winds add to the chill.

Use plants to build shelter. Consider planting a hedge or a sheltering belt of

Barriers, such as a fence, can reduce wind velocity for distances up to five times their height.

Trees and Shrubs for Wind Shelter

Plants can be a great alternative to a solid fence for dividing a property or blocking an unpleasant view. Open-branched trees are good dispersers of wind. These plants tolerate close planting to create an effective barrier or screen.

Araucaria heterophylla (Norfolk Island pine)
Cedrus spp. (cedars)
Cupressus spp. (cypresses)
Grevillea robusta (silky oak)
Ilex spp. (hollies)
Juniperus virginiana (eastern red cedar)
Lagunaria patersonii (Norfolk Island hibiscus)
Liquidambar styraciflua (liquidambar)
Melaleuca quinquenervia (broad-leaved paperbark)
Picea abies (Norway spruce)
Pinus spp. (pines)
Platanus orientalis (oriental plane tree)
Populus spp. (poplars)
Quercus palustris (pin oak)
Schinus molle (peppercorn tree)
Ulmus parvifolia (Chinese elm)

Holly

SHADY GARDEN CORNER You can lighten and brighten a shady area of the garden, such as a corner under an overhanging shade tree. First, paint the wall a pale color that will reflect light. Then plant a variety of golden-leafed, white-variegated or white-flowered plants.

trees and shrubs across the windiest border of your garden. Plant barriers can be most effective in providing shelter from strong winds, because solid barriers such as a wall can cause wind eddying that can damage your plants.

Shelter plants may well need protection as they develop. Erect temporary screens of loose-weave hessian or heavy-duty shade cloth on posts, either as a single, large screen or as a broad cylinder around individual plants.

You can also use woven fence panels as a temporary shelter to protect a growing hedge or windbreak. When the fence's useful life is over, the hedge should be well established.

When planting shelter, resist the temptation to plant only the fastest-growing trees. They can get out of control and unless you plan to clip them regularly, you might find less unruly plants much easier in the long term.

Shady Characters

A shade garden can be a place of quiet beauty and subtle colors, a cool retreat on a hot summer afternoon. While trees are

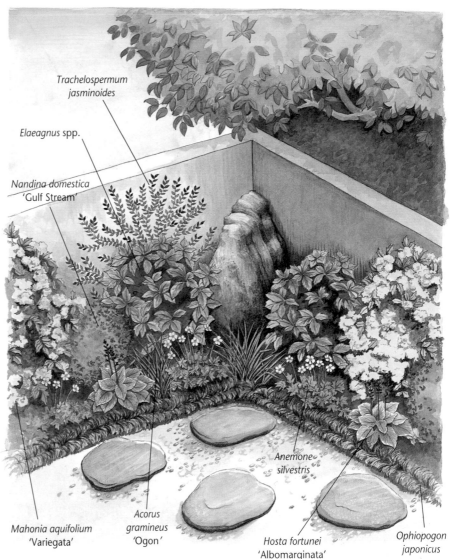

Trachelospermum jasminoides

Elaeagnus spp.

Nandina domestica 'Gulf Stream'

Mahonia aquifolium 'Variegata'

Acorus gramineus 'Ogon'

Anemone silvestris

Hosta fortunei 'Albomarginata'

Ophiopogon japonicus

the foundation of the shady garden, shrubs soften the edges, add privacy and provide a backdrop for flowering annuals, perennials and bulbs.

Success in shady sites, as in any kind of garden, depends on careful planning and on choosing plants that grow happily in such conditions. The two main factors that determine which plants can grow well in your shade garden are how much light the garden gets and how much water is available.

Hostas, such as *Hosta ventricosta*, are ideal for season-long interest in a shady, moist situation.

Sites that get a few hours of direct sun or a full day of filtered light can support a wider range of plants than a spot that's in deep shade all day. Gardens under deciduous trees may get lots of sun until early summer, when the developing tree leaves begin to block the light.

Shady gardens can also vary widely in the amount of moisture that's available. Plants that grow well in moist, woodland soils usually aren't happy in the dry shade under roof overhangs or shallow-rooted trees such as maples and beeches.

Direct traffic away from shallow-rooted trees and areas you wish to keep as deep shade, so you can replace scraggly lawn with groundcovers. Use stepping stones or heavily mulched paths to guide visitors around planted areas. A bench or an informal stone patio makes an inviting destination, and works well when sited in the deepest shade or beneath the most shallow-rooted trees.

A good supply of organic matter may mean the difference between death and survival in shade, especially dry shade. If you are gardening under trees, you can't just till in the organic matter or dump a thick layer on the surface; either way, you'll harm the tree roots. Instead, try digging and enriching individual planting pockets close to the tree trunk, where there are few feeder roots.

One quick solution for deep shade is simply to let more light into the garden— reduce the number of branches on overhanging trees, lengthen their bare trunks by removing lower limbs and pull out any high shrubs or greenery that are blocking light.

In a seaside dune garden, use plants such as sea holly *Eryngium amethystinum* to hold the sand in place.

Hills and Slopes

With a little imagination, you can transform a sloping site from a maintenance headache into an eye-catching landscape. Hillsides are awkward to mow and weed,

Bethlehem sage

so the best strategy here is to cover them with plants that take care of themselves.

If you like a casual look and you're willing to mow the slope once a year, consider turning it into a wildflower meadow. Or, if you're willing to invest time and money, you can build retaining walls or terraced beds that will safely support a wide range of attractive plants.

Another good option for sunny slopes is planting a mixture of sun-loving groundcovers, taller spreading perennials (such as daylilies) and low-growing, spreading shrubs, such as creeping juniper *Juniperus horizontalis*.

Building a rock garden is another effective solution for a sunny, well-drained slope. Place large rocks at irregular intervals throughout the area. Bury each so that over half is underground to keep it from rolling or washing away. Large, secure stones will give you a steady foothold so you can get into the garden for occasional weeding.

For very hilly areas of the garden, you can create level planting areas with a series of terraced beds.

On shady slopes, spreading species and cultivars of hostas make great groundcovers, either alone or combined with other plants. Other suitable companions include lily-of-the-valley *Convallaria majalis*, pachysandra *Pachysandra terminalis* and common periwinkle *Vinca minor*. For extra interest, add spring-flowering bulbs to get early color from groundcover plantings.

If the slope is shaded by deciduous trees, create a woodland garden by combining groundcovers such as ajuga and European wild ginger *Asarum europaeum* with early-blooming wildflowers. Creeping phlox *Phlox stolonifera*, wild bleeding heart *Dicentra eximia* and Allegheny foamflower *Tiarella cordifolia* are a few species that will bloom in spring before the trees leaf out fully and shade the area.

Coasting Along

Seaside gardens can have similar problems to merely windy gardens, but there are two additional problems—first, the wind that carries salt spray can be very damaging to plants and, second, sand can blow into the garden. However, coastal gardens are generally warmer than those inland in the same region and seaside gardens are usually frost-free.

Again, the solution is to develop shelter, but using salt-resistant plants. They will probably not grow as tall or lush as they might inland.

Mediterranean gardens are naturally at home on maritime sites in warmer climates, and in really sandy areas, think about a dune garden. Use grasses, sea hollies and other maritime plants to anchor the sand to one spot.

Wet Spots

Wet areas are generally caused by a high water table or poor drainage or both. You cannot do much about the first, other than to build up parts of your garden with raised beds, terracing and so on. If you excavate to change levels, you can develop contrasting wet and drier areas.

Poor drainage can be put right by installing a piped drainage system or by improving the soil's porous quality with bulky materials, such as compost, bark mulch or grit.

Often, water stands where soil has been compacted. Once the compacted layer has been broken up the water will run away more easily.

You can also incorporate plants that tolerate, or even welcome, damp or wet conditions. Most woodland plants and

Bee balm
(bergamot)

many wildflowers prefer moist soil. Many sun-loving wildflowers also grow happily in moist soil. If the area dries out enough to support grass, try a moist meadow garden.

For more ideas, check out natural marsh, pond or stream habitats in your area to see what is thriving there. (Just remember to gather ideas and inspiration from these natural areas, not the plants themselves. Many garden centers are expanding their selection into water-garden plants as well, so you should have no trouble buying the plants you need.)

If your problem site is underwater for much of the year, go with the flow—leave it as a wetland or convert it into a small pond and plant perennials to cascade over its edges. Trees and shrubs for wet conditions include *Amelanchier lamarckii*, birches, *Cornus alba*, mountain ash *Sorbus* spp., *Viburnum opulus* and willows (but be careful, because some are very vigorous).

Herbaceous plants to choose from include astilbes, daylilies, hostas, ligularia, bee balm (bergamot), *Mimulus* (monkey flower) and primulas.

Hot and Dry Sites

Positions in full sun, often on poor soil, tend to lose their reserves of moisture very quickly. By late spring, plants begin to wilt, growth stops and only the most drought-resistant plants survive.

Many silver-leaved species are particularly sensitive to winter wetness, but will get by comfortably in such a site. Select plant species

that relish hot, dry conditions. Again, this might be the perfect site for a Mediterranean garden.

The prettiest of the Mediterranean shrubs have aromatic leaves, fragrant blooms and often have silver foliage. Sage, rosemary, several species of lavender, *Phlomis* and *Cistus* (rock roses) will all grow well here. Use them with dark evergreens such as dwarf juniper. Dry landscaping, or xeriscaping, enhances the arid effect. Consider gravel or grit as a mulch and set out rocks to accentuate the desert look.

Frost Pockets

The more sheltered a garden, the more likely it is to hold a frost pocket, especially if that area does not get direct sunlight. Some frost pockets can be created when new structures are built or maturing trees and shrubs cast more shade. If possible, let more light in and develop greater air circulation. A gap in a hedge or wall, for example, can allow more air flow.

Avoid planting vulnerable, frost-tender plants species in frost pockets. A plant may be trying to produce delicate spring blooms only to have buds and flowers killed or stunted by one cool night and a ground frost.

The Art of Concealment

Most of us share at least a part of our gardens with parked cars, garbage and compost bins, fuel tanks, woodpiles, gas and electric meters, utility wires and all the other paraphernalia of daily life. Few of these objects actually add beauty to the landscape but they can be disguised in various ways.

Sometimes designing a really spectacular focal point in your garden can distract attention from the more unsightly utility areas. More common, however, is the careful deployment of garden structures, such as screens (especially when covered with vines and other climbers), hedges, tall feature plants and other barriers.

Purple loosestrife *Lythrum salicaria* 'Feuerkerze' is a perennial that is happiest in wet areas of the garden.

Designing Beds and Borders

An essential part of designing a bed or border is planning. The ideal is a planting scheme that will deliver a year-round, all-weather garden bed, or a border full of color and interest.

Not only will you be able to enjoy a long-running and changing show all summer, but when autumn comes, you can replant for winter greenery, which will burst into color as soon as the days begin to warm up again. Foliage, as well as flowers, will help to keep your bedding displays fresh and lively.

Planting out bedding plants is as near as you can get to instant gardening. When selecting plants in spring, many will be just coming into flower, giving you an almost immediate display. But you can do even better if you take some trouble with your designs.

Bedding is beautiful if arranged in formal patterns, however simple, and

ABOVE: Create a color-theme border, such as this spectacular blue and yellow, summer border.
BELOW: Mixing ornamental grasses into your border plantings adds height and year-round interest.

always looks best when colors are selected to work well together. Deciding on which plants are most likely to thrive in your conditions is important, too, so that your display does not let you down if the weather turns bad.

Resist the temptation to buy purely on impulse. Have a clear idea of what colors (and characters) of plants you want before you arrive at the nursery and then choose accordingly.

Choose a theme and then acquire the plants that suit it. A successful border or garden bed combines elements of color, texture, shape and height to form a harmonious composition.

Professional designers use this approach when planning a border. They may focus on specific types of plants (herbs, for instance) or mix two groups of plants together (such as grasses and perennials).

Garden Beds

Beds are often located closer to the house than borders, usually along the foundation or edging a patio. If you're going to put a bed where you'll see it all the time, choose your plants carefully for all-season interest.

High-visibility beds will also need either some extra work or carefully chosen, low-maintenance plants to look their best all the time.

Garden beds come in a wide variety of shapes and sizes. It's best to choose a shape and style (formal or informal) that matches or balances nearby features in the garden. The front of the bed can curve, even if the side up against the house is straight. Make the bed as wide as you can, but make sure you can reach all plants from outside the bed. An alternative is to place stepping stones in the bed for easy access.

Thrift

This informal, herb garden bed, featuring flowering chives, looks as if it has been cut out of the surrounding paved garden surface.

Garden beds work particularly well if they are arranged in patterns. These can be formal, with geometric shapes, or informal, with plants set out in drifts. Be bold in your overall design, but keep things simple. Two or three varieties arranged together will often be more effective than a fussy mixture.

When planting drifts, arrange bold swathes or blocks of color rather than a mixed-up effect, and suit your planting design to the shape of the bed.

Island Beds

Island beds are surrounded on all sides by lawn or paving. Often these are oval or odd kidney shapes but a definite trend is round—circles are in. Island beds are a great way to add color and height to a new property while you're waiting for trees and shrubs to mature. They can also be useful replacements for lawn under trees, reducing the need for trimming and making mowing easier.

Island bed

Locate your island bed in some open situation but do not just plunk it down in the middle of the lawn—unless this is part of a formal plan. Use an island bed to form an oasis of color in the back corner of the property, to echo the shape of shrub groupings elsewhere in the lawn or as a welcome garden at the foot of the drive.

As a general rule, make island beds three times as long as they are wide for the most natural effect. You also make one end wider than the other so you can grow taller flowers there, but balance the extra bed width by putting an appropriate group of bold plants in or near the narrower side.

Generally, in a garden border that will be viewed from the front, the taller plants are at the back.

Since you can view an island bed from all sides, normally, it's best to put the tallest plants in the center and surround them with low-growers. However, if you will see the bed primarily from one angle, make the highest point in the back. Then you can add extra tiers of mid-border plants and still have some low-growers on the far side.

Garden Borders

Borders are often rectangular, following property lines or formal paths and driveways, but you can also design them with gentle curves for a more informal look. Because they are often seen from only one side, borders generally have a distinct front and back, with taller plants located to the rear.

There is no limit to how long a border can be, but long borders may need a

A hot-color, summer border featuring crocosmia *Crocosmia* 'Lucifer', scarlet sage *Salvia splendens*, and marigolds *Tagetes patula* and *Tagetes erecta*.

shortcut of a couple of stepping stones so you can get to the other side without having to walk around either end.

The width of the border will take some thought. Four to 5 feet (1.2 to 1.5 m) is enough room to include a good mix of plant heights. Long borders that are deeper than 5 or 6 feet (1.5 or 1.8 m) are a challenge to maintain, because it is hard to reach more than 2 or 3 feet (60 to 90 cm) in from either side to weed, trim, or dig.

If you want a border more than 3 feet (90 cm) wide in front of a hedge or wall, leave space behind it for a grassy or mulched access path so you can get to every part of it. Should you plan to make your border longer than about 15 feet (4.5 m), make the access path as wide as your garden cart or wheelbarrow so you can easily haul in loads of manure or compost and cart out trimmings.

Constructing Beds and Borders

Building a bed or border is easy if you start with a plan and follow a few simple rules. A successful border is largely a matter of good marriages between plants. Whether you use traditional perennials and annuals or shrubs with interesting foliage, the goal is the same: Combine plants whose colors and textures look good together, and plan for an extended season with a succession of bloom or foliage texture.

Start with the tall, long-lived plants that will give form to the border. Fill in with the low, more rambling plants and then add your special features—for example, bulbs that might have a brief but spectacular blooming season.

Make sure you locate plants with similar water, soil and light needs together. When designing islands of low-water plants, target those areas where summer irrigation would be difficult.

As well as being ideal for gardens with a Mediterranean theme, many culinary herbs combine well with ornamental shrubs and perennials. Sited alongside a patio or near the kitchen door, a bed of mixed flowers, herbs, vegetables and fruit can be very welcoming and attractive, as well as useful.

Edging Away

It can be tough to mow around or along beds and borders without cutting into the

Summer border edged with *Lavandula angustifolia* 'Dwarf White' and *L. angustifolia* 'Princess Blue'.

Bed and Border Tips

As with many gardening and landscaping tasks, a systematic approach makes things a little easier. These tips for creating your own garden beds and borders reflect the experience of many landscape designers and gardeners.

- Ask the "why?" question. What is this bed or border actually for? Why do you want it?
- Select your location. Determine its exposure (sun, part-sun or shade) and other growing conditions. Be wary of maturing trees and other changes that might affect your new garden.
- Measure and sketch your site dimensions and any special features with which you will have to deal.
- Choose a theme, taking account of the color or style of your home, or from the types of plant that do well in your area. You can also choose a theme to suit a particular use—to attract birds or butterflies, for instance.
- Go for a variety of blooming times. Look around your neighborhood and public gardens to see what is in bloom throughout the year.
- Plant densely for a fuller, lusher effect.
  - Prepare your soil, mixing in generous amounts of compost or other soil amendment, and then smooth it out.
  - Arrange the plants, still in their pots, on the soil and adjust as needed before planting. For one-sided viewing, place tall plants at the back, short to medium growers in the middle ground, and ground-huggers in the front. To view from all angles, put the tall plants in the middle and lower-growers around them.
  - Plant in groups with several plants of the same kind together—odd numbers, such as threes or fives, usually seem to look best.
  - Incorporate accent plants. Use dramatic plants (tall grasses or succulents, for example) as features throughout the bed or border, to act as a focal point.

Goldenrod

'Red Baron' blood grass

and borders. Edging plants are small, neat, compact plants used at the front of the border, in the same way that shrubs or fences define the back of the border. Any plant can be used for edging if it can be kept within bounds of space and low height and suits the growing conditions in your bed or border. The job of edging plants is to frame or add contrast to surrounding borders, lawns or hardscapes by forming bands of color. They will also help conceal less than attractive garden edging materials of metal or plastic.

Once established, it is easy to keep your edges neat. Replace any dead or ragged plants, deadhead the flowers and prune the plants back a bit if they become unruly. If you keep your edging plants in good health, your whole landscape will appear neat, complete and well cared for.

bedding plants. The more formal your landscape plans, the more neat edges and tidy boundaries matter.

If you look at photographs of old garden beds, the problem of neat edging was dealt with in a number of ways, including terracotta sections in a wide variety of "spaded" or decorative shapes arranged between path or lawn and bed or border. Wire hoops and miniature wire fences were also used.

Home gardeners have also edged with many different materials: timber, stone, brick and cement in formal or informal sections, laid loose or fastened or cast in place, perhaps with a bagged or painted finish to match pathways.

In more recent times, edging systems of metal and plastic have been developed that lie under the desirable lawn grass height so that they can be mown over. Your local garden center or hardware store will either stock edging products or be able to order them for you, and it seems that terracotta edging sections are rather coming back into fashion, especially for gardens surrounding older houses.

Edging with Plants

You can also use tough, ground-hugging plants along the front of your flower beds

Spiky plants, such as spike gayfeather, look wonderful contrasted with low, mounded plants.

Special Plant Effects

Many plants are more flexible in cultivation than we might at first think. Over the centuries, gardeners have trained plants to get the greatest possible benefit from them and, in doing so, have created distinctive garden forms that may have a place in your landscape.

Fruit trees, such as apples, pears, apricots and plums, have been carefully cultivated to produce as much fruit as possible in the smallest space. It is possible to train these trees into a variety of shapes to fit almost any space. Keep this in mind as you plan planting schemes to enliven small side yards, cramped courtyards, tight property lines and landscape sites with walls and fences.

Experiment with Espalier

Espalier is a training technique that turns a normally bushy plant into a flat, almost two-dimensional form. Although the

technique requires persistent attention and fearless pruning, the results are tremendously rewarding. Use espalier training to cover a blank or nondescript wall, to create a leafy screen that gives privacy to a doorway, deck, patio or porch, or to grow faster-yielding fruit in a small space.

Before you choose the plants you want to train, think carefully about the exposure of the site where you plan to create the espalier. Training styles for espalier are limited only by your imagination. For a classical look, you might choose a formal U-shape, fan or interwoven Belgian fence pattern. Informal, free-flowing patterns are attractive, too, but they can be more difficult to train without having them look like a jumble of stems.

ABOVE LEFT: Two spiral boxwood *Buxus* spp. topiaries make a striking display at an entrance.
ABOVE RIGHT: A romantic "gateway" has been created by a topiarized yew *Taxus baccata* hedge.

Espaliered trees take time to train and maintain. You'll have to shape them carefully, choosing the best main branches and manipulating them into the right position. Then you'll have to thin out side growth and errant shoots to maintain the purity of the pattern you've established. The stunning results, however, more than repay the extra work.

Topiary Tales

Training shrubs, trees and vines into fanciful shapes is another practice that carries pruning into the realm of sculpture. A single example of topiary can be a graceful focal point in a small garden; multiple figures can transform a larger space into a magical land, peopled with strange and wonderful creatures and shapes.

Evergreen, small-leaved plants are usually the plants of choice for garden topiary projects. Yews *Taxus* spp. and boxwoods *Buxus* spp. are traditional favorites for this type of pruning.

FAR LEFT: Espalier is a training technique to use to add charm and beauty to a narrow space.
LEFT: Carefully trained fruit trees can produce a unique and effective fence that is also productive.

For best results, start with a young or newly planted shrub; older shrubs may require more drastic pruning to get them into the shape you want.

Topiaries are generally trained into either geometric or representational forms. Geometric shapes, such as boxes and spheres, take less time, thought and planning, as evidenced by the abundance of these in residential landscapes.

For a more whimsical look, you may shape your topiary into a more unusual form, such as a boat, bird, giraffe, dog, chair or wishing well. If you plan to try a complicated figure, it's helpful to sketch out the final shape you want; then you can refer to the sketch as you prune. Try to keep the figure fairly simple; it can be hard to maintain fine details.

Basic Bonsai

Bonsai is an art that attempts to replicate, in a container, the look of an old tree that has been shaped by time and the elements. The process of training beautiful bonsai requires time and patience, but the results can be stunning and gratifying.

Bonsai maple

Before you buy or begin a bonsai project, be aware that these plants will need some special care. Hardy bonsai normally prefer to be outdoors during the growing season. They enjoy the shelter of a lath house or some other shade-producing structure, where they will receive bright, indirect light and protection from the elements. One gust of wind can easily knock over small plants and undo months or years of care!

Bonsai generally grow in shallow pots, so you'll have to water them frequently—possibly as often as twice a day in hot weather—to keep the soil evenly damp. During the winter months, you'll need to protect bonsai from cold temperatures.

When choosing a young plant for bonsai, you don't need to pick a symmetrical, well-balanced specimen. Stems with bends, twists, scars or stumps can give a bonsai real character—even some dead wood can be desirable.

Pleaching

Pleaching is the interweaving of growing branches, vines and other climbing plants, and can be trained as a living wall or arbor as well as an avenue of trees.

Carefully selected trees are planted on a grid, like a small orchard. As they grow, the branches are pruned and trained along this grid, so that eventually the branch of one tree meets that of its neighbor. At this point, an incision is made in the bark of both branches and they are tied together. When these pleached branches mature to form substantial limbs, the trees are all connected together.

Pollarding

Pollarding is a way of imposing a formal look on a tree, and for controlling the size of an otherwise large-growing tree.

Lime trees *Linden* spp. are a popular tree for pleaching, as their young limbs are pliable and easily trained into the interlocked pattern.

In addition to creating a stylized appearance, the training technique known as pollarding can restrain the height of a large-growing tree, such as this mulberry *Morus* spp.

In winter, a pollarded tree is a trunk, topped by a rather clubbed head or very short limbs. In summer, a mass of vigorous shoots wildly bursts forth from the tree's head or limbs.

Deciduous, fast-growing trees that do not resent being pruned hard are ideal candidates for pollarding, for example chestnut, horse chestnut, linden, London plane tree, sycamore, eucalypt and willow.

You can create a pollarded tree by removing branches along the trunk of a young tree to give the tree a high head with at least 5 or 6 feet (1.5 or 2 m) of clear trunk.

A pollarded tree needs to be pruned every winter, or at least every second or third winter. Pruning is easy. Cut off all new stems back to within half an inch (1 cm) or so of where they grew the previous season.

Using Trees in the Landscape

The biggest investment in your garden landscape—in both time and money—is the selection, purchase and planting of trees. Trees dominate the landscape with their size and their effects on the surroundings. A landscape with trees has psychological benefits, too, by making you feel rested and peaceful.

Landscaping with Trees

Trees generally have a mature height ranging from 15–100 feet (4.5–30 m) or more. A small tree is defined as one that generally doesn't exceed 25–35 feet (7.5–10.5 m) in mature height. A medium-sized tree matures at 50–65 feet (15–19.5 m), and a large tree matures at 75–100 feet (22.5–30 m) or taller. Growing conditions, climate, competition with grass and other plants, mechanical or animal damage, and pollution can prevent a tree from reaching its mature height.

These versatile plants frame views, develop patterns for your landscape and unify your design. To get the most out of the trees you select, you should consider the following features and what they can add to your design.

Beauty

Trees serve as backdrops for other plants or garden features and as focal points, like large, living sculptures. You can use them to screen unwanted views and give you privacy. Your trees establish the walls and ceilings for your outdoor rooms. You can use them to soften the architecture of your house or to call attention to it.

Climate Control

By shading your house, trees keep things cool, reducing energy bills. (Don't plant evergreen trees for summer shade, though; they'll block the sun in winter, preventing passive solar heating of your house.) You can use trees as a windbreak, to intercept and buffer prevailing winds. If winter winds are your bane, needle-leaved evergreens are

Consider Growth Rates

Trees grow at different rates, ranging from less than 1 foot (30 cm) per year to several feet (about 1 m) per year. Species with a slow-to-medium growth rate, such as oaks, generally require less maintenance than fast-growing ones. Fast-growing trees, such as poplars and willows, are often short-lived, surviving only 20–30 years, and they also generally have weak wood, which is more susceptible to damage from wind, storms and pests.

the best choice for a windbreak. If you live near a seacoast, choose salt-tolerant species to soften the sea winds.

Livability

Trees absorb noise and reduce glare, and they purify the air you breathe. Patios or play areas become more usable during hot summers when shaded by trees. Many trees have edible fruits that can feed your family or attract wildlife.

Consider Form and Function

When you select trees, use your landscape plan to help you decide what shape of tree to select and how each tree will function in the landscape. The arrangement of the branches gives each species of tree a distinctively shaped crown.

Most needle-leaved evergreens, such as pines and spruces, tend to have more symmetrical or rigid shapes than deciduous trees, such as oaks or maples. Needle-leaved evergreens often display the familiar conical or pyramidal "Christmas tree" look. Deciduous trees and broad-leaved evergreens can be many shapes, including round, vase-shaped and columnar.

Trees are often classified according to their intended use—as specimens, shade trees or street trees. Choose

LEFT: Full-moon maple *Acer japonicum* (top) and Japanese maple *Acer palmatum* (bottom).

LEFT: Black locust trees (*Robinia pseudoacacia*) provide dappled shade for a garden setting.
RIGHT: A water view is framed by the branches of a gum tree.

magnolia *Magnolia* x *soulangiana* is showy for a couple of weeks during spring when in flower, but fades into the background during the remainder of the year. A kousa dogwood *Cornus kousa*, on the other hand, bears showy flowers in spring, red fruits in autumn and attractive peeling bark in winter.

your landscape trees according to their function. For an upright, narrow screen, for example, you might select either a tree with a columnar shape or a pyramidal needle-leaved evergreen.

Specimen Trees

Specimen trees are showy in some way. They may put on an eye-catching display of flowers in spring, such as a flowering crab apple, or blaze with autumn color, such as *Acer rubrum* 'October Glory'. Or they may have unusually colored leaves, such as purple smoke tree *Cotinus coggygria* 'Royal Purple', or bright berries, such as American mountain ash *Sorbus americana*.

Specimen trees are valuable as focal points in a winter landscape. Fruits that hang on the branches after the leaves drop, such as the fruits of crab apples, add color to the winter landscape. Trees with attractive winter silhouettes, such as flowering dogwoods, also make good specimen trees.

Select a specimen tree with multiseasonal interest. A saucer

RIGHT: Deciduous trees make ideal companions for early bulbs. Here snowdrops grow under a forsythia.

Shade Trees

Shade trees may be showy, but it's their cooling effect that's important. A tree with a round or vase shape is ideal as a shade tree. Decide the location of a new shade tree with care: Make sure the tree's shadow will shade the area you intend it to.

If you want filtered shade or want to be able to grow grass under your tree, use a tree with small, fine leaves, such as a thornless honey locust *Gleditsia triacanthos* var. *inermis*, not one with a dense canopy of large, overlapping leaves, such as a Norway maple *Acer platanoides*.

The price of an advanced tree will not seem cheap, but it is a good investment.

First you are paying for the growth the tree has achieved and, with the right care, trees will repay you by being the longest-lived and often the most maintenance-free plants in your landscape.

Street Trees

Street trees are tough species that withstand the difficult growing conditions along the street. They are heat- and pollution-tolerant, grow well in poor soils, and can stand drought. Their roots must grow in very limited spaces, and their crowns must fit under overhead utility lines. Street trees have to be neat: Look for trees that don't have messy fruit, falling twigs or large leaves that can block storm sewers.

In spite of these demands, a number of attractive trees are available for roadside planting. Among small trees, consider trident maple *Acer buergerianum*, thornless cockspur hawthorn *Crataegus crus-galli* var. *inermis* or golden-rain tree *Koelreuteria paniculata*. Suitable medium to large trees include thornless honey locust *Gleditsia triacanthos* var. *inermis*, Japanese pagoda tree *Sophora japonica* and silver linden *Tilia tomentosa*.

Using Shrubs in the Landscape

Shrubs are hardworking plants in any landscape. They can be used to add a touch of greenery at the foundation of the house, make a thick screen between neighbors, add seasonal color from flowers or fruit, or outline the garden rooms of a landscape design. Even in a well-planted landscape, shrubs sometimes go unnoticed. The glossy, dark green of common boxwood *Buxus sempervirens* makes an ideal backdrop for light-colored flowers, but few passersby appreciate the shrub. Instead, their eyes are drawn to the blossoms that the boxwood sets off.

Types of Shrubs

Shrubs are woody plants with multiple stems, ranging from a few inches (centimeters) tall to approximately 15 feet (4.5 m) when they reach maturity. Occasionally an individual shrub is trained to a single treelike stem, called a standard. And large shrubs are sometimes "limbed up" into small trees, by removing the lower branches.

Like trees, shrubs can be deciduous, evergreen or semi-evergreen. If all leaves drop each autumn, with new leaves each spring through summer, the shrub is deciduous. Deciduous shrubs, including such favorites as roses *Rosa* spp. and spireas *Spiraea* spp., often have attractive flowers. For heavy flower production, plant them in full sun.

Evergreen shrubs have leaves year-round, though each year some of the oldest leaves drop off and are replaced by new leaves. Shrubs with wide, often thick, leaves, such as camellias *Camellia* spp. and rhododendrons *Rhododendron* spp., are called broad-leaved evergreens. Shrubs with thin, narrow leaves, such as junipers *Juniperus* spp. and dwarf mugo pines *Pinus mugo* var. *mugo*, are classified as needle-leaved evergreens.

ABOVE: A planting of light-colored azaleas *Rhododendron* spp. helps to brighten up a shady area under trees.
LEFT: A fragrant combination of pink roses and lavender is ideal planted near a garden seat.

A few shrubs are semi-evergreen, holding some of their leaves well into the winter months.

Choosing and Using Shrubs

There are many ways to use shrubs creatively in your landscape. You can use them to define the border of your property, hide an exposed foundation on your house, or block an unwanted view. These useful plants can create privacy, show people where to walk, or just provide an attractive show throughout the year. They also filter noise, break the force of the wind, and provide shade. Of course you can plant a hedge composed of plants from a single species, but one of the most creative and ornamental ways to use shrubs in a landscape is in mixed plantings. Try combining deciduous and evergreen species, interplanting shrubs that bloom at different seasons, or adding flowering shrubs to a perennial border to create year-round interest.

Before making your selections, consider what you want the shrubs for and what season or seasons you need them to work for you. If you need to block the noise of traffic year-round, for example, plant evergreen shrubs, such as yews *Taxus* spp., hollies *Ilex* spp. or, in warm regions, camellias *Camellia* spp. If you need privacy only for summer barbecues, deciduous shrubs would be a fine choice.

Specimens

Shrubs make excellent specimen plants. Use them to highlight a special feature in your yard, such as the beginning of a path or the end of a border or patio. For specimens, look for shrubs that are attractive for as many months as possible. Many viburnums, for example, have attractive spring flowers, summer fruit and good autumn color.

Backdrops and "Walls"

You can use shrubs to mark the garden rooms or the parts of your landscape—to screen a quiet sitting area from an area designed for active play, or to wall utility areas off for trash or storage. You can also use shrubs as a backdrop for plantings of

flowers. But if you use shrubs in this manner, look for ones that will complement but not compete with your flowers. Choose green shrubs such as boxwoods or junipers, for example, and avoid those with showy blossoms of their own.

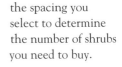

Hydrangea

Screens and Hedges

Shrubs are the perfect choice for hedges and screens, to block unattractive views or the sights and sounds of nearby neighbors and traffic. To calculate how many shrubs you need to buy for an effective hedge or screen, determine the mature spread of the species you've selected. Figure on spacing the shrubs closer together than their mature spread so that they'll form an unbroken line. For example, if a particular shrub has a mature spread of 5 feet (1.5 m), plan to space the plants 3–4 feet (90–120 cm) apart, depending upon how large they are when you buy them and how quickly you want a solid screen or hedge. Divide the total hedge length by

the spacing you select to determine the number of shrubs you need to buy.

Seasonal Attractions

In your landscape, shrubs can be utilitarian, but they can also be a focal point. Look for shrubs with multiseasonal interest—especially for use as accents or specimens. Oak-leaved hydrangea *Hydrangea quercifolia*, for instance, has interesting oak-leaf-shaped leaves that turn purple in autumn. Its showy clusters of off-white flowers dry on the plant and persist well into the winter. The peeling bark provides additional winter interest. The fruits on shrubs such as pyracanthas *Pyracantha* spp. and viburnums *Viburnum* spp. provide food for birds, while the plants serve as protective cover. Fruiting shrubs are also excellent for attracting wildlife.

Size Up Your Selections

If you want your shrubs to stay short, regular pruning will help to keep them in bounds. But a better approach is to choose shrubs that mature at the height you need. There are dwarf or miniature cultivars available of many popular shrubs. Dwarf cultivars of many trees—especially spruces *Picea* spp. and arborvitae *Thuja* spp.—are also commonly used as shrubs. Look for plants with names such as 'Prostrata', 'Nana', 'Compacta', 'Densa' and 'Pumila', but don't stop there. Be sure to verify mature height before you buy; compact forms of some trees and large shrubs may still be much larger than you want at maturity.

LEFT: Common box *Buxus sempervirens* is an ideal shrub for clipping into a formal hedge.

Using Vines in the Landscape

LEFT: Climbing plants can quickly grow to maturity to fill a garden landscape.

Vines, or climbers, are often used simply for the beautiful flowers and foliage they bring to the garden. But vines have functional uses as well: They are fast-growing and quickly lend an established look to the landscape. They can also soften or hide the harsh architectural lines of buildings, create or define garden spaces, provide privacy, screen unsightly views or noise, cover up ugly masonry, and break up the monotony of long fences and walls.

Types of Vines

While all vines twine or climb, there are three basic types of vines: annuals, herbaceous perennials and woody perennials. Most vines are fast growers, although some of the woody perennials may take a year or two to get established.

Annual vines, such as common morning glory *Ipomoea purpurea*, climb a lamppost or trellis in a hurry, making a good show in a single season. You'll need to replant annual vines each year, although

some will self-sow. Some vines grown as annuals in cooler areas, including black-eyed Susan vine *Thunbergia alata*, are perennial in warmer climates.

Herbaceous perennial vines, such as crimson starglory *Mina lobata*, die back to the ground every winter and regrow in spring.

Hardy woody vines include familiar species such as clematis *Clematis* spp., honeysuckles *Lonicera* spp. and wisteria *Wisteria* spp. Most hardy woody vines are deciduous, dropping their leaves each autumn but leaving a woody stem from which new leaves, flowers and fruits grow the following year. Others, including wintercreeper euonymus *Euonymus fortunei* and English ivy *Hedera helix*, are evergreen.

Choosing and Using Vines

You can find a vine for any type of soil—fertile or poor, wet or dry—and any

exposure from full sun to deep shade. Just as with trees and shrubs, the best course is to match the plant to your site rather than trying to alter your conditions to suit the plant. Most vines are adaptable plants and accept a wide range of growing conditions. A few vines require special conditions. Clematis, for example, need sun for good flower production but do best with cool roots, so plant them in full sun but shade their roots with a groundcover, low-growing perennial, or an organic mulch.

Climbing vines will soften the look of a raw, new fence or quickly screen an unsightly view. A hot, sunny porch becomes much more inviting when a trellised vine adds dappled shade. Vines trained on upright supports can fit in spaces too small for most trees and shrubs. They can be used as a vertical accent in flower or herb gardens or to mark the corners of an outdoor living area. Many vines also do well in containers on a deck or patio or in a courtyard garden.

Deciduous vines growing on the sunny sides of your house will shade the walls in summer, reducing your home's energy needs. Where garden banks are steep or grass is difficult to grow, evergreen vines make excellent groundcovers. Some vines, such as grapes and Chinese gooseberry *Actinidia chinensis*, also provide edible fruit for you or for wildlife.

Fast-growing Vines

Listed below are some particularly fast-growing vines that can cover a space quickly.

Actinidia spp. (kiwi fruit/Chinese gooseberries)

Ampelopsis brevipedunculata (porcelain ampelopsis)

Clematis maximowicziana (sweet autumn clematis)

Humulus lupulus (hops)

Mina lobata (crimson starglory)

Passiflora spp. (passionflowers)

Thunbergia alata (black-eyed Susan vine) pictured right

How Vines Climb

Vines either trail along the ground or climb appropriate supports. If you want your vines to climb, you'll need to know how they do it. Then you can choose an appropriate support for the vine you have in mind.

Some vines, such as passionflowers (*Passiflora* spp.) and sweet peas (*Lathyrus* spp.), climb by means of tendrils that grasp any objects they touch. These vines soon blanket a trellis or pergola, with little training. Vines that climb with tendrils need supports thin enough for their tendrils to grasp. Some tendrils will entwine themselves around supports, while others will loop around supports, then twine around themselves.

Other vines, such as wisterias, climb by twining their entire stems around supports. Twining vines need no encouragement to wrap themselves around a pole or porch post. These vines wrap themselves around slender supports, such as wires, railings or other

ABOVE: Large-flowered climbing rose, *Rosa* 'Lady Waterlow', disguises a brick column.
BELOW: Wisteria, Monet's garden, Giverny, France.

vines, as well as around large objects such as columns and tree trunks.

English ivy *Hedera helix*, wintercreeper euonymus *Euonymus fortunei* and climbing hydrangea *Hydrangea anomala* var. *petiolaris* use adhesive, aerial rootlets along their stems to cling to wood, brick, stone or other materials. Virginia creeper *Parthenocissus quinquefolia* and Boston ivy *P. tricuspidata* bear tendrils that end in adhesive discs.

A few plants, such as climbing roses, are often classified as vines even though they have no natural way to attach to a support. To help this type of vine climb, either weave its stems back and forth through a fence, trellis or arbor, or tie them to the support.

Climbing Supports for Vines

If you want your vines to grow upright, begin training them on supports as soon as you plant them. Use a structure big enough to support the mature plant, and put it in place before you plant the vine.

Buy or build freestanding supports that are constructed of sturdy, durable materials. Wood is a traditional and attractive choice for fan-shaped trellises, lattice panels, graceful arbors, or other supports. For longevity and durability, choose cedar or another naturally rot-resistant wood, or keep the support structure painted. Wire fencing framed with two-by-fours is a low-cost option that will give a vine years of sturdy support. Use galvanized or plastic-coated fencing to prevent rust. Copper or aluminum wire and tubing can also be fashioned into rustproof supports.

Training Vines

Use string to guide young vines to the structure you want them to climb. Fasten one end of the string to the support and tie the other end around a rock or a stick. Place the rock at the base of the plant, or poke the stick into the ground nearby, making sure to avoid the vine's rootball. Use string or soft fabric strips to tie vines to their supports until they begin to twine or cling by themselves.

Lawns, Grasses and Groundcovers

Lawn grasses, ornamental grasses and groundcovers play a key role in creating a practical and attractive landscape around your home. These adaptable plants protect your soil, provide areas for recreation and relaxation, and accent taller plants, such as perennials, shrubs and trees.

Easy-care Lawns

Here's a handy checklist of things you'll want to consider when planning your low-maintenance lawn.

Start small. Even the smallest lawn takes a certain amount of time to keep it looking good. If your time or energy is limited, plant lawn grass only on the amount of land you can easily maintain.

Plant grass where it grows best. Lawn grasses thrive with lots of sun, moisture and fertile soil. In shady spots and areas with wet, dry or infertile soil, it takes extra effort to keep the grass looking even halfway decent. Groundcovers and ornamental grasses are great choices for these problem areas.

Keep your lawn on the level. Smooth, level sites make for easiest mowing. Lawns on a gentle slope are fine, but steep grades make mowing exhausting and hazardous.

Plan for pathways. Constant foot traffic can wear out even the most durable grasses, so install gravel or paved paths where you want people to walk. Also make pathways between garden areas wide enough to push a mower through.

Keep clutter to a minimum. Anything in the middle of the lawn demands more time and effort for careful mowing and additional trimming. Keep swings, benches, birdbaths and other features around the outside of the lawn area.

Cluster plants for easy care. Group trees and shrubs into planting beds with groundcovers beneath them. That way you'll avoid having to mow and trim around individual plants.

Avoid fancy curves and tight angles. Keep lawn edges straight or gently rounded, avoiding sharp curves and narrow spots that are difficult to trim.

Plan for easy edge maintenance. Installing edging strips along fences, flower beds and walkways will eliminate almost all of those boring trimming chores.

Ornamental Grasses

Ornamental grasses are adaptable, easy-care plants that serve many kinds of landscape functions.

Ornamental grasses blend beautifully into traditional flower borders. Annuals and perennials add vibrant colors to the subtle, muted tones of grasses. The grasses, in turn, supply all-season interest and soothing backgrounds for delicate flowers.

Grasses look great with flowers in all parts of the garden. Spring bulbs such as daffodils, crocus, grape hyacinths, snowdrops and tulips make a colorful display early in the season; as they fade, the fast-growing grasses neatly camouflage the dying bulb foliage. In semiwild areas, wildflowers combine beautifully with the less showy grasses, including broomsedge *Andropogon virginicus*, tufted hairgrass *Deschampsia caespitosa*, switch grass *Panicum virgatum* and prairie cord grass *Spartina pectinata*.

Grasses with bright foliage go well with deep green, evergreen shrubs or gray-leaved perennials. The unusual, red-leaved 'Red Baron' blood grass *Imperata cylindrica* 'Red Baron' is spectacular against a background of greenery, for example. Clumps of grasses with variegated, yellow or silvery blue foliage are particularly striking when they accompany plants with green or gray leaves.

LEFT: Terracotta tiles, placed around the edge of a lawn, can make mowing much easier.
ABOVE: Ajuga and hostas are two tough, dependable groundcovers for easy-care gardens.

Site 'Red Baron' blood grass where the morning or afternoon sun can shine through the leaves.

The gray-green and white leaves of white striped ribbon grass make a good foil to pink blooms.

Planted at close spacings, blue fescue *Festuca cinerea* makes an unusual, attractive groundcover.

Tall ornamental grasses can provide a welcome change of texture and color from more rigid shrubs and trees. In large yards, big grasses, such as pampas grass *Cortaderia selloana* and eulalia grasses *Miscanthus* spp., provide spectacular backgrounds for shorter grasses, shrubs and flowering plants.

Tall-growing grasses also make excellent quick screens to provide privacy, eliminate unpleasant views, and cut down on street noise. Such screens can divide a larger area into separate "rooms" and also protect delicate plants from being buffeted by wind storms. Most grasses become fully established for screening purposes within 2 to 3 years—far more quickly than a standard hedge. This makes them ideal for new gardens where you need fast-growing plants to get an almost immediate effect. Grasses can also fill space while slower-maturing shrubs are getting started.

Great Groundcovers

Groundcovers offer a wealth of solutions to landscaping problems, but they're more than just practical—they're beautiful as well. Combining flowering and foliage groundcovers with each other and with bulbs, perennials, shrubs and other plants can give your yard year-round appeal.

Good Companions

Groundcovers group well with other garden plants. They provide a finishing touch by "tying" together mixed plantings of shrubs, trees, flowers and grasses.

Groundcovers are perfect foils for many bulbs, providing an interesting background for the blooms and covering the yellowing bulb foliage afterward. Tall spring-blooming bulbs, such as daffodils and tulips, are complemented by a backdrop of ivy or accented by a spring-blooming groundcover such as Bethlehem sage *Pulmonaria saccharata*. Tiny spring bulbs, such as snowdrops *Galanthus* spp., squills *Scilla* spp. and crocuses, are ideal company for low-growing groundcovers, such as fringed bleeding heart *Dicentra eximia*, cranesbills *Geranium* spp. and creeping phlox *Phlox stolonifera*.

Groundcovering shrubs, such as creeping juniper *Juniperus horizontalis*, shrubby cinquefoil *Potentilla fruticosa* and cotoneasters, are beautiful in groupings of one species, or combined with taller shrubs and trees. Vigorous groundcovers, such as ajuga *Ajuga reptans*, which could crowd out delicate perennials and grasses, are ideal companions for sturdy shrubs such as lilacs, shrub roses, hydrangeas and viburnums.

Plant a Tapestry

Although one species and color all by itself can be appropriate in a small space, large, solid splotches of one groundcover are likely to be visually monotonous. For a more exciting landscape, intermingle plants of different species or different cultivars of the same species, combining various colors, heights, textures and forms. An area covered with two or more different plants can change frequently during the gardening season, as each blooms in turn and as the foliage changes colors in autumn.

Even if you grow only a single species of groundcover, you can often choose among many different cultivars that have varying flower and foliage colors. A garden bed that features several compatible flower and foliage colors can be an eye-catching accent instead of a humdrum mass planting.

To combine groundcovers most effectively, you should choose kinds that are similar in vigor, such as pairing English ivy *Hedera helix* with common periwinkle, or foamflower *Tiarella cordifolia* with creeping phlox *Phlox stolonifera*. Otherwise, a vigorous spreading groundcover is likely to overpower the weaker one. When plants are evenly matched, the different species can weave in and out of each other's spaces in a natural way.

Fountain grass

Landscaping with Perennials

Any yard can be accented with perennials. A few clusters will bring colorful highlights to drab corners; a garden full of perennials will become a seasonal highlight. You can use perennials as accents, focal points, masses of color, or intriguing scenes of constant change as the perennial grows, flowers and dies down again at the end of its season.

Perennial Highlights

To get the most enjoyment and the greatest effect from these plants, you first need to establish a garden size and shape that looks natural in your landscape and fits in well with the existing elements, such as buildings and trees. Then choose perennials with colors, textures and forms that enhance your entire landscape.

Use large sweeps of bold perennials in beds and borders beside the lawn, beneath openings in trees, and in front of hedges and shrub plantings. Put smaller clumps of dramatic perennials in strategic locations to highlight the entrance to walks, the location of a door, or the view out a window. Consider nesting a trio of three gold-centered, broad-leaved hostas (such as *Hosta* 'Gold Standard') at either side of the entrance of a woodland path. Or use a large clump of red-hot poker *Kniphofia uvaria* to frame the top of a drive. A stand of elegant irises or plumed astilbes is an attractive feature near a Japanese bridge and water garden.

ABOVE: Variegated, evergreen hostas provide many months of interest planted either side of a gateway.
RIGHT: The yellow-lime flowers of euphorbia.

Picking the Right Perennials

Even experienced perennial gardeners can be a little overwhelmed by the thousands of perennials available. How do you begin to tell which are best for your garden? When you choose, weigh criteria such as height, color and shape. Here are some considerations to keep in mind.

Coordinating Heights and Habits

Mix perennials of varying heights to add visual interest to your garden design. Organize heights to progress from short to tall so no flowers will be hidden behind taller plants. If you view a garden from the front, put the tallest plants toward the back of the garden. Or with a bed that you see from all sides, cluster the tall plants near the center, and let the lower plants taper down in height toward the edges.

Many perennials have shapes or growth habits that make them particularly useful for certain purposes. Low-growing plants such as common thrift *Armeria maritima*, pinks *Dianthus* spp. and coral bells *Heuchera sanguinea* have neat foliage and make attractive edgings. Try full or tall types such as boltonia *Boltonia asteroides* or black snakeroot *Cimicifuga racemosa* to

hide unattractive views or to serve as a background for large beds and borders.

Combining Compatible Colors

When you're designing a perennial garden, approach it as you would your living room decor. Limit yourself to two main colors and possibly a third for accent. Also add some minor colors for small touches of diversity. If possible, match flower or foliage colors with other landscape elements, such as walkways, shutters, or flowers or berries on nearby shrubs. But keep the color scheme simple.

ABOVE: The lacy leaves of artemisia combine well with different flower forms and offer lasting color.

If you use too many colors, the garden will look fragmented and chaotic. (See "Combining Colors" on pages 52–55.)

Varying Shapes and Textures

In addition to their flowers, perennials have many different shapes and textures. Blend perennials with creeping, mounding and upright habits to make your garden design more interesting. For a more natural and informal arrangement, use creepers to edge the bed. You can emphasize mounded plants, using occasional upright foliage spikes or flower spires at strategic locations.

Perennial Beds and Borders

Two of the most common ways to group perennials are in beds and borders. Borders are long planting areas that create a visual edge to a lawn or other part of the landscape. They are usually sited so they're viewed from a distance. While they may stretch along a driveway, walkway, fence or the edge of woods, they don't really have to "border" anything; borders may merely create the illusion of a boundary to a "room" within the landscape.

Most perennial borders are designed to be seen primarily from the front, allowing you to set the shorter plants in the foreground and the taller plants in the back. You can plant a border exclusively with perennials to produce what is known as an herbaceous border, but more and more gardeners are enjoying the benefits of mixing their perennials with other plants, including shrubs, small trees, hardy bulbs, annuals and ornamental grasses. These plants complement perennials by adding extra height, texture and color to the border. Shrubs, trees, grasses and bulbs also add year-round interest, with early spring flowers, attractive autumn colors,

Dependable, Easy-care Perennials

Here's a list of some of the most trouble-free perennials you can grow. All of the plants below thrive in sun and average, well-drained soil with little fuss.

Achillea filipendulina (fern-leaved yarrow)
Alchemilla mollis (lady's-mantle)
Anemone tomentosa 'Robustissima' (Japanese anemone)
Armeria maritima (common thrift)
Asclepias tuberosa (butterfly weed)
Aster novae-angliae (New England aster)
Baptisia australis (blue false indigo)
Boltonia asteroides (boltonia)
Centranthus ruber (red valerian)
Coreopsis verticillata (thread-leaved coreopsis)
Echinacea purpurea (purple coneflower)
Echinops ritro (globe thistle)
Gaillardia x *grandiflora* (blanket flower)
Geranium sanguineum (blood-red cranesbill)
Hemerocallis hybrids (daylilies)
Iris sibirica (Siberian iris)
Leucanthemum x *superbum* (shasta daisy)
Liatris spicata (spike gayfeather)
Lilium hybrids (lilies)
Narcissus hybrids (daffodils)
Nepeta x *faassenii* (catmint)
Paeonia lactiflora (common garden peony, single-flowered cultivars)
Physostegia virginiana (obedient plant)
Platycodon grandiflorus (balloon flower)
Rudbeckia fulgida (orange coneflower)
Sedum spp. (sedums)
Salvia x *superba* (violet sage)
Veronica spicata (spike speedwell)
Yucca filamentosa (Adam's needle)

Balloon flower

ABOVE: Liven up mass plantings with a focal point. A bird bath adds interest to this group of mums.
LEFT: Orange coneflower *Rudbeckia fulgida*, surrounded by sage and ornamental grasses.

and showy fruits or foliage that may last well into winter.

Beds are often located closer to the house than borders, perhaps along the foundation or edging a patio. If you're going to put a bed where you'll see it all the time, choose your plants carefully for all-season interest. High-visibility beds will also need either some extra work or carefully chosen, low-maintenance plants to look their best all the time.

Perennial beds come in many shapes and sizes. Choose a shape and style (formal or informal) that matches or balances nearby features. The front can curve even if the side up against the house is straight. Keep the bed narrow enough to allow you to reach all the plants from outside the bed, or place stepping stones in it for easy access.

Beds surrounded by lawn are called island beds; often these are oval or kidney shaped. They are a great way to add color and height to a new property while you're waiting for the trees and shrubs to mature. Island beds are also useful for replacing the grass under trees, reducing the need for trimming and making mowing easier.

Like borders, island beds are usually designed to be seen from a distance. As islands are often viewed from all sides, the design needs to look attractive all around, like a table centerpiece. Since there's no "back," put tallest plants toward the middle and surround them with lower plants.

Succession of bloom is one reason the changeable nature of perennials is so appealing. By selecting plants carefully, you can have perennials blooming

ABOVE: Border with hostas and lady's-mantle.
BELOW: An island bed is designed to be seen from all angles, so taller plants are in the center, and shorter plants are at the front.

throughout the growing season, from early spring to late autumn. Let the beauty of the flowers create a shifting sequence of harmonies and contrasts.

Orchestrating All-season Interest

A good selection of spring-, summer- and autumn-blooming perennials, plus a few other plants with evergreen leaves for winter interest, will give you a garden landscape that is truly attractive all year

Super Perennials for Shade

Here's a list of just some of the great-looking, easy-to-grow perennials that will thrive in a shady garden.

Actea pachypoda (white baneberry)
Ajuga reptans (ajuga)
Aquilegia canadensis (wild columbine)
Arisaema triphyllum (Jack-in-the-pulpit)
Asarum europaeum (European wild ginger)
Astilbe x *arendsii* (astilbe)
Bergenia spp. (bergenias)
Brunnera macrophylla (Siberian bugloss)
Cimicifuga racemosa (black snakeroot)
Dicentra eximia (fringed bleeding heart)
Epimedium x *rubrum* (red epimedium)
Helleborus orientalis (Lenten rose)
Hosta hybrids (hostas)
Iris cristata (crested iris)
Lamium maculatum (spotted lamium)
Polygonatum odoratum (fragrant Solomon's seal)
Pulmonaria saccharata (Bethlehem sage)
Smilacina racemosa (Solomon's plume)
Tiarella cordifolia (Allegheny foamflower)
Uvularia grandiflora (great merrybells)

long. All-season interest starts with flower displays that spread beyond one season. Foliage and plant form are other features you can use to keep your garden looking beautiful as flowers come and go.

From spring through autumn, many perennials have attractive leaves—such as the maroon leaves of 'Palace Purple' heuchera *Heuchera* 'Palace Purple'— or interesting shapes, such as the starry leaves of blood-red cranesbill *Geranium sanguineum*. Unusual plant forms—such as the spiky leaves and flowers of yuccas, blackberry lily *Belamcanda chinensis* and spike gayfeather *Liatris spicata*—add drama, especially next to mounds such as cushion spurge *Euphorbia epithymoides*. Use different types of foliage and forms to add contrast, or repeat similar leaves and shapes to unify a planting scheme.

Your Spring Landscape

After a long, dreary winter, few things are more welcome than colorful spring flowers. In spring, Lenten rose *Helleborus orientalis* blooms before most of the garden shrugs off winter. Many wildflowers and shade-loving perennials bloom as trees leaf out, so spring is a good season to draw attention to areas that will be shady and green later on. Supplement early-blooming perennials with flowering shrubs and trees such as forsythias, azaleas, magnolias, dogwoods, flowering cherries and crab apples.

RIGHT: Summer border featuring sea holly and euphorbia.
BELOW: Bellflowers (*Campanula* spp.) cascade over and soften a stone wall.

A Wealth of Summer Color

As spring becomes summer, many perennials—including peonies, irises and columbines (*Aquilegia* spp.)—reach their peak, making it an easy time to feature flowers. Supplement these with early summer shrubs and vines, such as rhododendrons, roses, clematis, wisteria and honeysuckle *Lonicera* spp.

As summer progresses, daisy-like perennials and annuals—including blanket flower *Gaillardia* x *grandiflora* and coreopsis *Coreopsis* spp.— take center stage. Good-looking foliage keeps up appearances where early perennials have finished blooming. Silver leaves make dramatic partners for hot- or cool-hued flowers; yellow, purple or variegated foliage also attracts attention. Flowering shrubs for mid- to late summer include abelia *Abelia* x *grandiflora*, butterfly bush *Buddleia davidii* and hydrangeas. Sourwood *Oxydendrum arboreum* and Japanese pagoda tree *Sophora japonica* are large trees that bloom prolifically in late summer, as does the large trumpet creeper vine *Campsis* spp.

Combinations for Autumn

Asters, boltonia and Joe-Pye weeds *Eupatorium* spp. keep blooming after autumn frosts nip most annuals. As flowers fade, foliage brightens—and not just on trees or shrubs such as burning bush *Euonymus alata*. Leaves of peonies and common sundrops *Oenothera tetragona* turn beautiful shades of red, amsonias *Amsonia* spp. and balloon flower *Platycodon grandiflorus* leaves turn bright

yellow, and many ornamental grasses bleach to gold. White baneberry *Actea pachypoda* and Jack-in-the-pulpit *Arisaema triphyllum* are perennials with dramatic berries that may last into autumn.

Perennials for Winter Interest

After the leaves drop, attention turns to evergreen plants and those with interesting seedpods or fruits. Perennials with showy winter seedpods include blue false indigo *Baptisia australis*, coneflowers *Rudbeckia* and *Echinacea* spp., blackberry lily *Belamcanda chinensis* and astilbes.

Many crab apples and shrubs, such as viburnums, cotoneasters and deciduous and evergreen hollies *Ilex* spp., display fruits well into winter. Ornamental grasses remain attractive for months; cut them to the ground when they look tattered to make way for spring's new growth.

Annuals in Your Garden

Fast-growing and relatively inexpensive annuals are invaluable for providing quick color to new gardens. But don't forget that they can enhance an existing landscape as well. Repeated plantings of a particular type or color can provide a note of continuity to an established framework of shrubs and trees. Experimenting with new colors and combinations allows a new twist on the theme each year, without the expense of changing the framework itself.

If you have just moved into a house, you could fill the garden with annuals for a year or two while you decide on your long-term plans for the landscape. Annuals are also great for city gardens, since they can make the most of compact spaces and less-than-ideal growing sites.

Four-o'-clocks

LEFT: Planted in groups, compact zinnias provide a colorful, season-long show and are ideal for edging flower beds and borders. They also make great cut flowers.
BELOW: Mixed, hot-color border of annuals, perennials and bulbs, featuring moss pinks *Phlox subulata*, pot marigolds *Calendula officinalis*, pansies *Viola* x *wittrockiana* and ranunculus *Ranunculus asiaticus*.

Annuals Alone

In some places, you may choose to go with a basic all-annuals bed. Plants that have been bred or selected exclusively for a certain height or color are ideal for this kind of design. These compact, uniform annuals, such as dwarf marigolds, zinnias or scarlet sage *Salvia splendens*, lend themselves to lines as well as to mass plantings of geometric shapes.

A single color of one annual massed together makes an eye-catching accent. This kind of planting is useful for long-distance viewing (such as from the street), for marking drives or entry gates, or for drawing attention to a door or entryway. But keep in mind that color doesn't have to be shocking to get attention.

Annuals with Other Plants

Although they look wonderful by themselves, annuals have a lot to offer in groupings with other plants. In borders predominantly planted with perennials, bulbs and shrubs, you can use annuals as a formal or informal edging, suggesting a flowering necklace around the border.

While the other plants come in and out of bloom, the annual edging adds consistent color through most of the season. Repeating the same annual edging in different flower beds is an excellent way to link the separate beds into a complete garden picture.

Of course, you can also add annuals to the inside of borders as well. While the compact, uniform annuals that are excellent for formal bedding can look stiff and awkward next to perennials, many other annuals have a looser, more graceful habit. In fact, annuals and biennials such as larkspur *Consolida ambigua*, foxgloves *Digitalis purpurea* and Canterbury bells *Campanula medium* are so charming when mixed with perennials that they are often considered traditional parts of a perennial border. Tall annuals and biennials such as cosmos, cleome, hollyhocks and mulleins *Verbascum* spp. are ideal for adding height to the back of a mixed border. And shorter, airy annuals blend easily into border edgings; try plants like pot marigolds *Calendula officinalis*, annual candytuft *Iberis umbellata* and annual baby's-breath *Gypsophila elegans* with low-growing perennials and bulbs.

Annuals as Fillers

When you start any new garden, one of the hardest parts of the process is waiting for plants to fill in. This is especially true with perennial and shrub beds, since these plants can take 3 or 4 years to really get established. While you need to allow ample space for these plants to fill in as they mature, the bare soil in between is boring and empty, and it provides an open invitation for weeds to get started.

A few seed packets of quick-growing annuals provide color and excitement for minimal cost. Sweet alyssum *Lobularia maritima*, flowering tobacco *Nicotiana alata* and cornflower *Centaurea cyanus* are a few

LEFT: Sweet alyssum *Lobularia maritima* quickly fills the space between these paving stones. BELOW: These tall foxgloves *Digitalis purpurea*, make an ideal screen or natural "fence."

groundcovers may take over their allotted space in a few years, but a carpet of annuals is most welcome in the meantime. A few seed packets, or trays of seedlings, of your favorite annuals will be easy to plant, and the resulting flowers and foliage will provide infinitely more interest than a dull covering of bark chips.

Annuals for Screens

While the word "annual" commonly brings to mind compact, small plants, such as petunias and marigolds, there are a number of fast-growing annuals that can reach amazing heights of 6 feet (1.8 m) or more in a single season. There are also annual vines, the twining stems of which can quickly cover trellises for welcome shade and privacy.

Grow tall annuals in your yard to block or cover unattractive features, such as garbage bins, alleys or clothesline poles. Or plant a row or mass of tall annuals to create a "neighbor-friendly" temporary fence that delineates your property line or separates different areas of your garden. Some top-notch tall annuals include castor bean *Ricinus communis*, summer cypress *Kochia scoparia*, hollyhocks *Alcea rosea*, sunflowers *Helianthus annuus* and Mexican sunflower *Tithonia rotundifolia*.

great filler annuals that can quickly cover the soil and deprive weed seeds of the light they need to grow. Many annuals may also self-sow to provide cover in succeeding years, gradually yielding space to expanding perennials.

If you're looking for annuals to fill in around new perennial plantings, choose those with a similar range of heights and colors as the perennials. Select a few short or trailing annuals for the front of the border, a few medium-sized plants for the middle of the border, and a few tall annuals for the back.

Low-growing annuals such as sweet alyssum, rose moss *Portulaca grandiflora*

and baby-blue-eyes *Nemophila menziesii* can be excellent fillers for young groundcover plantings. Stick with one kind of annual for a uniform effect. While many low-growing annuals will self-sow, you may want to scatter some fresh annual seed over the planting for the first few springs until the groundcover fills in.

New foundation plantings also benefit from annuals the first few years as they develop. Shrubs and

Bulbs in Your Garden

Whether you enjoy growing bulbs in formal displays or more natural-looking plantings, you can add extra interest by choosing compatible companion plants. Ideal companions will enhance the appearance of the bulbs at bloom time and also help to cover the untidy ripening foliage later on.

Bulbs and Annuals

Showy bulbs, such as tulips and hyacinths, can make a dramatic feature when planted in rows or blocks. But it's even more exciting when you fill in between the bulbs with a pretty carpet of early-blooming annuals rather than leaving the soil bare or mulched. Good candidates for planting under bulbs include pansies, Johnny-jump-ups *Viola tricolor*, English daisies *Bellis perennis* and forget-me-nots *Myosotis* spp. As you choose companions, look for flower colors that complement those of your bulbs.

Summer-blooming annuals make great companions for bulbs in more informal plantings. As they grow, the annuals cover the bare soil and disguise the maturing bulb leaves. Self-sowing annuals are ideal for this purpose, since they will return year after year with little or no help from you. Good choices for sunny beds include California poppy *Eschscholzia californica*, corn poppy *Papaver rhoeas*, cornflower *Centaurea cyanus* and love-in-a-mist *Nigella damascena*. You can also use annual transplants to fill in around bulbs, tucking them in before or just after the bulb blooms fade. Ageratum, dusty miller and flowering tobacco *Nicotiana alata* are just a few good annuals to choose from.

Bulbs and Perennials

Tall bulbs, including lilies, ornamental onions *Allium* spp. and crown imperial *Fritillaria imperalis*, usually look best near the middle or back of a bed or border. Planting them in between clumps of slightly shorter perennials makes attractive combinations, especially if the perennials bloom at the same time as the bulbs. For instance, Asiatic lilies are

RIGHT: Daffodils under magnolia tree.
BELOW: A dramatic swathe of closely spaced, tiny, purple grape hyacinths *Muscari* spp.

especially pretty with shasta daisies *Leucanthemum* x *superbum*, coral bells *Heuchera sanguinea* and Cupid's dart *Catananche caerulea* at their feet. You can also combine bulbs with taller perennials, such as delphiniums, mulleins *Verbascum* spp. and meadow rues *Thalictrum* spp., for a colorful background.

Bulbs and Groundcovers

Combining bulbs with groundcovers is a great way to go. The groundcover provides a pretty backdrop for the bulbs' flowers and then remains to add interest when the bulbs go dormant. Most bulbs have no trouble poking their flowers through a carpet of creeping stems and leaves. Many low-growing, spreading perennials, including thyme, sedums, creeping baby's-breath *Gypsophila repens*, creeping veronicas *Veronica* spp., rock soapwort *Saponaria ocymoides* and sun rose *Helianthemum nummularium*, can be used as groundcovers. In shady areas, try common periwinkle *Vinca minor*, creeping Jenny *Lysimachia nummularia*, English ivy *Hedera helix*, spotted lamium *Lamium maculatum* and self-heal *Prunella* spp.

Bulbs and Shrubs

You can create stunning garden scenes by grouping flowering shrubs and bulbs with similar bloom times and colors. Forsythia creates a golden glow behind a mass of daffodils, while lilac beautifully echoes the colors of ornamental onions. The arching branches and fragrance of old-fashioned roses make them a classic companion for summer-blooming lilies. Viburnums *Viburnum* spp., mock oranges *Philadelphus* spp., hydrangeas, rhododendrons and azaleas are some other wonderful flowering shrubs that look super with spring bulbs.

Evergreen shrubs, such as junipers, yews *Taxus* spp. and arborvitaes *Thuja* spp., complement flowering bulbs throughout the year. Some evergreens have a gold, blue or reddish cast to their foliage; keep this in mind as you combine them with bulbs. White or pink tulips can create a soothing scene against the blue-gray cast of a juniper.

Tulips and forget-me-nots

Bulbs and Trees

Bulbs and trees can also make colorful garden groupings. Spring bulbs are especially well suited for growing under deciduous trees, since they can get the sunlight they need before the leaves shade the ground. Spring-flowering bulbs that perform well under trees include crocus, squills *Scilla sibirica* and *Puschkinia scilloides*, snowdrops *Galanthus nivalis*, glory-of-the-snow *Chionodoxa luciliae* and daffodils. Summer-flowering bulbs that prefer some shade include tuberous begonias and caladiums *Caladium* x *hortulanum*. For autumn interest, add hardy cyclamen *Cyclamen hederifolium* and Italian arum *Arum italicum*.

Bulbs for Naturalizing

Naturalizing means planting bulbs in random, natural-looking drifts under trees, in woodlands or in grassy areas. It's easy to do, and the results look better and better every year as the bulbs multiply to produce even more blooms.

Deciding Where to Plant

Naturalized bulbs are often best in low-maintenance areas, where you can enjoy the blooms but not be bothered by the sight of the ripening leaves. Very early bulbs, such as spring crocus, are sometimes naturalized in lawns to provide color. You may have to put off the first spring mowing for a week or two to let the bulb foliage turn yellow, but after that you can mow as usual. Autumn-blooming bulbs can also look good in grassy areas, but you'll have to stop mowing in late summer, as soon as you see the flower buds sprouting from the soil.

Thick grass may be too competitive for some bulbs, but a sparse lawn—especially under deciduous trees—is just the right environment to help bulbs take hold. The bulbs get plenty of spring sun and moisture before the trees leaf out, and the flowers add cheerful spring and/or autumn color to otherwise drab areas. If you have many trees, you can combine sweeps of naturalized bulbs with shade-loving annuals, perennials and shrubs to create a charming woodland garden with four-season interest.

Groundcovers make great companions for naturalized bulbs. The leaves and stems of the groundcovers support the bulb flowers, provide an attractive backdrop, help to keep soil from splashing onto the blooms, and mask the ripening bulb leaves. In turn, the bulbs provide a pretty seasonal show of flowers to make the groundcover more exciting.

Planting Naturalized Bulbs

The key to successful naturalizing is planting bulbs in random-looking arrangements rather than in straight rows or patterns. It's usually best to place them randomly over the planting area by hand until the arrangement looks right to you. Don't just toss out handfuls of bulbs from a standing position; the bulbs may get bruised or damaged as they fall and be prone to pest and disease problems.

ABOVE: Liven up the area under a spring-blooming tree with late-flowering plants, such as autumn crocus *Colchicum* spp.
BELOW: Crocus are ideal bulbs for naturalizing.

Herb Garden Design

Versatile, colorful and flavorful, herbs have a place in any landscape. Mix them with other perennials in beds and borders, or group them together in a separate herb garden. Either way, you can enjoy their delightful scents and colors in the kitchen as well as in the garden.

Choosing the Site

First decide where to locate your herb garden. You could reassign a section of your existing vegetable or flower garden, or perhaps create a whole new garden devoted to herbs. If you're starting from scratch, put as much thought as you can into site selection. You can avoid many problems by choosing a good location, especially if you plan to live in the same place for a while.

An ideal site will also correspond with your ideas of what a garden should be and where it should be. It may be most convenient for you to have your herb garden located near the kitchen door. Or perhaps you'll get most enjoyment from one that may be viewed from indoors through a window.

Choosing the Style

Regardless of the size or location of your herb garden, its style is a reflection of your

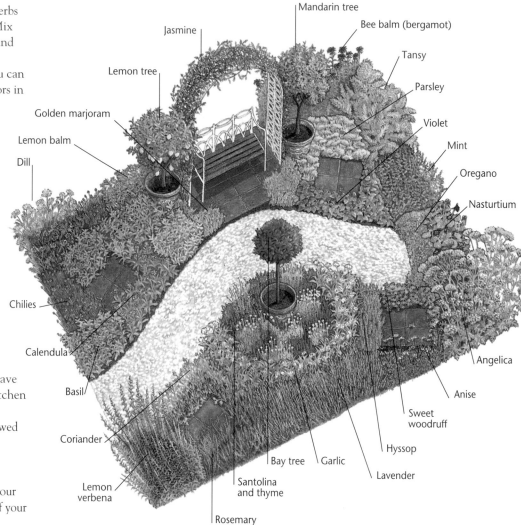

ABOVE: An informal herb garden, featuring a variety of herbs with other edibles and ornamentals.

ABOVE: Formal hedge herb garden, featuring an elaborate knot garden of clipped hedges.

own tastes. At one extreme are the formal gardens with their angular knots and pruned hedges, and at the other are random groupings of whatever suits the season. The number of possible herb-garden styles is limited only by your imagination and creativity. You can plan one or more theme gardens to concentrate on a particular aspect.

Seek inspiration from books and experienced gardeners. If you enjoy formal patterns, plan your garden along the lines of an Italian Renaissance garden or a knot garden, in which intertwining miniature hedges of different herbs create a knot-like shape. For something more informal, look for inspiration in a book about English cottage gardens. Perhaps you

would prefer to specialise and grow a kitchen garden full of culinary herbs, a medicinal herb garden, a scented garden or simply a wild garden of many herbs.

The simplest gardens to set out and manage are square or rectangular. If you must take advantage of every square inch of space, it makes sense that you will follow the general outline of your property, and land is most often sold in boxlike shapes. Laying out your herb garden with square or rectangular beds not only may be the most practical way, but can give the garden a formal look that appeals to many gardeners.

Of course, squares and rectangles aren't the only shapes. You may choose to lay your garden beds following the curve of a hill, stream, fence or stone wall, or design them to accent the shape of a building. If you want to be especially creative, garden within unusual boundaries such as circles or ovals. For even more formality, you could lay out the garden beds in geometric shapes, wheel spokes or intricate knots. You can make a garden in the shape of a spiral with one continuous bed beginning in the centre and spiraling out in circles.

Define the edges of formal beds with low, clipped hedges of bluish rue, green hyssop or silvery santolina—or even a combination of all three. Or be more casual and allow the herbs that are growing along the edge to sprawl a little onto the paved or gravel paths. For a traditional touch, plan a small, round bed in the center of the garden, and accent it with a sundial, statue, bird bath or a large potted bay *Laurus nobilis* or rosemary as a special focal point.

In culinary herb gardens, remember to include attractive, edible herbs, such as silver thyme and variegated sages, for color contrast. Add annual herbs and edible flowers such as purple basil, nasturtium

ABOVE: The stunning pink flowers of chives *Allium schoenoprasum* make an attractive accent in a predominantly foliage garden.

RIGHT: Parsley planted with purple petunias and other ornamentals.
BELOW RIGHT: A lavender-lined path is just one way to enjoy herbs.

and borage for even more color. If you don't have room for a separate herb garden, tuck your favorite herbs into other perennial beds and borders.

A number of herbs are also well suited to container gardening, so you can move potted herbs around to add fragrance and color wherever you need them.

Practicalities

If you're planting in beds, keep them under 5 feet (1.5 m) wide, not more than twice the distance you are able to reach from the side. Remember that single plants tend to become lost in the crowd; it's more effective to plant in clumps. It's generally best to plant the tallest herbs at the back, the shortest in the front.

Keep the following in mind when you plan your herb garden:

• Select herbs that flower at the same time or share the same color. Lavender and blue themes especially, are easy to create with herbs. Or focus on foliage, and plant blue-green or silvery herbs mixed with darker greens for contrast.

• It's a good idea to group the perennial herbs together since they tend to have similar requirements and this will help you avoid mistakes. If you're planning to grow invasive perennials, such as mint, among other herbs, plant them in buried containers such as clay drainage pipes or bottomless large pots that are at least 1 foot (30 cm) deep.

Fruits and Vegetables

LEFT: Freestanding espaliered fruit trees provide attractive screens and make effective boundary markers, too.
BELOW: Kiwi vines are excellent for covering trellises and arbors.

The options for including edibles in your yard are as extensive as your imagination. Here are some suggestions of ways you can add these beautiful and productive plants to your landscape plans.

Landscaping with Fruits

It's surprising that fruiting plants have been neglected so long for landscape use. After all, most of them have at least two outstanding features: attractive flowers and edible fruits. Many have other special features as well, such as showy autumn color or interesting bark. Some fruits can go where no plant has gone before—squeezing in next to walls, along fences, and in narrow areas where an ordinary bush would be crushed. That's because many fruiting plants are incredibly versatile. You can train them into a variety of shapes to fit almost any space. Keep this in mind as you plan planting schemes to enliven small side yards, cramped courtyards, tight property lines, and landscape sites with walls and fences.

Experiment with Espalier

Train dwarf fruit trees into an espalier that will grow flat along a trellis or wall, stretching horizontally and upward. You can give espaliered plants many fanciful shapes. (See "Espalier" on page 82 for complete details.) Espaliered plants paint a beautiful scene with greenery, flowers and fruits and appear especially prominent against the quiet backdrop of the wall. In addition, your espalier will soften the hard lines of a wall, blending it into the landscape.

Include Some Climbers

Vines are extremely flexibile when young, so you can manipulate them as you wish. Grow fruiting vines, such as grapes and hardy kiwis, on vertical trellises; or, if you have enough space and a vigorous growing vine, use broader V- or T-shaped wire trellises. A strongly growing grapevine can fill out a trellis to form a solid wall of foliage, making a handy summer screen for privacy. A less aggressive grower will still produce an abundance of greenery but will leave some sunny openings. For more fun with flexible plants, allow grapes, hardy kiwi or thornless blackberries to climb up and overhead on arbors, arching trellises or pagodas. Situate them at the entrance to your garden, over a sitting area, or anywhere you want shade, beauty and abundant fruit.

Fruits for Hedges

Hedges are handy for creating attractive screens and barriers to provide privacy, block ugly views or mark boundary lines.

And when you have a hedge of fruit-bearing plants, you have a landscape feature that's productive as well as pretty. Fruit- and nut-bearing shrubs work best as informal hedges, since the shearing needed to keep formal hedges neat will drastically reduce fruit production. Few fruiting shrubs are evergreen, so fruiting hedges will be most attractive and effective during the growing season. Good choices for edible hedges include red and white currants, American filberts, Nanking cherries, blueberries, blackberries, dwarf citrus trees, raspberries, wineberries, elderberries, dwarf figs, Manchurian bush apricots, gooseberries and currants. For an informal hedge, plant bush fruits close enough together so that their branch tips will intermingle when they mature.

You also can train some dwarf or compact-growing fruit trees into a highly productive trellised hedge. Commercial fruit growers developed this technique to make mechanical harvesting easy. But in the process, they discovered that trellis-trained hedges produce three times more fruit per acre (hectare) than individually planted trees. Dwarf apples, dwarf pears, dwarf peaches and European plums are all good candidates for this system.

To train a trellised hedge, set up a 5-foot (1.5-m) tall post-and-wire trellis where you want the hedge to be. Plant dwarf trees along it, spaced 4–6 feet (1.2–1.8 m) apart. Prune them to develop three or four main branches that fan out along the trellis. Hold the main branches in place as they grow to the top of the trellis by tying them loosely to the wires. Cut back side branches to about 1 foot (30 cm) long in summer, encouraging them to form a wall of greenery.

Vegetable Garden Design

The vegetable garden can be a decorative feature in its own right, especially if you incorporate attractive edibles, such as purple-leaved varieties, and include some flowering herbs and ornamentals. The style of your vegetable garden will depend on how much space and time you have. However, it needs careful planning, with easy access and efficient workflow in mind. You can

Vegetables for Garden Color

Add excitement to your vegetable garden by growing crops that are attractive as well as good-tasting. Listed below are just a few suggestions of colorful crops and cultivars.

Beans (stringless): 'Royal Burgundy', 'Royal Purple'.
Broccoli: 'Purple Sprouting'.
Cabbage: 'Mammoth Red', 'Preko'.
Kale: 'Peacock Pink', 'Cherry Gateau'.
Ornamental Cabbage: 'Dynasty Pink'.
Peppers (capsicums), Light green: 'Lady Belle', 'Yolo Wonder', 'Big Bertha', 'Park's Whopper', 'Pro Bell II', 'Ace'; **Golden:** 'Golden Bell', 'Golden California Wonder', 'Golden Summer'; **Yellow:** 'Gypsy', 'Banana', 'Hungarian Wax'; **Orange and red:** 'Tasty Hybrid', 'California Wonder', 'Tequila Sunrise', 'Banana Supreme', 'Anaheim'.
Squash: 'Burpee Golden', 'Gold Rush', 'Jersey Golden', 'Baby Blue'.
Tomatoes: 'Golden Boy', 'Yellow Plum', 'Yellow Cherry', 'Yellow Pear'.

garden in rows or beds, both of which have different advantages.

Row gardening involves planting vegetables in parallel lines. Rows might be the best way to garden if you have plenty of space and time for cultivating between rows. You'll find rows easy to plan and easy to plant, but you'll use space less efficiently since you'll need to have paths between rows.

Beds are raised areas for planting, and offer several advantages over row planting for vegetable gardening. Production is greater, since beds are more intensively planted and aren't subjected to compaction from foot

Ornamental onion

ABOVE: Orange marigolds and purple-leaved cabbages combine to stunning effect.

traffic. They are attractive, space-efficient and easy to organize and work within.

Container Vegetables

You can grow some common garden vegetables, such as potatoes, in containers. You can also grow dwarf cultivars of larger-sized vegetables in pots and barrels. A decorative effect can be achieved by mixing compatible vegetables and ornamentals.

Mixing Vegetables and Ornamentals

Vegetables and ornamentals can be mixed to beautiful effect. Attractive edibles, such as ornamental onions, ornamental cabbages and globe artichokes, make wonderful feature or accent plants in the flower garden. Edible nasturtiums add color to the vegetable garden, and annuals such as zinnias, cosmos, marigolds and sunflowers turn the kitchen garden into a cutting garden, too. Blue or red cabbages, and pale green or red lettuces can be used decoratively in row and bed plantings, painting geometric designs with their colorful leaves.

LEFT: Lady's-mantle and marguerites bloom next to lettuces and ornamental cabbages in a wood-edged raised bed.

Cacti and Succulents

Greatly valued for their unique variety of forms and their ease of maintenance, cacti and other succulent plants add a touch of drama and an unusual beauty to your garden. With their bold, geometric shapes, cacti and succulents are particularly suited to the modern garden. Some are grand enough to stand alone as architectural features.

Few cacti and succulents, however, tolerate excess moisture and even the toughest plants require good drainage. Sunny rock gardens and raised beds, where water drains away freely, are good locations. For once, rocky ground or sloping gardens with shallow soil are gardening advantages. Agaves, cacti, sedums and sempervivums all thrive, and their glaucous leaves fit naturally into the landscape.

A Sculptured Garden

For large banks with plenty of space, the huge rosette-forming *Agave americana* with its bold, gray-green, prickly leaves makes a dramatic landscape plant for a Mexican-style garden. In addition to the normal form, there are different variegated cultivars available, which grow to half the size of the species. These are suited to smaller spaces. But each of those sturdy leaves ends in a sharp spike, so they do need to be planted safely out of the way. More friendly is the smaller *Agave*

attenuata, which has fleshy, light green leaves without spines. It can be grown nearer to paths and, when planted in rows, makes a highly decorative border.

The slow-growing *Agave victoriae-reginae* is sometimes considered the most beautiful of the agaves—grow it in a raised bed where its perfectly domed rosette of white-marked, dark green leaves can be fully appreciated.

If you have lots of heat and little water, a striking desert garden can be created by using different types of cacti with neat, rounded forms and strong vertical lines. For greatest effect, clump a group of three or more plants of one species together. For good uniform shape, the popular globe-shaped, golden barrel cactus *Echinocereus grusonii* is a beautiful and fast-growing species to 3 feet (90 cm) in height.

The dramatic organ-pipe cactus *Pachycereus marginatus*, often grown as a living fence in Mexico, can be used for creating different vertical accents.

The towering tree-like euphorbias, such as the statuesque *Euphorbia canariensis* and *E. candelabrum*, with its fantastic branching arms, will give balance to the surroundings. Choose species that vary in color and form to make stunning arrangements. But it is important to select those that have similar light and water requirements.

When the cacti are in place, top with a dressing of small stones or other materials of a color that blends harmoniously with your surroundings. This dressing will enhance the appearance of the plants. It will also keep the weeds down, moderate soil temperatures and ensure that the area close to the base of the plant is dry.

A Colorful Border

Attractive, flowering succulents include the aloes and many members of the Crassulaceae family. Massed, like more conventional perennials or shrubs, they will give you flowers for months and interesting foliage year-round. The candelabra aloe *Aloe arborescens* is a good bloomer, sending up branched spikes of scarlet or yellow flowers in spring. The butterfly-attracting *Sedum spectabile* and its colorful cultivars have frilled, fleshy leaves and showy flower heads in late summer—these make excellent bedding plants. *Aeonium arboreum* has rosettes of bright green, fleshy leaves and clusters of golden-yellow, spring flowers. Add a decorator's touch

LEFT: The rosette-shaped leaves of Canary Island rose *Aeonium urbicum*.
ABOVE: Cactus garden featuring golden barrel cactus *Echinocereus grusonii*.

LEFT: The arresting, tubular flowers of *Aloe bromii* pictured with yucca and *Senecio scarposis*.
ABOVE: Some cacti, such as *Aloe vera*, have interesting blooms as well as their attractive leaves.

with the cultivar 'Zwartkop', which has striking, reddish black leaves.

With their profuse, brilliantly colored flowers, ice plants (*Lampranthus* spp.) can be used as a cheery sidewalk edging. If pastel shades are more to your liking, a more subtle edging can be created by planting the charming *Echeveria elegans* with its frosty blue-green leaves and nodding, pinkish red flower heads. Or try the sugar almond plant *Pachyphytum oviferum*, which bears orange-red or greenish flowers mainly in spring. It forms rosettes of white-frosted, swollen leaves providing interest year-round as a beautiful foliage plant.

Consider Containers

If space is at a premium, or climatic conditions not in your favor, you can still enjoy growing cacti and other succulents outdoors in containers. Most have shallow roots and can survive for years in the same pot. Choose containers that suit the shape and form of the plants—a shallow bowl, for example, is a natural choice for dwarf, cluster-forming species such as the houseleeks (*Sempervivum* spp.) and many of the mat-forming sedums.

RIGHT: The bold-shaped leaves of agaves look great growing in large terracotta pots or urns.

Cacti and succulents with stronger forms, such as the yuccas and agaves, are better suited to large pots or urns. For an eye-catching courtyard display, grow one of the large variegated agaves in a large stone urn raised on a matching pedestal so that the light can catch and highlight the variegation. Trailing succulents, such as donkey's tail *Sedum morganianum* and the Christmas cacti *Schlumbergera* hybrids, which produce their highly colored flowers from flattened weeping branches, are best displayed in hanging baskets.

In areas with wet winters, potted specimens can be moved to a warm, sheltered position such as a corner of a covered patio or against a wall under an overhanging roof to keep them drier. Where winters are severe, move frost-tender plants indoors during the cooler months. Watering once a month in winter is often enough, especially if the plants are kept in low temperatures. You'll need to take care when placing plants back outside—move them into the sun gradually.

Repotting

The size of the container should be only as large as necessary. Repot cacti and succulents in larger pots only when they have completely filled their containers with roots—no more than about every 3 years or so. Commercial cacti potting mixes are easy to use and can be purchased from your local nursery or garden center.

Right Plant, Right Place

For successful garden design, it is important to match plants with their preferred conditions. To help you make the best choices for the conditions you have, the following chart summarizes the specific needs of more than 170 popular annuals and biennials, bulbs, perennials, trees and palms, shrubs, vines, water and bog plants, accent plants and groundcovers. You can see at a glance exactly which plants prefer sun, and which prefer shade, and you can check if the plant will thrive in your particular climatic Zone. The chart also notes the season of interest for the plant, as well as its most common landscape uses.

Plant	Light Needs	Hardiness	Season of Interest	Landscape Uses
ANNUALS AND BIENNIALS				
Hybrid tuberous begonias *Begonia* Tuberhybrida hybrids	Half-day of sun or filtered sun	Zones 6–10	Flowers from summer until frost in all colors except blue.	Use as features in shaded beds, or to introduce color in hanging baskets.
Ornamental cabbage *Brassica oleracea*	Full sun to light shade	Zones 6–11	Leaves are marked with pink, purple or cream in autumn.	Add color to autumn gardens, or use in window boxes.
Canterbury bells *Campanula medium*	Full sun to light shade	Zones 6–10	White, pink or purple-blue flowers; spring to early summer.	Grow in small clumps in beds and borders, among annuals or perennials.
Cleome *Cleome hassleriana*	Full sun to light shade	Zones 9–11	White, pink or lavender flowers from midsummer to midautumn.	Plant at the back of flower beds or in cottage garden borders.
Cosmos *Cosmos bipinnatus*	Full sun to partial shade	Zones 8–10	White, pink or red flowers bloom from late summer through autumn.	Add height and color to beds, borders and meadows.
Common foxglove *Digitalis purpurea*	Full sun to partial shade	Zones 5–11	Spires of thimble-shaped flowers in early summer.	Tall spires are effective when massed in lightly shaded woodland.
California poppy *Eschscholzia californica*	Full sun	Zones 6–11	Orange, yellow, white, pink or red flowers appear from summer to autumn.	Colorful fillers, also excellent in meadow and water-saving gardens.
Common sunflower *Helianthus annuus*	Full sun	Zones 4–11	Large, yellow, red or orange flowers from midsummer to autumn.	Tall-growing screen along a fence, or to add height to a sunny border.
Impatiens *Impatiens* spp.	Full sun to partial shade	Zones 8–12	White, pink, purple, rose or red flowers appear from midsummer until frost.	Brighten shady corners in gardens, borders or hanging baskets.
Morning glory *Ipomoea tricolor*	Full sun to light afternoon shade	Zones 8–12	Purple flowers open every day throughout summer.	Let it climb through large shrubs, or on a trellis to create a summer screen.
Sweet pea *Lathyrus odoratus*	Full sun	Zones 4–10	Flowers in white, pink, red or purple bloom from midspring into summer.	Provide a tepee of bamboo stakes for plant to climb on. Looks good in a hanging basket.
Edging lobelia *Lobelia erinus*	Full sun to partial shade	Zones 7–11	Blue, violet, pink or white flowers appear in summer.	Grow at the front of beds and borders, or cascade from window boxes.
Sweet alyssum *Lobularia maritima*	Full sun to partial shade	Zones 7–10	White, pink or purple flowers appear from summer to autumn.	Edging for beds and borders, or use as a groundcover under shrubs.

Plant	Light Needs	Hardiness	Season of Interest	Landscape Uses
Baby-blue-eyes *Nemophila menziesii*	Full sun to partial shade	Zones 7–11	Sky-blue flowers with a white center bloom in summer.	Looks great trailing out of pots or among pavers.
Flowering tobacco *Nicotiana alata*	Full sun to partial shade	Zones 7–11	White, pink or red flowers bloom from summer until frost.	Plant around outdoor sitting areas to enjoy evening fragrance.
Love-in-a-mist *Nigella damascena*	Full sun to partial shade	Zones 6–10	Blue, pink or white flowers bloom in summer.	An unusual filler in beds, borders and cottage gardens.
Iceland poppy *Papaver nudicaule*	Full sun	Zones 2–10	White, pink, red, orange or yellow flowers bloom in early to midsummer.	Great for early color in beds and borders.
Zonal geranium *Pelargonium* x *hortorum*	Full sun	Zones 5–10	White, pink, red, salmon and bicolor flowers bloom from late spring until frost.	Grow in beds or borders as accents or fillers, or in containers.
Petunia *Petunia* x *hybrida*	Full sun; tolerates half-day sun	Zones 6–10	Single or double flowers in most colors of the rainbow from early summer until frost.	Ideal for hanging baskets and window boxes.
Scarlet runner bean *Phaseolus coccineus*	Full sun	Zones 3–10	Clusters of orange-red flowers from midsummer to frost.	Use for quick shade or to cover an ugly fence, or train up a tripod.
Rose moss *Portulaca grandiflora*	Full sun	Zones 6–11	White, pink, red, orange, yellow and magenta flowers bloom in summer and autumn.	A great groundcover for sunny, dry rocky slopes.
Black-eyed Susan *Rudbeckia hirta*	Full sun to light shade	Zones 3–10	Golden-yellow flowers bloom from summer into autumn.	Bright and cheerful in beds and borders.
Scarlet sage *Salvia splendens*	Full sun	Zones 6–10	Mostly red flowers bloom from early summer until frost.	Edging for beds and borders, or surround with green herbs and grasses.
Dusty miller *Senecio cineraria*	Full sun	Zones 8–11	Silver foliage with yellow flowers in summer.	Silver foliage ideal as edging or accent for beds and borders. Salt-tolerant.
Coleus *Solenostemon scutellarioides*	High, indirect light to moderate shade	Zones 8–12	Pale blue flowers appear from late spring to early summer.	Showy leaves bring all-season color to beds and borders.
Marigolds *Tagetes* hybrids	Full sun	Zones 5–11	Yellow, orange and red blooms appear in summer and autumn.	Summer edgings or fillers for beds and borders, or grow as a flowering hedge.
Nasturtium *Tropaeolum majus*	Full sun to partial shade	Zones 5–11	Flowers in a range of colors appear from early summer through autumn.	Grow as climbers on a trellis or over other plants.
Pansy *Viola* x *wittrockiana*	Full sun to partial shade	Zones 5–10	Pink, red, orange, yellow, blue, purple and near-black flowers bloom in spring and autumn.	Use to inject color into winter and spring gardens.

BULBS

Plant	Light Needs	Hardiness	Season of Interest	Landscape Uses
Giant onion *Allium giganteum*	Full sun to light shade	Zones 5–9	Round flower head with small purple flowers in early summer.	Show-stopping accent for the back of flower beds and borders.
Italian arum *Arum italicum*	Partial shade	Zones 6–10	Greenish yellow flowers bloom in mid- to late spring.	Plant in masses along streams or clumped near ponds.

Plant	Light Needs	Hardiness	Season of Interest	Landscape Uses
Caladium *Caladium bicolor*	Partial shade	Zones 10–12	Bushy clumps of arrow-shaped leaves from late spring to frost.	Summer color in shady gardens.
Showy autumn crocus *Colchicum speciosum*	Full sun to partial shade	Zones 4–9	Pink flowers bloom in late summer to early autumn.	Grow up through low groundcovers or under shrubs.
Hardy cyclamen *Cyclamen hederifolium*	Partial shade	Zones 5–9	Pink or white flowers bloom in early autumn.	Seasonal groundcover for shaded places under trees.
Dahlias *Dahlia* hybrids	Partial to full sun	Zones 9–10	Red, orange, pink, purple, white and yellow flowers bloom from midsummer through autumn.	Use for color at the front of beds. Use taller varieties for autumn interest.
Gladiolus *Gladiolus* hybrids	Full sun	Zones 8–10	Many-budded floral spikes from summer to early autumn.	Spiky blooms enliven middle and back of beds and borders.
Spanish bluebells *Hyacinthoides hispanica*	Full sun to partial shade	Zones 4–9	White, pink and purple-blue flowers bloom in spring.	Clumps in beds and borders, or combine with groundcovers.
Hyacinth *Hyacinthus orientalis*	Full sun	Zones 4–9	White, pink, red, orange, yellow, blue and purple flowers bloom in spring.	Cheerful color for beds and borders.
Reticulated iris *Iris reticulata*	Full sun	Zones 5–9	Blue, purple or white flowers bloom in early spring.	Delicate blooms beautiful when massed.
Lilies *Lilium* hybrids	Full sun to partial shade	Zones 4–10	Showy flowers in many colors by early to late summer.	Add height and color to planting schemes.
Grape hyacinth *Muscari armeniacum*	Full sun to partial shade	Zones 4–9	Dense spikes of small purple blooms in early spring.	Scatter bulbs liberally throughout beds and borders.
Daffodils *Narcissus* hybrids	Full sun to partial shade	Zones 4–9	Yellow or white trumpet-shaped flowers in spring.	Combine with other spring-flowering annuals and bulbs.
Tulips *Tulipa* hybrids	Full sun to partial shade	Zones 3–8	Spring-flowering, in a wide range of colors.	Mass in beds for pools of color, or use as edging or in containers.

PERENNIALS

Plant	Light Needs	Hardiness	Season of Interest	Landscape Uses
Fern-leaved yarrow *Achillea filipendulina*	Full sun	Zones 3–9	Yellow flowers bloom from early to midsummer.	Use on dry, sunny banks to control erosion.
Agapanthus *Agapanthus praecox* subsp. *orientalis*	Full sun	Zones 8–11	Long-stalked blue or white flowers during summer.	Edging for a lawn, fence, swimming pool or path, or as summer accent plant.
Hybrid columbine *Aquilegia* x *hybrida*	Full sun to partial shade	Zones 3–9	Flowers of many colors bloom in early summer.	Best in groups or drifts. Plant in formal beds or informal settings.
New England aster *Aster novae-angliae*	Full sun to light shade	Zones 3–9	The white, pink, rose, lavender and purple flowers bloom from summer through autumn.	Plant in formal and informal settings or in meadows at back of border.
Astilbe *Astilbe* x *arendsii*	Full to partial shade	Zones 3–9	Red, pink and white blooms in spring and early summer.	Plant in masses by ponds where blooms will be reflected.

Plant	Light Needs	Hardiness	Season of Interest	Landscape Uses
Hybrid delphinium *Delphinium* x *elatum* hybrids	Full sun	Zones 4–9	Flowers from white to true blue to lavender and purple appear in spring.	Rear of borders or by a wall or hedge where showy flower spires will stand tall.
Garden mum *Dendranthema* x *grandiflorum*	Full sun	Zones 3–10	White, pink, red, gold or yellow flowers bloom from summer through autumn.	Use to freshen appearance of annual displays.
Purple coneflower *Echinacea purpurea*	Full sun	Zones 3–9	Red-violet to rose-pink flowers from midsummer to autumn.	Formal gardens, or meadow and prairie gardens.
Globe thistle *Echinops ritro*	Full sun	Zones 3–10	Steel-blue flowers bloom in midsummer.	Middle or rear of borders, or use in cottage gardens or meadows.
Daisy fleabane *Erigeron speciosus*	Full sun or light shade	Zones 2–10	Flowers in white, pink, rose or purple bloom in early to midsummer.	Plant in front of beds, rock gardens beside steps and paths or among paving stones.
Amethyst sea holly *Eryngium amethystinum*	Full sun	Zones 2–10	Steel-blue flowers bloom in summer.	Use as accent in middle of a border, or as mass planting against a hedge.
Blood-red cranesbill *Geranium sanguineum*	Full sun to partial shade	Zones 3–10	Bright magenta flowers from late spring to midsummer.	Place at the front of a border or along paths or in rock gardens.
Lenten rose *Helleborus orientalis*	Light to partial shade	Zones 4–10	Reddish purple, pink or white flowers bloom from early winter through spring.	Shade gardens, woodland walks, spring borders, under trees.
Daylilies *Hemerocallis* hybrids	Full sun to light shade	Zones 3–9	Orange, yellow, red, pink, buff, apricot or green flowers appear from spring through autumn.	Mass plantings in beds and borders, in meadows and beside woodland.
Hostas *Hosta* hybrids	Light to full shade	Zones 3–10	Purplish or white flowers in summer or autumn.	Versatile plants to edge beds or cover the ground under shrubs and trees.
Bearded iris *Iris* bearded hybrids	Full sun	Zones 3–10	White, yellow, blue or purple blooms late spring to summer.	Looks great combined with ferns.
Common torch lily *Kniphofia uvaria*	Full sun	Zones 5–10	Yellow-white to red flowers from late spring to summer.	Vertical form adds drama to perennial borders and rock gardens.
Shasta daisy *Leucanthemum* x *superbum*	Full sun	Zones 3–10	Violet-blue flowers from spring through summer.	Plant in beds and borders, cottage gardens and meadows.
Catmint *Nepeta* x *faassenii*	Full sun to light shade	Zones 3–10	Lavender-blue flowers bloom from spring to midsummer.	Perfect for edging walks and beds or planting along rock walls.
Common garden peony *Paeonia lactiflora*	Full sun to light shade	Zones 2–8	Fragrant white, pink or red flowers from late spring to early summer.	Cottage gardens, beds, borders and mass plantings.
Oriental poppy *Papaver orientale*	Full sun to light shade	Zones 2–9	Flowers in shades of pink through red bloom in summer.	Use with other perennials in beds and borders.
Garden phlox *Phlox paniculata*	Full sun to light shade	Zones 3–10	Flowers of magenta to pink and white bloom from mid- to late summer.	Formal and informal beds, meadows and cottage gardens.

Plant	Light Needs	Hardiness	Season of Interest	Landscape Uses
Drumstick primrose *Primula denticulata*	Light to partial shade	Zones 3–9	Tight, globe-shaped clusters of lavender or pink flowers in early spring.	Grow along a stream, beside a pool or in a moist shade garden.
English primrose *Primula vulgaris*	Light to partial shade	Zones 4–9	Pale yellow flowers bloom in spring and early summer.	Grow in light shade in woodland or informal gardens.
Orange coneflower *Rudbeckia fulgida*	Full sun or light shade	Zones 3–10	Gold flowers with dark central cones bloom during summer and autumn.	Formal and informal beds, cottage gardens and meadows.
Violet sage *Salvia* x *superba*	Full sun to light shade	Zones 4–10	Violet-blue flowers appear in early to midsummer.	Formal or informal borders or rock gardens.
Showy stonecrop *Sedum spectabile*	Full sun	Zones 3–9	Small bright pink flowers bloom in mid- to late summer.	Formal borders, rock gardens, or mass plantings with shrubs.
Stiff goldenrod *Solidago rigida*	Full sun or light shade	Zones 3–9	Golden-yellow flowers bloom in late summer and autumn.	Plant along walls and fences, in beds and borders, or in formal gardens.
Foamflower *Tiarella cordifolia*	Partial to full shade	Zones 3–9	White flowers bloom in midspring.	Excellent groundcover for moist garden in cool to mild climate.

TREES AND PALMS

Plant	Light Needs	Hardiness	Season of Interest	Landscape Uses
Nikko fir *Abies homolepis*	Full sun to light shade	Zones 4–8	Coniferous evergreen with purplish cones summer to winter.	Specimen tree, screens, or evergreen framework for cold-climate gardens.
Maples *Acer* spp.	Full sun to partial shade	Zones 3–9	Vibrant autumn foliage, some also have spring color.	Shade trees for changing seasonal effect. Tall species are good street trees.
Parlor palm *Chamaedorea elegans*	Full sun to filtered light, afternoon shade	Zones 9–11	Tiny yellow flowers in panicles, from spring to autumn.	Dwarf palm used with other foliage plants for rainforest look.
European fan palm *Chamaerops humilis*	Full sun to bright light	Zones 8–10	Yellow, perfumed male flowers in dense panicles in late spring.	Large, clump-forming specimen plant for a lawn or entrance.
Lemon *Citrus limon*	Full sun	Zones 8–12	Highly fragrant, white flowers in spring followed by yellow fruit.	Feature tree in backyard orchard or vegetable garden.
Flowering dogwood *Cornus florida*	Full sun to partial shade	Zones 4–9	Showy white blooms in spring, brilliant red berries in autumn.	Specimen or lawn tree, singly or in groups, or massed as a woodland.
Smoke tree *Cotinus coggygria*	Full sun	Zones 5–9	Feathery pink, purple or gray plumes appear midsummer to autumn and persist many months.	Autumn and summer color for shrub borders.
Italian cypress *Cupressus sempervirens*	Full sun	Zones 8–10	Evergreen with small, nutlike cones turning brown in winter.	Useful as narrow screen, or use as an "exclamation point" in gardens.
Blue gum *Eucalyptus globulus*	Full sun	Zones 8–10	Clusters of creamy white flowers from winter to spring.	Shade or specimen tree, used for street tree or windbreak in warm climates.
European beech *Fagus sylvatica*	Full sun to partial shade	Zones 4–8	Dark green leaves turn copper-gold in autumn.	Specimen or shade tree, or train as a dense, deciduous hedge.

Plant	Light Needs	Hardiness	Season of Interest	Landscape Uses
Golden rain tree *Koelreuteria paniculata*	Full sun	Zones 5–9	Yellow flowers in midsummer. In autumn, leaves turn yellow and seedpods turn red.	Specimen tree for good midsummer and autumn color.
Golden chain tree *Laburnum* x *watereri*	Full sun	Zones 3–9	Golden-yellow flowers hang in long clusters in late spring.	Group against an evergreen background or train into arch or arcade by pleaching.
Crape myrtle *Lagerstroemia indica*	Full sun	Zones 7–10	White, pink, red or purple flowers in mid- to late summer.	Small tree for suburban garden or street plantings.
Magnolias *Magnolia* spp.	Partial shade	Zones 7–10	Both spring-flowering and summer-flowering species.	Specimen trees. Grow as shade or avenue tree in warmer climates.
Crab apple *Malus floribunda*	Full sun	Zones 4–9	White buds followed by pink flowers in spring. Red or yellow fruit ripens summer to autumn.	Specimen or shade tree for small gardens or to line a driveway.
Colorado spruce *Picea pungens*	Full sun	Zones 2–8	Evergreen conifer with reddish-brown flowers in late spring.	Screen planting, especially for cold climates when all else is bare.
Swiss mountain pine *Pinus mugo*	Full sun	Zones 2–7	Evergreen conifer with yellow or reddish flowers in late spring.	Foundation plant or low, evergreen hedge.
Poplars *Populus* spp.	Full sun	Zones 2–9	Greenish catkins in spring and butter-yellow leaves in autumn.	Screens, avenues and mass plantings, or an accent plant for large gardens.
Japanese flowering cherry *Prunus serrulata*	Full sun	Zones 5–9	Leaves turn yellow, orange and scarlet in autumn. Clusters of pink or white spring flowers.	Specimen tree, or create a spring walk.
Oaks *Quercus* spp.	Full sun	Zones 4–10	Some evergreen species, others deciduous with magnificent autumn color.	Specimen trees, particularly those with autumn color. Shade or avenue trees for large gardens, parks or golf courses.
Black locust *Robinia pseudoacacia*	Full sun to partial shade	Zones 3–10	Leaves turn yellow in autumn; white, pealike flowers in summer.	Grafted forms useful as accent trees for courtyards or small areas.
Weeping willow *Salix babylonica*	Full sun	Zones 6–10	Narrow leaves turn yellow in autumn; greenish catkins from late spring to early summer.	Effective near ponds, lakes, or in moist ground. Useful for bank-binding near streams and rivers.
American arborvitae *Thuja occidentalis*	Full sun	Zones 2–10	Evergreen with inconspicuous flowers in midspring.	Screens, hedges, or as accent plants in shrub borders or rockeries.
Chinese windmill palm *Trachycarpus fortunei*	Full sun to bright light	Zones 8–10	Small, yellow flowers emerge near leaf bases in early summer.	Large specimen plant for lawn or entrance, or among mixed foliage.
Chinese elm *Ulmus parvifolia*	Full sun	Zones 5–9	Deciduous in cooler climates; inconspicuous reddish flowers autumn to early winter.	Specimen, shade and street trees. Underprune to create shaded space for summer entertaining.

SHRUBS

Plant	Light Needs	Hardiness	Season of Interest	Landscape Uses
Marguerite *Argyranthemum frutescens*	Full sun	Zones 5–10	Abundant white, pink or yellow blooms from spring to autumn.	A low-care fast-grower for cottage gardens or perennial borders.
Japanese aucuba *Aucuba japonica*	Shade	Zones 6–10	Small, purple flowers in late winter to early spring.	Shrub borders, foundation plantings, containers, under trees.

Plant	Light Needs	Hardiness	Season of Interest	Landscape Uses
Japanese barberry *Berberis thunbergii*	Full sun to almost full shade	Zones 4–10	Leaves turn orange-red in autumn; small, yellow flowers in late spring.	Informal hedges or barrier plantings, shrub border for autumn color.
Orange-eye butterfly bush *Buddleia davidii*	Full sun	Zones 5–10	Purple flowers with orange eye from midsummer to early autumn.	Back of flower or shrub borders.
Common boxwood *Buxus sempervirens*	Full sun to partial shade	Zones 6–9	Evergreen with inconspicuous perfumed flowers in early spring.	Informal hedges, screens, foundation plantings, topiary.
Sasanqua camellia *Camellia sasanqua*	Full sun to light shade	Zones 7–10	Pink, red, white or lavender flowers from autumn to winter.	Formal or informal hedges, specimen shrub or small tree, espalier.
Mexican orange blossom *Choisya ternata*	Full sun to light shade	Zones 7–9	Small, white, fragrant flowers appear in spring and summer.	Low hedge, foundation planting, shady shrub border.
Red-osier dogwood *Cornus stolonifera*	Full sun to full shade	Zones 2–9	Red stems, with white flowers in late spring followed by red berries.	Winter color in shrub borders.
Burning bush *Euonymus alatus*	Full sun to partial shade	Zones 3–9	Leaves turn red, crimson, orange and scarlet in autumn.	Specimen shrub, shrub borders, and informal hedges.
Border forsythia *Forsythia x intermedia*	Full sun	Zones 5–9	Bright yellow flowers early to midspring on bare branches.	Specimen shrub, informal hedges, or in front of evergreen background.
Common fuchsias *Fuchsia hybrids*	Partial shade	Zones 9–11	White, pink, red, mauve and violet hanging flowers in late spring to autumn.	Informal hedges, standards, or hanging basket plants.
Common gardenia *Gardenia augusta*	Partial shade, protect from afternoon sun	Zones 9–11	Very fragrant white flowers in early to midsummer.	Foundation shrubs, specimen plants or low, formal hedges.
Chinese witch hazel *Hamamelis mollis*	Full sun	Zones 5–9	Leaves turn golden-yellow in autumn; fragrant yellow flowers in winter on bare branches.	Specimen plant, shrub borders, woodland plantings or city gardens.
Bigleaf hydrangea *Hydrangea macrophylla*	Partial shade, protect from afternoon sun	Zones 6–10	Large, flat flower clusters in pink or blue in midsummer.	Specimen shrub, shrub borders for shaded gardens, container plants.
English holly *Ilex aquifolium*	Full sun to light shade	Zones 5–9	Small, perfumed, white flowers late spring to early summer; red or yellow fruit on female plants.	Specimen tree or shrub, foundation plantings, hedges.
English lavender *Lavandula angustifolia*	Full sun	Zones 6–9	Tall spires of lavender-blue flowers in summer.	Shrub borders, mass plantings, low hedges.
Orange jessamine *Murraya paniculata*	Full sun or partial shade	Zones 9–12	Waxy, white, perfumed flowers appear several times a year.	Specimen planting, formal or informal hedges, background plantings, topiary.
Heavenly bamboo *Nandina domestica*	Full sun to dense shade	Zones 6–10	Leaves color in autumn; panicles of white flowers in midsummer.	Hedges, narrow spaces such as fence lines, foundation plantings.
Japanese pieris *Pieris japonica*	Full sun to light shade	Zones 4–9	Fragrant white flower clusters in spring.	Specimen shrub, shrub borders, foundation plantings.
Scarlet firethorn *Pyracantha coccinea*	Full sun to light shade	Zones 6–9	White flowers from late spring to early summer, followed by persistent red to yellow berries.	Specimen shrub, foundation plantings, espalier, hedges, screens. The berries attract birds.

Plant	Light Needs	Hardiness	Season of Interest	Landscape Uses
Rhododendrons *Rhododendron* spp. and hybrids	Light shade	Zones 4–10	White, pink, red, lavender, blue or yellow flowers in early spring to midsummer.	Foundation plantings, specimen shrub, massed plantings, containers.
Roses *Rosa* hybrids	Full sun	Zones 4–10	White, pink, orange, yellow, red, lavender or multicolored flowers, often fragrant, from late spring to early winter.	Shrub or flower borders, containers. Excellent for cutting gardens.
Common lilac *Syringa vulgaris*	Full sun to light shade	Zones 3–8	Very fragrant, lavender flowers in mid- to late spring.	Specimen shrub, shrub borders, screens or hedges.
Fragrant viburnum *Viburnum carlesii*	Full sun to partial shade	Zones 4–9	Fragrant heads of white flowers tinged with pink in midspring.	Specimen shrubs, shrub borders, screens or hedges.
VINES				
Common allamanda *Allamanda cathartica*	Full sun to partial shade	Zones 9–12	Trumpet-shaped, bright yellow flowers in summer.	Grow on fences, walls and around poles in warm climates.
Bougainvilleas *Bougainvillea* spp.	Full sun	Zones 9–12	Brilliant colored bracts of yellow, red, white or magenta all summer.	Cover trellises or clip into dense hedge.
Clematis *Clematis montana*	Full sun at top, shade at roots	Zones 6–9	White or pink, perfumed flowers in late spring or early summer.	Outstanding flowering vines for arbors or trellises.
Common white jasmine *Jasminum officinale*	Full sun to light shade	Zones 6–10	Clusters of pink buds opening to fragrant, white flowers in spring.	Excellent for trellises, arbors, or to scent a courtyard.
Woodbine honeysuckle *Lonicera periclymenum*	Full sun to partial shade	Zones 4–10	Fragrant yellow, white, red flowers in late spring to late summer.	Allow to clamber over bushes, fences and verandas.
Boston ivy *Parthenocissus tricuspidata*	Full sun to light shade	Zones 4–10	Leaves turn brilliant shades of red and purple in autumn.	The premier foliage vine to mask a wall and create autumn interest.
Blue passionflower *Passiflora caerulea*	Full sun to light shade	Zones 7–11	Blue or white flowers in summer, followed by inedible orange fruit.	Fast-growing screen or to hide a fence. Also understock for fruiting forms.
Crimson glory vine *Vitis coignetiae*	Full sun	Zones 5–10	Large, green leaves turn orange, scarlet and crimson in autumn.	Excellent cover for trellises and arbors, or to climb walls and fences.
Japanese wisteria *Wisteria floribunda*	Full sun to light shade	Zones 4–10	Fragrant mauve or white flower clusters appear in late spring.	Fine vines to climb on strong supports such as arches or pergolas.
WATER AND BOG PLANTS				
Sweet flag *Acorus gramineus*	Full sun or light shade	Zones 3–11	Evergreen perennial with inconspicuous flower spikes.	Small plant useful for edging, particularly in moist situations.
Marsh marigold *Caltha palustris*	Full sun to partial shade	Zones 2–8	Butter yellow flowers in open clusters in early to midspring.	Perfect for water gardens or along the low banks of a stream.
Papyrus *Cyperus papyrus*	Full sun or light shade	Zones 9–12	Fluffy head of green branchlets with brown flowers in summer.	Tall accent plant for shallow water.
Water iris *Iris pseudacorus*	Full sun to shade	Zones 5–9	Tall spikes of yellow flowers in spring and summer.	Grow in clumps at the edge of ponds. Contrast with creeping or floating plants.

Plant	Light Needs	Hardiness	Season of Interest	Landscape Uses
Yellow skunk cabbage *Lysichiton americanus*	Full sun	Zones 5–9	Yellow, lily-like flowers appear in early spring before the leaves.	Grow in clumps by water for the striking flowers and architectural leaves.
Lotus *Nelumbo nucifera*	Full sun	Zones 6–11	Fragrant, pink flowers on tall stems in summer.	Grow in ponds and lakes for dramatic flowering.
Waterlily *Nymphaea* hybrids	Full sun	Zones 5–12	Fragrant flowers in pink, yellow, white or blue in spring to autumn.	Ornament a pond or water feature.
Arum lily *Zantedeschia aethiopica*	Full sun to shade	Zones 8–11	Pure white flowers with yellow spadix in summer.	Beside water or in moist, shade areas.

ACCENT PLANTS

Plant	Light Needs	Hardiness	Season of Interest	Landscape Uses
Bromeliad *Aechmea* spp.	Warm sun to light shade	Zones 9–12	Long-lasting, exotic flowers produced in summer.	Brighten gardens with year-round leaf color and striking flowers.
Century plants *Agave* spp.	Full sun	Zones 3–11	Flowers in summer, though may take 15 years to bloom.	Small to large plants for dry gardens or modern landscapes.
Aloe *Aloe arborescens*	Full sun	Zones 9–11	Red, bird-attracting flowers in winter and spring.	Large mound-forming plants for hot and dry or seaside gardens.
Bamboos *Bambusa* spp.	Full sun to light shade	Zones 9–12	Fast-growing grass with woody stem and insignificant flowers.	Use for screens, accents, or for sound and movement in oriental gardens.
Queen's tears *Billbergia nutans*	Full sun to light shade	Zones 9–12	Navy blue and green flowers under pink bracts in spring.	Mass plant as understory in foliage gardens or among rocks.
Feather reed grass *Calamagrostis* x *acutiflora*	Full sun to light shade	Zones 5–9	Long, pinkish-green flower clusters from late spring.	Tall accent plant to add movement to the garden.
Giant saguaro *Carnegiea gigantea*	Full sun	Zones 9–11	May take decades to produce large white flowers in summer.	Mature plants produce striking silhouettes in arid gardens.
New Zealand cabbage tree *Cordyline australis*	Full sun or semi-shade	Zones 8–12	Fragrant white flowers in large panicles in spring and summer.	Accent plant or for color contrast in a foliage garden or by swimming pools.
Pampas grass *Cortaderia selloana*	Full sun to light shade	Zones 8–10	Plumelike white or pink flower heads from midsummer.	Dramatic screens, background clumps, or elegant specimens among lawns.
Soft tree fern *Dicksonia antarctica*	Light shade	Zones 8–12	Long, lacy fronds uncurl from top of trunk throughout the year.	Use to bring an exotic element to a shaded, moist or fern garden.
Dracaena *Dracaena marginata*	Light shade	Zones 9–12	Terminal panicles of white flowers in summer.	Mass in shaded areas under trees or in courtyards.
Hen and chickens *Echeveria elegans*	Full sun	Zones 8–11	Bell-shaped, pink flowers on long stem, late winter to early summer.	Mass in sunny areas or to edge paths.
Golden barrel cactus *Echinocactus grusonii*	Full sun	Zones 9–12	Ring of bright yellow flowers appears in summer.	Mass in hot and sunny, dry areas such as rockeries or succulent gardens.
Blue fescue *Festuca cinerea*	Full sun to light shade	Zones 4–10	Silver-blue, spiky evergreen foliage; insignificant flowers.	Attractive accent plant for borders, rock gardens and seaside plantings.
Japanese blood grass *Imperata cylindrica* 'Red Baron'	Full sun to partial shade	Zones 6–9	Red-tipped, green foliage turns red in summer, copper in autumn.	Dramatic mass planting or in borders, especially when backlit by sun.

Plant	Light Needs	Hardiness	Season of Interest	Landscape Uses
Mondo grass *Ophiopogon japonicus*	Full sun to shade	Zones 7–11	Lavender to white flowers in summer often hidden by leaves.	Groundcover or low accent under trees or beside paths.
Fountain grass *Pennisetum alopecuroides*	Full sun to light shade	Zones 5–9	Clusters of white to pinkish flowers in midsummer.	Excellent accents in borders, drifts or foundation plantings.
White-striped ribbon grass *Phalaris arundinacea* var. *picta*	Light shade	Zones 4–9	White flower spikes in early summer.	Spreading groundcover helpful for erosion control or to edge ponds.
Bamboos *Phyllostachys* spp.	Full sun	Zones 6–11	Evergreen clump-forming grass, some with colored stems.	Fast-growing screens, hedges or accents for oriental gardens.
Bamboo *Pleioblastus auricoma*	Full sun to light shade	Zones 7–10	Upright, evergreen, woody grass, rarely in flower.	Fast-growing screens, hedges or accents for courtyards.
Mother-in-law's tongue *Sansevieria trifasciata*	Sun to light shade	Zones 9–12	Grown for the stiff, fleshy, linear, green leaves banded with cream.	Mass plant for an eye-catching tall groundcover, or in clumps among rocks.
Bird of paradise *Strelitzia nicolai*	Full sun to partial shade	Zones 10–12	Spectacular white and blue birdlike flowers in summer.	Mass as tall screen or use singly as a dramatic specimen plant.
Adam's needle *Yucca gloriosa*	Full sun	Zones 7–10	Panicles of cream, bell-shaped flowers.	Use as focal point in succulent garden.

GROUNDCOVERS

Plant	Light Needs	Hardiness	Season of Interest	Landscape Uses
Wall rock cress *Arabis caucasica*	Full sun	Zones 3–9	Clusters of small, fragrant, pink or white flowers in spring.	Ornamental for rock gardens or crevices in a stone wall.
Dalmatian bellflower *Campanula portenschlagiana*	Full sun to light shade	Zones 4–10	Masses of lavender-blue flowers from late spring to midsummer.	Ideal groundcover in rock gardens, and on rocky slopes.
Snow-in-summer *Cerastium tomentosum*	Full sun	Zones 2–10	Abundant white flowers for several weeks in late spring.	Good groundcover for dry, sunny spots, where the spread won't be a problem.
Roman chamomile *Chamaemelum nobile*	Full sun to partial shade	Zones 3–9	Small, daisy-like white flowers appear in mid- to late summer.	Lawn alternative which becomes compact when mowed occasionally.
Treasure flower *Gazania rigens*	Full sun	Zones 9–11	Brilliantly colored flowers from midsummer to frost.	An explosion of colour for beds and borders.
English ivy *Hedera helix*	Partial to full shade	Zones 5–9	Evergreen vine in a range of leaf colors and patterns.	Use as erosion control on slopes, or as groundcover under trees.
Creeping juniper *Juniperus horizontalis*	Full sun	Zones 3–10	Dark-colored fruits on short stems in late summer.	Ideal for covering slopes, including steep slopes unsuited to other plants.
Forget-me-not *Myosotis sylvatica*	Partial shade	Zones 5–10	Sprays of blue flowers from midspring through early summer.	Spring color in shady gardens, or early-season groundcover under trees.
Lamb's ears *Stachys byzantina*	Full sun or light shade	Zones 4–10	Small, rose-pink flowers in early summer.	Felted, silvery leaves are a feature at the front of gardens or along paths.
Mother of thyme *Thymus serpyllum*	Full sun	Zones 4–10	Small, rose-purple flowers in late spring and summer.	Low, decorative edging in ornamental garden, or fast-spreader between stones.
Sweet violet *Viola odorata*	Full sun to shade	Zones 6–10	Fragrant, deep violet blooms in late winter to early spring.	Fragrant groundcover in wild gardens and under trees and shrubs.

Creative Garden Design

*If you are seeking inspiration, you'll find it in the following pages.
Any garden, whatever its size, from wide open spaces to the confines
of a balcony or courtyard, can have style and a unifying theme. A garden
may be designed with the wild, back-to-nature look of a meadow, or it can
capture the simple lines found in classical design. Seek inspiration from the
surroundings, the climate or a favorite place or era.*

Natural Gardens

If you do nothing at all to the patch of ground around your home, you will pretty soon have a "natural" garden. It may be unsightly, inconvenient—and possibly illegal, if prohibited weeds are flourishing and reproducing—but it will certainly be natural. However, there is another, better way to create a natural-looking garden.

Conventional gardening aims to create a perfect picture: a place where plants bloom prodigiously in expanses of perpetually green lawn, with neat trees and shrubs that grow quickly to just the height and shape you want and then stop.

As we usually find out fast, nature does not work like this. In order to act like nature, a garden must consist of plants that are suited to the conditions on the site, and which can thrive with minimal intervention by us, without being invasive and too dominant.

Natural gardeners tend to combine plants in "communities." This enables the plants to form mutually beneficial relationships with other plants, animals, insects and the site, encouraging them to prosper and reproduce. For an increasing number of gardeners, these bio-diverse gardens are more satisfying than the more conventional garden styles that need so much more time, effort and expense to maintain.

An autumn woodland scene with bracken *Pteridium* spp. growing beneath pine trees *Pinus* spp.

Woodland and Meadow Gardens

Available light determines the difference between an open meadow garden and a woodland garden. Woodland plants require partial or filtered sunlight for most of the day. Partial shade means about half a day of sun and half of shade, such as you would find at a woodland edge. Meadow gardens, on the other hand, require a sunny, open position to thrive.

Forget-me-nots

Wonderful Woodlands

Is there a moist, shady corner in your garden, perhaps shaded by a mature deciduous tree, where you think nothing will grow? This may be the perfect place to plant a woodland garden using compact native shrubs, ferns and early-blooming wildflowers.

Try to think like a forest—in a forest, nothing

is wasted. Dead leaves and twigs fall to the forest floor and return their nutrients to the soil. Most forests consist of three main layers, as follows:

- The canopy layer of tall trees
- The middle layer of shrubs and small trees, and
- The ground floor—groundcovers, perennials, biennials and some annual plants.

To recreate a natural woodland scene, your garden should include plants of all these kinds and, while forests are shady places, you do need some light, but just how much will depend upon the requirements of the plants you select.

If you want the lush plant growth we associate with woodlands, you need a fairly rich soil, full of nutrients and organic material.

If you want to transform a conventional lawn into a woodland garden, dig out all the grass and dig in lots of compost, well-rotted manure and some peat moss to a depth of at least 1 foot (30 cm). This is a good job for a rotary tilling machine—or a team of family and friends.

If you are moving into a newly built house, the builder has probably scraped

A delightful outdoor living area on a timber deck is surrounded by a woodland garden.

A mixture of annuals, perennials and grasses creates a cheerful and low-maintenance meadow garden.

away the topsoil, so you will probably need to get in loads of good garden soil and mix in extra compost, well-rotted manure and peat moss.

After you have boosted your soil in this way, you should be ready to start planting, but remember that soil-building will not stop. Continue to add compost every year to echo the leaf fall in natural woodlands—and remember, leaves and needles are dropping from trees for most or all of the year, not just in autumn.

You can also mulch your woodland with fallen leaves, grass clippings or shredded bark to conserve moisture, suppress weeds and to return nutrients and organic material to the soil.

Weeds are not usually a problem in the woodland garden, since most common weed species will not grow in shade. The faster the soil is covered with groundcover plants, the less likely it is that any weeds will take hold.

A bridge crosses a small stream in a shady woodland area of a large garden.

Woodland plants take a few years to get established and spread—they are definitely not instant gardens.

Marvelous Meadows

Meadow gardens are informal blends of flowers and grasses growing in a sunny, open position. They provide food and shelter for birds, beneficial insects and butterflies. They add a casual, country feeling to your home and, perhaps best of all, established meadows require very little maintenance.

Creating a vigorous, beautiful meadow involves more than simply shaking seeds onto a grassy or dusty spot. For best results, you'll need to give your meadow the same care you'd use to start any garden—prepare the soil well, choose the best-adapted perennials and plant them properly. Just follow these simple steps:

- Pick a site with well-drained soil and at least 6 hours of sun a day.
- In spring, summer or autumn, remove existing grasses and aggressive weeds; lawn grasses can spread vigorously and smother small, new plants. Skim off slices of turf with a spade. Compost the pieces of sod you remove or use them to fill holes in the remaining lawn.
- Spread 1–2 inches (2.5–5 cm) of compost over the area, and dig

Spike gayfeather

Meadow Plants

Magnificent meadow gardens are usually a blend of tough perennial flowers and noninvasive perennial grasses, with swathes of daffodils and other naturalized spring bulbs for early color.

Dry Meadow Perennials

Achillea filipendulina (fern-leaved yarrow)

Asclepias tuberosa (butterfly weed)

Echinacea purpurea (purple coneflower)

Gaillardia x *grandiflora* (blanket flower)

Helianthus x *multiflorus* (perennial sunflower)

Liatris spicata (spike gayfeather)

Oenothera tetragona (common sundrops)

Rudbeckia fulgida (orange coneflower)

Solidago rigida (stiff goldenrod)

Moist Meadow Perennials

Aster novae-angliae (New England aster)

Eupatorium maculatum (spotted Joe-Pye weed)

Eupatorium rugosum (white snakeroot)

Filipendula rubra (queen-of-the-prairie)

Helenium autumnale (common sneezeweed)

Lobelia cardinalis (cardinal flower)

Physostegia virginiana (obedient plant)

Thermopsis caroliniana (Carolina lupine)

Grasses

Andropogon virginicus (broomsedge)

Bouteloua curtipendula (sideoats grama grass)

Festuca spp. (fescues)

Schizachyrium scoparium (little bluestem)

Sporobolus heterolepis (prairie dropseed)

Corn cockle and other spreading perennials may be invasive in beds, but are perfect for meadows.

as soon as they appear. Established meadows don't require water, fertilizer or mulch. As the plants get established, your meadow garden will look different each year, but it will always be beautiful.

If you enjoy the informal look of meadow gardens but don't want to wait years for perennial plants to get established, try planting an annual meadow instead. Many catalogs are now selling seed mixes of meadow annuals, containing colorful, easy-care plants, such as corn poppy *Papaver rhoeas*, cornflower *Centaurea cyanus*, calliopsis *Coreopsis tinctoria* and California poppy *Eschscholzia californica*.

Creating a Cottage Garden

Possibly the ultimate in informality, cottage gardens display a glorious riot of colors, textures, heights and fragrances. Cottage gardens defy many gardening "rules." First, the plants are packed closely together, ignoring standard plant spacing; the colors are not organized into large drifts; tall plants pop up in front of shorter ones; and flowers are allowed to flop over

or till it into the top 4–6 inches (10–15 cm) of soil. Use a rake to remove any rocks and smooth the soil.

- To reduce the bank of weed seeds in the soil, water the area thoroughly to encourage surface weed seeds to sprout; then rake or hoe shallowly to kill the seedlings. Repeat the process several times before planting. Or use mulch instead of watering and hoeing; cover the area with black plastic or at least 12 layers of newspaper for an entire season.
- In autumn, set out your meadow perennials, grasses and bulbs, and mulch them well. By spring, the roots will be well established, and your plants will be ready to put on great growth.
- In spring, if you wish, rake away some mulch to sow annual wildflower seeds between the perennial meadow plants. Annuals will provide quick color the first year while the perennials are growing new roots and getting established.
- Through the first growing season, water your meadow when the top 1–2 inches (2.5–5 cm) of soil is dry, to help the growing young plants get established.

Foxgloves

Mow your meadow once a year to keep it looking good and to keep weeds, shrubs and trees from invading. Late autumn to early winter, after plants have formed seeds, is the best time. If you want to feed the birds, leave seed heads standing until late winter or early spring; just be aware that they'll be harder to mow after winter rain and snow have beaten them down.

Cut the whole meadow to a height of about 6 inches (15 cm). Use a sickle-bar mower for large areas; a string trimmer or hand clippers can handle small patches. A regular lawn mower won't work; it cuts too low. Leave trimmings in place so plants can self-sow, or collect them for your compost pile.

Aside from the yearly trim, your only maintenance is to dig out tree seedlings and aggressive weeds such as quack grass, poison ivy, bindweed and burdock

For many people, a cottage garden means romantic rose-covered arches and gateways.

and grow through each other to create a delightful, casual mixture.

Simplicity is the key. The simplest cottage gardens have a path straight to the front or back with beds or borders planted in profusion on either side of it. You can develop variations on this simple theme, increasing the number of paths, but most of the garden's appeal comes not from any elaborate design but from the planting.

Structural features or focal points can be supplied by trees—the older and more gnarled the better—old walls, and possibly a rose arch or pyramid and collections of potted plants.

While cottage gardens may appear effortless and unorganized, they need to be planned, planted and maintained just like any other perennial garden. In this section, you'll learn the tricks to capturing the informal cottage garden effect without creating a messy-looking mixture.

Locate cottage gardens next to the house, especially by a door. If your front or side yard is small, you may want to devote the whole space to the garden. In this case, a gravel, brick, stone or even cement path is essential; make it wide (at least 3 feet [90 cm]) to allow room for plants to spill out onto it.

Fragrant herbs are old favorites for a cottage garden. Mix them with annuals and perennials.

Cottage garden with a delightful swathe of pink catmint *Nepeta x faassenii,* roses and foxgloves.

To create a pleasing jumble rather than a chaotic mess, combine a variety of different flower shapes and sizes. Thinking of flowers in terms of their visual impact will help you get the right balance.

Cottage Garden Plants

Feature flowers are the ones that first catch your eye; they have strong shapes—like spiky lupines *Lupinus polyphyllus* and massive peonies—or bright colors. Filler flowers tend to be smaller and less obvious than the feature plants. Baby's-breath is a classic filler flower.

Edgers are low plants used in the fronts of beds or spilling over onto paths; think of thymes and catmint *Nepeta x faassenii.*

These categories aren't rigid: Lavender and the flowers of lady's mantle *Alchemilla mollis* make nice fillers, but both are often used to edge paths as well. Rose campion *Lychnis coronaria* works as a filler, but if set among flowers with contrasting colors, its bright magenta flowers may stand out as a feature. The key is to use some flowers that serve each purpose, so you don't have

all bright (and probably clashing) feature flowers, all small filler flowers, or all low edging plants.

As you choose plants for the garden, include some that have scented foliage or flowers; fragrance is a traditional part of the cottage garden feeling. It's also important to choose flowers that bloom at different times of the year for a continuous display.

Perennials aren't the only plants you can grow in your cottage garden: Annuals, herbs, shrubs, vines and bulbs all can have a place in your cottage garden, too.

Old-fashioned roses, either shrub types or climbers, are a classic ingredient and an important source of fragrant flowers. Climbing roses or honeysuckles look great trained over a door or archway; let clematis climb up lampposts or railings.

Including unusual and unlikely plants is a long-standing cottage tradition. Accent your cottage garden with dwarf fruit trees, and tuck in some other edibles for surprise: try colorful lettuces, curly parsley, red-stemmed 'Ruby' chard and maroon-podded 'Burgundy' okra.

One of the fundamentals of the classic cottage garden is the kitchen garden, often interspersed with flowering plants. This is a great combination because you can still have a garden that is beautiful in all seasons and one that is productive as well. Think about the vegetables, fruit trees, herbs, edible flowers and your favorite cutting flowers and the ways in which they can best be combined.

Wildlife Gardens

While it is probably impossible for any artificially designed landscape to reproduce all the integrity and complexity of an unspoiled ecosystem, we can create gardens that reflect the richness of natural environments.

Creating an ecological garden, while not necessarily easy, can be immensely satisfying. The aim is to create a private place for you and your family, that also provides shelter and support for the variety of plants and animals, birds and insects that make up a viable natural community.

There are many ways to help create a more bio-diverse landscape. City gardeners can simply add a few choice natives that are attractive to wildlife. In the suburbs, you might decide to reproduce a portion of the neighborhood's original landscape.

Most wildlife dislikes, and tends to avoid, disturbance, so keep any high-

maintenance areas of the garden close to the house, and plant your wildlife garden away from high traffic areas.

Reduce the size of your lawn— or eliminate it altogether. Think of lawn as outdoor living space, keep only as much as you really need and think about replacing high-upkeep lawn grass with a tougher prairie or field grass.

Take a look at the plants growing on your land. Decide which will stay, which should go and which can be moved to another location. There's no reason why some existing exotics cannot be incorporated into your new design. However, when it comes to wildlife-attracting plants, it's important to stick to natives. Birds, animals and insects spread the seeds of the fruits they eat so it would be much better for them to help reproduce native plants rather than exotics.

When it comes to the actual planting plan, think in terms of groups or natural associations of plants instead of a single shrub or tree. Firstly consider only the shapes and sizes of the plants you want, allowing ample room for the mature size of each tree or shrub that will form the skeleton of your garden.

Remember that layered plantings are most attractive to birds, which may sing, nest and

LEFT: The flowers of showy stonecrop are a magnet for a variety of butterflies, including tortoiseshells.
RIGHT: A rustic-style nesting box for small birds, hanging from a tree branch.

As well as attracting birds and butterflies, water in the garden can be appealing to small animals such as frogs and toads.

feed at different levels of the plant canopy. Choose plants for the cover and food they provide, as well as for the beauty of their flowers and foliage, so that wild creatures are attracted to your garden.

Avoid using insecticides and other chemicals while allowing room for the insects, leaf litter and dead wood many birds and animals need. Let a few herbaceous plants go to seed, and remember to include caterpillar food plants for butterflies as well as fragrant flowers.

Create a Butterfly Garden

One easy way to encourage wildlife in your garden is to create a landscape for butterflies. Choosing and growing the right perennials will supply the food butterflies need throughout their lives. You'll also want to provide water and shelter to encourage the butterflies that come to stay in your yard.

Vividly colored flowers, such as chives, will attract pollinating bees and other insects to your garden.

To find out what kinds of plants will attract the butterflies in your area, look for them in nearby gardens, old fields and at the edges of woods. Observe which flowers they prefer and where they stop to sun themselves. If you see a pretty butterfly sipping nectar from a particular flower, consider growing that plant. Imitating nature is the secret to successful butterfly gardening.

To have a great butterfly garden, you must get used to a few holes in the leaves of your perennials. You need to let the caterpillars feed in order to keep the adult butterflies around. Many "flowers" listed for butterfly gardens—including violets, parsley, hollyhocks *Alcea rosea* and milkweeds *Asclepias* spp.—are really food sources (leaves) for the caterpillars.

Adult butterflies that are ready to lay eggs are attracted by the plants that will feed their developing larvae. Some adult butterflies also feed on flower nectar. Plants that have clusters of short, tubular, brightly colored flowers are especially popular. Many annuals and shrubs— including butterfly bush *Buddleia davidii*

and abelia *Abelia* x *grandiflora*—are also natural choices for butterflies.

Along with growing their favorite food and nectar plants, you can take a number of steps to encourage butterflies to stay in your yard. Butterflies like sun and dislike wind, so plant flowers in sunny spots where fences, walls or shrubs act as windbreaks. Set flat stones in a sheltered, sunny spot for butterflies to bask on. Butterflies are attracted to shallow puddles and muddy soil. Dig a small, shallow basin, line it with plastic, and cover it with sandy soil and gravel to form a butterfly-luring water source.

Most butterflies have very specific tastes, so increase the variety of plants to provide a smorgasbord of food and nectar sources and attract many different species from early spring through autumn.

Avoid insecticides—one of the most important steps in having a butterfly haven is creating a safe, pesticide-free habitat. Even organically acceptable pesticides such as rotenone and pyrethrin kill butterflies and their larvae. BT, a biological control used against garden pests, is fatal to the larvae of desirable butterflies. Use safer techniques such as handpicking and water sprays to remove pests from plants. If you don't want butterfly larvae to munch on your vegetable garden (carrots, celery, cabbage, broccoli and parsley are a few favorite targets), protect those crops with floating row covers.

Feng Shui in the Garden

Feng shui literally means "wind water" and is an Oriental philosophy that has achieved a great deal of influence in some other cultures. According to believers, "chi," free flowing energy, is taken in from the surroundings and affects personal wealth, relationships, health and more.

Feng shui applies not only to the interiors and exteriors of our built environments but also to our gardens,

An informal yellow border edges a winding gravel pathway through a feng shui garden.

which are believed to enhance "chi" and are considered "the lifeblood of living earth," reflecting our personalities, emotions and much more.

It is important to create slow-moving or meandering "chi." Straight paths can allow too fast a flow of energy, while gently curving paths engender a more serene pace. If you already have straight paths or driveways, you can soften these by planting along the edges and allowing the plants to grow a bit irregularly.

Water is the other essential element in feng shui but there are a number of schools of thought on how auspicious water is when used in particular ways.

Secret gardens are another element in the feng shui garden. It is exciting to discover a carefully nurtured but secluded or concealed section of a garden. Such areas can be created using hedges, walls or fences or trees.

If you are interested in feng shui gardens, there is a great deal of specialized

information and much complexity that you might like to explore further.

This spiritual emphasis on the garden is reflected in many cultures. In Japan, for example, the garden is always an integral part in the aesthetics of any building.

Chinese gardens traditionally mirrored the natural landscape features surrounding the environment. The ideal garden would balance Yin and Yang, smooth and coarse textures, such as in rocks and water.

Different images or symbols can also create different feelings in the garden— a Buddha, a pagoda, a bridge or stream can create very different effects.

Moonlight Gardens

One of the most unforgettable experiences for many gardeners is exploring their garden by moonlight, and finding a different world. In sunlight some white or creamy flowers can seem rather dull, but there may be a reason why they are so muted in the day and yet seem literally to glow in the darkness.

As well as the reflected light, there is often a fragrance that lures moths and other nocturnal insects.

Plant pale lime-flowering, fragrant *Nicotiana* 'Domino Lime' for evening enjoyment.

Plants for Moonlight Gardens

When selecting plants for a moonlight garden, remember to look for the white or pale-blooming cultivars, as well as plants that are fragrant at night.

Achillea millefolium
Buddleia davidii
Cerastium tomentosum
Cistus salvifolius
Clematis armandi
Festuca ovina glauca
Gardenia spp.
Iberis sempervirens
Ipomoea alba
Jasminum polyanthum
Matthiola longipetala subsp. *bicornis*
Mirabilis jalapa
Nerium oleander
Nicotiana spp.
Oenoethera deltoides
Rosa banksia 'Alba Plena'
Spiraea prunifolium
Trachelospermum jasminoides
Yucca spp.
Zantedeschia aethiopica

Many cacti and other desert plants bloom at night when temperatures are cooler and flying insects (and other creatures, such as bats) are more numerous.

Some plants are even more curious— although yucca flowers, for example, are open during the day and popular with bees, they are not designed to be pollinated by them. Yucca flowers physically change at nightfall. During the day, the cuplike blossoms hang downward; at night, they turn up toward the sky and emit a fragrance that attracts the highly specialized yucca moths.

As well as plants which produce white, cream or yellow flowers, those with gray or silvery foliage are interesting additions to the moonlight garden because they too

The delicate, white flowers of *Clematis armandi* will seem to glow in the moonlight garden.

seem to glow at night. Since it is their leaves that reflect light, you can see this effect throughout the year.

You can also arrange garden lighting so that it subtly mimics moonlight and highlights special plants or other features.

Water-wise Gardening

The stony, sandy landscapes of coastal Mediterranean gardens are great examples of how gardeners can deal with low rainfall and soil so sandy that water drains away very quickly. Many Mediterranean plants are naturally drought-tolerant and actually flower more prolifically when given very little water. They are used to coastal temperatures, dry, rocky soils and little or no winter frost.

Most common culinary herbs, such as oregano, thyme, rosemary, sage, marjoram and basil, are Mediterranean natives— and so are other favorites, such as lavender, dianthus and grapevines.

Plants that suit dry or Mediterranean gardens are usually at their best from autumn to spring, but stop flowering or even become dormant over the hot, dry summer. These plants are commonly

Drought-tolerant cacti are ideal low-maintenance plants for a water-wise garden.

fragrant, attract birds and butterflies, and blend well with the natural environment.

Mediterranean gardens typically require minimal maintenance during the blooming season. Some late autumn maintenance and pruning is required to insure full, healthy growth during the next season.

Choosing drought-tolerant plants and using water-wise gardening techniques will save you more than just water—it can save you time and money—and you will be spared the disappointment of watching poorly chosen plants wither and die as heat and drought take their toll.

Water-wise gardening involves keeping the rain that you do get in the soil—or in storage—so that it is available to plants when it is needed. It also involves trying to reduce the total amount of water that your garden needs to thrive.

Channeling and storing rainfall are other ways to reduce the need for supplemental watering. Do not let valuable water get away—a large plastic trash can or a commercially available rain

barrel placed under a downspout will store rainwater for later use.

Regrading areas of your garden may help to keep rainfall from running off into the street, or at least to slow down the water so it has more chance to soak in. Building terraces is an effective way to slow or stop runoff on sloping sites.

At planting, set plants out in shallow depressions, so the crowns and the soil immediately around them are slightly below the normal soil level. Or use extra soil to form a shallow basin around each plant (new or established) to collect and hold available water.

Cutting down on the amount of water your yard actually needs is another important part of planning a water-wise landscape. Here are some ideas to try:

Rosemary *Rosmarinus* 'Tuscan Blue' is an attention-grabber for the Mediterranean garden. All types of rosemary are drought tolerant.

Rainwater barrel

• Mulch generously. A thick layer of organic mulch will help hold moisture in the soil, where plant roots need it.
• Reduce your lawn area. Lush lawns just aren't compatible with arid climates. Prairie and meadow gardens are better choices because they are adapted to drier conditions— once established, they don't need watering, and they need mowing only once a year.
• Group plants according to their water requirements. Locate thirsty plants closest to the house, rain barrel, or water faucet, where you can reach them easily. Landscape outlying areas with species that need little if any supplemental water.
• Leave a little extra space between all plants so their roots can reach farther for water without competing.
• Block or moderate drying winds with a hedge or a windbreak. Or locate your garden on the sheltered side of an existing structure.
• If you must water, do it early or late in the day, preferably using drip systems or soaker hoses.

Urban Solutions

Most of us live in cities, which means that many people have little or no ground space available for gardening. But with the right choice of plants and containers, your little patch can be as satisfying and as beautiful as any large-scale garden. Charming combinations and effects can be achieved and, if the sun is right, you can even grow herbs, vegetables and small fruit trees.

In a very small space, or a small, walled garden, don't bother to grow grass. Instead, transform the space into a delightful and secluded patio by laying paving stones, patterned brickwork, ceramic tiles, slate or even gravel. Once laid, a paved area needs less maintenance than grass, and plants can tumble over the edges without doing damage. And there is no lawn to mow.

A courtyard with low hedges of clipped boxwood surrounding beds of yellow and white irises.

Urban Garden Style

Every garden is different, and calls for its own design. Your garden design also reflects your personality and the relationship you want to have with your garden.

A small garden is usually viewed at close quarters from the house, so try to visually link the garden to the house, and keep it in harmony with the style of the interior.

The design of a contemporary house can be echoed with the use of contemporary or minimalist-looking paving material and bold clumps of architectural plants. In most modern gardens, and particularly in a small city

garden, it is often better to include several of one plant of the same type and color, rather than a number of different varieties. Small, tufty grasses and sedges planted in masses look great in modern gardens, with pebbles or rocks and perhaps a modern sculpture. In an arid climate, cacti and succulents are a natural solution.

If you live in a traditional building with country-style furnishings, a sunny, town garden can be turned into a small, charming cottage garden. Use the existing beds for taller-growing plants and rambling roses, and place masses of colorful flowering plants in pots, tubs and urns.

A green foliage garden is both stylish and trouble-free, and ideal for a small, shady town garden, whether it is contemporary or traditional.

A tropical foliage theme can also be used to good effect in a small seaside garden where an outsized oriental day bed on a veranda could set off a collection of bold, tropical-looking plants. To provide visual interest, use contrasting leaf shapes, textures and variegated foliage, set at different levels in the garden. Bamboos, for example, could be used to create an

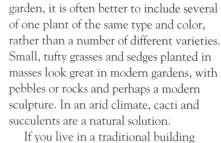

Spanish-inspired courtyard with square pond, ferns and topiarized boxwood in containers.

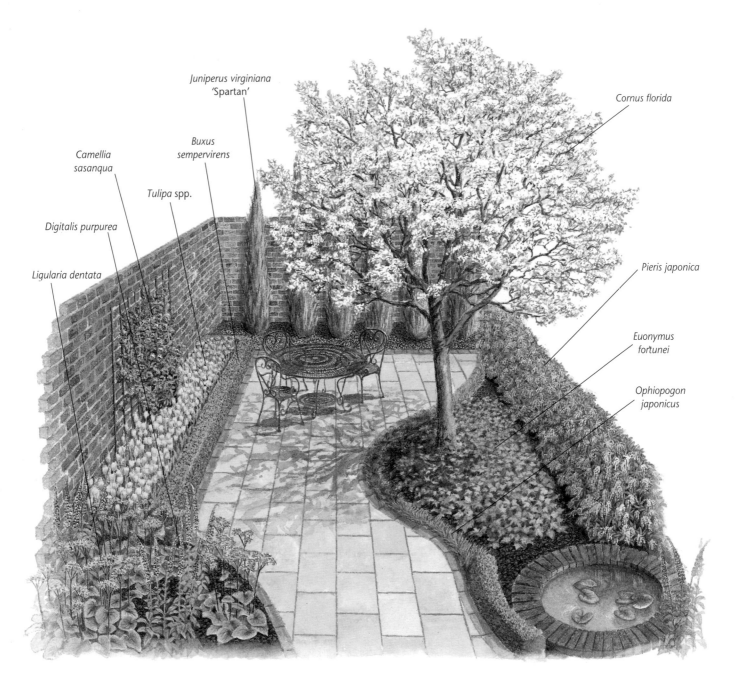

Juniperus virginiana 'Spartan'

Camellia sasanqua

Buxus sempervirens

Tulipa spp.

Digitalis purpurea

Ligularia dentata

Cornus florida

Pieris japonica

Euonymus fortunei

Ophiopogon japonicus

SUNNY COURTYARD WITH SHADE TREE This plan shows a paved, informal courtyard with a deciduous shade tree. A table and chairs are positioned in the shade of the tree. A shrub is espaliered along one wall and is edged with a low, boxwood hedge and infilled with spring bulbs. A row of narrow, evergreen conifers masks the rear boundary. Under the tree is a massed, low planting of groundcovers with taller shrubs behind. At the entrance to the courtyard is a water feature and a leafy planting with spire flowers.

effective vertical screen or a framework to the bold, kidney-shaped leaves of clumping ligularias. A tinkling water feature or an ornamental pot set among a profusion of green foliage will provide just the right focus to the lush jungle effects of the planting.

If terracotta tiles, pots, urns and a wall fountain appeal, and you have a climate to suit, you might like to create an informal Mediterranean-inspired garden. Here you

can grow grapevines, wisteria, lavender, roses, citrus, vegetables and plenty of lush and undisciplined herbs to create a relaxing, rustic atmosphere. If a formal, Italian garden is more your style, clipped boxwood hedges are always impressive in a small garden. Pots of citrus or clipped bay trees will provide dramatic accents along walls or on terraces, and a strategically placed classic sundial, urn, fountain or statue will complete the picture.

An espaliered fruit tree, such as this pear, is a thing of beauty, and makes good use of space.

entrances, verandas and balconies with potted plants and hanging baskets. Smaller pots can be moved around to create different displays, heights and colors, or to give the plants extra sun or shade according to their needs. Another advantage of a container garden is that you get a chance to grow some exotic gems that might otherwise be lost in an open garden bed, or that need to be overwintered in a greenhouse. But the best thing is that they are movable. This gives you an opportunity to create new looks, move pots with the season, or show off flowering plants at their peak. On the whole, plain containers are the most successful and have the advantage of suiting a variety of plantings.

Balcony Gardens

A balcony is always above ground level and often is the only garden available to people who live in apartments. Make sure that the balcony will safely support the weight of large containers and their soil. If your balcony is square or rectangular, choose containers that are firmly based and square. Troughs make excellent containers for balconies as their flat sides enable you to position them flush against the wall or front where they will not take up valuable space or be tripped over. And if wind is a problem, troughs are less likely to blow over than tall slender pots. Avoid

Wall Plants

In a small garden, you will probably have more wall space than ground space. Fences, walls, garages and railings provide the extra dimensions, so aim to cover them with climbing or trailing plants, such as wisteria, honeysuckle, clematis, climbing roses and solanum.

Espaliered plants, trained flat against walls, are ideal for making the most of space and, after the initial establishment period and the occasional removal of unwanted shoots, often prove far easier to manage in a small space than rampant climbers. Fruit trees are traditionally used, and when trained against a warm wall will crop prolifically, but sasanqua camellias are also beautiful, and their loose, pliable branches can be easily manipulated along a series of horizontal wires.

Although tall fences and trees prevent people from looking into your garden, or block out ugly views, they can cast a great deal of shade and give a restricted feeling. As an alternative, a small pergola clothed with grapevines, Virginia creeper or ivy will both screen you from nearby buildings and provide a shady private retreat.

Container Courtyard

Growing plants in containers is often the only successful way some people in cities can garden. It also gives greater flexibility to supplement the garden or to decorate windows,

Growing plants in containers allows you to move the plants around to experiment with various combinations.

A balcony garden with a trellis covered in *Ipomoea tricolor* 'Heavenly Blue' and *Thunbergia*.

it is difficult to water, consider some of the many succulents and silver-leaved plants that are able to withstand periods without water.

An extremely narrow balcony, viewed from a bedroom, could be transformed into a peaceful, oriental-style garden. Here you could cover the floor with stepping stones and pebbles and use a potted group of dwarf bamboos, one impressive bonsai, or a dwarf Japanese maple and a Japanese-inspired sculpture. A bamboo screen or blind could be used to hide an undesirable view.

Roof Gardens

A roof-top garden often solves the problem of space in a densely built environment, and at very least you should be able to grow plants in containers. You will need to check the weight that your roof can safely hold, and make sure that there is adequate floor drainage, because your plants will certainly need plenty of watering. The plants may also need protection from the wind and here you may want to erect some screens or windbreaks. Try to position these screens to also hide unattractive views, and also make sure they are securely anchored to withstand the wind.

Petunias in hanging basket

First of all, put in climbing and trailing plants to soften the hard outlines of surrounding walls and to cover structures and increase their effectiveness as windbreaks. Next, pot up shrubs, colorful flowers and herbs. It's best to place the containers along the sides so that the weight is evenly distributed

too many small pots, or they will detract from the overall design.

What you can successfully grow depends on the direction your balcony faces. Those that receive gentle, early morning sun can grow many palms, ferns, azaleas, fuchsias and camellias. A shady balcony may receive plenty of light, but no direct sun. Here shade-loving plants would be the happiest. If your balcony is protected from wind, you will be able to create a delightful mini-jungle using many lush, foliage plants. Popular ferns, such as fishbone, Boston and hare's foot fern, make spectacular hanging basket plants. Trailing ivies and vines can be grown up walls or made to spill out of wall-containers or pots.

A balcony that gets good direct sun for several hours is perfect for those who want to grow colorful flowering annuals, herbs, citrus trees in tubs, and vegetables. Bay trees are especially attractive as container plants; two or more, neatly clipped and in identical pots, could form the framework of a stylish semi-formal herb garden. In hot, dry areas, or where

This roof terrace has been transformed into a delightful, and private, outdoor living space.

at the strongest part. This is also probably the area where height is most needed to soften the straight lines of walls.

Decks

There is nothing like an above-ground timber deck for creating extra space, convenience and comfort. Decks are good for sloping sites, but also invaluable if your garden is shady, since often the extra height of the deck will give your plants longer hours of sunlight. A deck on the same level as internal floors makes entertaining easier and gardening a breeze if you want to relax outside in the evening after work. It's also an ideal place to grow culinary herbs, so that you can quickly snip them while you are cooking. Don't forget to raise all pots on feet or stands, so that excess moisture can drain away freely from the timber. If your deck is fairly high, make sure that the stairs leading to the rest of the garden are comfortable and wide enough to

allow for the traffic of pot plants, gardening equipment and potting mixes.

In a cool climate, a deck crowned with a pergola and roofed in clear, plastic glazing material will keep the wet weather away from the house and provide a dry, year-round entertaining area. It will also create a warm micro-climate for tender plants, such as palms, tree ferns and some interesting foliage plants. The pergola joists will give you some strong overhead support for suspending hanging baskets of Boston ferns, Christmas cactus and fuchsias.

Food at Your Fingertips

If your deck is large and sunny enough, it is possible to cultivate some fruit trees. In frost-free climates, citrus—such as kumquats, limes and lemons—make beautiful potted specimens, providing rich evergreen foliage, perfumed flowers and colorful fruit for the picking. Dwarf fruit trees such as apples, pomegranates and peaches can be also contained in large pots. Strawberries will tolerate a wide range of conditions and are the simplest fruit to grow in containers. They can also be hung in large baskets and will cascade decoratively down the sides.

Front Gardens

When designing with plants in the front garden, consider all the different angles from which they will be seen. Apart from being seen from the street, often the front garden is viewed from the upstairs or balcony. In a very small garden, think about the shapes you are creating. Boxwood hedges, for example, add impact by defining areas in an architectural way. These can be used in both traditional and contemporary garden plans. In a very small front garden, you could plan for a miniature boxwood-hedged garden to fit the shape of the land with an inner massed planting of one seasonal color, such as blue hyacinths for early spring, or white impatiens or petunias for most of summer.

A lawn path winds its way through colorful, curved garden beds to the house's entrance.

Summer window box with a cascade of lobelias, pelargoniums, helichrysum and Marguerites.

An easy-care front garden could be made with a combination of soil and square paving blocks set in a geometrical design. In the squares of soil where some height is needed, grow lightly clipped bushes of myrtle, bay, rosemary, *Murraya* and lavender. In the foreground squares, put in some low-growing bushes of variegated thyme or creeping thyme if you want some groundcover. If you have a picket fence, tuck in some nasturtium seeds along the edge for a pretty cascade of leaves and flowers that will peep out onto the footpath.

Modern condos or townhouses often offer little opportunity for a distinctive garden, and the simplest treatment is usually the most effective. Sometimes there is just a small raised bed built into the design. Here a flower bed could look good, with a bold planting of

Standard fuchsia

canna lilies backed by a clump of papyrus *Cyperus papyrus*. Or you may prefer a planting of easy-care Marguerite daisies or daisy-flowered felicias. If there is a narrow side bed leading to the front door, a neat row of dwarf conifers such as *Thuja occidentalis* 'Smaragd' can give you an instant formal look. Or if you have no garden at all, you could place a matched pair of dwarf conifers either side of the front door, or a standard flowering plant, such as a fuchsia. An extremely narrow bed could support a climbing fig to give a rich curtain of green to a stark wall.

Window Boxes

Window boxes are a delightful way to decorate bare walls, balconies and small city houses with colorful bulbs, annuals, perennials or other small trailing plants. They are especially invaluable to the apartment-dweller, who may have no outside space at all for regular gardening. Boxes and troughs can be bought in different sizes. When buying a window box, also get the bolts, brackets and screws to fix it securely into position, so that it does not become dislodged during windy weather.

Frequently used culinary herbs are a natural choice for a sunny window box outside a kitchen window. Thyme, prostrate rosemary, mint, parsley, chives and basil are easy, decorative and all smell and taste good. If you don't get a lot of sun, concentrate on such herbs as mint, chervil, parsley, lemon balm and chives that can get along on a little less. They will all need a good potting mix and regular watering.

Recycling Materials

With any new projects, try to match materials as closely as possible with your

A gravel path with a circular brick pattern, and steps made from wooden railway sleepers.

building and its style. Recycled local materials are not only cheaper, they are often preferable, because they tend to blend with the design and color of your home and offer a foolproof a way of retaining the integrity of your garden design.

Paving materials that echo the style of the house often look best in recycled materials. Old bricks, stone slabs, slate and old concrete slabs have a subtle weathered appearance and texture and are ideal for paved terraces and patios—often the main, permanent sitting areas in small gardens. Large slabs can act as stepping-stones and paths. Old bricks can also be used for sand-pits, barbecues, to define edges and as a raised sitting wall.

The appearance of some structures, such as pergolas, arches, privacy screens, fences, gates, seats and tables, can often be enhanced by using recycled timber that can be found at local timber yards.

Old railway sleepers are good for seats, raised beds, retaining walls or placed at intervals along a sloping pathway to make steps. They can also be laid relatively close together flush with the ground to form an effective and delightful rustic area of paving. A sturdy bridge over a pond or beautiful rounded river pebbles can easily be constructed using railway sleepers.

Wooden window boxes brimming with colorful *Pelargonium peltatum*, runner beans and petunias.

Low-maintenance Gardens

Just how much time can you devote to maintaining your new garden? Do you want to pay someone else to do it for you? It is possible to reduce or eliminate many of the maintenance chores that can make it much less of a pleasure.

Creating a low-maintenance garden doesn't mean settling for a second-best landscape. You can have a great-looking garden, except you won't have to spend nearly as much time as your neighbors do to keep your yard looking great.

A big part of making your garden low maintenance comes from working with the plants and conditions you have, rather than struggling to make poorly adapted plants grow.

Plants are healthiest, and require the least care from you, when they are well suited to the region and site where you plant them. In cool, humid regions, it's easy to grow woodland wildflowers in shady spots. In hot, dry areas, lavender cottons *Santolina* spp., penstemons and other heat- and drought-tolerant plants will thrive with little extra care.

A low-maintenance landscape does not mean exactly the same thing to every gardener. Maybe you hate mowing the lawn, but enjoy puttering in the flower garden. In that case, low maintenance would mean a small (or no) lawn, so you have more time for deadheading spent blossoms and pruning perennials.

Or maybe you find mowing relaxing but hate trying to keep up with ripe vegetables that must be harvested. In that case, low maintenance might mean a tomato patch surrounded by an acre of turf.

However, there are some principles that you can follow when designing your garden to reduce maintenance:
- Simple design
- Paving
- Small or no lawn areas
- No water features
- No plants that require clipping
- Reduce bedding plants and concentrate or shrubs or plants that self-sow
- Few pots or containers
- Choose low- or no-care plants
- Use native plants and plants you know do well in your area
- Use mulches for moisture control and to prevent weeds
- Install an underground irrigation system.

Make the most of a small site with a combination of paving and low-care plants, such as stonecrop.

Make an Anti-wish List

Planning a low-maintenance landscape is more than just deciding what you *do* want; it's also important to know what you definitely *don't* want. Take a realistic assessment of your landscape by picking up a notebook and a pencil and then taking a stroll around your yard. Jot down any problem areas—maybe it's that rocky patch in the backyard where nothing but weeds will grow; or perhaps it's the steep grassy bank along the sidewalk which is a real pain to mow.

Also look for high-maintenance elements that you may want to reduce or eliminate—perhaps you just can't stand the thought of clipping that privet hedge three times a year. Or maybe you enjoy having some fresh produce but are tired of tilling, weeding, and watering a huge vegetable garden every summer.

Add these notes to your "anti-wish" list. When you are finished, prioritize the list so that you can deal with those problems you find most annoying. That will help you form a practical action plan to converting your existing garden to a truly low-maintenance landscape.

Build raised beds to turn a wet site into a well-drained garden, so you can grow what you want.

For easy-care color all season long, fill your flower beds with a variety of self-sowing annuals.

Time-saving Trees and Shrubs

Once they're established, most trees and shrubs are the epitome of low-maintenance plants for your garden. You don't have to mow them, harvest them or pinch off their dead flowers. Most of the care they might require, such as pruning or raking, can wait until autumn or winter, when the rest of the garden is making few demands on your time.

However, it is important to avoid trees and shrubs with troublesome habits, such as brittle trees that drop twigs after every gust of wind. Others have messy fruit, such as practically any wild fig or the spiky, round seedpods of liquidambars.

Easy-care Lawns

Do you really need a lawn? If you do, you can reduce mowing chores by replacing some of the lawn with shrubs, trees or groundcovers—but don't plant trees and shrubs in your lawn, because you will actually increase your mowing difficulties.

Install mowing strips to cut down on edging chores and make maintenance easier by eliminating grass growing under or along fences and walls, on steep slopes, and under low-branching or shallow-rooted trees.

Quick Flower Gardens

"Low-maintenance" does not have to mean "no flowers." With a little planning,

A strip of bricks set into the soil around a flower bed lets you mow right up to the edge.

you can have a quick and colorful flower garden that is full of interest while you spend a minimum of time on routine garden maintenance.

Most garden flowers fall into one of three categories: annuals, biennials and perennials. It's useful to understand these three categories because they will influence how much and what kind of maintenance you need to put into the flowers you grow.

Annuals are plants that live only one growing season. Since the parent plants die off at the end of the season, you need to replace them every year with seeds or new plantings. Their strong points are that they are usually very easy to grow (even if you get a late start in spring planning and planting), they bloom for a long time, and they come in just about any color and height you want.

Biennials live for two growing seasons. The first year they form a rosette of leaves. The second year they send up a flower stalk, blossom, set seed and die. Some, such as pansies, are commonly grown as annuals. Some that reseed easily, like hollyhock *Alcea rosea*, are as dependable as perennials. Since it takes some planning and patience to get a good show from most biennials, they tend to be grown less frequently than annuals and perennials.

Perennials come back year after year (if they are planted in suitable conditions) so you don't have to buy and replant them each spring. Unlike annuals, most perennials only flower for a short while (days or weeks) each season but many do offer attractive forms and foliage, so they can look almost as good out of bloom as they do in bloom.

Most bulbs, such as daffodils, hyacinths and crocuses, are also perennials. They become dormant after flowering and can free up garden space for annuals or maturing perennial plants.

In the garden, you can choose to keep your annuals, biennials and perennials separate in different beds. Combining different kinds of plants, however, lets you enjoy the benefits of each kind, while minimizing the drawbacks—and this way you can also select plants that will produce a succession of color in the garden through most of the year.

Hollyhocks

Outdoor Living Areas

Today's gardens are often considered to be an extension of the house. Whether you have a large garden, or simply a balcony or small roof garden, you can create a delightful outdoor space for entertaining, activities or simply relaxing.

A garden landscape design is usually considered to be a success if it is beautiful in itself, and also enhances the visual appeal of the buildings set within it. However, your landscape can be even more attractive if it is also useful and functional, designed to meet the needs of family, friends and visitors.

With the high cost of interior floor space, outdoor living areas can add extra entertaining and living space. Even when not in use, well-planned, attractive decks and terraces, adjacent to the house, give a feeling of added space to interior rooms.

Some homes have several outdoor living areas. Small terraces adjacent to bedrooms, bathrooms and dining rooms are becoming more and more popular. A daybed under a covered veranda provides a delightful place for summer sleepouts. Or, for the ultimate in outdoor living, a screened-off shower, spa or

This gazebo, secluded among flowering trees and shrubs, is a delightful place to sit and relax.

plunge bath can extend out into the garden from the bathroom.

A terrace or outdoor living area may also be placed well away from the house to take advantage of a striking view, breezes or the shade of an unusually beautiful tree.

Attractive, long-lasting outdoor furniture and accessories, such as water features, sculpture and container plants, can be useful to decorate and enrich outdoor living areas.

Terraces, Patios and Decks

Most outdoor living and entertaining areas include a terrace, patio, veranda or deck of some sort. Locate these features where they will receive breezes and afternoon shade during hot summer weather. If sun is a problem, plant some

suitable shade or rig up overhead shading structures, such as sails or umbrellas.

Patios should be large enough to be useful. Small concrete slabs near the house are often rather cold and uninviting. Keep in mind the kinds of activities that will take place on your patio; it should be large enough to accommodate family and friends when entertaining. You may also need space for games, game tables and wheeled toys.

However, the patio can be made too large, so that it takes on the coldness of a parking lot. It's best to keep the size of your patio in scale with the size of your garden and house.

LEFT: Timber deck with outdoor setting under an umbrella, with containers of pickerel weed *Pontederia lancellata*.
RIGHT: Consider a wood-floored area for children's outdoor games.

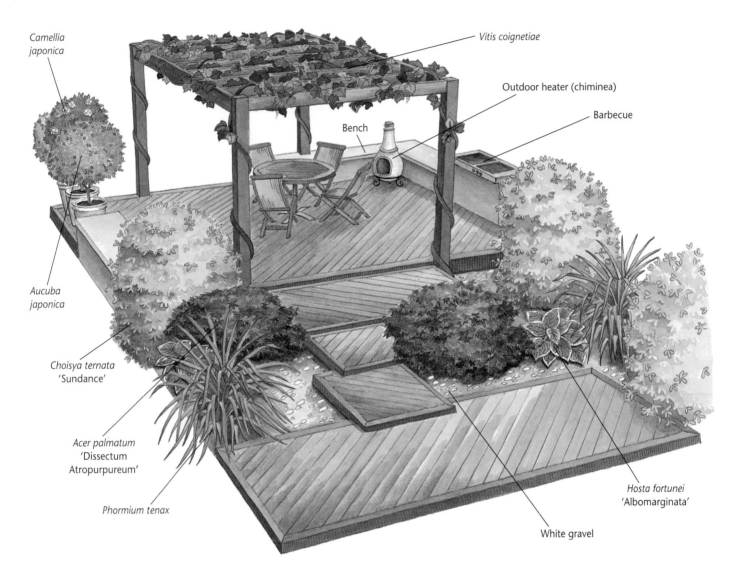

Camellia japonica

Vitis coignetiae

Outdoor heater (chiminea)

Barbecue

Bench

Aucuba japonica

Choisya ternata 'Sundance'

Acer palmatum 'Dissectum Atropurpureum'

Phormium tenax

Hosta fortunei 'Albomarginata'

White gravel

Outdoor living and entertaining areas are usually adjacent to the living areas of the house and can serve as a kind of transition between the interior of the house and the garden.

Children's Play Areas

Locate a children's play area close enough to the house so that adults can keep an eye on the kids. Sand piles and swing sets are popular, as are play houses, tree houses and paved areas for riding wheeled toys. Keep designs as simple as possible and make sure everything is easy to maintain. Consider how the area might be modified as children grow up and reused when the children no longer use it.

Active Sports and Recreation

Recreation or active sports areas, such as swimming pools or tennis courts, require considerable space, investment and planning. If such facilities are on your wish-list but will not be installed straight away, make them easier to build in the future by planning access and also leaving open lawn areas that can be easily removed when the time arrives. Spas, plunge pools and hot tubs require less space but still need careful planning.

OUTDOOR LIVING AREA This plan shows an outdoor living area under a pergola. An ornamental grapevine twines over the pergola, providing shade and shelter. (The grapevine grows out of the ground.) On either side of the pergola are two uncovered areas. Both of these have a low bench around a section, and the area on the right of the pergola has a raised barbecue. There are three large, potted plants on the left side of the pergola. Under the pergola cover is timber decking, which extends out to the garden via timber "stepping stones." Various low-growing plants, in contrasting colors, grow here. Around these plants and stepping stones is a groundcovering of white gravel.

Flower Lovers' Gardens

The garden created by the French Impressionist painter Claude Monet, at Giverny, north-west of Paris, must be one of the most influential gardens in landscape design. When Monet and his family settled in Giverny in 1883, the land sloping down from the house to the road was planted with an orchard and enclosed by high stone walls. From this, Monet created a garden full of perspectives, symmetries and colors. The land is divided into flower beds where flower clumps of different heights create volume. Fruit trees or ornamental trees dominate climbing roses, tall hollyhocks and banks of bedding plants.

Monet understood the complexities of color. In some areas he grew plants that explored gradations of shade in a single color—flowers ranging from pure white to soft pink, vivid red and the deepest crimson. Other places featured strong contrasts of, say, red tulips against cool blue forget-me-nots—seen from a

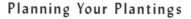

Campanula

distance, these become shades of violet, as in an Impressionist painting.

Monet saw that changes in light from the sky and reflections will also affect the colors of plants. The rosy glow of morning and evening light is well known to photographers, as are back lighting and side lighting which, shining through the petals of iris, poppy, roses or peonies, create an unforgettable effect.

Planning Your Plantings

Monet created the rich plantings at Giverney with the assistance of a head gardener and five assistants—and hardly any of us can count on this sort of labor. Trying to recreate this sort of profusion of color with fewer resources can be an interesting challenge.

Clearly, a lower-maintenance flower garden makes good sense and begins the same way that designing any landscape feature does—with a plan, however scribbled or sketchy.

From a distance, these red poppies and blue cornflowers merge to look like purple blooms.

Think about the shape and size of your beds. Do you want the straight lines of a formal garden or the curving outlines of an informal one? Or do you prefer informal massed plantings within a grid of straight paths, as Monet created in his flower garden? A rope or hose can be arranged on the ground to get a better idea of how possible bed outlines will look.

Scrutinize your plan to see if it will create maintenance headaches and how they can be avoided. Is the bed adjacent to lawn? Keep the grass out with a strip of bricks or some other easy-care edging.

For most people, deciding which flowers to grow is the most enjoyable part of the process. If you simply must have certain plants, such as pansies or peonies, you'll need to find a spot in your yard that provides the right growing conditions. Rethink your plant choices seriously if you can't provide the right growing conditions. No matter how much you want phlox or sunflowers, for example, a large shade tree in your backyard will block the sun those plants need to thrive.

Mass plantings of one kind of plant, or a combination of big groups of three or four types, are more effective than sprinklings of a few plants of a dozen different species.

To have something flowering most of the season, include plants that bloom early, late and in between. For early spring color, bulbs such as daffodils are easy.

A spring garden nook for the flower lover, featuring *Clematis montana* and rhododendrons.

Annuals provide dependable color during the summer and hide the browning leaves of early perennials. For the autumn, try late-bloomers such as chrysanthemums and Japanese anemone *Anemone* x *hybrida*.

With today's less formal gardening styles, you can plant whatever looks good to you. Some gardeners like to balance colors by using plenty of white flowers throughout the planting. Gray and pale yellow flowers are also helpful for blending different colors.

Hydrangea

The Fragrance of Flowers

Some gardeners believe that fragrance is as important an element in garden design as color and form. Whenever you walk along a garden path and catch an unexpected, magic scent, wondering from where it can be coming, you will certainly be more sympathetic to this point of view. Many fragrant flowers are also beautiful, so you can enjoy looking at them and smelling them as you walk around or work in the yard. Cutting these flowers for arrangements brings this pleasure indoors.

Traditionally, scented flowers were grown close to the house so that their fragrance could be appreciated through open doors and windows. They're equally nice near outdoor eating areas, patios, and porches—any place where people linger.

Roses, such as *Rosa* 'Ambridge Rose', are among the most prized of flowers, valued for their beauty and perfume.

Favorite fragrant flowers include sweet william *Dianthus barbatus* or china pinks *D. chinensis*, two carnation relatives noted for their spicy scents. Sweet alyssum *Lobularia maritima* is a common and easy-to-grow annual that's beloved for its fresh, honey-like fragrance. Mignonette *Reseda odorata* is an old-fashioned favorite with small, insignificant flowers but a powerful and delightful fragrance.

A few annuals withhold their scents until the sun sets, then release their sweet perfume on the evening breeze. Night-scented stock *Matthiola longipetalis* subsp. *bicornis*, sweet rocket *Hesperis matronalis* and flowering tobacco *Nicotiana sylvestris* carry remarkably potent night scents.

The real key to having a scented garden that you enjoy is smelling flowers before you buy them. The fragrance that a friend raves about may be undetectable or even unpleasant to you. Visit nurseries or public gardens when the plants you want are blooming, and sniff the flowers to see what you think. Different cultivars of the same plant may vary widely in their scents, so smell them all before you choose.

Just as a bed of many different flower colors can look jumbled, a mixture of many strong fragrances can be confusing or even unappealing. As you plan your garden, try to arrange it so that just one or two scented plants bloom at any one time. That way, you can enjoy different fragrances without being overwhelmed by too many at once.

Yellow roses

A Garden for Cutting

If you enjoy bringing loads of flowers indoors to decorate your home, consider adding a special cutting garden to your landscape

The bright flowers and ferny foliage of cosmos are excellent additions to summer arrangements.

design. A cutting garden is simply one or more beds where you grow flowers just for arrangements. You can then collect beautiful blooms from your cutting garden without raiding your carefully planned garden displays elsewhere in the garden.

Few people have enough space to put a cutting garden truly out of sight, but the more removed it is, the less you'll worry about making it look nice. Some gardeners turn over a corner of their vegetable garden to cut flowers; others create separate cutting beds along a garage, in a sunny side yard, or in a sheltered corner of the backyard.

Wherever you put your cutting beds, you want them to be easy to reach and maintain. Prepare the soil well, and mulch and water as needed to keep plants vigorous and blooming. Stake floppy or long-stemmed flowers, including peonies, baby's-breath, and delphiniums, to keep the stems upright and the flowers clean.

Selecting plants for your cutting garden is much like choosing any planting. The key is to pick plants that will thrive in your growing conditions; if they aren't growing well, they won't produce many

Favorite Perennials for a Cutting Garden

Here's a list of some of the best perennials you can grow in your cutting garden.

Aster novae-angliae (New England aster)

Boltonia asteroides (boltonia)

Delphinium x *belladonna* (belladonna delphinium)

Echinacea purpurea (purple coneflower)

Echinops ritro (globe thistle)

Eryngium amethystinum (amethyst sea holly)

Gaillardia x *grandiflora* (blanket flower)

Gypsophila paniculata (baby's-breath)

Helenium autumnale (common sneezeweed)

Iris spp. (irises)

Liatris spicata (spike gayfeather)

Lilium hybrids (lilies)

Monarda didyma (bee balm/ bergamot)

Narcissus hybrids (daffodils)

Paeonia lactiflora (common garden peony)

Phlox paniculata (garden phlox)

Platycodon grandiflorus (balloon flower)

Rudbeckia fulgida (orange coneflower)

Salvia x *superba* (violet sage)

Veronica spicata (spike speedwell)

LEFT: Strawflowers are great for cutting gardens and you can use the papery blooms in both fresh and dried flower arrangements.
RIGHT: Pasque flower *Pulsatilla vulgaris.*

flowers for cutting. Here are some other things you'll want to consider when you're deciding what to include:

- If space is limited, concentrate on growing flowers in your favorite colors; if you have lots of room, you can plant a variety of colors to have more options.
- Grow flowers that have different shapes to keep your arrangements from looking monotonous. Include spiky flowers and foliage for height, flat or round flowers and leaves for mass, and small, airy flowers and leaves for fillers.
- Look for plants that produce blooms on long stems. Cultivars described as dwarf or compact may be great for ornmental plantings, but their stems are usually too short for convenient flower arrangement.
- Include fragrant flowers.
- Add foliage—it adds body and filler to arrangements. Use subtle greens and silvers to emphasize individual flowers or colors; variegated leaves make striking accents.
- To add extra excitement to your arrangements, include other plants— annuals, grasses and hardy bulbs— in your cutting garden. Cosmos, snapdragon, larkspur *Consolida ambigua* and calendula *Calendula officinalis* are a few of the easy-to-grow annuals that are wonderful for fresh arrangements. Ornamental grasses are great for both flowers and foliage. Spray their delicate flowers with lacquer or cheap hairspray to make them last longer.

Taking a little extra care when you collect your flowers and foliage will help them look great over a longer period. In the cool of the morning, harvest flowers that haven't fully opened using sharp secateurs, garden scissors or a knife and immediately plunge the stems into a bucket of warm water. As you arrange the flowers, cut stems to their final lengths underwater so no air bubbles enter. Remove leaves that will be below the waterline in the finished arrangement.

After arranging your flowers, fill the vase to the top with water; refill as soon as the level drops. Add a shot of lemon-lime soda or a commercial floral preservative to

Himalayan blue poppy *Meconopsis betonicifolia* is a stunner for the cool-climate garden.

Grow fragrant plants, such as lavender, around a favorite garden bench, to enjoy the perfume.

keep the water fresh. Flowers will last longest in a cool room out of direct light.

The Plant Collector's Garden

Do you find it hard to resist buying new and interesting plants? It does not take long to build up a collection of odds and ends that can take up a lot of room until you eventually work out what you are going to do with all those plants.

The original plant collectors were botanists or explorers who spent months or years in remote areas of the world searching for new plant specimens— and you can now buy at your local garden center descendants of the plants they collected. That's part of the problem— we can obtain very exotic plants, for very little, near to home.

Professional plant collectors are not as prominent as they once were, because

most new plant varieties are developed through breeding practices such as hybridization. Unfortunately, a lot of otherwise well-meaning gardeners act as if they were amateur plant collectors, taking plants from the wild. Native populations of certain plants, especially wildflowers, have become extinct, so this practice is discouraged or actually illegal in most countries.

One of the keys to building a plant collection is to specialize. First, try to buy only those plants that suit your garden. This sounds obvious, but it is amazing how often you can buy a plant totally unsuited to your garden—and what is on sale at the local garden center may not necessarily suit local conditions.

Even if you make this a condition for collecting a new plant, you might consider specializing further into a particular type of plant or a single plant family, genus or species, or its hybrids and cultivars.

However, the true plant collector will probably continue to hanker after the difficult customers and even the downright weird.

Wonderfully bizarre plants are now readily available to home gardeners in formerly unheard-of quantities. And price is no object either—indeed, sometimes the most

LEFT: A clever design feature, these baskets of *Clematis* 'Sunset' and *C.* 'Silver Moon' are suspended from a tree branch.
RIGHT: Deadheading pansies will extend their blooming season for extra color.

expensive specimens sell very fast because of their apparent rarity.

Flowers All Year Round

If you want color in your garden all year round, get out your calendar and your plant charts and work out how you can plant for a succession of bloom through the seasons.

Remember that blooming times will vary according to local climates, orientation and other factors. In an existing garden, you can get some idea of how close the plant calendar is to your own conditions by matching the "official" flowering time against what your plants are actually doing at that time.

It is easier to plan for year-round color in certain climates. In the tropics, for example, there is scarcely any dormancy, while in much colder climates, your choices are more limited.

Sometimes in cool climates there will simply be very little—or nothing— in bloom. "Everlastings" are flowers, such as strawflowers and statice, that produce papery flowers or showy seedpods that hold their color when they are dried. They can be used in either fresh or dried arrangements, although most people grow them specifically with drying in mind. For best results, pick flowers for drying in the morning, before they are fully open.

Contemporary and Avant-garde Designs

One of the most important things about any landscape design is that it should feel right for its setting. How far is it stretching disbelief to build a natural-looking pond in the middle of a metropolis? Is it likely that your "authentic" rockery was left untouched when everything else between here and the horizon has been bulldozed? In the inner city, the standard suburban garden beds, trees and a large lawn can seem out of place or are just not possible.

Cities also tend to be crucibles where styles from all over the world are fused and used to generate new ideas. This is clearly apparent in architecture and interiors, so it would actually be rather surprising if it were not having an influence in landscaping and gardening.

This contemporary garden design shows the use of steel for pergolas, rather than the traditional wood.

Material Considerations

New materials, especially new sorts of surfaces, and old materials used in new ways, are transforming the ways we think about landscape design. One of the influences at work here is urban chic—straight lines (although round shapes, such as perfect circles, are also making inroads), minimalist plantings and adventurous use of textures, shapes and colors, often employing surprisingly basic

materials. Urban gardens, both residential and commercial, are where contemporary garden design is most quickly evolving.

Modern materials such as concrete, glass, plastics, polymers and metals can be used by themselves, in combination with each other or blended with natural stone, terracotta and wood in building a landscape. Glass is being used as sheets, windows and as mirrors as well as being recycled as blocks or pebbles which can be used for paths and as a non-decaying mulch. Neon lighting and other exotic effects can be used to highlight the artificial nature of the landscape being created using, say, resin-bonded artificial marble or synthetic stone. Galvanized and stainless steel is being used in gardens—including as pavers and as cables joining elements of the garden together (or just holding it up). Quite a few designers also like having old iron in the landscape somewhere, rusting away. All these materials are available for

Spectacular, blue-themed roof garden, pictured at night, showing neon strip lighting and other lighting effects.

structural work as well as for furniture, ornaments and other decorations.

The use of some less orthodox materials can depend on your climate, as well as personal taste. Metal surfaces can be interesting and attractive in warm or temperate Zones but where it gets very hot or very cold, they may be unsuitable, uncomfortable or even dangerous. Also, nothing dates quite so quickly as contemporary design—what was avant-garde last year can seem a bit tired now.

New materials are also being developed from recycling and the greater awareness of the environmental impact of waste products. Building and industrial materials are being recycled as landscaping materials in unprecedented volumes.

Japanese Influences

Since the late 19th century, Japanese-style gardens have played an important role in the development of Western gardens and landscape design. It's an influence that continues to be strong in 21st-century design. The influence of Japanese garden design principles and of their choice of traditional materials is strong in many contemporary garden designs. Modern designs that are inspired by traditional Japanese concepts reflect

LEFT: Green bamboo *Phyllostachys utilis*.
RIGHT: The restrained coolness and simplicity of Japanese design is shown in this garden featuring a *Pinus sylvestris*, timber gate, raked white gravel, stone bridge and rocks.

the idea of harmony and balance, which is probably the most important objective of Japanese garden design. Features, such as stones, gravel and water, that so often occur in modern designs, are integral parts of Japanese gardens where they are used to create spaces of beauty and, often, of great symbolism. Along with traditional plants and pruning techniques, these materials introduce movement and art to the landscape or are combined to form places for stillness and meditation, again ideas adapted from Japanese garden design through history.

The key to traditional Japanese garden design, and to many contemporary Western schemes, is not so much what specific material is used, but how it is used. Often the individual beauty of a single plant or garden feature is high-lighted, as opposed to the Western taste for lush abundance and overall effect.

As important as the initial design is, so too is ongoing maintenance and the ways in which plants and garden features are shaped and trained. Plants must be kept sculpted and shaped properly if the original effect is to be preserved.

The principles and intention behind creating this sort of space can be applied to other types of gardens as well. However, many Japanese-style gardens in the West are mere overlays of quasi-Japanese elements on a landscape.

To build a satisfying garden, it is necessary to observe nature closely enough to be able to distil sights, sounds and fragrances and express them with absolute economy of means—a simple grouping of rocks, plants and water. The result must be an elegant balance of opposites: mass and emptiness, light and dark colors, smooth and rough textures, sound and silence, and revealing and hiding.

Flat Gardens

Flat gardens, or *hira-niwa*, are constructed without hills or water; the flat ground level symbolizes water. The ground is usually covered with pebbles, raked in circles and lines to give the impression of water ripples. These gardens contain stones, trees, stone lanterns and wells and are representative of the seaside or of grand lakes. Carefully selected and placed groups of stones symbolize islands; sometimes a waterfall is suggested by upright oblong stones. The garden design is very subtle; the

Closeup showing raked gravel in a Japanese garden, in the pattern of water ripples.

placement of stones often suggests far-off lands and mystical locales.

Modern flat gardens also often contain wells and stone lanterns. The wells usually have a purpose in these gardens: namely purification of those who wish to observe the gardens. These wells are typically constructed from wood, and have either a pulley system or a large spoon for drawing out the water. Stone lanterns are not only ornamental, but also serve to illuminate the gardens at night.

Hill Gardens

The Japanese name for hill gardens, *tsukiyama-sansui*, means "hills and water": the foundations of a classic hill garden. Such a garden is like a three-dimensional picture. Whereas traditional gardens were viewed from only one point, modern gardens are designed with winding paths throughout them, to display the garden to full advantage. Usually these paths are made of carefully selected flat stones.

Water plays a very important role, and nearly every garden contains a waterfall and a pond. Waterfalls are an essential part of hill gardens, as they not only help

Oriental garden scene in autumn with maple tree *Acer* spp. with stunning orange leaf color, white summerhouse, stone lantern, path and pond.

water flow down the hill, they also provide great symbolism. They are usually constructed with two large stones, giving the appearance of great distance and size. They are often shaded by several tasteful bushes or trees which form a partial screen. The *ike*, or pond, is meant to represent a sea, lake or pond in nature. It is usually rimmed with stonework piling, and always contains an island.

Islands have great symbolic significance in Japanese hill gardens. The islands are built with rocks as their base and dirt piled neatly on top, in order for plants to grow. Sometimes a garden designer will include a bridge to an island. If so, often there will be a stone lantern or other object of reverence.

Irises

The general layout of this type of garden is designed to give the appearance of great distance and expansiveness, as if the whole world were contained in this one garden. Some have suggested that this is because there is so little space in Japan. A more philosophical viewpoint is that the creators of these gardens wish to present the essence of nature, or nature boiled down to its essential components.

Tea Garden

The modern form of Japanese tea garden is the one most well-known around the world. The Japanese tea garden plays an integral part in the tea ceremony, and as the ceremony has grown more elaborate through the years, so have the tea gardens. Japanese tea gardens now comprise two parts: the *soto-roji* (outer garden) and the *uchi-roji* (inner garden).

The outer section consists of a place where guests wait for the master to appear; the inner section contains the tea house itself. Stone lanterns light the pathway, which is made of either gravel or flat stones, between these two sections. The tea garden is usually made in a style similar to a hill garden, but is different in several respects.

First of all, the tea garden contains a wash basin, or *tsukubai*. The *tsukubai* is surrounded by *yaku-ishi* (literally "accompanying stones"), one in front, which is used for standing on, one on the right, and one on the left.

The basin itself can be any shape, as long as it can be easily used. In fact, broken stone lanterns are often put to use as new wash basins. The tea garden also contains a resting place, for breaks in the tea ceremony. This resting area was not in the original tea gardens. The resting place's principal purpose is to convey the spirit of *wabi*, or quiet solitude in nature.

While the outer garden contains deciduous plants and trees and is open and spacious, the inner garden is densely filled with evergreens, symbolizing its everlasting peace. The tea gardens of today have relatively few stones; flowering plants and extravagant designs are avoided, in favor of indigenous plants and materials found commonly along Japanese roads and in the countryside. Again, garden designers seek to find the essence of nature, and present it as a contemplative subject.

Contemporary Minimalism

The philosophy of minimalism, rooted simultaneously in classicism and modernism, has had a strong influence on architecture and interior and graphic design, as well as landscape. Minimalist gardens, with their emphasis on clean

Japanese-style garden with a bridge over a slate riverbed, with tea house on a patio in the background.

LEFT: Creative garden design with metal dish surrounded by clipped boxwood hedge. The metal dish is echoed in the metal strips on the painted magenta wall.
RIGHT: Japanese-style courtyard.

lines, pure form and a strong sense of place, are closely related to contemporary architecture and lifestyles.

New trends in more relaxed and ecologically aware planting have contributed greatly to the development of such green spaces, and the creative use of trees and hedges to define and control space is often an important design element.

The principle of "less is more" when applied to the garden can avoid it looking untidy and give it a feeling of space and a certain tranquillity. In addition, strong design can provide a clear guide as to what you need to do to build and maintain your garden—and what distractions you should avoid.

Minimalism in design has been reworked over the past few decades, and owes much to Japanese and European— especially Scandinavian—esthetics.

A minimalist garden can be a flexible space in which to play, work, read, relax, meditate, entertain, and so on—but one that always looks good. Key concepts relate to boldness, simplicity (even austerity) and cleanliness rather than fuss, mess and pointless elaboration. This can require a certain discipline, not least in being ruthless about what does—or, mostly, does not—fit in. Spaces are sharply defined and kept free of clutter.

Futuristic garden design with rill (small stream) that ends in a large round, metallic pool.

When buying plants, for example, you will not choose nine different kinds and plant them any old way. It may be a new discipline and at first rather hard to do, but a group or line of nine specimens of the same plant—or three clusters of three—will certainly have much more design impact on your landscape and bring greater cohesion to your garden.

Avant Gardening

Traditional gardens are usually more popular with the public and most gardeners, but contemporary gardens are great places to find new ideas and inspiration for garden design.

Some of these ideas will inevitably fall by the wayside and it takes time to see which trends or fashions will prove influential, popular and long-lasting.

Split-level timber decks, for example, are becoming increasingly popular. Decks have been around for a long time but people have been cautious about where to put them. Now decks are being used much more often, whether to go up over a hill, over water and to create different levels. Another trend is the strong coordination, including color, of interior and exterior spaces.

Contemporary garden design is evolving all the time. Go to garden shows and see what new ideas appeal to you and how you can adapt them to your landscape.

Garden Features

A garden's landscape elements play both a decorative and a functional role. The right element will work as part of a larger picture for a complete and well-considered look, but will also suit the purpose for which it was intended.

Garden Floors

Most gardens have some sort of open space at their heart—a focal "floor" among the flower beds, borders and shrubs that surround it. Because landscape design is increasingly seen as an extension of or parallel to interior design, it is a fair question to ask what sort of floor surface your garden "rooms" will have.

Until recently, the choice would have overwhelmingly been for lawn—the landscaping equivalent of wall-to-wall carpets. If it wasn't lawn, the "floor" was a courtyard, patio, deck or, maybe, the ragged area under the trees where the lawn would not grow. Today the choice is less obvious, and the variety of materials available can at first seem overwhelming.

Choosing Surfaces

First, it's wise to look at the exterior texture of your home to assess what sorts of surfaces will complement and extend what you have already achieved (or are planning to do) inside your home.

Hard surfaces, including gravels, pavers and pebbles, are now available in an increasing array of colors, so it shouldn't be too difficult to find materials to suit your chosen color scheme.

However, much will depend on what you want to use your landscape for—outdoor entertaining, relaxing in the sun, reading a book, or children's games.

Material Considerations

Garden floors can be roughly divided into those that will receive a lot of traffic (even vehicles), those that receive some traffic, and those that will hardly have to carry any weight at all. The heavier traffic areas need the most careful preparation. In some cases, it will be prudent to employ professional tradespeople to do the job, but not if you are just spreading a super-thick layer of mulch between your plants.

Heavier, more formal types of garden surfaces require substantially more preparation and, whatever surface materials you select, you should take into account the cost and difficulty of solid, safe installation.

Dirt, gravel and concrete blocks are heavy to move around. If you are doing this work yourself, avoid over-exertion and working in extreme heat. Wear eye protection when cutting or chipping masonry blocks or pavers, or even when spreading wood chips or mulch.

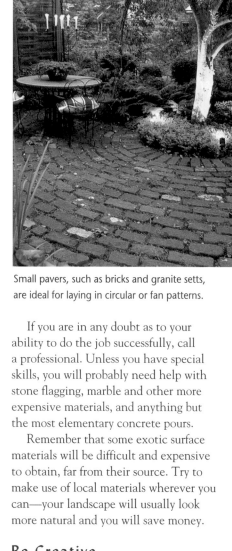

Small pavers, such as bricks and granite setts, are ideal for laying in circular or fan patterns.

If you are in any doubt as to your ability to do the job successfully, call a professional. Unless you have special skills, you will probably need help with stone flagging, marble and other more expensive materials, and anything but the most elementary concrete pours.

Remember that some exotic surface materials will be difficult and expensive to obtain, far from their source. Try to make use of local materials wherever you can—your landscape will usually look more natural and you will save money.

Be Creative

Using one type of material to surface an area creates a mass of just one color. While using one material will help to create unity, it can look a little boring or overwhelming. There are ways to create more interesting effects.

You can combine materials in novel ways. An area of paving—concrete, pavers or whatever you like—could be

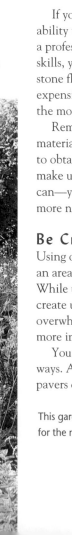

This garden floor of cobbles is a perfect match for the natural, cottage garden look.

edged with a line (or lines) of differently colored paving material, or interspersed with areas of other colored materials.

A patchwork of different, but complementary, colors (such as different-colored bricks or pebbles), mixed at random, will create an attractive and informal effect. It is usually safer to limit your range of colors and keep patterns simple—a blizzard of colors and shapes can look too busy and may divert attention away from the rest of the garden.

Also consider the effect of the color you choose on the surrounding plants, garden features and buildings. Decide whether to use hot or cool colors, bright or subdued colors, and one or several different colors, according to the mood you wish to create.

If an area is too dark, you might like to use light-colored surfacing materials. If an area is open and glare is a problem, try darker-colored surfacing materials.

A Range of Surfaces

There is a huge range of materials available for garden floors and surfaces. Here is a rundown of some of the more popular, and a few unusual, surface materials from which to choose.

Concrete

Concrete pavers and blocks are the modern version of old-fashioned paving stones. For constructing a permanent walkway, precast concrete blocks are just the thing. No cement or mortar is necessary. Since they are uniform in size and shape, they're also easy to fit together. Concrete block paving can match the look of natural stone setts, cobbled surfaces and handmade bricks, yet it costs significantly less. Pavers can be laid in a variety of bonds, and patterns can be laid by any competent DIY-er.

Concrete is often rejected or overlooked as a potential pavement surface, mostly because of its lack of color or interest. However, plain concrete can be useful in areas where a decorative look is not required, since it is utilitarian and inexpensive. By combining plain concrete with a more decorative edging material, such as brick, it can be made to look more attractive. Modern concrete technology has led to the development of fiber-reinforced concretes that create high-strength pavements without the need for steel reinforcement.

Decorative finishes now include polished-surface, coarse-textured and

A mosaic pattern has been incorporated into this paving design to add interest and color.

exposed aggregate. Some products combine color and finish, so it is possible to specify, say, a coarse-textured flag in a buff color, or an exposed aggregate in a red matrix color. There is also a choice of aggregate types, with various colored granites being a popular specification. But there are also flags with blue or green glass nodules as the exposed aggregate.

Poured concrete A variety of pigments can be added to avoid the gray drabness associated with solid concrete. Imprinted concrete is also available in various patterns, but larger surfaces, such as driveways and patios, must contain movement joints to prevent the concrete from cracking. If access to underground pipes or cables is needed, the pattern and color of the destroyed surface area might be difficult to replicate.

Brick Pavers

The fired earth colors of brick paving mellow with age. It is best to only use engineering bricks or special clay pavers with frost-resistant designations to avoid flaking and uneven surfaces. Clay or

The rough, informal look of these weathered brick pavers suits a natural-looking, informal garden.

terracotta bricks can look too rich for some tastes over a large area. Concrete counterparts can replicate the colors of clay and generally cost less.

Stone

Stone lends a timeless appearance and a feeling of permanence and beauty to the landscape, but is invariably expensive. Reclaimed stone flags, salvaged from old streets, yards or wherever, usually have more immediate character than newly cut flagstones, and are considerably cheaper. Newly cut flagstones will develop their own character over time, as they become weathered and worn, but they look pristine when just laid. Reclaimed flagstones add instant charm to period properties. Even if the stone can be excavated onsite from your own property, it still requires special skills and equipment to move it and to work with it.

Stone is commercially available in six forms—fieldstone, flagstone, dimension stone, rubble, crushed stone and stone dust.

Fieldstone is weathered, irregularly shaped stone found in fields (not quarried). Flagstone is flat slabs of stone that has been sliced 1 inch (2.5 cm)

thick or more. Dimension stone is cut to specific sizes, and either left rough or polished smooth. Rubble is rough fragments of quarried stone. Crushed stone, as its name suggests, is quarried stone that has been crushed into small, roughly uniform size, while stone dust is crushed fragments of stone less than 1/4 inch (6 mm) thick.

Slate

Slate is a fine-grained rock that can easily be split into thin, durable sheets. The building industry uses slate for roofing and flagstone because the rock is weatherproof and long-lasting. Slates are a naturally cleft material and are typically used for flooring or roofing applications. Most slates are suitable for exterior and interior applications. Be careful when specifying green slates, because their color may change or fade with time.

Sandstone

Sandstone is a type of rock composed mainly of sand that has been "bonded" together by pressure or by minerals. The

The wooden furniture works well with the wooden floor, and seems to be part of this overall design.

color of sandstone ranges from cream or gray to red, brown or green, depending on the cements and impurities in the sand. Sandstone was a common building material for larger structures before reinforced concrete came into use. Most sandstone is suitable for both interior and exterior application.

Marble

Marble is widely used in buildings, monuments and sculpture. The purest calcite marble is white. Marble containing hematite has a reddish color. Marble that has limonite is yellow, and marble with serpentine is green. Marble does not split easily into sheets of equal size and must be mined carefully. Large blocks of colored marble are used for columns, floors and other parts of buildings inside and out. Crushed, or ground, marble is used in paving.

Gravel

Gravel refers to small stones, generally 1/4–1 1/2 inches (6–30 mm) in diameter, that may be angular or rounded. Angular gravels are usually sourced from quarries and are a by-product of the stone crushing processes, whereas rounded gravels are from a source such as river beds, beaches and channel dredging.

Gravels can be of almost any color, depending on the parent rock type, or

Natural floors, such as bark chippings, work well in a woodland garden design. They also make useful soft surfaces for children's play areas.

the inaccessible space under low decking can accumulate litter and provide a breeding ground for undesirable animals.

Shredded Bark

Shredded bark can be used as a landscaping surface where a very informal look is desired, such as in a native garden or as a safe surface for children's play areas. It is usually recommended that the loose-fill bark or wood chips be at least 1 foot (30 cm) thick and retained with an edging. Areas beneath swings and at the foot of slides are prone to having loose-fill kicked away, reducing effective cover, and requiring regular maintenance.

Unusual Materials

Resin-bonded paving systems are a recent introduction to the market, made possible by advances in polymer and epoxy resins. Decorative or colored gravel is bonded to an existing solid surface using transparent or colored resin. The result is an extremely hard-wearing surface that is suitable for indoor as well as exterior use, weed- and maintenance-free, and resistant to temperature changes, stains and fading.

Tumbled glass pebbles are nodules that are rounded like marine or river gravel. Colors are limited only by the color of the original glass, with clear, blue, brown and green the most popular. These can be quite expensive.

Metallic nodules are, most commonly, made from copper and aluminum and are used for detailing special or feature paving areas. Aluminum nodules can also be used as a jointing detail. Unlike colored gravels and tumbled glasses, which are laid like normal gravels, at around 1½ inches (3.75 cm) thick, these metal dressings are laid just thick enough to cover the surface, usually around ¼ inch (6 mm).

a multicolored blend. The gravels most commonly used as a loose surface dressing range from ¼–¾ inch (6–20 mm) in size. Anything less than ¼ inch (6 mm) is more akin to a grit, and is too easily disturbed, and anything over ¾ inch (20 mm) can be difficult to walk upon. In general, the smaller gravels would be used for footpaths and the larger gravels for driveways. Small, fine gravel can be compressed to form a hard surface, such as compacted granite.

Tarmac

Tarmac, otherwise known as asphalt or blacktop, can be used as a driveway surface on a hardcore sub-base. The monotony of tarmac can be reduced by the addition of colored pigments. Initially cheaper to install than block paving, blacktop can prove costlier in the long run as resurfacing will eventually be required. Tarmac is prone to softening in hot weather and can be deformed by heavy vehicles.

Wood

Low- or high-level decking provides useful terrace space next to the house and can instantly transform a garden area. There are drawbacks, however. Efficient maintenance is needed to avoid a limited lifespan, and a moist climate can make the timber slippery underfoot. The raised platform can constitute a hazard for children or old or disabled people, while

Gravel is available in a huge variety of colors, from pinkish, as shown above, to white and jet black.

Walls

Good fences, so they say, make good neighbors, and no boundary is more solid than a well-constructed wall. Solid privacy walls separate peaceful, residential areas from the busy, noisy, intrusive world around them. Walls can also conceal unappealing views, and they can also provide a backdrop against which a garden can be beautifully displayed. Walls provide protection against winds and form suntraps in cooler climates, so that you can grow plants that would not normally survive in the open.

Walls can be free-standing, or used to retain a bank or terrace. You can also make hybrid versions, so that a retaining wall can become free-standing at its top, forming a terrace boundary.

Types of Wall

Stone and brick walls are functional, yet they add an architectural and sculptural element to a landscape. Although they are expensive to build, they are long-lasting and relatively maintenance-free.

Stone walls come in many forms—mortared or dry, split or sawn-block. The use of brick enables builders to add detailing and texture to a wall. A variety of bonding patterns can be applied to match any architectural theme. Brick is so versatile that it can be set in gentle curves and even formed into serpentine walls whose winding shape provides strong, lateral support, while adding flowing, graceful lines.

Tiles, found objects, pebbles, glass and much else can be combined to produce unique, artistic mosaics and other effects. In seaside areas, shells and pebbles can be incorporated into poured concrete walls.

Planning a Wall

Before planning any boundary wall, make absolutely certain about your property line—you do not want to encroach on your neighbors' land. If there is any doubt, get a new survey done and use that as the basis for the new wall. After all, it is a lot harder to adjust a wall than a hedge or even a wooden fence.

Have your local building regulations on hand—look at the maximum height for boundary walls, any required distance from the street and any other special local requirements. You may find that walls over

The cascading pink aubrieta is a perfect foil for this natural-looking stone wall.

a certain height require special permission and must be professionally built. (Height is an important factor for any boundary structure, since the higher the wall, the greater the area of shade that will be cast.)

If you have drainage problems, it may be best to consult a building contractor. A masonry wall can act as a dam, and in retaining walls, the higher the wall and the heavier the soil behind it, the greater the pressure on the wall itself, creating a situation where the wall may collapse.

Building a Drystone Wall

A drystone wall provides a natural-looking frame for any garden. It projects a feeling of old world charm, as well as being functional and cost-effective.

Building such a wall yourself may seem daunting, but by doing the appropriate planning and taking your time in the construction process, you can put together a drystone wall to be proud of.

The trick with a drystone wall is to get it as stable as a conventionally built wall, but without the cementing. To accommodate this, many stone walls are built with a taper, having a wide base of heavy, flat stones that gradually decrease in width as the wall gets higher.

Gently curving walls add interest to the garden, but flexible materials or small units are necessary.

The selection of stones is vital to the success of the project. You should look for flat stones in a variety of sizes. Make sure that some of them are wide enough to take in the full width of your wall.

Make sure each stone is stable when it goes into the wall by using smaller stones as packing behind it. The stone can also be bedded in soil. Pack the dirt firmly into the crevices between the bricks as you layer your way upward. It is not advisable to build a drystone wall higher than about 3 feet (1 m).

Select stone that complements materials already used for the house, and for other surfaces, such as paths and patios. It is also preferable to use the stone that is naturally occurring in your area, because it harmonizes with the environment. Limestone, sandstone and granite are most common, but slate and bluestone can also be used.

There are a few basic principles to follow when building a stone wall. The base of the wall has to be at least half as wide as it is tall.

The rule "end in, end out" means the longest part of the stone runs into the wall rather than along the length of the wall.

A lavender hedge has been planted on top of this drystone wall for a naturalistic effect.

Pink bougainvillea *Bougainvillea glabra* growing against a sandstone wall.

The lean on a retaining wall is called the batter and is usually about 1 in 4. This type of wall uses gravity as its support.

A Hedge of Stone

Stone-faced earth banks are sometimes called "stone hedges". (Similar banks can also be faced with turf.) Stone hedges can be thought of as two drystone retaining walls with an earth core between them.

A standard, free-standing, stone hedge usually stands about 4½ feet (1.5 m) high, but boundary stone hedges are half as high again.

The base width is normally equal to the total wall height. Stone hedges are often built with straight-battered sides, giving a lifespan of around 10 to 15 years. However, a concave-face stone hedge could last up to 200 years.

The infill for stone hedges should be granular earth, compacted at least every 6 inches (15 cm). The top, or cap, of the stone hedge may be finished with turf (most commonly), cope stones, or a combination of the two. The caps of stone hedges are considered "tender" until vegetation is well established.

Softening the Look

Although a long stretch of newly built wall often looks a bit raw, once planting begins, the wall is transformed. Walls can be dressed with vines or shrubs that grow from the base, or let trailing plants cascade from planters along the top of the wall. If your wall is particularly attractive, let it show.

Walls can also provide a sheltered, warm position against which can be trained espaliered apple, pear or other fruit trees. Not

Wall planted with flowers

only will the trees produce fruit in a very small space, but their elegant shapes provide great visual interest.

If your wall is less than totally attractive   perhaps one of those blank, boundary-edge, garage walls, common in older suburbs—think about bolder treatment, vivid paint colors, or maybe even a mural.

Wall Safety

Garden and boundary walls should be inspected regularly to see if they need repairs. Besides general deterioration and aging of a masonry wall over time, walls may be affected by increases in wind load, heavy rain, felling of nearby mature trees or planting of new trees close to the wall, nearby building work, changes in adjacent traffic, or alterations to the wall itself, whether deliberate or accidental (such as being hit by a motor vehicle).

Fences and Gates

Fences perform many tasks. They provide privacy, shelter you and your garden from the weather and keep children or pets in and intruders out. Fences can also look good, providing a strong, attractive framework for your landscape design. Fence designs are available as single-sided (having a definite front and back) or double-sided (having the same appearance from either side).

Planning a New Fence

Building fences doesn't require quite the level of investment of time and expense as building masonry boundary walls, but it is still important to be sure of your boundaries. Make sure you know exactly where your property lines are, and if you do not, have a surveyor mark them for you.

It is also a good idea to consult your local building regulations to find out if there are any restrictions on fence construction and height where you live. Check provisions regarding setbacks from the street to see if you can build right to the property line. Also check for buried cables or pipes—most utility companies will mark these for you, so that you can avoid unfortunate, expensive accidents when excavating to build.

When planning a new fence, there are several things to consider. One of the most important things to determine is which material is best for your needs and which will suit your home and neighborhood and still meet your budget.

Consider the amount of wear and tear your fence will have to endure. You may not need the best hardwoods, for example, if you live in a mild climate and you do not have animals or children that may be leaning or climbing on your fence.

If you want a fence that is a little out of the ordinary, think about designing your own, instead of relying on standard, prefabricated materials or builders' patterns. Observe fences where you live, and ransack books and magazines for ideas. Keep an eye out for books and magazines with pictures of buildings and places that appeal—travel magazines, for instance, can contain a lot of good ideas that may be right for you.

Also keep an eye on what leading landscape designers, architects and builders are up to. Professional designers display their work in magazines, at home exhibitions, on web sites and, of course, on the ground. It's hard to keep a good-looking fence secret.

You might also get ideas from historic precincts in your area. Historical sites or museum houses often have fences that are suitable for your region and have stood

This blue fence, with overhanging barberry in complementary yellow, becomes a design feature.

the test of time. Look for practical responses to climate, creative use of local materials, or simply designs that "look right" in your neighborhood.

Types of Fence

While any sort of fence can be used to establish boundaries, the most popular choice is probably the rail fence. Rail fences can be architectural in design, or blend in with the background and be virtually invisible.

Rail fences with metal mesh attached can be a good choice where you want to have a more open feel, or to retain an attractive view. Combine rail fences with solid privacy fences, if there is an area you want to block out.

Privacy fences are not only used to prevent people from looking in, but also to block the view of something unsightly. A fence—whether a simple stockade fence or an architecturally designed trellis fence—can transform part of the garden not previously conducive to use into a new area to enjoy. Another advantage to privacy fences is the protection that they offer from a busy street or other source of outside noise. These fences are designed to complement other styles of fence, where a combination is desired.

The ever-popular white picket fence can be enhanced with a gently curving top.

Another traditional choice is picket fences. These provide an open view, while not allowing young family members—or their toys or pets—to get through.

Although any fence can be used to enclose a sports or games area, the most common choice is a chain link wire fence—especially where flying tennis or golf balls are inevitable. They are available in many colors and styles.

Most fence types add safety and security to your garden but some situations require a thorough knowledge of the local building codes. Swimming pool fences, for example, may need to comply with exact technical details as to height and materials used, as well as the precise type of gate and lock.

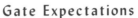

Apple tree espalier along a fence

Cast metal fencing is strong and available in a wide range of picket grades, heights, colors and styles. Standard patterns can be modified by the addition of decorative castings, such as rings, finials, ball caps and scrolls.

Aluminum fencing systems are long-lasting, maintenance-free and allow you

This stunning display of purple wisteria makes a spectacular entranceway to the house during spring or early summer.

to match the fences with pedestrian and driveway gates.

Wrought-iron fences and gates are suitable for period houses and gardens, and a range of traditional designs is being manufactured for the restoration market. However, wrought iron needs priming and painting, and ongoing maintenance.

If maintenance is a problem, consider vinyl (PVC) fencing. With many of the same applications as wood fencing, PVC fencing is available in picket, privacy and post-and-rail fence styles. Although the initial cost of PVC can be greater than wood, upkeep costs are minimal. Besides its strength, PVC fencing never has to be painted, does not rot and rarely has to be replaced. Most PVC fencing manufacturers guarantee their product for 20 years—some even guarantee it for life.

Gate Expectations

Gates need to open and close easily. If they don't, you will have problems—either the gate will never be properly closed or never opened, becoming a de facto wall or fence.

The choice of timber gates can present a challenge. Although a good timber fence can be constructed that will last for 10 or 20 years, with little more trouble than restaining, repainting or replacing the occasional warped picket, the gate will usually be the first part of the fence to fail.

Solid wooden gates are prone to sagging, within the frame itself, or when the bolts in the hinges pull through the wood. Some fence timbers are soft, and bolts or screws can pull out of the wood, especially if the gate is under a lot of pressure. Gates made of oak or cedar may, in the long run, be a cheaper choice than apparently more economical softwoods.

A cottage-garden entrance, with lattice-patterned, white, timber gate, framed with climbing roses.

It will be worth the investment when you aren't replacing it every few years.

Gate posts and timbers may need to be more durable than the fence timbers. Posts and framing timbers without knots will perform better over time. Weather-treated wood is worth the extra cost but look closely at any warranties provided with prefabricated fencing materials to see precisely what is, and isn't, covered.

Use caps for wooden gate (and fence) posts. Exposing the ends of the wood to rain will encourage moisture that may cause premature rotting.

Metal-framed timber gates are available and you can buy frames and kits to make your own. Wrought and cast metal gates are also commonly used in timber fences because of their strength and reliability.

Always consider gate safety at the outset. Wooden gates, for example, are quite heavy, and small children or frail people could be seriously injured by a slamming gate. Leave ample space on the latch side so as not to allow little fingers to get caught in pinch points and make sure that gates can be secured whether they are open or shut.

Trellises and Hedges

No matter how carefully we order our gardens, there will generally be some area that you would rather not see—or be seen in. The solution is a screen. Garbage or utility areas are prime candidates for screening. Screening is also used to separate different "garden rooms" or to separate garden areas of various styles.

In addition, blank garden walls are not to everyone's taste. You can screen them off or use them to support trellises—a curtain of lush greenery and colorful blooms may be a much better solution.

And since many of us live in urban areas, it is sometimes necessary to use fences, hedges or screens to get some element of privacy in our gardens.

A hedge of scarlet runner bean makes an unusual change from the more common hedge plants.

Trellises

Trellises can be fashioned into arches and used to link buildings or fill up peculiar, discordant spaces in the garden. Handcrafted trellises made from metal and wood are available at garden centers, builders' suppliers and by mail order. These are usually easy to set up. Simply push the feet into the soil next to a wall or in a planter box, plant a vine nearby and wrap the growing stems around the

Morning glory

supports, using plant ties if necessary. Alternatively, you can make your own trellis, and this design can be as simple or as grand as you wish.

Wooden trellises are usually bought in natural wood finishes but can look good painted as a complement or contrast to other garden structures.

At the simpler end of the scale, string or wire can be used to weave a trellis structure over a bare wall or between two or more supports.

One useful trellis material is fishing line. It is nearly invisible as well as durable (if you use a good-quality, monofilament line). It is also very flexible, so you can create interesting patterns—fans, fountains and other shapes—simply by tracing the pattern onto a wall or fence and positioning screws, screw eyes or nails at the appropriate points. You can also use this method to create a kind of false espalier.

Depending on the plants you choose, trellises need solid support. Free-standing, they can be used as screens as the vegetation grows.

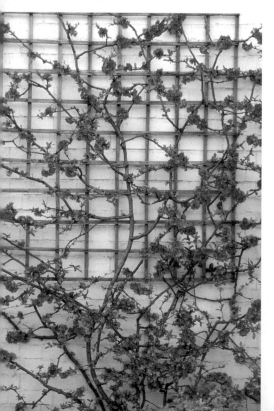

LEFT: Red flowering quince *Chaenomeles* spp. trained up a trellis.

When fixed to a solid surface, wall or fence, make sure that there is a gap behind the trellis. It will be easier to

Flowering Hedges

A flowering hedge can provide seasonal or year-round interest. Flowering shrubs generally look best when you let them grow in their natural arching or spreading forms. Avoid heavy pruning as this can remove flower buds and reduce or eliminate flowering altogether. Try one of the following:

Abelia x *grandiflora* (glossy abelia)
Camellia sasanqua (sasanqua camellia)
Chaenomeles speciosa (flowering quince)
Deutzia spp. (deutzias)
Forsythia spp. (forsythias)
Hibiscus syriacus (rose-of-sharon)
Hydrangea paniculata var. *grandiflora*
Philadelphus coronarius (sweet mock orange)
Prunus laurocerasus (cherry laurel)
Rosa spp. (roses)
Spiraea spp. (spireas)
Syringa spp. (lilacs)
Viburnum spp. (viburnums)

Forsythia

Formal Hedges

If you are willing to invest the maintenance time, a closely trimmed hedge can add a dramatic touch to the landscape. A formal hedge is a perfect way to enclose a garden, providing wind protection and serving as a background for colorful flowers. These plants can stand the severe pruning needed to produce dense hedges.

Berberis thunbergii (Japanese barberry)

Buxus sempervirens (common boxwood)

Carpinus betulus (European hornbeam)

Chamaecyparis lawsoniana (Lawson cypress)

Fagus sylvatica (European beech)

Ilex crenata (Japanese holly)

Photinia spp. (photinias)

Pyracantha coccinea (scarlet firethorn)

Taxus spp. (yews)

Thuja spp. (arborvitae)

Tsuga canadensis (Canada hemlock)

anchor your plants and allow better air circulation so that the supporting surface is not perpetually damp.

Hedges

Hedges give a garden a strong, handsome, year-round structure. They can be tall or short, formal and clipped, informal and shaggy, or something in between.

A healthy, well-maintained hedge can become a superb landscape design feature. Hedges combine beauty with usefulness, and are ideal for providing privacy and creating shelter. Tall hedges can act as efficient windbreaks and can reduce noise. As a bonus for wildlife gardeners, hedges also can provide food and shelter for birds and a wide variety of beneficial

A hedge of copper beech *Fagus sylvatica* 'Atropunicea' capped with snow.

The beds in this formal herb garden, featuring lavender cotton, fescue and lavender, are framed with low, clipped hedges of boxwood *Buxus* spp.

insects, amphibians, reptiles and other small animals.

Hedges come in a range of styles and you can combine a few of them for different purposes. You can choose from:

- Formal hedges: Clipped into neat geometric shapes (high maintenance).
- Informal: Usually trimmed and tidied up on a regular basis (moderate to low maintenance).
- Rough screens or shelter belts: Rows of vigorous shrubs, occasionally cut back hard but usually free to flower and fruit (low- or no special maintenance).
- Miniature hedges: Boundary or border hedges, low enough to step over (moderate to high maintenance).
- Topiary: Formal hedges or single specimens clipped into a geometrical or artistic shape resembling sculpture (very high maintenance).

Planting Your Hedge

If you are thinking about planting a tall hedge on the boundaries of your property,

it's a good idea to discuss it with your neighbors first. Well-grown hedges can be around for a long time—and so can a neighbor's irritation at a favorite view or sunlight being blocked.

Like all new plants, a hedge is vulnerable in its first growing season. Water will be the main limiting factor, so water your new hedge regularly, especially through its first summer.

Very close planting tends to make plants grow taller as they compete for sunlight. Regular mulching and watering are essential to keep the soil in good condition and to maintain healthy growth, both above and below ground.

Paths and Steps

Paths form the skeleton of most garden designs. They divide your garden space and frame plantings, as well as directing the ways in which people move through the landscape. Steps are essential to link two different levels in the garden. Although they are functional items, try to think of paths and steps as being major garden features, and give plenty of thought as to materials and design.

Path Finding

If you do not make proper garden paths, they tend to be made for you by the footsteps of people traversing your garden in the most direct way. If you save time by cutting across the lawn to get the mail, or to add to the compost pile, or hang washing, soon a trail of flattened grass marks your new path.

Every path maps out a journey, even if it is just a short path that you use many times a day. Ideally, a good pathway combines the virtues of beauty and function, taking you from one point to another in a graceful way on the surface most appropriate for the situation.

If you rarely use a path, the mere fact that you don't use it very often will stimulate your senses when you do. A much-used path is the perfect spot for scented flowers, pots of bulbs and special plants that spark interest as they change throughout the gardening year.

You can add interest to routine journeys by building a pergola over the path or by using distinctive materials. Trees planted along a path will have the same effect—if you are a little imaginative about the journey between the kitchen and the compost heap or garage, it can become something to look forward to rather than mere drudgery.

Making a Path

When creating a path, the first consideration should always be safety. You do not want a path that is slippery when wet, or treacherously uneven, nor do you want any obstacles that might cause someone to trip. The most durable paths are designed for use in all weathers—with good drainage in the wet and good traction in frosts.

When deciding what materials to use in creating a path, there are three main categories of choice:

* Suitability of materials
* Original cost
* Maintenance costs.

A path of mown grass is not suitable if it is going to be used every day. Even if the grass is able to withstand the amount of traffic,

LEFT: Stepping stones connect two separate paved patio areas.
RIGHT: Cottage garden and mulch path.

Paths in strong, linear patterns lead one through areas of the garden to a visual conclusion.

grass is slippery when wet and the moisture will soak through many shoes.

Grass paths are inexpensive to install but the grass will need to be mowed every 10 days or so during the summer, and it will need to be edged in some way—either by trimming the edges, or by installing some sort of edging to separate the grass from planting beds. Mowing strips are a great solution. If they are set flush with the grass, you can run one wheel of the lawn mower along the strip and your edging is done.

Bricks or concrete pavers are ideal materials for a path which is used often. Poured concrete can be made more attractive with colored oxides, or by stamping it with a paving pattern.

Flagstone is expensive and can be slippery when wet, but if you live in an area with lots of rocks, a flagstone path will harmonize well with the environment.

Another alternative is to create a path of stepping stones, using stones or concrete pavers.

It is best to use solid paths (brick, concrete, pavers or stone) for routes that you are likely to travel barefoot (the path from the hot tub or swimming pool to the house, for example), so you won't pick up dirt on wet feet.

Use bark or gravel in places that call for a more natural look. Gravel paths require less maintenance than mown grass, but gravel paths may need to be treated for weeds during the growing

Circular sections of sawn-off tree trunks create imaginative as well as functional steps.

Again, remember access issues for people who are less mobile—a ramp or gentle slope may be useful.

Reclaimed railroad ties or railway sleepers are popular for quick construction of steps and low terraces, but they can cause problems for gardeners who may not have considered the tar, oil, creosotes and whatever else was used to preserve the timbers. New hardwood can often be less troublesome.

Whatever you decide to use, the timber slabs should be laid on a concrete bed 2–4 inches (5–10 cm) thick. For extra security, steel pins or stakes can be driven in front of or through each tie or sleeper.

Constructing flights of more than three or four steps can be tricky if you are inexperienced, and in such cases it may be better to seek the advice of a professional builder or break up a steep change in levels into two or more smaller rises.

season. This can be tricky if you have plants along the edges of your paths.

People seem to like gently curved paths, but the keyword here is "gently"— don't over-complicate the construction of curves. If the curved paths go around an obstacle that obscures the walker's destination, you add some mystery to your landscape, leading visitors through the garden and inviting them to explore further. However, too many intersecting paths can just be confusing.

Weeds in paving

If you have an informal path, plant groundcovers between pavers to soften the hard edges, and to prevent weeds from growing there instead. Floppy, trailing plants spilling over and onto your paths have a similar effect, but make sure they cannot cause slipping or tripping.

Plan to make your paths wide enough for two people to walk side by side— 4–5 feet (1.2–1.5 m) in width is good.

Also consider access for wheelchairs, prams and wheelbarrows. Wheelchairs and walkers require a 4-foot (1.2-m) wide path in order to make a 90-degree turn without backing up; 5 feet (1.5 m) allows a 180-degree turn without reversing. Ideal paths for people with mobility problems are level, non-skid, and require minimal upkeep to stay in good condition.

Stepping Out

If there is a change of level in your pathways, with a little imagination, steps can add interest, as well as functionality, to the most ordinary of paths.

Do not expect visitors to be focused when they are walking along your garden path, since they will be looking at your plants, so it is best to not just have one step when there is a change in levels— a set of three steps is more noticeable and less likely to cause people to trip.

The simplest, most stable type of stone steps are made from large stones or concrete blocks.

Remember that the top of each riser has to be flat and level and all the risers have to be more or less equal height.

A flight of weathered, stone steps winds its way uphill. Plants at the edges soften the look.

Arches, Arbors and Pergolas

If you have an uninteresting long path, a boring wall or garden topography devoid of even the hint of a bump, you can transform your landscape by building dramatic garden structures such as garden arches, arbors and pergolas.

Each of these features has a specific look, as well as a specific purpose, and can complement just about any outdoor space. You can buy cheap kits—especially of garden arches—at chain stores, or you can spend thousands in creating uniquely beautiful constructions. Most gardeners settle for something in between.

Arches

Arches frame garden views, often in both directions, and can be free-standing or part of a wall, fence or trellis. Materials can be metal, wood, brick, stone or a lattice of metal or wood. Kit arches vary greatly in size and elaborateness. They can be round-topped, elliptical, a Gothic pointed arch, or any other shape through which you can pass.

Arches are the archetypal supports for climbing roses, but they can also be used for any vine, often at entrances or transition points in the landscape.

Arbors

Arbors are also plant-supporting structures that are used to create an entryway, but some experts believe that an arbor is a destination rather than a passageway. Arbors are usually lightweight structures, and the ones that definitely are destinations are partially enclosed to form an outdoor seating area or focal point.

Pergolas

Lastly there is the pergola. Although often a large-scale structure that fits well into a substantial property, a pergola can also serve as a means to support different types of flowering vines and climbing plants. Sometimes a pergola is attached to another structure and acts as an extension of that building. Pergolas also create a pathway within a landscape, giving strong direction from one area to the next as well as a sense of shelter.

A pergola could be a good way to separate a flower garden from an

Passion flower

A glorious, shady and natural, arched walkway created with European filbert *Corylus avellana*.

ornamental vegetable garden, because they would both be visible yet each would have its own clearly defined space.

Gardening Upward

Arches, arbors and pergolas allow you to explore the vertical dimension of your garden with powerful planting schemes. A pergola can serve as a colorful entryway to your home and garden. Arbors make sturdy supports or trellises for many attractive climbers, such as wisteria or roses. Larger arbors that cover patio or picnic areas can support grapes, passion flower, clematis or hanging baskets.

There is an enormous range of climbing, twining, clinging and trailing plants that will do well growing on high. Check your local garden centers to see what flourishes in your area, and also investigate nearby gardens, to see what plants or varieties do well in your area.

Two all-time favorites for arches are clematis and climbing roses, often grown

An archway is a delightful way of linking two separate areas, or "rooms," of a garden.

together. Clematis prefers full sun, but likes to have cool roots. Place clematis among other plants that will shade its roots, or apply a thick layer of mulch. As the shoots grow, wrap them around a vertical structure or tie them to the structure.

Climbing roses, with their stunning blooms and tall canes, give a garden a romantic feeling. They do not have clinging tendrils, so you will need to tie them to the structure for support.

Design Considerations

If you are thinking about including an archway, arbor or pergola in your garden, you should consider whether you want this structure for purely aesthetic reasons or to be more utilitarian. Or will it be a combination of both?

If you are shading an outdoor seating or dining area, you will need to consider wind and shade as well as temperature and rainfall, especially during the summer months, when you will likely be spending most time outdoors.

You should also consider whether local building regulations will cover the kind and size of structure you are planning.

Pergolas, arbors and archways may be custom-designed to fit almost any garden space or style of architecture. Choosing

A rose-covered archway is one of the most romantic features you can include in your garden design.

which structure best fits your landscape depends, however, on several issues, including budget, function, space and your capacity and interest in maintaining such a structure. Reasons for including such structures include:

- Adding vertical interest to the garden
- Forming a transition space from garden to house or other buildings, or to another part of the garden
- Extending and integrating architectural details from buildings into the garden
- Providing a shady spot in the garden or on a patio or terrace
- Providing shelter from winds and other climatic conditions
- Providing support for vines
- Screening unattractive views or providing privacy.

If you are going to construct an arbor or pergola yourself, be honest with yourself about your abilities. A rustic archway or arbor can be charming, while a failed attempt at magnificence is an embarrassing eyesore—and may be unsafe as well.

Clematis

Depending upon your level of building skill, you may want to design and build a structure yourself (it can be a big job) or buy a professional plan and either build it yourself or get a professional to construct it for you. Alternatively, you can adapt a commercial plan to your site or get a structure custom-designed and professionally built.

Remember that just as flower beds need weeding and watering, these structures also need regular attention. The amount of maintenance depends on the materials used. Regular maintenance generally includes sealing, painting or staining the wood, adjusting screws or bolts, rust proofing all metal pieces and repairing or replacing damaged wood.

Some of the popular choices of building materials for these structures include pressure-treated pine, cedar, redwood, fiberglass, PVC, aluminum and galvanized pipe. Fiberglass and metal frames are durable and virtually maintenance free. Frame supports can be constructed of any of the above materials, or of masonry, such as stone, brick or cement blocks.

A pergola is a major garden structure and can be directional, or purely decorative, as shown above.

Water Features

Water adds a new dimension to any landscape. Surrounding plants and the sky above are mirrored in water surfaces, while moving water adds gentle sounds and shimmering lights. Fish and aquatic plants can thrive in the simplest garden ponds, and even a fairly modest fountain can produce charming effects.

While it is ideal if an entire landscape—including your water garden—can be designed as a whole, the reality is that most ponds and other water features are fitted into an existing landscape.

A water feature can range from a small pond or recycling fountain, to a large pond, dam or lake. Indeed, a water feature can be as simple or complex as you like.

Ponds and Pools

The heart of most water gardens is a pond, and you can add one to your garden in a day or so by using a preformed, fiberglass or plastic shell. Installing one is easy, but it does require a good shovel and a fairly strong back. You just dig a hole, drop in the shell, check that it is level, then fill it with water and plants. Edged with stones and low-growing plants, the pond becomes graceful and invitingly natural-looking very quickly.

Preformed ponds come in a variety of shapes, sizes and depths. Despite their bulk, most shells are light in weight. Some have smooth, vertical sides, while others imitate natural rock. Some have shelves at different depths to hold water plants.

The size of the pond is important. The smaller the pond, the greater the impact of seasonal and daily temperature fluctuations, and the less stable the overall pond environment will be.

Maximum pond depth should range from 18–24 inches (45–60 cm). Depths over 3 feet (1 m) are usually not necessary and could cause maintenance and safety problems. In some areas you may find that bodies of water over a certain depth need to be fenced. Check with local garden centers or your building regulatory body.

If the pond is to achieve its potential for your landscape, the shape of the pond

Marsh marigold

should complement the shapes dictated in your landscape. If your landscape is formal in style, then the angles, lines and curves should be repeated in the shape of the pond.

If your landscape is informal, then this freedom of line and form should be reflected by a less rigid design. If the pond is constructed of flexible liners, your options are almost limitless. However, if you elect to use a preformed shell liner, your options are more limited.

Edging materials help to tie the water feature into the overall scheme of the garden. Use the colors, textures and form of the individual pieces of edging material to complement or reinforce the position that your pond occupies in the overall scheme of your landscape.

Choice of materials for your pond should take into account the cost, life expectancy of the material, installation requirements, availability in your area and the ways in which these materials will blend with the rest of your landscape.

The liner is generally the most important and most expensive component of the water garden. Some popular examples of liners and their life expectancy are:
- PVC (pond grade): 5–15 years
- Butyl or rubber (pond grade): 30 years
- Fiberglass: 50 years or more
- Concrete: 50 years or more if properly constructed.

Plan your pond so that you can easily add a waterfall or a second pool in the future. Most new water gardeners improve and experiment as they gain expertise.

Aquatic Wildlife

Fish are an essential element in most water gardens, feeding on the mosquito eggs and larvae that would otherwise collect in standing water. Most aquatic

Lighting and water features used together create spectacular design effects.

Irises, such as this purple rabbit-ear iris, will provide year-round color in shallow water.

plants require relatively warm water, so schedule your installation for a time when the air temperature in your area has reached a reliable 70°F (22°C). Before adding fish or plants, let the water warm and dechlorinate for at least 24 hours. Using a fine spray to fill the pond from the mains water supply will help disperse added chlorine. Alternatively, add a dechlorinator, available from your local water garden or aquarium supplier.

If you live in a very cold climate where the ground freezes, you may have to overwinter your plants and fish indoors. However, a shallow crust of ice will harm neither fish nor most plants.

If the ice does not melt during the day, an effective trick is to put a smooth rubber ball into the water before the freeze, remove it after the ice has formed and then siphon some water out of the pond. The ice and air space combine to give a cosy greenhouse environment for the plants and fish below.

Water lily

Plants

Plant selection for the pond is a major consideration, and, in new ponds fitted into an existing landscape, plants chosen for the water garden should complement

existing plants in the landscape. Some design aspects to keep in mind when attempting to match or contrast the pond to your landscape are: plant texture, flower color, duration of bloom, foliage color, texture, evergreen or deciduous, overall form, height, density, growth habit and longevity.

Water lilies are the most popular water plants. Most are white, red, pink or yellow, and hardy lily blooms open during the day and close in the late afternoon. Some tropical water lilies bloom at night and some are fragrant. They like 12–15 inches (30–40 cm) of water above their rootstock.

Deep-water aquatics, such as nymphoides *Nymphoides peltata* and thalia *Thalia dealbata*, are useful plants for areas of the pond with moving water or partial shade.

Submerged oxygenators, such as Canadian pond-weed *Elodea canadensis* and

A simple, geometric-shaped pond, complete with fish.

hornwort *Ceratophyllum demersum*, are plants that can be rooted in soil or float around under the water. You do not need to go to a specialist plant nursery for these— many are available at local pet stores and aquarium suppliers.

Marginal plants, including marsh marigold *Caltha palustris* and water irises, such as *Iris pseudacorus* or *I. laevigata*, are planted in containers placed on shallow shelves at the pond's edge. Most marginals prefer shallow water.

Bog plants, such as astilbes, hostas and skunk cabbage, like to be constantly damp, but not waterlogged.

Once your water garden is growing, it will require little maintenance. The most crucial job is to top up any water lost to evaporation (let it warm for a few hours in a bucket before adding it to the pond), and to remove spent flowers or brown foliage.

Fish

Goldfish are the most popular garden pond fish, since they do not require special water filtration and are compatible with

Juniperus 'Sky Rocket'

Rosa 'Iceberg'

Iris pseudacorus

Alyssum maritima

Buxus 'Suffruticosa'

Iris pseudacorus

Gardenia augusta

Gardenia augusta

FORMAL GARDEN WITH WATER FEATURE The above garden plan shows a garden with a screening wall at the far end on which is mounted a water fountain. Behind this wall are hidden a shed (which contains the electrical connection for the fountain) and a utility area. Also behind this screening wall is a row of conifers. From the fountain, the water overflows and runs along a rill (small stream) that ends in a small pool, and this is carried back to the fountain via underground pipes. In the pool is a containerized water iris. On either side of the rill are two symmetrical, formal beds. These are edged with a low, clipped hedge. White roses feature in the beds and are surrounded by a groundcover of sweet Alice. At the near end of the garden is a pergola-covered entertaining area. However, this plan shows only the curved step up to this paved area. On either side of the curved step is a row of fragrant gardenias.

water plants. Koi, also popular in ponds, need sophisticated filters to keep their water clean and healthy.

If you have created a good pond eco-system, your fish colony may expand at a dizzying rate. If not, and you want to introduce more fish, do so a few at a time to make sure everything is working well.

To add new fish, float the unopened bag they came in on the surface of your pond to equalize water temperatures. Let the bag sit in the water for an hour or so before opening it slowly, letting the water mix and your new fish gradually to swim out into their new home.

You can feed the fish with commercial goldfish food, but do not over-feed.

A Container Water Garden
A small water garden adds a special sparkle to any collection of container plants. As a bonus, the open water will attract birds, insects, frogs and toads. You can use any large container—an old bathtub or sink, a half barrel or glazed pot (properly sealed), or a special plastic tub sold complete with a filter and small fountain.

Most garden centers and some chain stores now stock a selection of small (and not so small) water garden kits, fountains and the plants to put in them. These kits are available in a range of styles.

This garden is separated from the swimming pool by a wall.

Set the container on your patio or deck, or sink it into the ground for a natural pool effect. A filter usually isn't necessary for a small water garden if you include a few oxygenating plants, such as *Elodea canadensis*, to help keep the water clear.

Swimming Pools in the Landscape
Unless you have a very large garden, it will be difficult to make any swimming pool look relatively unobtrusive or "natural" in your landscape. Choosing dark waterline tiles instead of the usual electric blue pool interiors can make a pool seem more like a natural pond. While a pool can be made to fade into the landscape, it is far easier to keep the pool at the center of your landscape plan.

In many localities, there are regulations governing swimming pool fencing, so you should check on these.

Swimming pool landscaping is all too often something of an afterthought. You need to consider such things as types of plants, potential maintenance, sunlight patterns and shading from trees before you start planting. You should also consider your lifestyle and activity level. If you really want a garden around the pool, you need to recognize that plants will always shed leaves and bark, and this means more maintenance.

Avoid plants with thorns and prickles and trees with invasive root systems. Make sure runoff water from flower beds

Moss pink

Water features can incorporate sculptural elements, such as this water spout head.

does not drain into the pool and consider using gravel (rather than bark) to mulch beds close to the pool. Do not plant anything that will actually grow over the perimeter of the pool and, wherever possible, use groundcovers and grasses as alternatives to larger plants.

Most plants will tolerate occasional splashes of properly maintained pool water. However, heavily chlorinated water will take its toll over time and can raise the soil salt content. Periodic flooding and flushing with regular tap water avoids salt build-up. Use container plants or raised beds with retaining walls to protect plants from chlorinated or otherwise chemically rich pool water.

You might like to play up the essentially formal shape of most swimming pools with complementary plantings. Low-growing plants, groundcovers and lawns can ring the pool site in a neat border, leading to taller plantings further from the pool itself.

Many gardeners like tropical plants near swimming pools. While many of these plants are not hardy everywhere, you can still use a few for their strong effects. If you live in a cool-climate Zone, you may be able to able to grow these plants in containers, protecting them indoors through the winter.

Rock Features

Gardening with rocks and stones is immensely satisfying. Rocks have a natural, sculptural beauty and an air of permanence. A successfully designed rockery should appear as if it has been there forever.

A rock garden is a combination of rocks and plants; it is not simply a place for displaying attractive rocks. It is through the selection and placement of plants that the harmony of a rock feature becomes complete.

Of course, some initial planning, expense and some very hard work will be involved to get rocks into your garden or at least moved to a suitable location within your property. But once the design is set and the rocks are in place, the feature is relatively easy to maintain and, in many instances, the mat-forming plants that are at home in a rockery tend to keep the weeds out.

A Suitable Site

Almost every garden has at least one site suitable for a rock feature. It can be any size, from a tiny corner in a courtyard garden, to an area as large as you can comfortably maintain.

Usually it is much easier to develop an attractive landscape by using the existing natural features in your garden, so you are off to a good start if you have natural rocky outcrops on your lot.

Effective rockeries can be constructed on sites that are naturally uneven or sloping. Because a rockery provides support for the soil, it also helps to prevent erosion. However, a rock feature can bring interest to a flat piece of land. To develop attractive contours, introduce rock and subsoil as a gentle undulation, not a hill. Fill in the spaces with good topsoil for planting.

In a small, city garden, thoughtfully placed rocks and plantings can add height

Natural rocks, lit from below, are the perfect ornament for this Japanese-style garden that features bonsai and a bamboo fence.

and contour to an otherwise flat area. High walls built for privacy often deny sunlight to small urban gardens, so your range of plants may be limited. However, ferns may solve the problem. They will tolerate shade; their lacy fronds will drape over the rocks, providing year-round greenery; and they rarely grow too big. You could even add a sculpture to complete the picture.

Selecting the Right Rocks

If you are introducing rocks to a landscape, select those that blend with the immediate surroundings. Rocks that have a weathered look are preferable to newly quarried material, which will take a long time to mellow. Try to use the same type of rock throughout the construction, and if stepping-stones are required, they should be also of the same colored stone.

When you wish to create a bold effect, start by acquiring the larger pieces of rock or boulders first. Smaller pieces of rock may be added later to add variety, but don't make the finishing rocks too small or the feature will look bitty.

A rock feature is ideal to combine with a water feature, such as a waterfall, as pictured above.

A small pool surrounded by rocks is a beautiful feature in a garden that has a floor-covering of rock paving.

is nearly vertical, a low wall may be required. To prevent movement, each rock must be firmly seated, resting on the rocks below and partly embedded in the soil. Allow for the possibility of heavy rain and for the eroding effect that can have on new soil.

Arranging the Rocks

Place large rocks so that they all flow in the same direction (usually horizontally), burying them to between a fourth and a third of their height. Rounded rocks are best set in groups and should be fairly deeply embedded to hide the inward curve on the underside. Soil must be firmly packed under and around rocks to prevent movement, and also in any cracks and crevices which could provide homes for unwanted pests.

If a slope is exceptionally steep, a few larger rocks may have to be completely embedded to provide support for the remaining rocks. Or, when the change

Use a rock feature as a more unusual and attractive way of edging a garden bed.

Rock Garden Settings

The art of rock gardening originated in attempts to cultivate rare alpine plants in gardens at lower altitudes. These little plants, the wildflowers of the mountains, are the natural dwellers of bare scree, rocky hillsides and alpine meadows.

If you live in a cool climate and your rock feature is set in an open, sunny position with excellent drainage, you will be able to provide the ideal growing conditions for alpine plants.

Among the many favorites are alpine phlox, arabis and aubretias. These are robust, spreading plants that will form carpets and provide many colorful flowers in spring. Hebes, saxifrages, stonecrops and garden pinks will also thrive in this environment. Several *Arenaria* species are attractive cushion-forming plants useful as groundcover or edging. The rampant snow-in-summer *Cerastium tomentosum* is an indispensable carpeting plant for spilling over large boulders and walls.

Shrubs will give the rock feature a framework, and obvious choices are found among the conifers. *Juniperus conferta* and *J. horizontalis* are effective, low-growing, creeping shrubs that reach no more than 1 foot (30 cm) in height.

In warmer climates, you may prefer to grow plants based around a particular theme. Mediterranean plants with aromatic and silvery leaves and fragrant flowers will all enjoy the warmth and drainage a rock garden provides. Here you could include groups of *Lavandula*

angustifolia, rosemary, salvias, santolinas, silver artemisia and golden marjoram. Or start a collection of thymes, ranging from the bushy garden thyme *Thymus vulgaris* and lemon-scented thyme to the very low-growing, woolly thyme that can be used as a carpet between stepping stones.

Lavender

An all-succulent garden is another appealing plant community for a sunny rock garden. Select species compatible with your climate and those that enjoy the same growing conditions. Often a well-drained raised bed or steep slope with shallow soil is all that many succulents require. Aloes, agaves and yuccas will provide a backdrop for bushy species of *Aeonium* and *Sedum*. Small pockets of soil can be filled with houseleeks, carpeting sedums and echeverias that will all multiply and form carpets of foliage in the most delightful way.

Hens and chickens *Echeveria secunda* are the perfect plants for a rock garden in a hot, dry spot.

Container Gardens

The great thing about gardening in containers is the flexibility you get. Because the plants aren't rooted in the ground, you can place them exactly where you want them. You can create a miniature landscape filled with your favorite plants right around your deck or patio, where you get to relax and really enjoy their beauty and fragrance. If you live in a high-rise apartment building or condo, where you have no ground for a garden, you can create a lush, green oasis on a tiny balcony or outdoor stairway. City dwellers can grow large gardens entirely in containers on building rooftops. Even if you have nothing but a wall and windows to call your own, you can fill hanging baskets with trailing plants and pack window boxes full of flowers, herbs and vegetables.

With plants in containers, you can rearrange and replace each pot as needed, maintaining a garden that always looks picture-perfect. While the plants are flowering, you can place the container where you'll see it best and enjoy it most. Then, as the blooms fade, you can retire the pot to the basement or garage until next year. Or, if your season permits, you can re-pot it with fresh plants.

Variegated ivy

Types of Container

Anything that can hold soil securely can be used as a garden container. From classic terracotta pots and tubs to colorful ceramic pots and much more, the range of containers now available means that your selection of container shape, material, and color is greater than ever.

More specialized container types include hanging baskets, which can be made of plastic, with drainage saucers or, less obtrusively, of a wire or plastic frame lined with wet sphagnum, bark, peat moss or synthetic basket liners. But remember that hanging baskets with well-grown plants can become heavy, especially when they have been fully watered, so ensure that the weight will be supported.

Window boxes are popular but they must also be well secured. They can be made of wood, metal, terracotta, fiberglass or plastic. Such boxes should ideally be lightweight, durable and easily handled.

There's no need to limit yourself to commercially produced containers. As

long as the container provides enough drainage, markets and garage sales can offer antique, quaint or just plain crazy containers that you can adapt to a new life holding your favorite plants—kettles, basins, barrows, or even old boots are just a few examples. Remember, too, that you can conceal plants in utilitarian plastic pots by hiding them inside larger, much more decorative outer containers.

Container Garden Design

A container planting can be as simple as one pot of flowers or as lush and full as a garden border. You'll get the best results from your potted plants when you choose and group them to match your setting.

Choose the Right Size

Plants in single, small containers can look puny and out of place all alone on a deck or patio. To get the best effect, you want your container plants to be in proper scale with the great outdoors. Whenever possible, opt for larger containers, at least 10 inches (25 cm) in diameter; generally

Large containers make the strongest statement, such as this pot with cascading campanulas.

the bigger, the better. Using larger pots will cost a little more up front, but the plants will grow better, you'll have to water less often, and the overall effect of the container garden will be more dramatic.

If you prefer to grow your plants in smaller containers, group them together to create an eye-catching effect. It also makes regular watering and maintenance much easier, since all the plants are in the same place. For extra interest, it's a good idea to vary the heights of plants in a group of pots. You can use short plants in smaller pots for the front and taller plants in the back. Or use concealed bricks, plastic crates, or upside-down pots to vary the height of individual pots in a grouping.

Consider the Colors

Don't forget to think about color combinations when buying plants for containers. Groupings look best when one or two colors dominate. For example, a yellow accent (maybe dwarf marigolds) works well with a group of blue flowers such as ageratum. White is also a good accent color, and it looks good with every color. Sweet Alice *Lobularia maritima* is an excellent white trailing plant that always looks good as it spills loosely over the sides of the pots.

Flowers for Pots and Planters

Nothing says summer like pots and planters filled to overflowing with lush foliage and beautiful blooms. Create your

FAR LEFT: Japanese maple *Acer palmatum*.
LEFT: Potted cranesbill *Geranium argenteum*.

own colorful container gardens with a bounty of annuals and dependable, blooming perennials, selecting companions with the same growing needs.

The easiest and longest-flowering plants you can grow in containers are flowering annuals. Most annuals do extremely well in containers; the many compact cultivars of marigolds, petunias, impatiens, begonias and ageratum are especially good. These annuals begin blooming early and put on a nonstop show of color all season long.

Some perennials work well in containers, too. Top choices include those with a long season of bloom, such as compact, golden orange 'Stella d'Oro' daylily. Other perennials that look especially nice in containers are those with interesting foliage, such as hostas, ornamental grasses, lady's mantle *Alchemilla mollis* and heart-leaved bergenia

Snapdragons and campanulas

Bergenia cordifolia. Try using some of these plants in large containers, mixed with annual flowers to provide constant color.

Trees, Shrubs and Vines for Containers

In many situations, one large tree or shrub in a pot is all you need to add a spectacular focal point to your courtyard or garden. A maple looks great with an understory of low-growing annuals, and you get the bonus of the maple's beautiful red leaves in autumn.

There are many shrubs ideally suited to containers, no matter what your climate. Some of the prettiest gardens are those featuring traditional cottage garden shrubs, such as roses, pelargoniums and lavender cotton spilling unhindered from containers.

Vines grown in containers have the added attraction of providing quick shade or privacy for an exposed porch or patio. These larger container plants will need some pruning to control their size and keep a pleasing shape.

Large planters can hold a whole garden on a deck or patio. This large, shallow container contains a seasonal display of daffodils surrounded by hyacinths, together with a few primroses.

Garden Furniture and Ornament

Good design in furniture and ornament is just as important outside as inside. As we are spending more and more time entertaining outdoors, the distinction between indoor and outdoor use is blurring. Furniture and ornaments designed for the garden are increasingly being used indoors and in transition spaces such as sunrooms, balconies, conservatories and verandas.

Furniture

Whatever your decorating style and budget, you now have a wider range than ever from which to choose. Larger dining tables, seating six to eight or more, capacious end tables, bigger and more comfortable chairs and even couches, love seats and much more are available.

Manufacturers have improved on old favorites, such as wicker, to make them more durable, and have found ways to give inexpensive plastic, acrylic and metal products a more handsome appearance and greater durability.

Bird bath

Wood

The classic material, wood, remains very popular, with hardwoods such as teak and jarrah becoming much more widely available. These are virtually maintenance-free and can be kept in the open throughout the year in most climates. Exposure to the weather actually enhances their beauty—jarrah is naturally reddish-brown and teak is a sandy beige when new, but they weather to subtle silvery-gray shades over time.

Pine outdoor furniture is less expensive than teak and jarrah but is also less durable and requires a little more maintenance. Recommended for covered areas only, pine furniture will need to be stripped and repainted or revarnished on a regular basis.

Traditionally, wicker has been an indoor or under-awning material only, but some manufacturers have developed new finishes that make wicker much tougher, tolerating heat and moisture much better. If you buy untreated wicker—or rattan and rustic tree or sapling—furniture, you will still need to keep them out of the rain, preferably indoors, except when you are actually using them. These less robust materials are still popular choices for sunrooms, verandas and conservatories that have a dryish floor.

Wooden furniture need not be plain brown, as this set of colorful blue furniture shows.

Metal

Another classic garden furniture material is iron, whether wrought or cast. Iron is generally quite ornate in design and always very solid, and can last forever if it is properly looked after. Because of its tendency to rust when the finish gets scratched or chipped, immediate touch-ups and repairs will reduce the need for a yearly scraping down and repainting. You can use cans of spray anti-rust enamels to touch up minor damage—most colors can be matched, especially if you check out the vehicle repair section of your local hardware or auto parts store.

If you want the look of iron but do not care for the maintenance involved, strengthened cast aluminum may be the solution. There is a wide variety of designs available in furniture as solid and durable as iron, but rustproof. Different finishes are available and you may have to shop around for special pieces, and be prepared to pay to get exactly what you want.

If your budget is a touch more modest, or if you simply need robust, knock-about garden furniture, tubular aluminum furniture may suit you. It is less expensive

A wooden bench strewn with cushions makes an appealing seat in this shady spot of the garden.

A garden bench made from a natural material, such as stone, is ideal in a naturalistic garden.

than most other materials, but now is available in more stylish designs than it once was. Manufacturers are now producing aluminum furniture frames in darker, matt finishes and colors, and are using real or fake wicker seats or acrylic slings (such as those in a director's chair) in pleasing colors and textures.

Other Materials

There are now also plastic ranges of furniture designed to simulate wicker and other natural materials. It is possible to find some stylish, modern furniture in perspex or fiberglass that particularly suits the contemporary style of garden.

The Garden Bench

Some people consider a simple garden bench—or even two or three—an essential garden item. Benches come in a wide variety of materials, colors and styles, from natural or painted wood, to stone or twiggy prunings. There are traditional British teak benches and wrought-iron reproductions of Victorian classics available, but you are not limited to store-bought items—well-placed boulders, long, stone slabs or wooden planks can also be used to provide seating for the garden.

Most department and homeware stores, and some garden centers and bigger hardware stores, sell outdoor furniture and

accessories, but you will usually find the best selection at local, outdoor furniture specialty shops.

Essential Accessories

Decorative items, such as statuary, bird baths, bird feeders, gazing balls, sundials, wall plaques, wind chimes, urns, mirrors, tubs and planters in a variety of materials and finishes are now widely available. However, the range can be overwhelming, to the extent that you can even buy bird feeders that are species-specific.

One way to focus is by careful planning. This way you will be less likely to end up with a bitsy collection of oddments, all of which you like (or liked) but which just do not seem to fit together.

Another is to select favorite themes or interests and try not to stray from them. Some people like mythical figures—gods and goddesses can cavort in your garden without any of the traditional mayhem. You

may also like to explore the world of the gargoyle, whether Gothic and weird, or contemporary or classic reproductions.

Yet another way to avoid a bitsy look is to think big rather than small. A pair of large urns flanking a path or gateway will have much more impact than a collection of smaller items.

One role of garden ornaments is to draw people from one garden area to another. Place your first garden ornament by your entrance, then consider where you want visitors to go next. Draw them from one location to the next with a striking garden ornament, a collection of plants in containers, a built structure such as a pergola or arbor, a garden bench or a handsome combination of plants.

LEFT: A hammock, strung up with chains between two strong trees, is perfect for lounging around on lazy days outdoors.
RIGHT: An ornamental raised stone pond with fountain.

Garden Buildings

Garden buildings are important elements in any landscape. Some buildings are free-standing, such as summerhouses, gazebos, sheds, most glasshouses and some garages. Others, such as garages, conservatories, porches and verandas, are attached to the house on one of their sides. Still others are an integral part of the house, such as a sunroom that opens out to the garden. There are also more individual constructions, such as children's playhouses, pool houses and changing rooms, aviaries, or even tree houses.

Garden tents with fabric ceilings and sides are a way to create a garden room without elaborate construction. These tents are not made for camping, but rather are semi-permanent structures made of handsome, sturdy materials that are often carried on lightweight, demountable metal frames.

Any gardener and landscaper, or householder and parent, usually needs more storage space—especially for big items such as mowers. Kit sheds are one solution. They are cheap and functional, but you may do better with a custom design, or one of the many commercial plans now available.

Conservatories are suntraps, and provide delightfully warm places to sit in cool-climate areas.

Treehouses today are undergoing a renaissance. Some specialist companies undertake the whole process from design to construction. Whether you want a rather whimsical refuge and retreat, a place for peaceful study or meditation, or even a permanent home, building up into the trees might be a solution. A treehouse can be just a simple deck with a rope ladder, or an ambitious, multistory structure with a living area, bedrooms, bathroom and kitchen (but check building regulations before you begin).

Design Considerations

Many of these structures can be bought as kits, but if you have unusual conditions, such as severe winds or extreme cold, it may be wise to seek professional advice. Buildings that are specially designed for your particular garden will be much more likely to match the style and materials of your house than any kit you can buy.

A gazebo can provide a place to sit, admire a view or shelter from the elements.

On a severely sloping landscape, some form of terracing must usually precede the building of substantial garden structures. Gravel terraces, for example, have been part of domestic landscapes in southern France for centuries. Gravel is very economical compared to other paving materials, easy to maintain and provides a dry floor for most garden structures.

Floors and footings are important considerations. The type depends upon what uses you have in mind for your buildings, as well as what garden floor surfaces are already in place or planned.

Wooden structures must also be adequately protected against the ravages of climate, pests and damp.

Paradise for Plants

You can add a sunroom or conservatory to your house to create a warm, sunny place for plants and people, or turn a family room or a sunny nook off the kitchen into a garden room, with a few carefully chosen plants, furnishings and accessories. Conservatories and sunrooms

Porch, Veranda and Deck Success

- Avoid fussy, delicate detailing. Simple, sturdy elements look more at home in the great outdoors and require less maintenance.
- Choose materials and finishes that blend with the natural setting. If your house is painted, finish part of your new structure to match.
- Create privacy walls with drapery, standing screens or latticework, covered in growing vines.
- Keep a trunk or basket of cotton throw-rugs or light quilts handy, in case the air gets chilly at night.
- Make the entry appealing. Flank steps or doorways with plant-filled urns, statuary or other decorative details.
- Repaint floors in an interesting color or pattern or refinish the floor in something more appealing, such as pavers, brick or timber. Use hard-wearing rugs made of seagrass or sisal.
- Select a design detail or motif from your house and repeat it in your new structure.
- Set built-in lights on dimmers. Use side lamps, candles and lanterns outdoors for effective accent lighting.
- Treat walls as you would interior ones and hang inexpensive or durable artworks and mirrors.
- Use containers filled with plants to add color and layers to the decor. Remember to use plants that are shade-tolerant, if this is an issue.
  - When selecting color schemes, consider the colors of your exterior walls and any adjacent rooms.

Cyclamen

Some conservatories can be joined onto the house on one side.

are ideal for cool-climate gardeners who like to try growing tropical plants that wouldn't survive in the garden.

For the best environments for keeping plants happy "semi-indoors", take account of these factors:

- **Humidity** Dry heat is fine for cacti and succulents, but tough on tropicals such as African violets, bromeliads and orchids. To raise humidity levels, mist plants every other day with a fine spray of tepid water.
- **Light** To thrive, most indoor plants need at least some natural light and most can do with as much diffused light as you can provide. Blooming plants such as orchids need more light than palms and other plants grown mainly for their foliage.
- **Screening** To protect plants from intense sunlight, put up translucent curtains, blinds or screens.
- **Temperature** Like people, most indoor/outdoor and houseplants thrive in average temperatures about 68–72°F (20–22°C) during the day, and no lower than 55°F (12°C) at night. Some plants, such as dwarf citrus, cyclamen, cymbidium and miniature roses, like a temperature as low as 60°F (15°C) during the day, and 50–55°F (10–12°C) at night. Keep plants out of drafts and away from airconditioners, fireplaces and heaters.
- **Waterproof flooring** Brick, tile and gravel are most tolerant of water spills and moisture. Hardwood flooring is fine for garden rooms as long as pots and saucers do not touch the floor directly.

Permission to Build

Once you have decided what structures you want, it is wise to check that what looks good to you also passes muster with your local building and zoning department. In most communities, building permits are required for new homes and some remodelling projects. Check with your local department for details regarding application procedures, fees and the rest. Projects that may require permits include:

- Adding bay windows or dormers
- Building a deck, patio or fence
- Building a garage
- Building a shed or gazebo
- Converting a garage to livable space
- Demolishing the whole or part of a permanent structure
- Home additions
- Installing a swimming pool
- Tree removal.

Don't forget to use plants to accent your garden structures. Foxgloves add charm to this well.

Lighting Effects

Landscape lighting goes beyond safety and security. It helps to blend interior and exterior space, draws attention to particular features and can even make your home feel larger. Lighting also extends the time in which your garden or patio can be enjoyed, and the drama of light and shadow can add a lot to your enjoyment of home and garden.

Effective lighting is usually a team effort—different fixtures perform different duties to define and enhance your outdoor space. Lighting plans can be made up of zones, with different light intensities— a foreground of medium brightness, a middle area with varying levels of light and shadow, and a background containing some bright sections to draw your eye through the garden.

A well-located lighting fixture should call attention not to itself, but to an element in the landscape. And the lighting fixture should not be obvious.

Subtle lighting is usually much more effective for security purposes than glaring lights—and it is a lot more attractive.

Effective lighting brings this small, simply designed urban roof garden alive at night.

Lighting Effects

Uplighting accentuates shapes, from tree trunks and branches to the over-arching leaf canopy, which can reflect light back to the ground. For maximum effect, use two or more light fixtures placed at different points around a tree.

Backlighting (or silhouetting) emphasizes the form of a tree, shrub, sculpture or some other feature. Place the fixture between the object and a broad background surface, aiming the light at the background so that you see the object's dark silhouette.

Shadowing uses a spotlight in front of plants that stand against or near a high wall, making immature plants seem dramatically larger.

Grazing takes advantage of walls or objects that have textured surfaces— position the light fittings 6–8 inches (15–20 cm) from the surface, and let the light wash across it to create a high-contrast pattern. Wall-washing is similar to grazing, but the light source should be

farther from the wall, and should have a frosted diffuser to give a more even light.

Downlighting uses light sources placed above the featured area and mounted on trees, arbors or under eaves on buildings. Downlights have different beam patterns so that you can design focused accent lighting, or broader, softer light for areas that need general illumination.

Moonlighting gives one of the most natural appearances to a patio or path under trees. Mounted high in a tree, light sources are aimed downward through leaves, so they cast shadows and pools of light on the surfaces below, simulating the light of the full moon.

Low-voltage Lighting

Low-voltage lighting systems allow landscape designers to experiment with fixture placement and the location of cable and transformers, before burying the cable. (The other option is a standard-voltage system, which can produce brighter light levels but is more costly, has bulkier fixtures, provides less flexibility in final placement, and can require cable in conduit and professional installation, depending on local regulations.)

Low-voltage outdoor lights can be strategically positioned to highlight the plants and features you want emphasized.

LEFT: This contemporary, mailbox-style fountain is lit up at night, while candles float in the pool.
RIGHT: Yellow, tubular light in blue pebbles.

Bamboo against a red-painted wall is lit from beneath with lights mounted in stone mulch.

door. Wall-mounted, decorative fixtures can overpower the yard and put a bright light source at eye level. People will often spend a lot of money on a fine carriage lamp, for example, but at night all you really see is a cheap light bulb.

The big mistake made with this fixture style is trying to use it to light the whole landscape, when all it should be doing is marking the entrance with a friendly glow. The real light at the front door would be more effectively produced by concealed light sources under the eaves.

Path lighting defines walkways, steps and changes of level. The best fixtures of this type have a cap that shields the light source from direct view. It is a good idea to locate such lights in garden beds, because putting them in or near the lawn may mean mower trouble. If you want footlights along pathways, go for brass and metal over plastic—they are safer, longer-lasting and fairly easy to install.

Old Flames

Lanterns can be hung outside in the garden during spring and summer, and brought inside in winter or heavy weather. They come in a variety of shapes, sizes and colors, and are made from a wide range of materials, including glass, metal, earthenware, volcanic stone and wood, making it easy for you to select a style that suits your landscape design.

There is a lantern to suit every decor style and hanging a lantern—or a sea of them, as in some Buddhist temples—is the best way to show off their attractions.

Votive candles in short, glass holders can create a firefly-like effect by being suspended from tree branches near an outdoor dining area. You can also float candles in a bird bath or water bowl. They will bob about, with the gently moving lights producing a calming effect.

At ground level, candles or lanterns can provide gentle but dramatic illumination for an eating area or path. Or emphasize their shimmering light by placing them in front of a mirror.

They can also be used for safety, such as to illuminate paths, steps and dark areas.

Low-voltage systems are also easy for homeowners to install themselves. Most home centers offer sets that combine light fixtures, a transformer and timer as well as connecting wire. You might also consider installing an indoor switch and timer combination so that you can bypass any automatic controller and turn the lights on or off whenever you wish.

Lighting an Entryway

Effective entryway lighting should promote safety and security, and yet be esthetically pleasing at the same time. The key principles are simple: Shield the light source and keep the light level low and balanced.

Shielding the light source becomes a bigger problem when you get to the front

Lanterns and candles are a highly evocative way of lighting outdoor living areas at night.

Plants for Every Purpose

Plants are the fun part of gardening. With the hard landscaping features in place, plants of all shapes and sizes finish the picture with their color, shape, texture and seasonal interest. They also modify your garden's environment by providing shade, privacy and shelter. The key to success is to select the right plants for the job. In this guide, you'll find plants to bring your landscape to life from the ground to the treetops. Working at ground or "floor" level are annuals, perennials, bulbs and groundcover plants. For the green "walls" and "roof" of your garden, select from shrubs, trees, palms and vines. To create the impact and individuality you are looking for, consult the special sections on accent plants and water and bog plants. You'll find pictures, concise descriptions and all the information you need on the height, spread, climate, site and growing conditions in order to enjoy great results.

Alcea rosea
MALVACEAE

HOLLYHOCK

The tall flower spires of hollyhocks bring height and boldness to a garden. Grown as annuals or biennials, they self-sow if spent flowers are left to form seeds.

Description Flower stalks rise from green, leafy clumps. Expect blooms from summer until autumn (the buds open progressively up the stem). The hibiscus-like, single or double flowers are up to 5 inches (12.5 cm) wide in white or shades of red, pink and yellow.

Height and spread Height 3–6 feet (90–180 cm); spread to 2 feet (60 cm).

Best climate and site Zones 4–10 (cool to mild summer climates); full sun; average, well-drained soil; shelter from strong winds (stake in exposed areas).

Landscape uses Use the tall spires of hollyhocks as accents in a flower border, or mass plant along a wall or fence. Hollyhocks give a cottage garden feel.

Growing guidelines Plant seedlings or small, potted plants into garden beds after risk of frost has passed, setting plants 1½–2 feet (45–60 cm) apart. Remove spent plants in late summer to autumn.

Good companions Cottage garden plants.

Cultivars Named, double-flowering hollyhocks; dwarf varieties reach 3 feet (90 cm) tall.

Comments Hollyhocks are prone to rust, a fungal disease that produces orange spots on leaves. Spray with fungicide or remove affected plants.

Begonia Semperflorens-cultorum hybrids
BEGONIACEAE

WAX BEGONIA

Wax begonias provide massed color in shades of pink or white for many months from summer to autumn. For contrast, look for cultivars with chocolate-brown or bronze leaves.

Description All parts are fleshy, including the succulent leaves and flowers with their waxy sheen. Single or double in red, pink or white, the flowers are 1½ inches (3.5 cm) across and bloom from summer to autumn.

Height and spread Height 6–8 inches (15–20 cm); spread 6–8 inches (15–20 cm).

Best climate and site Zones 9–11; partial shade to sun (morning sun and afternoon shade best in hot-summer areas). Although grown as tender annuals in cold climates, begonias grow year-round in warm, frost-free gardens.

Landscape uses Ideal edging for beds, pots or window boxes, or use for long-lasting mass displays.

Growing guidelines Plant seedlings or small, potted plants after last frost with temperatures above 50°F (10°C) at night. Space 6–8 inches (15–20 cm) apart. Dig in extra organic matter before planting and keep plants well watered.

Good companions Vincas, sweet alyssum, foliage plants.

Cultivars Named single colors; cultivars with bronze to chocolate-brown leaves.

Comments Watch for powdery mildew on leaves in humid climates or in shade. Move to a sunnier spot or spray with fungicide.

Begonia Tuberhybrida hybrids
BEGONIACEAE

HYBRID TUBEROUS BEGONIAS

Hybrid tuberous begonias make eye-catching baskets or potted displays of luscious flowers that come in a wide range of colors and patterns. The full, double flowers resemble roses.

Description Begonias are succulent, bushy plants laden from summer to autumn with gorgeous, single or double flowers up to 4 inches (10 cm) across. The green to brown, serrated leaves are also attractive.

Height and spread Height to 1½ feet (45 cm); spread 1–1½ feet (30–45 cm).

Best climate and site Frost-hardy in Zone 10; elsewhere, grown as annuals or stored indoors in winter. Partial shade; moist, well-drained soil.

Landscape uses Plants are beautiful features in shaded beds, or use to introduce color in hanging baskets.

Growing guidelines Hybrid tuberous begonias grow from flattened, circular, light brown tubers. Buy in flower or grow from tubers, starting them in pots in bright light. Set plants out 1½ feet (45 cm) apart when night temperatures stay above 50°F (10°C). Water and use mulch to keep the soil evenly moist. Liquid feed monthly during the growing season.

Good companions Ferns, impatiens.

Cultivars Many named varieties; start a collection.

Comments To keep tubers over winter in cold areas, lift them before or just after the first frost, to store in a frost-free place.

Brachyscome iberidifolia
ASTERACEAE

SWAN RIVER DAISY

The fine, lacy leaves of Swan River daisy are as much a feature of this dainty groundcover as its daisy flowers. It's a cheerful choice for a sunny, fuss-free garden edging.

Description This half-hardy annual forms bushy mounds of thin stems and lacy, finely cut leaves. From midsummer until frost, plants bear many 1-inch (2.5-cm), rounded, daisy-like flowers in shades of blue, purple, pink and white, with a golden or dark center.
Height and spread Height to 1 foot (30 cm); spread to 1½ feet (45 cm).
Best climate and site Zones 8–11; full sun; light, well-drained soil.
Landscape uses Use as an edging plant, or trail over rocks or spill from window boxes and hanging baskets.
Growing guidelines Buy small plants in flower to plant out after last frost. In warm, frost-free areas, plant year-round. Space plants 8 inches (20 cm) apart to form a solid carpet or edging. Use good quality, free-draining potting mix for containers. Dig organic matter into garden bed.
Good companions Sweet alyssum, osteospermum, or mix with other trailing plants in baskets.
Cultivars Named single colors, including white, purple, pink and blue.
Comments Drought-tolerant when established. To maintain a compact, bushy shape, lightly clip over after flower flushes.

Brassica oleracea Acephala Group
BRASSICACEAE

ORNAMENTAL CABBAGE

Don't restrict these to the vegetable patch. Ornamental cabbages add a colorful accent to late-season gardens and even potted displays. They withstand frost and look good well into autumn.

Description Grown for its rosettes of colorful foliage in the colder months. The smooth, blue-green leaves are marked with pink, purple, cream or white. As temperatures cool, the leaves in the center become more colorful and dominant.
Height and spread Height 1–1½ feet (30–45 cm); spread to 1½ feet (45 cm).
Best climate and site Zones 6–11; full sun to light shade; average, well-drained soil.
Landscape uses Use to add color to autumn gardens as other annuals finish. Effective when massed into bold patterns as a feature. Use to add color to a potager. Try one as an outdoor table decoration in a pot, or add to a large window box.
Growing guidelines Plant seedlings or small pots in late summer and early autumn, spacing 1 foot (30 cm) apart and deep enough to cover the stem up to the lowest set of leaves.
Good companions Asters, pansies.
Other common names Flowering cabbage, kale.
Cultivars Named varieties have colored and patterned leaves; some are frilly.
Comments If caterpillars damage leaves, pick the pests off by hand or spray with a biological control.

Campanula medium
CAMPANULACEAE

CANTERBURY BELL

Plan ahead for next year's flowers by starting seed during the summer, or buy overwintered container-grown plants in spring for blooms the same year.

Description The rosettes of leaves grow for a year before the slender flower stalks appear. These produce loose spikes of bell-shaped blooms in white, pink or purple-blue. The spring to early-summer flowers may be single or surrounded by a larger, colored cup.
Height and spread Height 1½–3 feet (45–90 cm); spread 1 foot (30 cm).
Best climate and site Zones 6–10; full sun in mild climates; average, well-drained soil.
Landscape uses Canterbury bells are naturals for cottage gardens. In beds and borders, grow them in small clumps with later-blooming annuals and perennials that can fill in the spaces left after you remove spent plants in midsummer.
Growing guidelines These biennials need two growing periods from seedling to flowering. Sow the seed outdoors in summer in pots. Cover seed lightly and keep soil moist until seedlings appear. Transplant in autumn or early spring, spacing plants 1 foot (30 cm) apart.
Good companions Larkspur, baby's breath.
Cultivars Look for named double, dwarf and pink varieties.
Comments Pinch off spent blooms to prolong flowering. Pull out plants that have finished blooming.

Cleome hassleriana
CAPPARACEAE

CLEOME

Cleome is a must for butterfly gardens; it's also popular with bees. Plant it in large groupings to show off the spidery white, pink or lavender flowers.

Description Cleome is a fast-growing, half-hardy annual. Its tall, sturdy stems and palmlike leaves are slightly prickly, as small spines grow on the stems and undersides of leaves. From midsummer until midautumn, enjoy globes of spidery, pink or white four-petaled flowers. These are followed by long, narrow seedpods that split to scatter seed.

Height and spread Height 3–4 feet (90–120 cm); spread 1½ feet (45 cm).

Best climate and site Zones 9–11; full sun to light shade; well-drained soil with added organic matter.

Landscape uses Try cleome in the back of flower beds, cottage garden borders or in the center of a round bed, for height and color.

Growing guidelines Grows easily from seed scattered in garden beds, or look for nursery seedlings for planting after the last frost date. Space transplants or thin seedlings to 1 foot (30 cm) apart. Cleome usually self-sows prolifically.

Good companions Roses, asters, daisies, cosmos and other summer-flowering, cottage garden plants.

Other common names Spider flower.

Cultivars Compact named varieties grow less than 3 feet (90 cm) tall.

Comments Deadhead to encourage side blooms and reduce seeding.

Cosmos bipinnatus
ASTERACEAE

COSMOS

Use fast-growing cosmos to fill spaces left by early-blooming annuals and perennials. Pick flowers or pinch off spent blooms for more buds.

Description From late summer to autumn, cosmos has pink or white, daisy-like blooms on tall, finely leafed stems. The flowers can be 4 inches (10 cm) across with golden centers.

Height and spread Height 3–4 feet (90–120 cm); spread to 1½ feet (45 cm).

Best climate and site Zones 8–10; full sun to partial shade; average to moist, well-drained soil in a sheltered spot.

Landscape uses Cosmos adds height and color to beds, borders and meadows and grows quickly to fill gaps left by spent spring annuals.

Growing guidelines Plant seedlings in spring or, after last frost date, scatter seed where plants are to grow. Space or thin seedlings to 6–12 inches (15–30 cm) apart. Push sturdy pieces of twiggy brush into the soil around young plants to support stems as they grow, or stake individual stems as needed. Or just let the plants sprawl; they'll send up more flowering stems.

Good companions Dahlias, roses and summer- to autumn-flowering plants.

Cultivars Named dwarf forms. The yellow cosmos is *C. sulphureus*.

Comments Will self-sow. Adapts to hot, dry summers. Great for cut flowers.

Dianthus barbatus
CARYOPHYLLACEAE

SWEET WILLIAM

Sweet William plants may rebloom the following year if sheared back after flowering, but you'll get a better show by starting new plants each year.

Description This short-lived perennial is grown as a frost-hardy biennial or annual. An old-fashioned favorite, it forms clumps of narrow, lance-shaped, green leaves. The stems are topped with dense, rounded clusters of small flowers in early to mid-summer. The five-petaled flowers are red, pink or white, some with eyes or zones of contrasting colors.

Height and spread Height 12–18 inches (30–45 cm); spread to about 8–12 inches (20–30 cm).

Best climate and site Zones 4–10; full sun to partial shade; average, well-drained, slightly alkaline soil.

Landscape uses Sweet William looks super as an early summer filler for beds and borders.

Growing guidelines For earliest bloom, grow as a biennial: Sow seed outdoors in pots or in a nursery bed in summer, then move plants to their garden position in autumn, or plant seedlings after frost has passed. Space transplants 8–10 inches (20–25 cm) apart. Sweet William will self-sow once established.

Good companions Roses, cottage flowers.

Cultivars Look for dwarf cultivars (6 inches [15 cm] tall), with bicolored flowers in white, pink, rose and red.

Dianthus chinensis
CARYOPHYLLACEAE

CHINA PINK

China pinks look equally lovely in beds, borders and containers. Pinching off spent flowers can be time-consuming, but it will prolong flowering.

Description A biennial or short-lived, tufty perennial in warm climates, in cool Zones it is usually grown as an annual, although it is frost-hardy. The upright stems bear 1-inch (2.5-cm) wide, flat flowers with broad petals that are fringed at the tips. Leaves are narrow and gray-green and flower color includes white, red, pink, mauve and rose.
Height and spread Height 8–12 inches (20–30 cm); similar spread.
Best climate and site Zones 7–10; full sun but with afternoon shade in hot-summer areas; average, well-drained, slightly alkaline soil.
Landscape uses A cottage garden favorite; grow to spill over rocks, or to soften path edges. Try a few in pots, too.
Growing guidelines Buy plants in spring, or sow seed directly into the garden around 2–3 weeks before the last frost date. Thin seedlings or set transplants to stand 6–8 inches (15–20 cm) apart.
Other common names Rainbow pink, Indian pink.
Cultivars Many named varieties, including fringed flowers.
Comments The white, pink or red summer flowers are seen almost year-round in warm gardens.

Digitalis purpurea
SCROPHULARIACEAE

COMMON FOXGLOVE

Cut down the spent flower stems to keep the garden tidy, or allow the seeds to form so plants can self-sow. All parts of this plant are poisonous.

Description Foxgloves have spires of thimble-shaped flowers. The 2–3-inch (5–7.5-cm) blooms may be white, cream, pink or pinkish purple and often have contrasting spots on the inside. As foxgloves are biennials, the flowers bloom in the second year of growth.
Height and spread Height 3–5 feet (90–150 cm); spread to 2 feet (60 cm).
Best climate and site Zones 5–10; full sun to partial shade (afternoon shade in hot-summer areas); well-drained but moisture-retentive soil.
Landscape uses The tall spires are effective when plants are massed in lightly shaded woodlands. Grow foxgloves in the back of borders, where other plants will fill the space left in midsummer.
Growing guidelines Grow as biennials. Sow seed in late summer or allow existing plants to set seed after flowering. Plant out seedlings in autumn 1 foot (30 cm) apart. Tall cultivars may need staking.
Good companions Deciduous trees, forget-me-nots, spring annuals, bulbs, perennials.
Cultivars Dwarf and apricot varieties.
Comments Plants can dry out in warm climates if the rosette of gray, felty leaves stops water reaching the root zone. Watch for aphids and two-spotted mite on leaves.

Erysimum cheiri
BRASSICACEAE

WALLFLOWER

Fragrant wallflowers are normally orange or yellow in color, but they also bloom in shades of red, pink or creamy white. They are lovely to pick for a fragrant posy.

Description This perennial is commonly grown as a half-hardy annual or biennial for late winter or spring color. The bushy clumps are topped with clusters of 1-inch (2.5-cm) wide, four-petaled, fragrant flowers from late winter to early summer.
Height and spread Height 1–2 feet (30–60 cm); spread to 1 foot (30 cm).
Best climate and site Zones 7–10; full sun to partial shade; well-drained soil, ideally neutral to slightly alkaline.
Landscape uses Grow in masses for spots of early color and scent. Also good for window boxes and growing in walls.
Growing guidelines Sow seed or plant seedlings. To grow as annuals, sow outdoors in early spring. Set plants out 8–12 inches (20–30 cm) apart around the last frost date. In frost-free areas, grow wallflowers as biennials. Sow seed in pots or in a nursery bed in early summer; move plants to their flowering position in early autumn. Pull out plants when they have finished blooming.
Good companions Tulips, pansies, forget-me-nots.
Cultivars Dwarf cultivars available.
Comments Water during dry spells to keep the soil evenly moist.

Eschscholzia californica
PAPAVERACEAE

CALIFORNIA POPPY

The flowers of California poppy open during sunny days but close in cloudy weather and at night. Pinch off developing seedpods to prolong flowering.

Description Usually grown as a hardy annual. Plants form loose clumps of deeply cut, blue-green leaves. The thin stems are topped with pointed buds that unfurl into single, semidouble or double flowers up to 3 inches (7.5 cm) across from early summer to autumn. The silky-looking petals are usually orange or yellow, but they can also bloom in white, pink or red.
Height and spread Height 1–1½ feet (30–45 cm); spread 6–12 inches (15–30 cm).
Best climate and site Zones 6–11; full sun; average to sandy, well-drained soil.
Landscape uses Colorful, easy-to-grow fillers that are also excellent in meadow and water-saving gardens.
Growing guidelines Transplants poorly, so sow seed directly into the garden in very early spring (or autumn in frost-free areas). Thin seedlings to 6 inches (15 cm) apart. Plants usually self-sow in mild-winter areas but may revert to orange.
Good companions Cottage garden plants, including lavender, dusty miller, succulents and roses.
Cultivars Single colors available.
Comments If blooms are sparse by midsummer, cut plants back by about one-third to encourage a new flush of flowers.

Euphorbia marginata
EUPHORBIACEAE

SNOW-ON-THE-MOUNTAIN

Shrubby snow-on-the-mountain forms showy clumps of white-marked leaves by late summer. Use this old-fashioned favorite as a filler or accent.

Description This shrubby annual is grown for its showy foliage. Young plants produce upright stems with oblong to pointed, green leaves. In mid- to late summer, the stems begin to branch, and the upper leaves are edged with white. At the branch tips, flower clusters are surrounded by white, petal-like bracts.
Height and spread Height 2–4 feet (60–120 cm); spread to 1–1½ feet (30–45 cm).
Best climate and site Zones 4–10; full sun; well-drained soil.
Landscape uses A foliage accent in flower beds, borders or rockeries. Use them to highlight pathways and entrances.
Growing guidelines Grows readily from seed (and may self-sow), or plant seedlings after last frost. Thin seedlings or space transplants to 1 foot (30 cm). Plants may lean or flop by late summer. Overcome this by staking young plants in early to midsummer, or grow compact varieties.
Good companions Hibiscus, daylilies, geraniums, late-flowering annuals.
Cultivars Compact varieties only grow to around 1½ feet (45 cm) tall.
Comments Handle cut stems carefully; they leak a milky sap that can irritate skin, eyes and mouth.

Helianthus annuus
ASTERACEAE

COMMON SUNFLOWER

Common sunflowers are child-friendly plants, much-loved for their large, showy blooms (and often for their tasty seeds as well).

Description This easy-to-grow plant has large, sturdy stalks with coarse, heart-shaped leaves. From midsummer to autumn, the stems are topped with flat, daisy-like flowers to 1 foot (30 cm) wide or more. The flower heads normally have a purple-brown center, with yellow, bronze, mahogany-red or orange petals.
Height and spread Height 2–8 feet (60–240 cm) or more; spread 1–1½ feet (30–45 cm).
Best climate and site Zones 4–11; full sun; average, well-drained soil.
Landscape uses Great as a tall-growing screen along a fence, or to add height to a sunny border. A fun plant for children to grow from seed.
Growing guidelines Fast-growing plants to grow from seed sown directly in the garden, or seedlings planted after your last frost date. Thin seedlings to 1 foot (30 cm) apart. Keep well-watered.
Good companions Nasturtiums, daisies, vegetables and cottage garden plants.
Cultivars Dwarf varieties grow to around 2½ feet (75 cm) tall. Also some forms have double flowers.
Comments Sunflowers can drop their lower leaves, so hide bare "ankles" with a low plant. Seeds attract birds.

Impatiens spp.
BALSAMINACEAE

IMPATIENS

New Guinea impatiens (above left) has attractively colored leaves and iridescent flowers. There are double-flowered varieties of busy Lizzie (above right) that resemble clusters of tiny rosebuds.

Description These are tender annuals or perennials grown as annuals. The 1–2-inch (2.5–5-cm) wide, single or double flowers bloom from midsummer until frost (or year-round in warm, frost-free climates). Flowers are white or shades of pink, rose, mauve, purple, coral, orange or red and are almost iridescent on New Guinea impatiens. Some impatiens have a flower with a colored eye. Petals have a silky sheen.

Height and spread Height 2–2½ feet (60–75 cm); spread to 1½ feet (45 cm).

Best climate and site Zones 9–12 in sun to partial shade; average to moist, well-drained soil with added organic matter.

Landscape uses Use these easy-going plants to brighten shady corners in gardens, containers or hanging baskets. Balsam, particularly the double-flowered forms, has an upright growth that gives an old-fashioned flavor to the garden. For the best show, set out three or more plants to form lush clumps. Busy Lizzie can be used for a massed floral display for summer color in sunny or shaded garden beds. White-flowered varieties in particular brighten dull corners. Also choose them as an accent plant for pots or window boxes. New Guinea impatiens, especially forms

with boldly colored and patterned leaves, add a lush tropical feel to shady gardens, ferneries or as hanging baskets.

Growing guidelines Impatiens is sold as seedlings or potted plants, or can be grown from seed or cutting. Many will also self-sow once established and, in warm climates, can become weedy. Sow seed or plant seedlings directly into garden after last frost date (or year-round in warm, frost-free climates). Thin seedlings or space transplants 12–16 inches (30–40 cm) apart. Water daily during dry spells, or if plants are in containers or growing in a hot, sunny situation. Water-stressed plants will tend to wilt.

Good companions Shade-loving plants, such as azaleas, camellias, ferns and large-leaved foliage plants.

Other common names Balsam; busy Lizzie (also patient Lucy, patience, sultana).

Cultivars Much variety in flower color, plant size and leaf pattern. For a strong bedding display, select compact, dwarf varieties. Propagate distinctive forms by taking cuttings, to maintain particular flower color or leaf pattern.

Comments Impatiens that self-sow freely can become weedy in warm, frost-free gardens. The common name of busy Lizzie comes from the way the ribbed, swollen seedpods burst open at the slightest touch, scattering seeds far and wide.

Ipomoea tricolor
CONVOLVULACEAE

MORNING GLORY

Morning glories grow slowly at first, then really take off when the weather heats up in midsummer. Established vines are generally problem-free.

Description A tender, perennial vine grown as a tender annual in cool to mild Zones. This fast-growing climber has twining stems and heart-shaped leaves. Buds open in early morning to reveal trumpet-shaped flowers up to 5 inches (12.5 cm) across. Each flower lasts only 1 day, but new buds open every day through the summer.

Height and spread Height to 8 feet (2.4 m) or more; ultimate height and spread depend on the size of the support.

Best climate and site Zones 8–12; full sun to light afternoon shade; average, well-drained soil.

Landscape uses Morning glory makes a quick-growing screen for shade or privacy through the warmer months. Let it climb through large shrubs or roses, or on a trellis or wall behind a cottage garden.

Growing guidelines Grow from seed sown directly into the garden or pot after the last frost. Set plants or thin seedlings to 8–12 inches (20–30 cm) apart.

Good companions Roses, cottage garden plants, summer annuals.

Cultivars Look for named varieties, including bicolored cultivars, such as sky blue flowers with a white center.

Comments Some species of morning glory are invasive weeds in warm climates.

Lathyrus odoratus
FABACEAE

SWEET PEA

Dozens of sweet pea cultivars are available in a range of heights and colors. Many modern cultivars aren't very fragrant; check catalog descriptions.

Description Sweet peas flower from winter to spring and into summer in cooler climates. Colors from white to shades of pink, red or purple.

Height and spread Height usually 4–6 feet (1.2–1.8 m); spread to around 6–12 inches (15–30 cm).

Best climate and site Zones 4–10; full sun with afternoon shade in hot-summer areas; evenly moist soil with organic matter and a handful of lime.

Landscape uses Train sweet peas up a tripod as an accent, or grow on a trellis, against a brick wall or a fence. Dwarf varieties can be used in window boxes, hanging baskets and pots.

Growing guidelines Plant seed into moist soils in autumn (or early spring in cold climates) and don't water again until shoots appear, usually 7–10 days. Plant seedlings in autumn in warm Zones or after last frost date in cool climates (or plant seedlings in midspring). Space plants 4–6 inches (10–15 cm) apart. Water when dry and pull out vines when they stop blooming.

Good companions Cottage garden plants and bulbs.

Cultivars There are named scented and dwarf, non-climbing varieties available.

Comments Plants are prone to mildew.

Lobelia erinus
CAMPANULACEAE

EDGING LOBELIA

If you grow edging lobelia from seed or buy seedlings in trays, transplant them in clumps (rather than separating them into individual plants) to avoid damaging the stems.

Description This tender perennial is often grown as a half-hardy annual. Plants form trailing or mounding clumps of slender stems with small, narrow, green leaves and are covered with ½–¾-inch (12–18-mm) wide flowers from late spring until early autumn. The five-petaled flowers bloom in white, blue, purple and pinkish red.

Height and spread Height 6–8 inches (15–20 cm); spread 6–10 inches (15–25 cm).

Best climate and site Zones 7–11; full sun to partial shade; well-drained soil with added organic matter.

Landscape uses Grow at the front of beds and borders or as a filler. Cascading types make attractive fillers for containers, window boxes and hanging baskets.

Growing guidelines Plant seedlings or small, potted plants in spring, 6–8 inches (15–20 cm) apart after danger of frost has passed. Water when dry. Shear plants back by half after each flush of bloom and fertilize to promote reflowering.

Good companions Cottage garden plants, annuals such as sweet alyssum, marigolds or violas, and bulbs.

Cultivars Many blue, mauve, violet, pink or white-flowered cultivars. Some are more compact, others trail.

Lobularia maritima
BRASSICACEAE

SWEET ALYSSUM, SWEET ALICE

Sweet alyssum is a long-lasting annual. It may stop blooming during summer heat, but will start again when cooler conditions return. Shear off spent flowers and water thoroughly for new growth.

Description Sweet alyssum is a tender perennial grown as a hardy annual. Plants form low mounds of clusters of many ¼-inch (6-mm) blooms in summer and autumn. The sweetly scented, four-petaled flowers bloom in white, pink and purple. Sweet alyssum is also listed in seed catalogs as *Alyssum maritimum.*

Height and spread Height 4–8 inches (10–20 cm); spread to 10–12 inches (25–30 cm).

Best climate and site Zones 7–10; full sun to partial shade (especially in hot-summer areas); well-drained soil.

Landscape uses Grow as an edging or filler in flower beds and borders or as a groundcover under roses and shrubs. It also grows well in pots and window boxes.

Growing guidelines Plant seedlings or small, potted plants in spring, or sow seed directly into the garden in mid- to late spring. Space plants or thin seedlings to 6 inches (15 cm). Plants usually self-sow.

Good companions Cottage garden plants; good as a contrast to blue flowers.

Cultivars There are many named, single colors available.

Comments Hardy and easy to grow.

Matthiola incana
BRASSICACEAE

COMMON STOCK

The fragrant, single or double flowers of common stock have white, pink, red, yellow and purple blooms. Their perfume is wonderful in the garden or indoors in flower arrangements.

Description The fast-growing, bushy plants have upright stems and lance-shaped, grayish leaves. The stems are topped with spikes of four-petaled, 1-inch (2.5-cm) wide flowers in summer.

Height and spread Height 1–2 feet (30–60 cm); spread to 1 foot (30 cm).

Best climate and site Zones 6–10; full sun; well-drained soil with some added organic matter.

Growing guidelines Plant seedlings 6–8 inches (15–20 cm) apart in late winter. Mulch plants to keep the roots cool and moist. Liquid feed as plants grow. Water when dry.

Landscape uses Use as a filler in beds and borders near your house or outdoor sitting areas, where you can enjoy the fragrance. Dwarf varieties can be used as border plants.

Good companions Cottage garden plants, especially pansy, viola and sweet alyssum and spring bulbs.

Cultivars Dwarf plants in many colors.

Comments Stocks are prone to aphids, and fungal diseases such as mildew and root rot. Treat fungal problems with fungicide or remove affected plants. Deadhead or pick the flowers. Stocks should not be grown in the same spot year after year.

Nemesia strumosa
SCROPHULARIACEAE

NEMESIA

Nemesia usually stops flowering in warm weather, but plants may recover and rebloom if you cut them back by half, water thoroughly, and give them a dose of fertilizer.

Description Nemesia forms clumps of brightly colored flowers in spring and summer. The 1-inch (2.5-cm) wide trumpet-shaped flowers are white, pink, red, orange, yellow, lilac and light blue.

Height and spread Height 1–2 feet (30–60 cm); spread 6–8 inches.

Best climate and site Zones 9–11 but best in cooler summer climates; full sun to partial shade; evenly moist, well-drained soil with added organic matter. Nemesia needs a long, cool growing season; it does not tolerate heat or humidity.

Growing guidelines Set nemesia plants out 4–6 inches (10–15 cm) apart after the danger of frost has passed. Short pieces of twiggy brush stuck into the soil around young plants help support the stems as they grow. Promote branching and more flowers by pinching out growth tips.

Landscape uses Nemesia makes an attractive edging for beds and borders or as mass planting in the garden, window boxes or containers.

Good companions Plant among summer-flowering bulbs.

Comments Nemesia needs good drainage, regular watering, liquid feeding, and protection from winds.

Nemophila menziesii
HYDROPHYLLACEAE

BABY BLUE-EYES

Sow baby blue-eyes among the emerging shoots of spring bulbs to form a colorful, fast-growing carpet that will cover the ripening bulb foliage after bloom.

Description Baby blue-eyes forms sprawling mounds of slender, trailing stems. The 1-inch (2.5-cm) wide, bowl-shaped, summer-blooming flowers are sky blue with a white center.

Height and spread Height 6–8 inches (15–20 cm); spread to 1 foot (30 cm).

Best climate and site Zones 7–11; full sun to partial shade (morning sun and afternoon shade is ideal); moist, well-drained soil with added organic matter.

Landscape uses A charming filler around spring bulbs or an edging for shady flower beds and borders. Also looks super trailing out of pots or among pavers.

Growing guidelines Grows quickly from seed sown directly into the garden. Make first sowings in early spring (or in autumn in mild-winter areas) and successive sowings every 3 weeks until summer to extend flowering. Thin seedlings to 6 inches (15 cm) apart. If plants stop blooming in midsummer, shear them back halfway and water thoroughly to promote rebloom.

Good companions Roses, spring bulbs.

Cultivars Usually sold in mixed colors but a named white variety with black speckles is available.

Comments Grow from seed as seedlings don't transplant well. Plants often self-sow.

Nicotiana alata
SOLANACEAE

FLOWERING TOBACCO

Hybrids and red-flowered types of flowering tobacco often have little or no scent, but old-fashioned, white-flowered types are fragrant, especially at night.

Description The trumpet-shaped flowers in white, pink, purple and red grow from a rosette and open toward evening. Main flowering occurs in summer to early autumn.

Height and spread Height 1½–3 feet (45–90 cm); spread to 1 foot (30 cm).

Best climate and site Zones 7–11; full sun to partial shade; average to moist, well-drained soil with added organic matter.

Landscape uses Grow some in the garden for fresh flowers. Plant fragrant, white-flowered types around outdoor sitting areas for evening enjoyment. Try compact types in containers.

Growing guidelines Buy seedlings in spring and plant them out 10–12 inches (25–30 cm) apart after the danger of frost has passed. Water during dry spells and liquid feed regularly. Cut out spent stems to prolong the bloom season. Plants may self-sow.

Good companions Cottage garden plants; blue petunias.

Cultivars Dwarf forms are available as well as a perfumed, lime green cultivar.

Comments Watch out for snails and caterpillars, which can be a problem. Use snail baits to protect small plants, but keep baits well away from pets and wildlife.

Nigella damascena
RANUNCULACEAE

LOVE-IN-A-MIST

Sowing every 3 to 4 weeks from early spring to early summer can extend the bloom season of love-in-a-mist through the summer into autumn.

Description A fast-growing, hardy annual that forms bushy mounds of slender stems with fern-like, bright green leaves. Single or double, 1–2-inch (2.5–5-cm) wide flowers of blue, pink or white are followed by decorative, swollen, striped seedpods with short, pointed horns.

Height and spread Height 18–24 inches (45–60 cm); spread 6–8 inches (15–20 cm).

Best climate and site Zones 6–10; full sun to partial shade; average, well-drained soil; shelter from winds and hot sun.

Landscape uses An unusual filler in beds, borders and cottage gardens. Allow flowers to mature into the puffy seedpods as these prolong the display and can also be used as cut floral decoration.

Growing guidelines Sow directly into the garden from early spring and thin seedlings to 6 inches (15 cm) apart. Established plants are care-free. Plants may self-sow.

Other common names Fennel flower, devil-in-the-bush.

Cultivars There are double forms.

Comments These are best sown in the garden as seeds because love-in-a-mist does not transplant well. Allow some of the flowers to mature so plants can self-sow, but deadhead to prolong flowering if seedpods are not required.

Papaver nudicaule
PAPAVERACEAE

ICELAND POPPY

Enjoy bunches of poppies indoors as they are excellent cut flowers. Picking or removing spent flower stems will also mean the plants flower longer.

Description Poppies have attractive, furry green buds held on slender, leafless stems above clumps of gray-green leaves. The buds pop open to release colorful, cup-shaped flowers with silky petals. Flowers are up to 2–4 inches (5–10 cm) wide.

Height and spread Height 1–1½ feet (30–45 cm); spread 4–6 inches (10–15 cm).

Best climate and site Zones 2–10; full sun and protected from wind; rich, well-drained to dry soil. Grows poorly in hot weather. In warm-winter climates, Iceland poppy flowers in late winter; in cold-winter zones, they flower late spring to summer.

Landscape uses Great for early color in beds and borders.

Growing guidelines Grow from seed sown directly into garden or plant seedlings. Plant in late autumn or very early spring for summer bloom. In hot-summer areas, sow late summer to early autumn for late winter to spring bloom. Thin seedlings to about 6 inches (15 cm) apart. Liquid feed when buds appear and then fortnightly.

Good companions Cottage garden plants, freesias, ranunculus.

Cultivars Poppies are available in many colors and some dwarf forms.

Comments Drooping stems indicate fungal disease.

Papaver rhoeas
PAPAVERACEAE

CORN POPPY

Corn poppies are meadow flowers grown as hardy annuals for their late spring to summer, mostly scarlet, cup-shaped flowers.

Description The cup-shaped flowers of four silky, crinkled petals open from plump, hairy buds. The 2–4-inch (5–10-cm) wide, summer blooms are most often a glowing scarlet with a black center. Shirley poppy is a strain selected for single or double flowers in white, pink, red and bicolors.

Height and spread Height 2–3 feet (60–90 cm); spread 6–8 inches (15–20 cm).

Best climate and site Zones 5–9; full sun; well-drained soil.

Landscape uses Corn poppies add sparkle to meadow gardens or use them as fillers in beds and borders.

Growing guidelines Corn poppy is easy to grow from seed sown directly into the garden in late autumn or early spring. In cool seasons, a second sowing in midspring can help extend the bloom season. Thin seedlings to 6–8 inches (15–20 cm) apart.

Good companions Meadow plants, cottage garden plants, California poppies.

Other common names Flanders poppy, Shirley poppy.

Cultivars Shirley poppy has a pale heart instead of the black center of the corn poppy and there are double-flowered varieties.

Comments Plants will self-sow.

Pelargonium x hortorum
GERANIACEAE

ZONAL GERANIUM

Colorful and dependable, zonal geraniums are a mainstay of summer flower gardens. You can also bring them indoors in the autumn.

Description In cold-winter areas these tender perennials are grown as annuals. Their pungent leaves can be marked with dark green or brown zones. The single or double flowers (2 inches [5 cm] across) bloom in clusters from late spring until frost in white, pink, red, salmon and bicolors.

Height and spread Height 1–2 feet (30–60 cm); spread usually 1–1½ feet inches (30–45 cm).

Best climate and site Zones 5–10; full sun; average, well-drained soil.

Landscape uses Grow in beds and borders as accents or fillers; or grow in containers, hanging baskets and window boxes.

Growing guidelines Plants grow readily from cuttings taken in spring or autumn, and can be raised from seed or seedling. Plant geraniums after all threat of frost has passed. Space plants about 1–1½ feet (30–45 cm) apart. To bring the plants inside for the winter, leave them in their pots when you set them into the soil; then you can lift the plants easily in autumn.

Cultivars Many cultivars are available in a wide range of heights and colors.

Good companions Lavender or lavender cotton, succulents, colorful annuals.

Comments During the summer, pinch off spent flower stems to promote rebloom.

Petunia x hybrida
SOLANACEAE

PETUNIA

Petunias are tender perennials usually grown as half-hardy annuals. They may self-sow, but the seedlings seldom resemble the parent plants.

Description Both the leaves and stems are hairy and somewhat sticky. Funnel-shaped, single or double flowers bloom from late spring to early summer until frost, in nearly every color of the rainbow; some have stripes, streaks or contrasting eyes.

Height and spread Height 6–10 inches (15–25 cm); spread to 1 foot (30 cm).

Best climate and site Zones 6–10; full sun, light shade; average to moist, well-drained soil.

Landscape uses Petunias are favorites for flower beds and borders. Massed together or mixed with other plants, they fill gaps left by spring-flowering annuals and bulbs. They look great spilling out of containers, hanging baskets and window boxes.

Growing guidelines Petunias are popular annuals, and many types are sold each spring. Plant seedlings 8–12 inches (20–30 cm) apart after danger of frost has passed. Pinch tips when plants are 6 inches (15 cm) high for compact shape.

Cultivars Petunias are available in an amazing range of flower forms and colors: There are single and double forms, single colors, multicolors, ruffles, and compact and taller varieties.

Good companions Annual phlox.

Comments Snails can be a problem.

Phaseolus coccineus
FABACEAE

SCARLET RUNNER BEAN

Scarlet runner beans are equally at home in the flower and vegetable garden. The fast-growing vines produce showy blooms and edible seedpods.

Description This tender, perennial climber is grown as a half-hardy annual. The twining stems produce clusters of 1-inch (2.5-cm) long, orange-red flowers that bloom from midsummer until frost. The pealike flowers are followed by long, silvery green pods.

Height and spread Height 6–8 feet (1.8–2.4 m); ultimate height and spread depend on the size of the support.

Best climate and site Zones 3–10; full sun; average, well-drained soil.

Landscape uses Use for quick shade, privacy, to hide an ugly fence or as a garden accent trained up a tripod.

Growing guidelines Before planting, erect a support of stout posts or plant along an existing fence. This fast-growing vine is easy to start from seed sown directly into the garden. Wait until 12 weeks after the last frost date, when the soil is warm; then plant the seed 1 inch (2.5 cm) deep. Thin seedlings to 8 inches (20 cm) apart.

Good companions Salvias, daylilies, ornamental silverbeet, vegetables.

Cultivars White-and-red and white-flowering varieties, and dwarf forms that don't climb.

Comments Bean set may be erratic in warm climates.

Phlox drummondii
POLEMONIACEAE

ANNUAL PHLOX

Annual phlox is a hardy annual grown for its colorful flowers. If plants stop blooming, cut them back by half and water thoroughly; they should resprout and rebloom in autumn.

Description From midsummer to autumn, these bushy clumps are topped with clusters of flat, five-petaled flowers, each ½–1 inch (12–25 mm) across. The flowers bloom in a wide range of colors, including white, pink, red, pale yellow, blue and purple; some have a contrasting eye.

Height and spread Height 6–18 inches (15–45 cm); spread 6–8 inches (15–20 cm).

Best climate and site Zones 6–10; full sun; average, well-drained soil.

Landscape uses An excellent filler for beds and borders. Try compact cultivars in container gardens and window boxes.

Growing guidelines Plant annuals in spring or sow seed directly into garden in clumps after danger of frost has passed. Set plants or thin seedlings to 6 inches (15 cm).

Good companions Cottage garden plants, petunias and other summer-flowering annuals.

Cultivars There are dwarf varieties available that grow to 4–6 inches (10–15 cm) high and many colors, some with contrasting eyes and pointed petals.

Comments Water around the plants, not over the flowers, since this can cause fungal problems; mulch around the plants to keep the roots cool.

Portulaca grandiflora
PORTULACACEAE

ROSE MOSS

Rose moss comes in many vibrant colors, including white, pink, red, orange, yellow and magenta. The flowers tend to close by afternoon and stay closed on cloudy days.

Description A low-growing, tender annual that forms creeping mats of fleshy, reddish, many-branched stems with small, thick, almost needle-like leaves. Single or double, 1-inch (2.5-cm) wide flowers bloom from early summer through autumn.

Height and spread Height to 6 inches (15 cm); spread 6–8 inches (15–20 cm).

Best climate and site Zones 6–11; full sun; average, well-drained to dry soil.

Landscape uses A great groundcover for sunny, dry, rocky slopes. It is also charming as an edging for sunny beds and borders or cascading out of pots and hanging baskets.

Growing guidelines Plant seedlings about 6 inches (15 cm) apart or sow seed directly into the garden after the danger of frost has passed; keep the soil moist until seedlings appear. Thin seedlings only if crowded. Established plants may self-sow. Water when dry. Plants are drought-hardy.

Good companions Succulents.

Other common names Sun plant, pig face.

Cultivars There are many cultivars available in bright colors, and single and double flowers. Modern varieties may stay open more reliably in cloudy weather.

Comments The flowers close on dull days and at night.

Rudbeckia hirta
ASTERACEAE

BLACK-EYED SUSAN

The daisy-like blooms of black-eyed Susan have golden yellow outer petals and a purple-brown or black, raised center. They are excellent cut flowers.

Description These plants grow from clumps of long, hairy leaves and flower from summer to autumn. The large, daisy-like, yellow flowers are up to 2–3 inches (5–7.5 cm) wide.

Height and spread Height 2–3 feet (60–90 cm); spread to 1 foot (30 cm).

Best climate and site Zones: 3–10; full sun to light shade; average, well-drained to dry soil.

Landscape uses Bright and cheerful in beds and borders. They're also a natural choice for meadow gardens.

Growing guidelines Plant seedlings 1 foot (30 cm) apart in early spring. Sow seed directly into garden in early spring for plants that flower the following year.

Good companions Summer- and autumn-flowering cottage garden plants, dahlias, globe amaranth, gray-toned foliage plants.

Other common names Gloriosa daisy, marmalade daisy, coneflower.

Cultivars There are cultivars available in yellow, orange, brown and reddish brown, and single, semidouble and double flowers; also named dwarf varieties growing to 14 inches (35 cm).

Comments Plants often self-sow; to prevent self-seeding, remove spent flowers before they set seed.

Salvia splendens
LAMIACEAE

SCARLET SAGE

Compact cultivars of scarlet sage tend to flower mostly in summer; taller types generally start blooming in midsummer and last until frost. Pinch off faded spikes.

Description The showy spikes of colorful, petal-like bracts and long, tubular flowers grow from clumps of upright stems. Usually, fire-engine red, scarlet sage also flowers in tones of white, pink, salmon and purple.

Height and spread Height 1–2 feet (30–60 cm); spread to 1 foot (30 cm).

Best climate and site Zones 6–10; full sun; well-drained soil.

Landscape uses If you enjoy mixing bright colors, grow scarlet sage as an edging or filler for flower beds and borders. For a somewhat more restrained effect, surround scarlet sage with leafy, green herbs and ornamental grasses.

Growing guidelines Plant seedlings after the danger of frost has passed; space them 8–12 inches (20–30 cm) apart. Fertilize several times during the summer.

Good companions White flowers, such as sweet alyssum or petunias, or silver foliage plants, such as dusty miller. Use as a colorful filler within a formal box hedge.

Cultivars Named cultivars in colors from white to pink, red and purple are available.

Comments Salvias suffer if they are overwatered.

Senecio cineraria
ASTERACEAE

DUSTY MILLER

Dusty miller can live through mild winters, but second-year plants tend to be more open. Where uniformity is important (as in an edging), start with new plants each year.

Description A silver foliage shrub that has clusters of yellow, daisy-like flowers in summer. The silver leaves are deeply lobed. Dusty miller is also listed in seed catalogs as *Cineraria maritima*.

Height and spread Height 8–24 inches (20–60 cm); spread to 1 foot (30 cm).

Best climate and site Zones 8–11 (but not very humid or wet-summer regions); full sun; average, well-drained soil.

Landscape uses Dusty miller's silvery foliage is invaluable as an edging or accent for flower beds, borders and all kinds of container plantings. It contrasts well with white and pastel flowering plants. Also useful in seaside gardens as it is salt-tolerant.

Growing guidelines Plant seedlings 8 inches (20 cm) apart after danger of frost has passed. Pinch out stem tips in early summer to promote bushy growth and to check flowering (flowers of dusty miller are generally unwanted).

Good companions Cottage garden plants, roses, or drought-tolerant plants in gravel gardens.

Cultivars Some cultivars have finely cut leaves.

Comments The silvery leaves and stems of dusty miller are good for drying.

Solenostemon scutellarioides
LAMIACEAE

COLEUS

Keep favorite coleus plants from year to year by taking cuttings in summer; they'll root quickly in water. Pot up the cuttings for winter; then put them outdoors in spring.

Description These tender perennials are grown as bushy, tender annuals. Their sturdy, square stems carry showy, patterned leaves with scalloped or ruffled edges. Each leaf can have several different colors, with zones, edges or splashes in shades of red, pink, orange, yellow and cream.
Height and spread Height 6–24 inches (15–60 cm); spread 8–12 inches (20–30 cm).
Best climate and site Zones 8–12; partial shade; average to moist, well-drained soil with added organic matter.
Landscape uses Coleus brings all-season color to beds, borders and containers. Groups of mixed leaf patterns can look too busy when combined with flowering plants, so grow them alone in masses.
Growing guidelines Plant seedlings or small, potted plants 8–12 inches (20–30 cm) apart after danger of frost has passed. Water regularly so soil is damp. Pinch off spikes of the pale blue flowers to promote leafy growth. Plants are perennial in subtropical and tropical frost-free gardens.
Good companions Ferns, tropical shrubs.
Cultivars Some named cultivars with strong leaf color are available.
Comments Used for displays in conservatories in cool-summer areas.

Tagetes hybrids
ASTERACEAE

MARIGOLDS

Marigolds can add bright color to any sunny spot. Mix them with other annuals and perennials, or grow them alone in masses.

Description Marigolds are grown for their bright, summer and autumn flowers. There are two main species. African marigolds (*T. erecta*) are large plants, with 1½–3-feet (45–90-cm) stems and large, usually double, yellow or orange flowers. French marigolds (*T. patula*) are daintier, with smaller, single or double flowers in yellow, orange or red on 1-foot (30-cm) tall plants.
Height and spread Height 6–36 inches (15–90 cm); spread 6–18 inches (15–45 cm).
Best climate and site Zones 5–11; full sun; average, well-drained soil.
Landscape uses Grow marigolds as summer fillers or edgings for flower beds, borders, vegetable gardens and containers, or as a flowering hedge.
Growing guidelines Plant seedlings of dwarf types 6–8 inches (15–20 cm) apart; leave 1–1½ feet (30–45 cm) between larger cultivars. Sow seed of small types directly into the garden after frost.
Good companions Vegetables and salad greens, herbs, cottage garden plants.
Cultivars Tall, dwarf, single and double flowers, in shades of cream, yellow, orange, mahogany, brown and red.
Comments Marigold roots may release substances fatal to soilborne pests, so are often used as companion plants.

Tropaeolum majus
TROPAEOLACEAE

GARDEN NASTURTIUM

Garden nasturtiums have brightly colored flowers on climbing succulent stems. Bushy types are great as edgings or fillers for beds and borders. Nasturtiums may self-sow.

Description Plants are either vines or bushy mounds with showy, fragrant blooms of cream, rose, red, orange and yellow. Flowers are 2 inches (5 cm) wide with a prominent spur and bloom.
Height and spread Height of climbing types to about 8 feet (2.4 m), bush types to 1 foot (30 cm); spread 6–12 inches (15–30 cm).
Best climate and site Zones 5–11; full sun to partial shade; average, well-drained to dry soil.
Landscape uses Climbers quickly cover trellises or make interesting groundcovers. Compact types are suited to containers or as edgings or fillers in beds and borders.
Growing guidelines For climbers, grow on a support or trellis or plants will scramble over other plants. Sow seed directly into the garden 12 weeks before last frost date. Plant seedlings 6–12 inches (15–30 cm) apart. In shaded areas expect leafy growth and fewer flowers.
Good companions Vegetables, herbs, bold-colored flowers.
Cultivars Single colors, double flowers and variegated-leaf forms are available.
Comments The leaves and flowers are edible and can be added to salads.

Verbena x *hybrida*
VERBENACEAE

GARDEN VERBENA

Grow garden verbena alone in masses, or mix it with other flowers for all-season color. Pinch off the stem tips in early summer to promote branching and more flowers.

Description The stems are topped with rounded clusters of bright, ½-inch (12-mm) wide flowers from early summer until frost. The flowers may be white, cream, pink, red, blue or purple; they often have a contrasting white eye.

Height and spread Height 8–12 inches (20–30 cm); spread to 1 foot (30 cm).

Best climate and site Zones 8–10; full sun to partial shade; average, well-drained soil.

Landscape uses Use the upright forms as fillers or edgings for beds and borders; grow the trailing types as groundcovers or in window boxes and hanging baskets.

Growing guidelines Plant seedlings 8–10 inches (20–25 cm) apart in spring after the danger of frost has passed. Do not overfeed or overwater as verbena resents overwet conditions but can tolerate dry soils and hot temperatures. Cut back after flowering to promote more blooms.

Good companions Geraniums.

Cultivars Cultivars come in shades of white, orange, pink, mauve, violet and red.

Other species *Verbena bonariensis* is a tall-growing perennial, usually seen as an annual for late summer to autumn flowers.

Comments Not easy to grow from seed, so look for seedlings and small plants.

Viola x *wittrockiana*
VIOLACEAE

PANSY

To keep pansies happy, mulch the soil and water well, especially during dry spells to keep the roots moist. Picking flowers or pinching off spent flowers prolongs bloom.

Description Plants form tidy clumps of flat, five-petaled flowers, mainly in spring but sometimes in autumn. The 2–5-inch (5–12.5-cm) wide flowers bloom in a range of colors, including white, pink, red, orange, yellow, purple, blue and near black; many have contrasting faces.

Height and spread Height 6–8 inches (15–20 cm); spread 8–12 inches (20–30 cm).

Best climate and site Zones 5–10; full sun to partial shade (especially in hotter Zones); moist, well-drained soil.

Landscape uses Pansies are invaluable for injecting color into winter and spring gardens. Use them as fillers, as an edging or in containers. Follow them with summer bloomers, such as impatiens and begonias.

Growing guidelines Plant seedlings 6–8 inches (15–20 cm) apart in autumn for winter to spring flowers and in spring to flower through to autumn.

Cultivars Numerous cultivars are available in all colors and combinations, some with ruffles and blotches.

Other species *Viola tricolor* has single-colored flowers.

Comments Aphids can be a problem (control with a systemic spray); snails and slugs can be removed by hand, or set baits.

Zinnia elegans
ASTERACEAE

COMMON ZINNIA

Common zinnias are excellent for replacing early-blooming annuals and filling in gaps left by dormant, spring-flowering bulbs and perennials. They also make great cut flowers.

Description The stiff, sturdy stems are topped with blooms from midsummer until frost. Flowers in every color except true blue from 1–6 inches (2.5–15 cm) across. The single or double blooms may have petals that are quilled (curled), ruffled or flat.

Height and spread Height 6–36 inches (15–90 cm), depending on the cultivar; spread usually 1–2 feet (30–60 cm).

Best climate and site Zones 8–11; full sun; average, well-drained soil with added organic matter.

Landscape uses They add welcome color to any sunny landscape. Use the tall types as background plants, the medium-sized ones as fillers, and the compact types for edgings or container plants.

Growing guidelines Quick from seedlings or seed sown directly into the garden 1–2 weeks after the last frost date. Plant seedlings of compact types about 1 foot (30 cm) apart; leave 1½–2 feet (45–60 cm) between tall cultivars.

Good companions Marigolds, salvias.

Other common names Youth-and-old-age.

Cultivars Look for mildew-resistant forms. The green-flowered form is called 'Envy'.

Comments Zinnias cope well with heat but not humidity.

Allium giganteum
LILIACEAE

GIANT ONION

Make a statement in your garden by planting the large bulbs of giant onion. In early summer the showy flower heads stand tall among other plants.

Description A tall, slender stem with a round flower head that's densely packed with small, purple flowers in early summer. The leaves yellow and die back by midsummer.

Height and spread Height of leaves usually 6–12 inches (15–30 cm); flower stems grow to 5 feet (1.5 m). Spread to about 1 foot (30 cm).

Best climate and site Zones 5–9; full sun to light shade; fertile, well-drained soil.

Landscape uses A show-stopping accent for the back of flower beds and borders. Clumps of six or more giant onions look super with shrubs or perennials.

Growing guidelines Plant bulbs in early to midautumn or in early spring 8 inches (20 cm) deep, 8–12 inches (20–30 cm) apart. In Zones 5 and 6, protect bulbs over winter with a loose mulch, such as straw or evergreen branches, that can be removed in spring. Leave established bulbs undisturbed.

Good companions Lilac, other tall bulbs, such as lilies. Follow with perennials or summer-blooming annuals to fill in when the bulbs go dormant.

Comments Remove spent flower stems, unless you want to collect seed or use the seed heads in floral arrangements.

Arum italicum
ARACEAE

ITALIAN ARUM

By late summer, the spring flowers of Italian arum mature into columns of reddish orange berries. These colorful spikes look dramatic and bare until the new leaves appear in autumn.

Description Italian arum grows from tubers with a greenish white, hoodlike flower (called a spathe) sheltering a narrow column known as the spadix. These unusual spring flowers are interesting, but the plant is mainly grown for its late-summer berries and arrowhead-shaped, semiglossy, dark green leaves that are marked with creamy white.

Height and spread Height 1–1½ feet (30–45 cm); spread to 1 foot (30 cm).

Best climate and site Zones 6–10; partial shade; well-drained soil with plenty of organic matter.

Landscape uses Looks marvelous in masses along streams, clumped near ponds and in shaded, woodland or bog gardens.

Growing guidelines Divide and plant the tubers in late summer or early autumn 2–3 inches (5–7.5 cm) deep, 8–12 inches (20–30 cm) apart. Keep the soil moist during leaf growth and flowering.

Good companions English ivy, common periwinkle, hellebores, snowdrops, snowflakes and love-in-a-mist.

Cultivars Look for cultivars with boldly patterned leaves.

Comments This is the true arum, not the white arum lily *Zantedeschia aethopica*.

Caladium bicolor
ARACEAE

CALADIUM

Caladiums are grown for their boldly colored, heart-shaped leaves. These shade-loving plants thrive in heat and humidity.

Description Caladiums grow from tubers and produce bushy clumps of long-stalked, arrow-shaped leaves from late spring until frost. The lush leaves are shaded and veined with various combinations of green, white, pink and red.

Height and spread Height 1–2 feet (30–60 cm); spread to 2 feet (60 cm).

Best climate and site Frost-hardy in Zones 10–12; elsewhere, grown as annuals or stored indoors for winter; partial shade; moist but well-drained soil with added organic matter.

Landscape uses Caladiums provide summer color in shady gardens. Grow them in containers for a tropical touch on decks, porches and patios.

Growing guidelines Grow the tubers with the knobby side up in moist potting mix in spring in a warm, bright spot. Plant out when night temperatures stay above 60°F (16°C); space about 1 foot (30 cm) apart. When the leaves die, dig up the tubers and store them in a warm place.

Other common names Angel wings, elephant's ears.

Cultivars Look for forms with boldly colored leaves.

Comments In summer, pinch off the small, hooded flowers.

Colchicum speciosum
LILIACEAE

SHOWY AUTUMN CROCUS

Autumn crocus grow from large, plump corms. Once established, each corm produces leafless clumps of showy pink flowers in late summer to early autumn.

Description Pink, 4-inch (10-cm) wide, goblet-shaped flowers rise directly from the ground in late summer to early autumn, followed by strappy leaves in winter.

Height and spread Height of leaves to about 8 inches (20 cm); flowers 4–6 inches (10–15 cm) tall. Spread to about 6 inches (15 cm).

Best climate and site Zones 4–9; full sun to partial shade; well-drained soil.

Landscape uses Showy autumn crocus is beautiful but a little tricky to site effectively. It's usually best growing up through low groundcovers or under shrubs, where the coarse spring leaves won't detract from, or smother, other flowers.

Growing guidelines Plant corms in mid- to late summer about 4 inches (10 cm) deep and 6 inches (15 cm) apart. Divide just after the leaves die down only if needed for propagation.

Good companions Low groundcover plants, such as species geraniums, and other autumn-flowering bulbs, including cyclamen. Autumn crocus will also flower without soil and can be grown as curiosities indoors in paper bags or bulb bowls.

Cultivars White and double-flowered pink varieties are available.

Comments All parts of plant are poisonous.

Crocus vernus
IRIDACEAE

DUTCH CROCUS

Dutch crocus are a welcome sight after a long, cold winter. After bloom, the leaves elongate until they ripen and die back to the ground in early summer.

Description Dutch crocus grow from small corms. Plants shoot in late winter to early spring, with leaves and flowers at the same time. Goblet-shaped, stemless flowers up to 3 inches (7.5 cm) across bloom just above the grasslike leaves. The flowers can be white, lavender, purple or yellow.

Height and spread Height of leaves to 8 inches (20 cm); flowers usually to 4 inches (10 cm) tall. Spread 1–3 inches (2.5–7.5 cm).

Best climate and site Zones 3–8; full sun to partial shade (under deciduous trees and shrubs is ideal); average, well-drained soil.

Landscape uses Great for early color in gardens, naturalized in lawns or under trees, or grown in containers.

Growing guidelines Plant the corms in autumn, pointed-side up and set 2–4 inches (5–10 cm) deep and 2 inches (5 cm) apart.

Good companions Early spring-flowering annuals and bulbs, including anemones and daffodils.

Cultivars There are many vigorous, large-flowered cultivars available, including those striped in contrasting colors.

Comments If naturalized in lawns or under trees, remember to wait until late spring (when leaves have turned yellow) before mowing.

Cyclamen hederifolium
PRIMULACEAE

HARDY CYCLAMEN

Hardy cyclamen grow well under shrubs and trees—even in dry, summer shade—and are attractive in flower in autumn and in leaf until late spring.

Description Hardy cyclamen grow from smooth tubers. They bloom in early autumn, with leafless flower stalks topped with pink or white flowers. The 1-inch (2.5-cm) long, nodding flowers have upward-pointing petals with heart-shaped, silver-marked, green leaves.

Height and spread Height and spread of flowers and foliage 4–6 inches (10–15 cm).

Best climate and site Zones 5–9; partial shade; average, well-drained soil.

Growing guidelines Buy in autumn in flower or plant dormant tubers shallowly in summer, making sure the smooth, unmarked side is on the bottom. The top of the tuber should be about 1 inch (2.5 cm) below the soil surface and 6–8 inches (15–20 cm) apart. Top-dress with a thin layer of compost in late summer. A mulch of gravel is ideal for keeping excess water away.

Landscape uses Hardy cyclamen look good massed as a seasonal groundcover for shaded spots such as under trees. Excellent for potted color over autumn and winter.

Good companions Ferns, hellebores, deciduous trees and shrubs.

Cultivars When buying potted plants, select forms with patterned leaves.

Comments Tubers increase in size with age. Plants readily self-sow.

Dahlia hybrids
ASTERACEAE

DAHLIAS

Pinch off stem tips in early summer to promote bushy growth and more (but smaller) flowers. Or, to get the largest flowers, pinch off side shoots to leave one or two main stems.

Description Dahlias range from bedding plants to tall, large-flowered plants that bloom from midsummer through autumn. Flowers are 1–8 inches (2.5–20 cm) across in almost every color and shape.

Height and spread Height varies from 1 foot (30 cm) for bedding types to 5 feet (1.5 m) for border types. Spread to 1 foot (30 cm) for bedding types and 4 feet (1.2 m) for border types.

Best climate and site Hardy in Zones 9 and 10; elsewhere, grown as summer and autumn annuals; full sun; well-drained soil.

Landscape uses Bedding dahlias add cheerful color to the fronts of beds and borders, as well as to pots and window boxes. Tall-growing types are excellent for late summer and autumn interest and make good cut flowers.

Growing guidelines Plant seedlings in the garden 1–2 weeks after the last frost, 10–12 inches (25–30 cm) apart. In warm Zones plant tubers in spring, setting neck 3–4 inches (7.5–10 cm) deep.

Good companions Marigolds, daylilies.

Cultivars Countless cultivars of all forms and shades of flowers are available.

Comments When planting tall dahlias, insert a stake at planting time.

Dierama pulcherrimum
IRIDACEAE

FAIRY FISHING ROD

The wiry, yet graceful, arching stems of fairy fishing rods are hung with bell-shaped flowers through late spring and summer.

Description Fairy fishing rod corms form large, grassy, evergreen clumps with arching flower stems in late spring to summer. The white or pink, 1-inch (2.5-cm) flowers hang in clusters for 3–4 weeks.

Height and spread Leafy clumps stand around 1½–2 feet (45–60 cm) tall, but flowering stems can be 5–6 feet (1.5–1.8 m) tall; clumps are 1½ feet (45 cm) across.

Best climate and site Zones 8–10; full sun to semi-shade; well-drained, moist soil.

Landscape uses Use to frame a path or entryway. Makes a graceful contrast to upright plants. Fairy fishing rod makes a bold statement arching over a fence or growing beside a pool or pond.

Growing guidelines Plant corms or pot grown plants in autumn or early spring. Keep soil moist during spring and summer. Plants resent disturbance.

Good companions Intermingle with silver-foliaged plants such as lavenders and lamb's ears.

Other common names Wandflower, angel's fishing rod.

Cultivars Dwarf forms lack the drama and impact of the tall-growing species. There are named, white and purple forms.

Comments Remove old leaves in early spring to tidy clump.

Fritillaria imperalis
LILIACEAE

CROWN IMPERIAL

Crown imperials are striking in flower. Often tricky to grow, they may take a few seasons to establish and bloom but they are worth it as mature clumps live for many years.

Description By mid- to late spring, these large, fleshy bulbs produce tall stems topped with a tuft of green leaves and hanging, bell-shaped, yellow, orange or red flowers about 2 inches (5 cm) long.

Height and spread Height 2–4 feet (60–120 cm); spread to 1 foot (30 cm).

Best climate and site Zones 5–9; full sun; average to sandy, well-drained soil.

Landscape uses They make striking spring accents for beds and borders.

Growing guidelines Plant bulbs in late summer or early autumn about 8 inches (20 cm) deep, loosening the soil at the base of the hole for good drainage. When planting, tilt bulb slightly to one side to discourage water from collecting in the depression at the top. Space bulbs 1 foot (30 cm) apart then leave them undisturbed. Keep soil dry in summer and allow plants to die back and become dormant.

Good companions Honesty, forget-me-nots, daffodils and later-blooming annuals.

Cultivars Many named varieties.

Other species Checkered lily *F. meleagris* has smaller, but interestingly marked flowers in colors from white to purple.

Comments All parts have a musky (some say skunklike) odor.

Gladiolus hybrids
IRIDACEAE

GLADIOLUS

Gladioli bloom in nearly every color but true blue; many have spots or splashes of contrasting colors. For cut flowers, pick them just as the bottom bud begins to open.

Description Gladioli form tall fans of sword-shaped, green leaves. The flower stem is topped with a many-budded spike that blooms from the bottom up. The buds produce open, funnel-shaped flowers up to 4 inches (10 cm) across.

Height and spread Height 2–5 feet (60–150 cm); spread 6–12 inches (15–30 cm).

Best climate and site Usually frost-hardy in Zones 8–10, elsewhere grown as annuals or stored indoors over winter; full sun; fertile, well-drained soil.

Growing guidelines Plant corms after the last frost 4–6 inches (10–15 cm) deep, 4–6 inches (10–15 cm) apart. To extend flowering, plant more corms every 2 weeks until midsummer. Tall-flowering types benefit from staking. In Zone 7 and colder areas, dig and store the corms before or just after the first frost.

Landscape uses The spiky blooms add excitement to the middle and back of beds and borders and are excellent cut flowers.

Good companions Agapanthus, liliums and other summer-flowering perennials and bulbs.

Cultivars Many named, fancy cultivars.

Hyacinthoides hispanica
LILIACEAE

SPANISH BLUEBELLS

Once established, Spanish bluebells increase quickly to create a flowering carpet that looks stunning in early spring under deciduous trees.

Description Upright, leafless flower stems, topped with spikes of many bell-shaped blooms appear in late spring. The ¾-inch (18-mm) wide flowers are white, pink or shades of purple-blue. Plants are dormant by midsummer.

Height and spread Height of flowers 1–1½ feet (30–45 cm); leaves usually to 8 inches (20 cm) tall. Spread 4–6 inches (10–15 cm).

Best climate and site Zones 4–9; full sun to partial shade; average, well-drained soil with added organic matter.

Landscape uses Include clumps in beds and borders, combine them with groundcovers, or naturalize them in woodlands and low-maintenance areas.

Growing guidelines Plant the bulbs in autumn, 3–4 inches (7.5–10 cm) deep, 4–6 inches (10–15 cm) apart. Plants will self-sow and naturalize readily.

Good companions Evergreen azaleas, forget-me-nots and daffodils.

Cultivars Compact forms with pink-lilac flowers are available.

Comments Spanish bluebells are sold under former names, including *Scilla campanulata*, *Scilla hispanica* and *Endymion hispanicus*. Take care when handling the bulbs, since they are poisonous when fresh.

Hyacinthus orientalis
LILIACEAE

HYACINTH

Treat these sweetly flowered bulbs as annuals for a striking floral display each spring. Their perfume is overwhelming and can be enjoyed indoors or out.

Description Hyacinths grow from plump bulbs. By midspring, each stalk is topped with a dense spike of starry, 1-inch (2.5-cm) wide, powerfully fragrant flowers. The single or double flowers bloom in a wide range of colors, including white, pink, red, orange, yellow, blue and purple. Hyacinths go dormant in early summer.

Height and spread Height 8–12 inches (20–30 cm); spread to 4 inches (10 cm).

Best climate and site Zones 4–9; full sun; average, well-drained soil with added organic matter.

Growing guidelines Plant bulbs in midautumn 5–6 inches (12.5–15 cm) deep, 6–10 inches (15–25 cm) apart. Double-flowered types may need some support. Remove spent flower stalks but leave plants to die down naturally.

Landscape uses Hyacinths contribute cheerful color to spring beds and borders. They grow well in containers for spring bloom outdoors or winter forcing indoors. Bulbs grown indoors in bulb vases or shallow bowls are highly decorative.

Cultivars Many named varieties, including an apricot-colored hyacinth.

Good companions Primroses and pansies.

Comments After the first year, bloom spikes are smaller or may not bloom at all.

Iris reticulata
IRIDACEAE

RETICULATED IRIS

Reticulated irises return year after year to grace your garden with their delicate spring flowers. Tuck them into beds, borders and rock gardens.

Description Reticulated irises grow from small bulbs. The dainty blue, purple, yellow or white, early spring flowers have three upright petals (known as standards) and three outward-arching petals (known as falls). The falls have gold and/or white markings. Leaves are short at flowering time but develop after flowering.
Height and spread Height of flowers 4–6 inches (10–15 cm); leaves to about 1 foot (30 cm) tall. Spread to around 2 inches (5 cm).
Best climate and site Zones 5–9; full sun; average, well-drained soil.
Landscape uses The delicate, lightly fragrant blooms are beautiful when massed. Reticulated irises grow well in pots for spring bloom outdoors to decorate patios or decks. They can be used for winter forcing indoors. Choose scented plants for pots.
Growing guidelines Plant bulbs in autumn, 3–4 inches (7.5–10 cm) deep. For propagation, lift and divide clumps after the leaves turn yellow.
Good companions Combine with *Anemone blanda* and early spring crocus.
Cultivars Many named varieties in a range of blue shades.
Comments Bulbs can rot if overwatered or in poorly drained soil.

Lilium hybrids
LILIACEAE

LILIES

Lilies are tall, exotic plants to include in any planting and make excellent potted or cut flowers; pick them when the first one or two buds open.

Description Lilies grow from scaly bulbs. By early to late summer (depending on the hybrid), the long, plump flower buds open to showy, flat or funnel-shaped flowers.
Height and spread Height 2–5 feet (60–150 cm) depending on hybrid; spread usually 6–12 inches (15–30 cm).
Best climate and site Zones 4–10 (depending on species); full sun to partial shade; average, well-drained soil.
Landscape uses Lilies add height and color to any planting scheme. They are elegant mixed into foundation plantings, grouped with shrubs, or naturalized in woodlands. Use them as tall, potted plants.
Growing guidelines Handle the scaly bulbs gently, planting them in autumn or early spring, depending on species. Dig planting areas 6–8 inches (15–20 cm) deep, and loosen the soil in the bottom. Use groundcover plants or mulch to keep the bulbs cool and moist. Water when dry, especially before flowering.
Good companions Combine them with mounding annuals and perennials.
Cultivars There are many species and varieties in a range of sizes and colors.
Comments Growing a range of species and varieties will extend flowering period from late spring to early autumn.

Lycoris squamigera
AMARYLLIDACEAE

MAGIC LILY

The magic lily gets its common name from the way the bare stems burst into flower in late summer or autumn before the leaves appear.

Description In late summer to early autumn slender, greenish brown, leafless stems are topped with loose clusters of funnel-shaped, rosy pink flowers up to 4 inches (10 cm) long with prominent stamens. Leafy growth follows flowering.
Height and spread Height of flowers to 2 feet (60 cm); leaves to 1 foot (30 cm). Spread to 6 inches (15 cm).
Best climate and site Zones 5–9; full sun to partial shade; average, well-drained soil.
Landscape uses They grow best when naturalized on slopes, or in among groundcovers or rockeries.
Growing guidelines Plant bulbs in midsummer 4–5 inches (10–12.5 cm) deep and 8 inches (20 cm) apart. Water during dry spells in autumn and spring. In cold Zones, protect the leaves over winter with a loose mulch, such as evergreen branches, pine needles or straw. For propagation, divide bulbs in early to midsummer, when leaves die; otherwise, leave the bulbs undisturbed to form large clumps.
Good companions Nerines, autumn crocus.
Other common names Resurrection lily, spider lily.
Other species *Lycoris aurea* has golden-colored flowers.
Comments Liquid feed while in growth.

Muscari armeniacum
LILIACEAE

GRAPE HYACINTH

Grape hyacinths are trouble-free bulbs that naturalize well under trees and shrubs, and they look attractive combined with groundcovers or mass planted with spring bulbs.

Description Grape hyacinths grow from small bulbs. The clumps are accented by short, leafless stems topped with dense spikes of grapelike blooms in early spring. The individual purple-blue, white-rimmed flowers are only ¼ inch (6 mm) wide.
Height and spread Height of flowers and foliage 6–8 inches (15–20 cm); spread 3–4 inches (7.5–10 cm).
Best climate and site Zones 4–9; full sun to partial shade (under deciduous trees and shrubs); average, well-drained soil.
Landscape uses Scatter the bulbs liberally throughout flower beds and borders.
Growing guidelines These easy-to-grow bulbs are planted in early to midautumn, 2–3 inches (5–7.5 cm) deep and about 4 inches (10 cm) apart. For propagation, divide just after the leaves die back in early summer. Otherwise, leave the bulbs undisturbed to form sweeps of spring color.
Good companions Primroses, pansies, daffodils and tulips.
Cultivars Several cultivars are available with double or white-rimmed flowers.
Comments Grape hyacinths are used extensively in large landscape displays to create a river of blue among other spring-flowering bulbs and annuals.

Narcissus hybrids
AMARYLLIDACEAE

DAFFODILS

It's hard to imagine a garden without at least a few daffodils for spring color. Grow them in borders, plant them under trees, or naturalize them in low-maintenance areas.

Description Daffodils grow from large, pointed bulbs. Clumps of green leaves emerge in early spring and die back in summer. Flowers are yellow or white, trumpet-shaped blooms held on tall stems.
Height and spread Height of foliage and flowers 6–20 inches (15–50 cm); spread usually 4–8 inches (10–20 cm).
Best climate and site Zones 4–9; full sun to partial shade; average, well-drained soil with added organic matter.
Landscape uses Create unforgettable combinations by grouping daffodils with spring-flowering annuals and bulbs. Grow some daffodils in containers for spring bloom outdoors.
Growing guidelines Plant bulbs in early to midautumn 4–8 inches (10–20 cm) deep, depending on bulb size. Space small types 3–4 inches (7.5–10 cm) apart and large types 8–10 inches (20–25 cm) apart.
Cultivars There are early-, mid- and late-spring flowering cultivars. Blooms are single or double in white or yellow, with pink, green or orange parts or markings.
Good companions Pansies, crocus, grape hyacinths.
Comments Groundcovers mask dying leaves, which can look unsightly.

Tulipa hybrids
LILIACEAE

TULIPS

Stately tulips are an indispensable part of the cool-climate spring garden and can be grown alone in containers or massed with other bulbs and annuals.

Description Tulips grow from plump, pointed bulbs. In spring, broad, dusty green leaves appear. The slender flower stems bear showy single or double flowers up to 4 inches (10 cm) across.
Height and spread Height from 6–30 inches (15–75 cm), depending on the cultivar; spread 6–10 inches (15–25 cm).
Best climate and site Best in Zones 3–8 (to grow in Zones 9 and 10, treat as annuals and plant pre-cooled bulbs each year in late autumn). Full sun to partial shade; well-drained soil that's dry in summer.
Landscape uses Mass in display beds for pools of spring color, use as edging, or grow in containers.
Growing guidelines Plant bulbs in mid- to late autumn. Set them in individual holes or larger planting areas dug 4–6 inches (10–15 cm) deep. Space bulbs 6 inches (15 cm) apart.
Good companions Daffodils, pansies, primroses, grape hyacinths, forget-me-nots.
Cultivars Many unusual colors including black, striped and multicolored flowers. There are also exotic forms including ruffled flowers.
Comments Pick tulips when the flowers are fully colored, but still in bud.

Acanthus mollis
ACANTHACEAE

BEAR'S-BREECH

Bear's-breech is a robust plant with lustrous, toothed, evergreen leaves that can be used as a bold feature in shaded gardens. Its tall flower spikes are a bonus.

Description A broad, clumping plant that spreads by rhizomes, with large, glossy, evergreen, divided leaves. The 1-inch (2.5-cm) flowers with three white petals and overarching, purple hoods are carried in tall spikes in late spring or summer, opening sequentially up the spike.
Height and spread Height 2½–4 feet (75–120 cm); spread 3 feet (90 cm).
Best climate and site Zones 8–10; full sun to partial shade; evenly moist, humus-rich soil (can tolerate dry shade).
Landscape uses Use in foundation plantings or as bold accents in formal and informal gardens. An excellent choice along walls or in courtyards.
Growing guidelines Plant in spring. In cold areas, mulch after the ground freezes in winter and remove mulch gradually in spring to protect plants from heaving. Keep moist because dry soil will reduce the size of the leaves. Sensitive to winter frost and to hot, humid weather. Produces foliage in colder Zones but the flower buds die.
Good companions Yarrow, cottage garden plants, arum lilies.
Other common names Oyster plant.
Comments *Acanthus* leaves were carved on Corinthian columns in Classical times.

Achillea filipendulina
ASTERACEAE

FERN-LEAVED YARROW

Fern-leaved yarrow is a tough, adaptable perennial that looks great in herb gardens, perennial borders, wildflower meadows and containers.

Description This aromatic herb with deeply incised, ferny, olive-green leaves grows from fibrous roots. The wide-spreading plants have many tall, leafy stems of flattened flower clusters. The 4–5-inch (10–12.5-cm) heads contain dozens of tightly packed, golden-yellow flowers in summer that last for weeks.
Height and spread Height 3–4 feet (90–120 cm); spread 3 feet (90 cm); forms broad, tight clumps.
Best climate and site Zones 3–9; full sun or light shade; average, dry to moist, well-drained soil.
Landscape uses Plant at the front or middle of formal perennial borders or in meadows and other informal gardens. Use on dry, sunny banks to control erosion.
Growing guidelines Plant in spring or autumn. Plants spread rapidly and need frequent division. Lift and divide clumps every 3 years in early spring or autumn. Deadhead regularly.
Good companions Combine with drought-tolerant perennials, such as catmints *Nepeta* spp., pinks *Dianthus* spp. and globe thistle *Echinops ritro*, as well as ornamental grasses.
Comments In hot, humid areas, plants may develop fungal problems.

Actaea pachypoda
RANUNCULACEAE

WHITE BANEBERRY

Mature clumps of white baneberry in full fruit are stunning in the autumn garden. The red-stalked berries are poisonous to people but savored by birds.

Description Plants grow from a woody crown with wiry, yellow roots. The spring flowers lack petals and comprise a fuzzy cluster of broad stamens. The blooms are carried on sturdy stems above deeply dissected, compound leaves. The oval, white fruits, a feature of the plant, are ¼ inch (6 mm) long and borne on showy, red stalks in late summer to autumn.
Height and spread Height 2–4 feet (60–120 cm); spread 3 feet (90 cm).
Best climate and site Zones 3–9; partial to full shade; moist, humus-rich soil.
Landscape uses Plant for dramatic accent at the edge of a path in a woodland garden or at the end of a shady walk. Mass plantings are breathtaking among ferns and foliage plants.
Growing guidelines Top-dress with compost or shredded leaves in spring or autumn. Plants seldom need division but can be grown from seed.
Good companions Combine with wild bleeding heart *Dicentra eximia* and violets. In autumn, the berried plants look great with ferns, cardinal flower *Lobelia cardinalis*, blue lobelia *Lobelia siphilitica*, white wood aster *Aster divaricatus* and monkshoods *Aconitum* spp.
Comments Bird-attracting in autumn.

Agapanthus praecox subsp. orientalis
AMARYLLIDACEAE

AGAPANTHUS

The blue or white flowers are a summer feature, but the evergreen foliage of agapanthus is handsome year-round as an informal border against a fence or around a swimming pool.

Description Evergreen clumps of pale green, strappy leaves are topped with long-stalked, blue or white flowers during summer. The small, lily-like flowers form a large cluster on top of a thick stem. Flowers are followed by green seedpods.
Height and spread Varies with cultivar, but leafy clumps to around 1½ feet (45 cm) tall and wide. Flower stems to 3 feet (90 cm).
Best climate and site Zones 9–11; full sun; any soil.
Landscape uses Edge a lawn, fence, path or driveway, or use as an accent plant for summer color around a swimming pool or in containers.
Growing guidelines Plant anytime. Divide existing clumps in late winter to early spring. Remove spent flower stems in late summer to tidy plant.
Good companions Other blue-flowered summer plants, such as hydrangeas, or combine with strong orange or yellow cosmos, hibiscus or dahlias.
Other common names African lily.
Other varieties Many named varieties. including miniature and compact forms.
Comments Plants that fail to flower are growing in too much shade.

Alchemilla mollis
ROSACEAE

LADY'S-MANTLE

Lady's-mantles form mounded clumps of pleated foliage. The 4–6-inch (10–15-cm) pale green leaves are covered in soft hair that collects beads of water like jewels on velvet.

Description Plants grow from stout, creeping crowns with fibrous roots. Pale green leaves with soft hairs and small, greenish yellow flowers in foamy clusters cover the plant in spring and early summer. The foliage forms a distinctive, soft green carpet throughout the season.
Height and spread Height 6–12 inches (15–30 cm); spread 1–2 feet (30–60 cm).
Best climate and site Zones 4–9; sun or shade; humus-rich, evenly moist soil. Where summer heat and humidity are high, provide afternoon shade.
Landscape uses Choose lady's-mantle for the front of formal and informal beds and borders or for edging walks.
Growing guidelines Set the stout crowns at the soil surface. Divide existing crowns in spring or autumn. If the leaves look tattered after flowering, cut plants to the ground; new foliage will appear. Mulch to keep soil evenly moist.
Good companions Combine with other moisture lovers, such as Siberian iris *Iris sibirica*, astilbes and primroses. Plant with large-leaved perennials, such as ligularias *Ligularia* spp. and hostas.
Comments The greenish yellow flowers add light to the garden in evening.

Anemone x hybrida
RANUNCULACEAE

JAPANESE ANEMONE

In autumn, Japanese anemones produce clouds of flowers on slender stems and suit a woodland garden or lightly shaded cottage garden.

Description This stout, herbaceous perennial with thick, tuberous roots has deeply divided, dark green, slightly hairy leaves, usually around the base of the plant. Flowers are held on tall stems and range from white to pink and rose and may be single or double blooms. They occur in late summer to autumn.
Height and spread Height 3–5 feet (90–150 cm); spread 2–3 feet (60–90 cm).
Best climate and site Zones 5–10; full sun to light shade (more shade in hot Zones); humus-rich, evenly moist soil.
Landscape uses Extend seasonal interest in a woodland garden with late-season perennials and ornamental grasses. Plant with shrubs or ferns in moist, open shade.
Growing guidelines Spreads by creeping, underground stems to form broad clumps once established. Thin overgrown clumps in spring if bloom wanes. Replant into soil that has been enriched with organic matter. Mulch plants in colder Zones.
Good companions Deciduous trees, such as maples, or with deciduous shrubs.
Other common names Windflower.
Other varieties Named varieties with single, semidouble or double flowers.
Comments Protect the plants from hot afternoon sun.

Angelica archangelica
APIACEAE

ANGELICA

Tall-growing angelica forms a striking clump of broad, lobed leaves. The sweetly scented, greenish flowers bloom in midsummer, and attract beneficial insects to gardens.

Description A fast-growing and very tall herbaceous perennial with deeply divided, deep green, shiny leaves and umbels of greenish yellow, honey-scented flowers in summer.

Height and spread Height 5–8 feet (1.5–2.4 m); spread 3 feet (90 cm).

Best climate and site Zones 4–9; half shade or filtered sunlight; moist, fertile, well-drained soil.

Landscape uses A striking plant for flower borders, herb or vegetable gardens, or for foliage contrast in beds.

Growing guidelines Can be difficult to germinate, so plant potted plants in spring or summer. The plant dies after flowering in its second or third year. Cutting off the flower stalks as they form will help prolong the life, but then you won't get the benefit of the flowers. To have a continuous crop, set out plants for the first few seasons, then let plants self-sow.

Good companions Herbs, vegetables, other perennials.

Comments Plant angelica where its tall stems won't shade out lower-growing plants. However, in the vegetable garden, angelica provides effective shade for summer lettuces.

Aquilegia x hybrida
RANUNCULACEAE

HYBRID COLUMBINE

Hybrid columbines are graceful plants with curious, nodding flowers. These plants self-seed readily for massed displays.

Description Plants grow from a thick taproot. The ferny foliage has many fan-shaped leaflets, often blue-green in color. Each flower has five spurred petals surrounded by five petal-like sepals, 4 inches (10 cm) long, in spring and early summer.

Height and spread Height 2–3 feet (60–90 cm); spread 1–2 feet (30–60 cm).

Best climate and site Zones 3–9; full sun or partial shade; in light, average to rich, well-drained soil. Tolerates heat and cold.

Landscape uses Columbines look best in groups or drifts. Plant in formal beds and borders or informal settings, such as cottage gardens, woodlands and meadows.

Growing guidelines Hybrid columbines generally live only 2–4 years, but plants self-sow readily.

Good companions Combine with spring and early-summer perennials, tulips and daffodils. In light shade, combine them with wildflowers, ferns, forget-me-nots and hostas.

Other common names Granny's bonnet.

Other species *A. caerulea*, Rocky Mountain columbine, has upward-facing blue-and-white flowers with long spurs.

Comments Will hybridize readily.

Artemisia absinthium
ASTERACEAE

COMMON WORMWOOD

The silvery foliage of common wormwood adds a cool touch to perennial borders, herb gardens and shrub plantings. It can reach shrublike proportions.

Description The deeply lobed, aromatic foliage is covered with soft hairs, creating a soft, gray-green tone. The inconspicuous yellow flowers are borne in compound, terminal clusters in late summer and autumn and can be removed if desired.

Height and spread Height 2–3 feet (60–90 cm); spread 2 feet (60 cm).

Best climate and site Zones 3–9; full sun; average, sandy or loamy, well-drained soil.

Landscape uses Use in formal or informal dry-soil gardens, cottage and herb gardens or rock gardens. The silver foliage is a useful color contrast. Also suited to containers.

Growing guidelines Thrives in all but the most inhospitable garden spots. Avoid overly rich soil, which encourages weak growth. If plants become floppy or open in habit, prune back by at least half to encourage compact growth. Grow from cuttings (a new shoot with a piece of older stem at the base) in late summer.

Good companions Combine with yarrows, sages *Salvia* spp., ornamental onions *Allium* spp. and other drought-tolerant perennials. The soft foliage is lovely with ornamental grasses or conifers.

Comments Grown mainly for leaf color.

Aster novae-angliae
ASTERACEAE

NEW ENGLAND ASTER

As they mature, New England asters form broad, bushy clumps topped with pastel-colored, daisy-like, autumn flowers. Cultivars vary from white to purple, pink and rose.

Description New England aster is a tall, stately plant with hairy stems and lance-shaped leaves. The 1–2-inch (2.5–5-cm) lavender to purple flowers have bright yellow centers in late summer to autumn.
Height and spread Height 3–6 feet (90–180 cm); spread 3 feet (90 cm). Forms broad, bushy clumps when mature.
Best climate and site Zones 3–9; full sun or light shade; moist, humus-rich soil. Plants tolerate moist soil.
Landscape uses Plant in formal and informal settings or in meadows at the back of the border. Dwarf selections can be grown in pots.
Growing guidelines Divide clumps every 3–4 years in spring. Plants may need staking. Cut down after flowering.
Good companions Combine with autumn perennials, such as sunflowers *Helianthus* spp., garden mums and sedums, as well as the foliage of artemisias and ornamental grasses.
Other common names Michaelmas daisy, Easter daisy.
Other species *A. novi-belgii* has single or double flowers in a rainbow of colors. Zones 3–10.
Comments Useful as a cut flower.

Astilbe x arendsii
SAXIFRAGACEAE

ASTILBE

Astilbes are lovely plants for moist shade gardens or beside pools. The airy plumes of red, pink, rose, lilac, cream or white flowers add grace and motion to the garden.

Description Plants grow from woody crowns with ferny leaves. The emerging spring shoots are red-tinged. The plumed flower clusters bear tightly packed, fuzzy blooms in spring and early summer.
Height and spread Height 2–4 feet (60–120 cm); spread 2–3 feet (60–90 cm).
Best climate and site Zones 3–9; full to partial shade; moist, slightly acid, humus-rich soil.
Landscape uses Plant masses beside a stream or pond where their plumes are reflected in the water. In beds and borders, plant them at the front or toward the center, depending on their size.
Growing guidelines These heavy feeders benefit from an annual application of balanced organic fertilizer. If crowns rise above the soil, top-dress with compost or lift and replant the clumps. Divide clumps every 3–4 years.
Good companions Combine with ferns, daylilies, lady's-mantle *Alchemilla mollis* and other plants that like moist soil.
Other varieties Many named varieties in colors of pink, lavender, red and white.
Comments The foliage is a season-long asset, and the dried seed heads are attractive in a snowy landscape.

Bergenia cordifolia
SAXIFRAGACEAE

HEARTLEAF BERGENIA

Grow bergenias under shrubs for a glossy, green groundcover, or use them in borders or containers. Plant with ferns and small-leaved hostas.

Description Bergenias are handsome foliage plants with broad, leathery, evergreen leaves. The 10–12-inch (25–30-cm) leaves emerge from a stout, creeping rhizome. Fleshy pink or rose flowers are carried on thick stems in late winter or early spring. Foliage turns red in autumn and stays attractive till winter.
Height and spread Height 12–14 inches (30–35 cm); spread 1 foot (30 cm).
Best climate and site Zones 3–9; sun or partial shade (in warmer Zones, plants need afternoon shade); moist, humus-rich soil. Plants are drought-tolerant once established.
Landscape uses Use as accents in narrow beds and borders, at the base of walls or along paths.
Growing guidelines As clumps age, they become bare in the center. Lift plants in spring and remove old portions of the rhizome with a knife; replant into amended soil. Protect with winter mulch.
Good companions Combine with small-flowered plants, such as bellflowers *Campanula* spp., pinks *Dianthus* spp., cranesbills *Geranium* spp. and asters.
Other varieties Many named varieties, some with good autumn leaf color.
Comments Excellent in winter shade.

Campanula persicifolia
CAMPANULACEAE

PEACH-LEAVED BELLFLOWER

Peach-leaved bellflower is a dependable favorite for cottage gardens and borders. The blooms are also long-lasting as cut flowers for indoor arrangements.

Description Peach-leaved bellflower produces mounds of narrow, 8-inch (20-cm), evergreen leaves from a fibrous-rooted crown. Tall, narrow stalks carry a profusion of open, bell-shaped, lavender-blue flowers in summer.
Height and spread Height 1–3 feet (30–90 cm); spread 2 feet (60 cm).
Best climate and site Zones 3–9; full sun to partial shade (provide protection from hot afternoon sun in warmer Zones); moist soil.
Landscape uses Place toward the middle or rear of border. Use in drifts as an accent along a stone wall or garden fence.
Growing guidelines Peach-leaved bellflower is a tough, easy-care plant that spreads slowly by sideshoots from the central crown. Plants may be short-lived in warmer Zones and can be replanted in winter or spring.
Good companions The flower spikes combine well with yarrows, Russian sage *Perovskia atriplicifolia*, cranesbills *Geranium* spp., bee balm (bergamot) *Monarda* spp., phlox and others. Use with shrubs and climbers, such as roses and clematis.
Other common names Willow bell, peach bells.
Comments Prefers cool summers.

Canna x *generalis*
CANNACEAE

CANNA

Cannas are grown for both their bold summer flowers and their attractive, often multi-colored leaves that bring height and interest to the garden.

Description Cannas grow from thick rhizomes. They produce tall, sturdy stems with large, oval, green or reddish purple leaves from spring until frost. The stems are topped with showy clusters of broad-petaled flowers up to 5 inches (12.5 cm) across from mid- to late summer. The flowers bloom in shades of pink, red, orange and yellow, as well as bicolors.
Height and spread Height 2–6 feet (60–180 cm); spread 1–2 feet (30–60 cm).
Best climate and site Zones 8–12; full sun to partial shade; moist soil. In colder Zones, grown as annuals or stored indoors in winter.
Landscape uses Grow alone in masses, or plant with annuals and perennials in beds and borders. Adds a tropical lushness to a cold-climate garden. Dwarf cannas grow well in containers.
Growing guidelines Plant in spring, after frost. In Zone 7 and colder, dig rhizomes before frost and store them indoors for winter. In warm areas, rhizomes can be left in the ground but should be divided every 3–4 years in spring.
Good companions Perennials, grasses and foliage plants.
Comments Good for seaside conditions.

Clivia miniata
AMARYLLIDACEAE

CLIVIA

These evergreen, leafy clumps can be massed in any shady spot as a tall groundcover. The late-winter to spring flowers are a bonus.

Description An evergreen perennial with green, strappy leaves. In late winter to spring, tall, stout stems with clusters of lily-like flowers appear above the foliage. Flowers are up to 3 inches (7.5 cm) across and are usually salmon with a pale throat. Recent breeding has produced cream, yellow, red, pink and striped flowers.
Height and spread Height 1½ feet (45 cm); spread 3 feet (90 cm).
Best climate and site Zones 8–12 (elsewhere a container plant or for conservatories); partial to deep shade; well-drained soil.
Landscape uses A plant to mass under trees or against a shady wall. Can also be grown in a container.
Growing guidelines Plant in spring (or year-round in warm climates). Drought-tolerant once established. Divide when crowded every 3 years.
Good companions Other shade-loving plants, including aucuba, azaleas, camellias, cinerarias and ferns.
Other common names Kaffir lily.
Comments As plants take several years to flower and are often seed-grown, buy unusual colors in flower or select plants that have been propagated by division, to be assured of color.

Cynara cardunculus
ASTERACEAE

CARDOON

This thistle-like plant, related to the globe artichoke, is grown for its towering size, which brings drama and excitement to the garden. It can also be eaten for its blanched stalks, which are used like celery.

Description A thistle-like plant with coarse, gray stems, large, pointed and divided leaves, and topped from summer to autumn with clusters of large, mauve flowers much like a thistle.
Height and spread Height 5 feet (1.5 m); spread 4 feet (1.2 m).
Best climate and site Zones 6–10; full sun; well-drained, moist, fertile soil.
Landscape uses A dramatic addition to any herbaceous bed or border to add architectural interest.
Growing guidelines Grow from offshoots planted in spring or start seedlings indoors if season is short; otherwise, direct-seed 1–2 weeks before last frost. Thin to 2 feet (60 cm) apart. If the plant is to be blanched, tie the leaf stalks together in autumn and wrap with burlap or heavy paper to exclude sunlight and whiten the stalks. Stalks are blanched in 3–4 weeks. In areas where cardoon is perennial, spring shoots may be blanched.
Good companions Other bold perennials such as echium, sea holly or grasses.
Other varieties Named dwarf cultivars.
Comments You can also dig and eat the main roots.

Delphinium x *elatum* hybrids
RANUNCULACEAE

HYBRID DELPHINIUM

Hybrid delphiniums are tall, stately border plants with dense flower clusters atop straight stems with deeply cut, lobed leaves.

Description Plants grow from stout crowns. They produce deeply cut, palmately lobed leaves and tall flower stems from spring to summer. Showy flowers range in color from white through all shades of true blue to lavender and purple. Five petal-like sepals surround two to four small, true petals that are often called the "bee." The top sepal has a long spur.
Height and spread Height 4½–6 feet (1.3–1.8 m); 2–3 feet (60–90 cm) wide.
Best climate and site Zones 4–9; full sun; evenly moist soil.
Landscape uses Plant delphiniums at the rear of borders or against a wall or hedge, where their showy spires will tower over other perennials.
Growing guidelines Set out new plants in early spring. Thin the clumps to three to five stems as they emerge to promote strong growth. Often short-lived in warm climates. Feed in spring. Deadhead and divide overgrown plants.
Good companions Phlox, lilies, lupins and bellflowers *Campanula* spp.
Other species *D.* x *belladonna* hybrids are hardy, heat-resistant, compact plants. Zones 3–9.
Comments May rebloom in autumn.

Dendranthema x *grandiflorum*
ASTERACEAE
(Syn. *Chrysanthemum* x *morifolium*)

GARDEN MUM

The bright flowers of mums signal the end of summer. They bloom in a variety of colors, from white, pink and red to gold and yellow.

Description Garden mums have lobed leaves and grow from clumps with tangled, fibrous roots. Flowers are seen in late summer through autumn. Blooms range from 1–6 inches (2.5–15 cm), often with highly ornate forms.
Height and spread Variable, depending on the cultivar. Height 1½–5 feet (45–150 cm); spread 1–3 feet (30–90 cm).
Best climate and site Zones 3–10; full sun; well-drained soil.
Landscape uses Breathe new life into tired annual displays. Place mums in informal beds and borders or cottage gardens. They also grow well in pots.
Growing guidelines Pinch the stems once or twice in late spring to summer to promote compact growth. Divide the fast-growing clumps in spring every 1–2 years to keep them vigorous. Take tip cuttings in late spring or early summer.
Good companions Asters, goldenrods *Solidago* spp., sedums and Japanese anemones *Anemone* spp. for a showy autumn display. Use with foliage plants, such as yuccas and ornamental grasses.
Other common names Chrysanthemums.
Comments Garden mums can be trained into fans and cascades.

Echinacea purpurea
ASTERACEAE

PURPLE CONEFLOWER

The bright blooms of purple coneflower add a splash of color to ornamental grasses and combine well with most perennials.

Description Purple coneflowers grow from deep roots and are showy, summer- to autumn-flowering daisies with sparse, 6-inch (15-cm), oval or broadly lance-shaped leaves on stout, hairy stems. The rose-pink flowers from midsummer to autumn have broad, drooping rays (petal-like structures) surrounding raised, bristly cones. There are also white forms.
Height and spread Height 2–4 feet (60–120 cm); spread 1–2 feet (30–60 cm).
Best climate and site Zones 3–9; full sun; average to rich, moist, well-drained soil.
Landscape uses Plant in formal gardens or meadow and prairie gardens.
Growing guidelines Purple coneflowers increase from basal buds to form broad, long-lived clumps. Division is seldom necessary and is not recommended.
Good companions Combine with fine-textured flowers, such as yarrow, baby's-breath *Gypsophila paniculata*, Russian sage *Perovskia atriplicifolia*, border phlox *Phlox paniculata* and coreopsis. In meadows and prairies, plant them with goldenrods *Solidago* spp. and a generous supply of ornamental grasses.
Comments Drought-tolerant once plant is established.

Echinops ritro
ASTERACEAE

GLOBE THISTLE

The unusual steely coloring of these small, thistle-like flowers is a welcome addition to the perennial garden through summer, especially where it's hot and dry. The leaves are also highly decorative.

Description Globe thistles are stout, coarse perennials with erect stems clothed in shiny, lobed leaves. They grow from thick, deep-branched roots. Small, five-petaled, steel-blue flowers are packed into 1–2-inch (2.5–5-cm), spherical heads in midsummer.
Height and spread Height 2–3 feet (60–90 cm); spread 2–3 feet (60–90 cm).
Best climate and site Zones 3–10; full sun; average to rich, well-drained soil. Good drainage is essential.
Landscape uses Position near the middle or rear of border, or use in cottage gardens or meadows. The round heads are perfect for cutting or for drying.
Growing guidelines Globe thistles are tough plants. They are drought-tolerant once established and thrive for many years without staking or division.
Good companions Combine with other drought-tolerant perennials, such as sedums, Russian sage *Perovskia atriplicifolia*, catmints *Nepeta* spp., oriental poppy *Papaver orientale*, fine-textured ornamental grasses, baby's-breath *Gypsophila paniculata* and asters.
Comments Butterflies and bees relish the flowers.

Erigeron speciosus
ASTERACEAE

DAISY FLEABANE

Daisy fleabane is lovely teamed with low grasses in dry meadow gardens, to spill over rockeries or to soften the edges of steps or paving.

Description Fleabanes form low clumps of hairy, 6-inch (15-cm), lance-shaped leaves. The 1-inch (2.5-cm) aster-like flowers have white, pink, rose or purple rays surrounding bright yellow centers in early to midsummer.
Height and spread Height 1½–2½ feet (45–75 cm); spread 1–2 feet (30–60 cm).
Best climate and site Zones 2–10; full sun to light shade; moist but well-drained, average to rich soil.
Landscape uses Plant at the front of beds, in rock gardens, beside steps and paths or among paving. Use to soften hard edges. Also useful in containers and hanging baskets.
Growing guidelines These long-lived perennials benefit from division every 2–3 years. They can also be grown readily from seed sown in spring or autumn. Tolerant of heat and cold but must be kept well-watered.
Good companions Summer-blooming perennials, such as pinks *Dianthus* spp., cranesbills *Geranium* spp., cinquefoils *Potentilla* spp., evening primroses *Oenothera* spp. and phlox.
Other varieties Many large-bloomed or colored, named varieties.
Comments Can self-sow.

Eryngium amethystinum
UMBELLIFERAE

AMETHYST SEA HOLLY

The architectural shape and spiny flower bracts of amethyst sea holly add excitement to any perennial planting. These trouble-free plants tolerate heat, cold and drought.

Description Amethyst sea holly is an architectural plant with stiff, summer-flowering, blue stems and basal leaves. The small, steel-blue, globose flower heads are surrounded by thin, spiny bracts. The flowering stems are also blue.
Height and spread Height 1–1½ feet (30–45 cm); spread 1–2 feet (30–60 cm).
Best climate and site Zones 2–10; full sun; average, well-drained soil; extremely drought-tolerant once established.
Landscape uses Plant in the middle of the border as an accent, or use it as a mass planting against a hedge or wall. The showy, blue bracts combine well with yellow-leafed shrubs.
Growing guidelines Set plants out in their permanent location while they are young; older plants resent disturbance. Division is seldom necessary.
Good companions Combine with goldenrods *Solidago* spp., asters, phlox and ornamental grasses. Surround with fine-textured plants, such as sea lavenders *Limonium* spp., baby's-breath *Gypsophila paniculata* and coral bells *Heuchera* spp.
Other species Miss Willmott's ghost, *E. gigantium*, has silvery bracts. Zones 6–9.
Comments Attractive, glossy foliage.

Euphorbia polychroma
EUPHORBIACEAE

CUSHION SPURGE

Cushion spurge blooms at the same time as tulips, so create striking color combinations with the two plants. The plants are long-lived garden residents that need little care.

Description Cushion spurge is a creeping plant with thick stems clothed in succulent, blue-gray, wedge-shaped leaves. The stems grow from fleshy, fibrous roots. The unusual spring flower heads consist of tiny, yellow flowers surrounded by showy, funnel-shaped, yellow bracts (modified leaves).
Height and spread Height 6–10 inches (15–25 cm); spread 1–2 feet (30–60 cm).
Best climate and site Zones 3–9; full sun or light shade; average to rich, well-drained soil. Plants grow in gravelly soil.
Landscape uses Plant at the front of the border, in a sunny rock garden or in a rock wall.
Growing guidelines Divide congested clumps if they overgrow their position.
Good companions Combine with early-blooming perennials, such as columbines *Aquilegia* spp., rock cresses *Arabis* and *Aubrieta* spp., creeping phlox *Phlox stolonifera* and daisy fleabane *Erigeron speciosus*. Use them with bulbs, such as ornamental onions *Allium* spp., tulips, fritillaries *Fritillaria* spp. and daffodils.
Comments The lush foliage is handsome all summer and turns apricot and orange in autumn.

Filipendula rubra
ROSACEAE

QUEEN-OF-THE-PRAIRIE

Mature clumps of queen-of-the-prairie make an arresting display in bloom. If the leaves look tattered after flowering, cut plants to the ground; new leaves will emerge.

Description Queen-of-the-prairie is a towering perennial with huge flower heads on stout, leafy stalks. The showy, 1-foot (30-cm) leaves are deeply lobed and starlike. Plants grow from stout, creeping stems. The small, five-petaled, pink flowers are crowded into large plumes in late spring and early summer.
Height and spread Height 4–6 feet (1.2–1.8 m); spread 2–4 feet (60–120 cm).
Best climate and site Zones 3–9; full sun to light shade; evenly moist but well-drained, humus-rich soil.
Landscape uses Plant at the rear of the border, along streams, beside ponds or in moist, meadow gardens.
Growing guidelines Plants need division every 3–4 years to keep them from overtaking their neighbors. Plants spread more slowly in drier soil. Cut back in winter in cold climates.
Good companions Combine with shrub roses, irises, daylilies and phlox. Use beside ponds with ferns, ornamental grasses and bold foliage plants, such as hostas and rodgersias.
Other common names Meadowsweet.
Comments Plants will not tolerate prolonged dryness.

Gaura lindheimeri
ONAGRACEAE

WHITE GAURA

White gaura is a shrubby perennial with fine, arching stems with airy flower clusters that are pink in bud, opening to white.

Description White gaura is a shrubby perennial and grows from a thick, deep taproot. Unusual white flowers borne on wiry stems with small, hairy leaves are tinged with pink. They have four triangular petals, long, curled stamens, and dance in slender spikes above the foliage throughout summer into autumn.
Height and spread Height 3–4 feet (90–120 cm); spread 3 feet (90 cm).
Best climate and site Zones 5–9; full sun; well-drained soil. Heat-tolerant.
Landscape uses White gaura is a lovely addition to formal and informal gardens alike. The flower clusters look like a swirl of dancing butterflies.
Growing guidelines An easy-care perennial. Plants bloom nonstop all summer despite high heat and humidity. Periodically remove old bloom stalks, cutting back to ground level for the new flowers in 6–8 weeks. Cut to the ground when flowering has finished.
Good companions Combine with low-mounding perennials, such as verbenas *Verbena* spp., cranesbills *Geranium* spp. and sedums. Looks striking with lavender and ornamental grasses.
Other common names White butterfly.
Comments Will self-sow.

Geranium sanguineum
GERANIACEAE

BLOOD-RED CRANESBILL

Even when blood-red cranesbills aren't in flower, you can still enjoy the finely cut foliage all season. The leaves turn burgundy-red in autumn.

Description Blood-red cranesbill is a spreading to low-mounding plant with deeply cut, five-lobed leaves arising from a slow-creeping, fibrous-rooted crown. The bright magenta, saucer-shaped flowers are carried singly above the foliage in late spring to midsummer.
Height and spread Height 9–12 inches (22.5–30 cm); 1–1½ feet (30–45 cm) wide.
Best climate and site Zones 3–10; full sun or partial shade; evenly moist, well-drained, humus-rich soil.
Landscape uses Place cranesbills at the front of the border to tie plantings together, or use them as an edging along paths or in rock gardens.
Growing guidelines Plant 2 feet (60 cm) apart in spring. Divide clumps in spring or autumn when the plants overgrow their position.
Good companions Combine with sundrops *Oenothera* spp., catmints *Nepeta* spp., bellflowers *Campanula* spp., phlox and irises.
Other species *G. macrorrhizum*, bigroot cranesbill, is a fast-spreading plant with fragrant, seven-lobed leaves and bright pink flowers. Zones 4–9.
Comments Plants commonly known as geraniums are in the genus *Pelargonium*.

Helleborus orientalis
RANUNCULACEAE

LENTEN ROSE

Lenten roses may take 2–3 years to become established; after that, they'll bloom dependably every spring. Try them as a groundcover under shrubs and flowering trees.

Description Lenten roses have deeply lobed, leathery leaves growing from a stout crown with fleshy roots. The reddish purple, pink or white flowers have five petal-like sepals surrounded by green leafy bracts. They flower from early winter through spring. The flowers fade to soft pink and green with age.
Height and spread Height 1–1½ feet (30–45 cm); spread 1–2 feet (30–60 cm).
Best climate and site Zones 4–10; light shade; evenly moist, humus-rich soil.
Landscape uses Shade gardens, along woodland walks and spring borders. Excellent under trees, or where viewed from below (such as along a shaded retaining wall).
Growing guidelines In spring, remove damaged leaves. Lift clumps after flowering in spring and separate crowns (divide only for propagation). Replant the divisions immediately. Established plants tolerate dry soil and deep shade.
Good companions Early-spring bulbs, wildflowers, lungworts *Pulmonaria* spp., ferns, shrubby dogwoods with colored stems, such as *Cornus sericea*.
Other common names Hellebore.
Comments A must for shade gardens.

Hemerocallis hybrids
LILIACEAE

DAYLILIES

Each daylily flower lasts only one day, but a profusion of new buds topping multiple bloom stalks keeps the plants in bloom for a month or more.

Description Daylilies grow from dense clumps and have straplike leaves (some varieties are evergreen, others deciduous). The flowers bloom from spring to autumn, each lasting only 1–2 days. The majority of wild species are orange or yellow.
Height and spread Height 1–5 feet (30–150 cm); spread 2–3 feet (60–90 cm).
Best climate and site Zones 3–10; full sun or light shade; evenly moist, average to rich soil.
Landscape uses Mass plantings in beds and borders, in meadows and at the edge of woodland with shrubs and trees.
Growing guidelines Plant container-grown or bareroot plants in spring or autumn, placing the crowns just below soil surface. Some of the older selections and species will bloom in partial shade.
Good companions Summer-blooming perennials and ornamental grasses.
Other varieties Modern hybrids come in a rainbow of colors, except blues and true white. Many have blazes, eyes and blotches on the petals. Flower shape varies from the traditional form to narrow-petaled, spider-like forms and fat, tubular or saucer-shaped flowers.
Comments In cold-winter areas, grow deciduous forms.

Hibiscus moscheutos
MALVACEAE

COMMON ROSE MALLOW

The showy flowers of common rose mallow are borne in profusion on a shrublike plant that grows from a thick, woody crown.

Description This herbaceous, shrublike plant grows from a thick, woody crown with unbranched stems and broad, oval leaves. The 6–8-inch (15–20-cm), five-petaled flowers are white to pink with bright red centers and a prominent column of stamens. Flowering extends through summer.
Height and spread Height 4–8 feet (1.2–2.4 m); spread 3–5 feet (90–150 cm).
Best climate and site Zones 5–10; full sun; evenly moist, humus-rich soil. Tolerates some dryness once established.
Landscape uses Use for a bold dash of color or as accent plants.
Growing guidelines Space young plants 3–4 feet (90–120 cm) apart to accommodate their eventual spread. Once established, clumps dislike disturbance. Keep well watered and fertilize every 6 weeks during the growing season.
Good companions Plant with ornamental grasses and summer perennials.
Other varieties Many named varieties with large, brightly colored flowers, including rose pink.
Comments Enjoy rose mallow where climates are not warm enough for Hawaiian hibiscus *H. rosa-sinensis*.

Hosta hybrids
LILIACEAE

HOSTAS

Hostas are indispensable foliage plants for shaded gardens. Hundreds of cultivars are available; many have striking leaf colors and textures.

Description The thick, pleated or puckered leaves vary in color and size from 1 inch (2.5 cm) to 3 feet (90 cm) or more. Lavender, purple or white flower spikes in summer or autumn. The foliage is decorative and often golden in autumn.
Height and spread Varies widely. Height 6 inches (15 cm) to 3 feet (90 cm) or more in leaf or flower; spread from 6 inches (15 cm) to 5 feet (1.5 m).
Best climate and site Zones 3–10; light to full shade; moist, humus-rich soil.
Landscape uses Versatile plants to edge beds or cover the ground under shrubs and trees. Giant forms create drama among a mixed planting.
Growing guidelines Allow room to accommodate their ultimate size. New spring shoots are slow to emerge, so take care not to damage them.
Good companions Ferns and shade perennials with contrasting foliage, such as spiky Siberian iris *Iris sibirica* and daylilies *Hemerocallis* spp.
Other common names Plantain lily.
Other varieties Many named and unnamed variegated and colored leaf forms including chartreuse, gold and blue.
Comments Protect plants from hot afternoon sun.

Iris bearded hybrids
IRIDACEAE

BEARDED IRIS

Bearded irises are old-fashioned, cottage garden favorites. Their beautiful flowers range in color from white and yellow to blue, violet and purple.

Description Bearded irises produce broad fans of wide, flattened leaves and thick, flowering stems from rhizomes. The flowers have three segments, called falls, each with a fringed "beard." The flower center boasts three slender segments called "standards." Flowers bloom late spring to early summer.
Height and spread Height 1–3 feet (30–90 cm); spread 1–2 feet (30–60 cm).
Best climate and site Zones 3–10; full sun; well-drained soil.
Landscape uses Formal or informal gardens to extend seasonal interest.
Growing guidelines Plant in late summer, or container-grown plants from spring to autumn. Plant with the top half of the rhizome above the soil line. Plants are more stable when newly planted if leaves are cut back by half. Remove dead foliage in spring and autumn. Divide every 3–4 years in summer.
Good companions Combine with peonies, yarrows and pinks *Dianthus* spp. Excellent with roses.
Other varieties Many named varieties in a rainbow of colors.
Comments Gently remove spent flowers to make way for more blooms, as flowers may only last 1–2 days.

Kniphofia uvaria
LILIACEAE

COMMON TORCH LILY

Common torch lily is a commanding perennial with tufts of narrow, evergreen leaves from a fleshy-rooted crown. The flower spikes add a dramatic accent to summer gardens.

Description Thick, channeled leaves and densely packed, tubular flower that form slender spikes on stout stems. The lowest flowers on the spike are yellow-white; the upper ones are red. Flowers seen late spring to summer.
Height and spread Height 3–5 feet (90–150 cm); 2–4 feet (60–120 cm) wide.
Best climate and site Zones 5–10; full sun; average to humus-rich, well-drained soil. Established torch lily plants are quite drought-tolerant.
Landscape uses The vertical form of common torch lilies adds drama to perennial borders and rock gardens. An accent beside fences, gates or entrances.
Growing guidelines Set out young plants 2–2½ feet (60–75 cm) apart. Leave established plants undisturbed. Plants increase to form broad, floriferous clumps. Remove spent spikes.
Good companions Combine with ornamental grasses, wormwoods *Artemisia* spp., sundrops *Oenothera* spp. and other summer perennials.
Other common names Red-hot poker.
Other species Some species flower in autumn and winter.
Comments Highly bird-attractant.

Leucanthemum x superbum
(Syn. *Chrysanthemum* x *superbum*)
ASTERACEAE

SHASTA DAISY

Shasta daisies look delightful in borders, cottage gardens and meadows. The plants are extremely heat- and cold-tolerant.

Description Shasta daisies are showy, summer-blooming plants with dense clusters of shiny 10-inch (25-cm), deep green, toothed leaves from short, creeping, fibrous-rooted stems. The 3-inch (7.5-cm) white daisies have large, bright yellow centers carried on stout, leafy stems throughout the summer.
Height and spread Height 1–3 feet (30–90 cm); spread 2 feet (60 cm).
Best climate and site Zones 3–10 (exact Zones vary by cultivar); full sun; average to rich, well-drained soil.
Landscape uses Plant in beds and borders, cottage gardens and meadows.
Growing guidelines Deadhead plants to promote continued bloom. These easy-care plants grow quickly but may be short-lived, especially in warmer Zones. Divide and replant clumps every 3–4 years to keep them vigorous.
Good companions Combine with summer-blooming perennials, such as yarrows, daylilies, irises and poppies. In a seaside garden, plant them with blanket flowers *Gaillardia* spp., butterfly weed *Asclepias tuberosa*, grasses and coreopsis.
Comments Shasta daisy is a classic cottage garden choice.

Ligularia dentata
ASTERACEAE

BIG LEAF LIGULARIA

Big leaf ligularias are bold accent plants for moist-soil gardens. Combine them with spiky or rounded plants to contrast or complement their broad leaves.

Description Big leaf ligularia has 1–2-foot (30–60-cm), round or kidney-shaped, leathery leaves on long stalks. Plants grow from stout crowns with thick, fleshy roots. The spires of 3-inch (8-cm) bright orange-yellow flowers are carried in open clusters in late summer.

Height and spread Height 3–4 feet (90–120 cm) tall and wide.

Best climate and site Zones 3–9; full sun or partial shade; average to rich, moist soil.

Landscape uses Use near ponds, beside a fountain, along a stream, or in informal and shaded borders.

Growing guidelines The huge leaves lose water rapidly. In hot sun, the plants go into dramatic collapse, but they recover as temperatures moderate in the evening or when water is applied. Although ligularias form big clumps, they do not need frequent division.

Good companions Ferns, irises and grasses for contrast, or hostas and umbrella plant *Darmera peltata* as a complement.

Other species *L. przewalski*, Chinese rocket, has deeply divided leaves and slender flower spires. Zones 4–9.

Comments Watch for slugs and snails.

Macleaya cordata
PAPAVERACEAE

PLUME POPPY

The imposing plume poppy is treelike in stature, with 10-inch (25-cm) lobed leaves clothing erect stems. Plants grow from stout, creeping roots that can quickly become invasive.

Description This tall, treelike perennial grows from creeping rhizomes and has large, lobed, gray-green leaves on erect stems. The 1-foot (30-cm) plumes consist of small, cream-colored flowers in summer that give way to showy, flat, rose-colored seedpods.

Height and spread Height 6–10 feet (1.8–3 m); spread 4–8 feet (1.2–2.4 m).

Best climate and site Zones 3–10, full sun to partial shade; moist, average to humus-rich soil. Stems are not as sturdy on shade-grown plants.

Landscape uses Place at the back of borders. Plant them as accents along stairs or fences or use them like shrubs as a focal point.

Growing guidelines Established clumps of plume poppy can double in size each season. Control is inevitably necessary to avert a total takeover. Chop off the creeping roots with a spade as soon as you see new stems emerging. Cut back spent stems to the ground in autumn.

Good companions Other tall-growing summer perennials and shrubs, such as fuchsias, or grow among trees.

Comments This plant can overwhelm smaller perennials.

Nepeta x faassenii
LAMIACEAE

CATMINT

Catmint is a low, groundcover perennial that produces soft gray leaves and misty purple-blue flower spires that rise above the leaves from spring to early summer.

Description A bushy, clump-forming, low perennial with fibrous roots and aromatic, gray-green leaves. Violet-blue flowers are carried in whorls on slender spikes above the leaves from spring through summer.

Height and spread Height 1½–3 feet (45–90 cm); spread 2–3 feet (60–90 cm).

Best climate and site Zones 3–10; full sun to light shade; average to humus-rich, moist, well-drained soil. Plants tolerate poor, dry soil.

Landscape uses Catmints are perfect for edging walks and beds or for planting along rock walls.

Growing guidelines Clumps get rangy after bloom. Cut back finished flower stalks to encourage fresh growth and repeat bloom. Select a well-drained site.

Good companions In borders combine with bellflowers *Campanula* spp., cranesbills *Geranium* spp., coreopsis, peonies, ornamental grasses and roses.

Other species *N. mussinii*, Persian nepeta, grows 1–1½ feet (30–45 cm) tall with a 2-foot (60-cm) spread. Lavender-blue flowers cover the plants for months. Zones 3–8.

Comments Highly attractive to bees.

Oenothera fruticosa
ONAGRACEAE

COMMON SUNDROPS

Young plants of common sundrops start out small but quickly form large clumps, so leave ample space at planting. Cut them back after flowering to promote rebloom.

Description Common sundrops are showy perennials with narrow, bright green leaves on upright to slightly sprawling stems. The bright lemon-yellow flowers bloom in late spring and early summer and are saucer-shaped and 3–4 inches (7.5–10 cm) wide and open during the daylight hours. Plants spread by creeping stems to form broad clumps.
Height and spread Height 1–2 feet (30–60 cm); spread 1–3 feet (30–90 cm).
Best climate and site Zones 3–10; full sun; average, well-drained soil. Established plants are drought- and heat-tolerant.
Landscape uses Use in the front or middle of borders, as a groundcover for sunny cottage gardens, or in rock gardens and meadow plantings.
Growing guidelines Plant anytime, spacing 1 foot (30 cm) apart. Cut back over winter; divide rosettes in late winter to early spring.
Good companions Sweet William *Phlox maculata*, cranesbills *Geranium* spp., catmints *Nepeta* spp., yarrows *Achillea* spp. and other early-summer perennials.
Other species *O. speciosa*, white evening primrose. Zones 5–10.
Comments Can become invasive.

Paeonia lactiflora
RANUNCULACEAE

COMMON GARDEN PEONY

Peonies are among the most popular of all flowers. As well as beautiful flowers, the red, new shoots look great with spring bulbs, while the rich green foliage is a foil to later-blooming perennials.

Description Peonies have sturdy stalks clothed in compound, shiny, green leaves with huge, fragrant, white, pink or red flowers in late spring to early summer.
Height and spread Height 1½–3 feet (45–90 cm); spread 3–4 feet (90–120 cm).
Best climate and site Zones 2–8; full sun or light shade; moist, well-drained, humus-rich soil.
Landscape uses Favorites for cottage gardens, beds, borders and mass plantings.
Growing guidelines Plant container-grown peonies in spring or autumn. Place the "eyes" (buds) 1–1½ inches (2.5–3.5 cm) below the soil surface and 3–4 feet (90–120 cm) apart. Apply an annual winter mulch where winter temperatures dip below 0°F (–18°C). Lift plants in autumn; divide, leaving at least one eye per division, and replant. Water well from spring to late summer.
Good companions Spring and early-summer perennials such as irises, foxgloves *Digitalis* spp., columbines *Aquilegia* spp., as well as oriental poppies and roses.
Other common names Chinese peony.
Comments Tall, shrubby forms are called tree peonies.

Papaver orientale
PAPAVERACEAE

ORIENTAL POPPY

Oriental poppies are prized for their colorful, paper-like flowers. Combine with bushy perennials to fill the gap when the poppies go dormant in summer.

Description Plants produce rosettes of hairy, lobed, bluish green foliage. The 3–4-inch (7.5–10-cm), early-summer flowers have crinkled petals with black spots at their bases. They surround a raised knob that becomes the seedpod.
Height and spread Height 2–3 feet (60–90 cm); spread 2–3 feet (60–90 cm).
Best climate and site Zones 2–9; full sun or light shade; average to rich, well-drained, humus-rich soil. Established plants are tough.
Landscape uses Use with other perennials and ornamental grasses in beds and borders. The showy flowers are favorites with cottage gardeners.
Growing guidelines In most areas, plants are dormant after flowering, leaving a bare spot in the garden. In autumn, new foliage rosettes emerge; divide overgrown plants at this time.
Good companions Combine with bushy plants such as catmints *Nepeta* spp., cranesbills *Geranium* spp., yarrow and asters to fill the gap left in summer.
Other common names Peony poppy.
Comments Related to opium poppies, these cottage plants are prohibited in some countries.

Penstemon hybrids
SCROPHULARIACEAE

PENSTEMON

Penstemons are a natural choice for meadow gardens, but also blend well into formal borders. Enjoy the flowers, which come in a range of jewel-like colors, from spring to summer.

Description Flowering stems and foliage rosettes arise from crowns. Penstemons are showy with upright, foxglove-like flower spikes in white, mauve or red and are clothed in shiny, broadly lance-shaped leaves. The 1–1½-inch (2.5–3.5-cm) flowers bloom from spring to summer.
Height and spread Varies with cultivar. Height 2–4 feet (60–120 cm); spread 1–2 feet (30–60 cm).
Best climate and site Zones 3–10 (but varies with selection); full sun to light shade; average, moist, well-drained soil.
Landscape uses Formal or informal gardens, rock gardens, hillsides, low meadows or the edge of a woodland.
Growing guidelines Plant in winter or spring. Plants benefit from division every 4 years. Cut back in summer if untidy to encourage reflowering. Some are frost-hardy but others need to be cut to the ground in winter.
Good companions Combine these spiky flowers with rounded plants, such as cranesbills *Geranium* spp., yarrows and coral bells *Heuchera* spp.
Other common names Beard tongue.
Comments Most penstemons are native to North America.

Phlox paniculata
POLEMONIACEAE

GARDEN PHLOX

Garden phlox is a beautiful and versatile garden perennial. It forms broad clumps that need dividing every 3–4 years in spring or autumn.

Description Garden phlox is a summer-blooming perennial with domed clusters of fragrant flowers atop stiff, leafy stems arising from fibrous-rooted crowns. The tubular flowers have flared, five-petaled faces in mid- to late summer. Color varies from magenta to pink and white.
Height and spread Height 3–4 feet (90–120 cm); 2–4 feet (60–120 cm) wide.
Best climate and site Zones 3–10; full sun or light shade; moist, well-drained, humus-rich soil.
Landscape uses Plant in formal and informal beds as well as cottage gardens. It is lovely in meadows and on the edges of lightly shaded woodlands.
Growing guidelines Set out plants in clumps with the crowns at soil level 8–12 inches (20–30 cm) apart in autumn to spring. Cut off spent flowers regularly. Divide clumps every 3–4 years.
Good companions Combine with daisies, bee balm (bergamot) *Monarda* spp., daylilies, meadow rues *Thalictrum* spp., asters, goldenrods *Solidago* spp. and ornamental grasses.
Other common names Summer phlox, perennial phlox.
Comments Look for mildew-resistant cultivars of garden phlox.

Polygonatum odoratum
LILIACEAE

FRAGRANT SOLOMON'S SEAL

Greenish flowers dangle from the arching stems of fragrant Solomon's seal in spring. The cream-edged leaves of the variegated form extend the interest throughout the season.

Description Plants spread from thick, creeping rhizomes to form wide clumps with graceful, arching stems and broadly oval, blue-green leaves arranged like steps up the stem. The tubular, white and green, fragrant spring flowers hang in pairs below the leaves from the nodes (leaf joints). Showy, blue-black fruits form in late summer.
Height and spread Height 1½–2½ feet (45–75 cm); spread 2–4 feet (60–120 cm).
Best climate and site Zones 3–9; partial to full shade; moist, humus-rich soil; tolerates dry soil.
Landscape uses The arching flower stems provide grace and beauty to the shade garden, or to overhang a pond. They also grow well in containers.
Growing guidelines Keep well watered through summer. Cut back to the ground after flowering in autumn, since plants are dormant during winter. Divide in spring or autumn.
Good companions Combine with hostas, lungworts *Pulmonaria* spp., irises and ferns. Use massed plantings under tall shrubs or in the dry shade of mature trees.
Comments Other species are taller, but all love moist shade.

Primula denticulata
PRIMULACEAE

DRUMSTICK PRIMROSE

Drumstick primroses have distinctive flowers that add a fun touch to the early-spring garden. Combine them with ferns and moisture-loving perennials for all-season interest.

Description Drumstick primroses have narrowly oval leaves arising in a whorl from a crown of thick, fibrous, white roots. The leafless, but thick and hairy flower stems bear tight, globe-shaped clusters of lavender or pink flowers in early spring.

Height and spread Height 6–12 inches (15–30 cm) in flower; leaves 6–8 inches (15–20 cm) tall. Plants 10–12 inches (25–30 cm) wide.

Best climate and site Zones 3–9; light to partial shade; humus-rich, moist soil.

Landscape uses Plant along a stream, beside a pool or in a moist shade garden. In a low spot, use them in mass plantings with moisture-tolerant shrubs, such as red-osier dogwood *Cornus sericea*.

Growing guidelines Drumstick primroses are heavy feeders, so mulch with compost or well-rotted manure in early spring or summer to provide extra nutrients.

Good companions Combine with astilbe, ferns, wildflowers and other primroses. In wet soils, plant with irises, hostas and rodgersias *Rodgersia* spp.

Comments There are many species, including some that are grown as annuals for cool-season color.

Primula vulgaris
PRIMULACEAE

ENGLISH PRIMROSE

The flowers of English primroses are excellent companions for spring-blooming bulbs and wildflowers in woodlands and under shrubs and trees.

Description English primroses have flat, five-petaled, pale yellow, scented flowers in spring and early summer. The broad, crinkled leaves rise directly from stout crowns with thick, fibrous roots.

Height and spread Height 6–9 inches (15–22.5 cm); spread 1 foot (30 cm).

Best climate and site Zones 4–9; light to partial shade; evenly moist, humus-rich soil.

Landscape uses Grow primroses in light shade in woodland and informal gardens.

Growing guidelines Mulch plants in winter to minimize the alternate freezing and thawing that can push plants out of the soil. Divide overgrown clumps after flowering.

Good companions Plant scattered clumps and drifts with spring bulbs, such as daffodils, tulips and Spanish bluebells *Hyacinthoides hispanicus*. Combine with early-blooming perennials, such as hellebores *Helleborus* spp., lungworts *Pulmonaria* spp., forget-me-nots *Myosotis* spp. and cranesbills *Geranium* spp. Wildflowers, ferns and sedges *Carex* spp. are other excellent companions.

Comments The flowers and fruits of English primrose contain a toxin and can irritate some skins.

Rodgersia pinnata
SAXIFRAGACEAE

RODGERSIA

Rodgersias are big, bold perennials with large, divided leaves that develop a pinkish tinge and look fabulous beside water.

Description This moisture-loving plant grows from rhizomes and has large, emerald-green leaves. The small, buff to pink flowers are carried in 1–2-foot (30–60-cm) plumelike clusters in late spring and early summer.

Height and spread Height 3–4 feet (90–120 cm); spread 4 feet (1.2 m).

Best climate and site Zones 4–9; in partial to full shade; moist, humus-rich soil. Protect from hot afternoon sun.

Landscape uses Mass plant in bog and water gardens or along streams.

Growing guidelines Rodgersias form huge clumps from large crowns that can remain in place for years. Provide at least 3–4 feet (90–120 cm) of room for each plant. Keep soil moist and regularly improve with layers of organic mulch and compost. Water regularly when hot or dry. Cut back flowered stems.

Good companions Moisture lovers, including filipendulas, hostas, irises, astilbes, ferns, ligularias *Ligularia* spp. and primroses.

Other common names Rodger's flower.

Other varieties White, salmon-pink flowers and bronze-tinted foliage.

Comments A dramatic plant choice for moist shade.

Rudbeckia fulgida
ASTERACEAE

ORANGE CONEFLOWER

Orange coneflowers, also called black-eyed Susans, are tough, long-lived perennials for late summer and autumn color in formal borders, meadow gardens or even containers.

Description Plants grow from fibrous-rooted crowns. The oval to broadly lance-shaped, hairy leaves are alternate on stiff stems. The cheery daisies have yellow-orange rays (petals) and raised, dark brown centers. Plants bloom from late summer to autumn.

Height and spread Height 1½–3 feet (45–90 cm); spread 2–4 feet (60–120 cm).

Best climate and site Zones 3–10; full sun or light shade; average, moist, well-drained soil. Heat-tolerant.

Landscape uses Plant in formal and informal beds and borders, cottage gardens and meadows.

Growing guidelines Plant while dormant in autumn to winter, or potted specimens anytime. Orange coneflowers spread outward to form large clumps. Their exuberant growth depletes the soil; the edges of the clumps are the most vigorous. Divide clumps every 2–4 years in spring or autumn and replant into amended soil. Deadhead after flowering.

Good companions Combine with other daisies, penstemons, sedums, phlox, bee balm (bergamot) *Monarda* spp. and ornamental grasses.

Comments Good drainage is important.

Ruta graveolens
RUTACEAE

RUE

Rue is a traditional favorite for herb gardens, but its lacy, blue-gray foliage also looks super in ornamental plantings with bold, colorful flowers.

Description The aromatic, blue-gray leaves are divided into many small, fan-shaped leaflets that look good year-round. Small, yellow, buttercup-like flowers are carried in open clusters above the foliage in summer. Plants grow from a woody crown.

Height and spread Height 1–3 feet (30–90 cm); spread 2–3 feet (60–90 cm).

Best climate and site Zones 4–10; full sun or light shade; average to rich, well-drained soil. Tolerates dry, sandy soil.

Landscape uses Choose rue for herb and knot gardens or for the front or middle of beds and borders. It is also beautiful for edging beds or bordering walks.

Growing guidelines Rue forms broad, dense clumps that seldom need division.

Good companions Combine with hyssop *Hyssopus officinalis*, yarrows, ornamental onions *Allium* spp. and ornamental grasses. Contrast the fine-textured foliage with bold flowers, such as balloon flower *Platycodon grandiflorus*, orange coneflowers *Rudbeckia* spp. and blanket flowers *Gaillardia* spp.

Other common names Herb of grace.

Comments While rue may irritate the skin of some people, it is also said to be useful to repel flies.

Salvia x superba
LAMIACEAE

VIOLET SAGE

The spiky blooms of violet sage combine wonderfully with rounded perennials, such as cranesbills. Cut back the stems after flowering to promote rebloom.

Description The bushy, well-branched plants have aromatic, triangular leaves and grow from a fibrous-rooted crown. Violet sage is covered with colorful flower spikes in summer. Below each flower is a leaflike bract.

Height and spread Height 1½–3½ feet (45–105 cm); spread 2–3 feet (60–90 cm).

Best climate and site Zones 4–10; full sun or light shade; average to rich, moist, well-drained soil. Plants are drought-tolerant once established.

Landscape uses Plant violet sages in formal or informal borders or in rock gardens. Use them in cottage gardens or in mass plantings. The plants also grow well in containers.

Growing guidelines Plants bloom nonstop for a month. After flowering wanes, shear off the spent flowers to promote fresh growth and renewed bloom. Plants seldom need division.

Good companions Combine with early-summer perennials, such as yarrows, lamb's ears *Stachys byzantina*, daylilies, coreopsis and ornamental grasses.

Comments There are many forms of salvia to bring blue, red or white flowers to gardens. Many are highly attractive to nectar-eating birds and insects.

Scabiosa caucasica
DIPSACACEAE

PINCUSHION FLOWER

Pincushion flowers are old-fashioned perennials that are regaining the popularity they had in Victorian gardens. Plant in groups to increase visual impact.

Description The stems are loosely clothed in lance-shaped to three-lobed leaves. The pale blue or pink, summer flowers are packed into flat, 2–3-inch (5–7.5-cm) heads.

Height and spread Height 1½–2 feet (45–60 cm); spread 1–1½ feet (30–45 cm).

Best climate and site Zones 3–10; full sun to light shade; average to humus-rich, moist but well-drained soil. Plants are sensitive to high temperatures. They also will not tolerate wet soils.

Landscape uses Beds and borders or cottage gardens.

Growing guidelines Plant in autumn or spring for good-sized clumps in 1–2 years. Divide in spring if plants become overcrowded. Remove spent flowers to promote continued bloom.

Good companions The airy flowers seem to dance above low, mounded plants, such as cranesbills *Geranium* spp., phlox, pinks *Dianthus* spp. and yarrows. They also combine well with bee balm (bergamot) *Monarda* spp., daylilies and columbines *Aquilegia* spp.

Other common names Perennial scabious.

Comments Cut back to ground level in cold Zones.

Sedum spectabile
CRASSULACEAE

SHOWY STONECROP

Easy-to-grow showy stonecrop is a dependable addition to beds and borders for year-round interest. It also looks great alone in mass plantings, or with ornamental grasses.

Description Showy stonecrops have thick stems clothed in broad, gray-green leaves growing from fibrous-rooted crowns. Small, bright pink flowers are borne in 4–6-inch (10–15-cm) clusters in mid- to late summer. The pale green buds are attractive in summer, and the seed heads hold their shape all winter.

Height and spread Height 1–2 feet (30–60 cm); spread 2 feet (60 cm).

Best climate and site Zones 3–9; full sun; average to humus-rich, well-drained soil.

Landscape uses Plant in formal borders, informal gardens and rock gardens. Stonecrops are also good for mass plantings with shrubs. They can be used in containers.

Growing guidelines Clumps get quite full with age and may flop open, leaving a bare center. Divide overgrown plants from spring to midsummer.

Good companions Combine with yarrows, shasta daisies *Leucanthemum* x *superbum*, purple coneflowers *Echinacea* spp., cranesbills *Geranium* spp., coreopsis and ornamental grasses.

Comments Extremely heat-, drought-, cold- and frost-tolerant.

Solidago rigida
ASTERACEAE

STIFF GOLDENROD

A bold, golden yellow flower to brighten the late summer and autumn garden, but best in a wild or meadow garden.

Description Stiff goldenrod is a showy wildflower with flattened clusters of bright yellow, fuzzy flowers on leafy stalks that grow from a crown with thick, fleshy roots. The basal leaves are oval to lance-shaped and may reach 1 foot (30 cm) in length. The stem leaves are oval and decrease in size near the top of the stem. The foliage is attractive in summer and turns ruby red in autumn. The seed heads are silvery.

Height and spread Height 3–5 feet (90–150 cm); 1–2 feet (30–60 cm) wide.

Best climate and site Zones 3–9; full sun or light shade; average, sandy or loamy, well-drained soil. Plants in rich soil produce weak, floppy growth.

Landscape uses Plant stiff goldenrod in beds and borders, along walls and fences, or in meadows and prairies. The stiff, upright form and showy blooms make them suitable for formal settings as well.

Growing guidelines Spreads rapidly and needs frequent division.

Good companions Combine with autumn flowers, such as asters, garden mums, anemones *Anemone* spp., sneezeweed *Helenium autumnale* and ornamental grasses.

Comments Can become invasive.

Tiarella cordifolia
SAXIFRAGACEAE

FOAMFLOWER

Foamflowers are elegant woodland wildflowers with fuzzy flowers and rosettes of dainty leaves. They make an excellent groundcover choice.

Description Plants grow from fibrous-rooted crowns and creeping stems. The plant has heart-shaped, hairy leaves. The small, starry, white flowers are borne in spikelike clusters in spring. They are often tinged with pink.

Height and spread Height 6–10 inches (15–25 cm); spread 1–2 feet (30–60 cm).

Best climate and site Zones 3–9; partial to full shade; evenly moist, humus-rich, slightly acid soil.

Landscape uses Foamflowers are consummate groundcovers. Their tight foliage mats discourage weeds under shrubs and flowering trees. An excellent choice for a moist, woodland garden in a cool to mild climate. Can also be grown beside shaded paths.

Growing guidelines Divide and plant in spring. Foamflowers spread by creeping stems to form broad mats. Divide plants to control their spread.

Good companions In woodland gardens combine them with bulbs, ferns, fringed bleeding heart *Dicentra eximia*, bloodroot *Sanguinaria canadensis*, as well as hostas, heucheras and irises.

Comments These plants are closely related to heucheras and, if planted together, may hybridize.

Tradescantia Andersoniana Group
COMMELINACEAE
(Syn. *T.* x *andersoniana*)

COMMON SPIDERWORT

Common spiderworts are succulent-like plants with bold, satiny flowers that open in the morning and fade in the afternoon.

Description Plants grow from thick, spidery roots with succulent stems and grasslike leaves. The 1–1½-inch (2.5–3.5-cm) flowers have three rounded blue, purple or white petals. They are borne in clusters at the tips of the stems from spring to early summer.

Best climate and site Zones 3–10; full sun to partial shade; moist but well-drained, average to humus-rich soil.

Height and spread Height 1–2 feet (30–60 cm); spread 2 feet (60 cm).

Landscape uses An excellent choice in any moist or shaded planting. Plant for color contrast in informal gardens. In formal gardens, combine common spiderwort with spring-blooming perennials and bulbs.

Growing guidelines Plant in autumn or spring. After flowering, plants tend to look shabby, so cut them to the ground to encourage new growth. Plants in dry situations go dormant in summer.

Good companions Bellflowers *Campanula* spp., columbines *Aquilegia* spp., hostas and ferns.

Comments Still sold as *T.* x *andersoniana* or *T. virginiana*.

Verbascum chaixii
SCROPHULARIACEAE

NETTLE-LEAVED MULLEIN

Nettle-leaved mullein produces clumps of crinkled green leaves and tall stems topped with spikes of yellow flowers. They are an excellent contrast to mounded perennials.

Description Nettle-leaved mullein has tall, thick flower spikes that appear in summer and stout stems with broadly oval, pointed leaves. The small, five-petaled yellow flowers are tightly packed into dense clusters up the spire.

Best climate and site Zones 4–9; full sun to light shade; thrives in well-drained, moist garden soil.

Height and spread Height 2–3 feet (60–90 cm); spread 1–2 feet (30–60 cm).

Landscape uses Plant as an accent in borders with fine-textured plants, or combine with mounded plants in informal gardens, meadows or gravel plantings.

Growing guidelines Divide in winter, or plant fresh plants in spring or autumn. Plants spread slowly and often self-sow.

Good companions Perennials, including thread-leaved coreopsis *Coreopsis verticillata*, cranesbills *Geranium* spp. and meadow rues *Thalictrum* spp., or mounded plants, such as catmints *Nepeta* spp. and ornamental grasses.

Other varieties There is a variety with white flowers and purple eyes.

Comments Verbascums also grow well in containers.

Abies homolepis
PINACEAE

NIKKO FIR

The Nikko fir is an attractive, evergreen conifer that grows best in cool, moist climates. It has a conical habit and whorls of glossy, needle-like leaves.

Description A tall and highly ornamental, coniferous, evergreen tree with attractive, horizontal branches. The insignificant, green or yellowish flowers in spring are followed by upright purplish cones in summer to winter.

Height and spread Height to 100 feet (30 m); spread to 30 feet (9 m).

Best climate and site Zones 4–8; full sun to light shade; deep, moist, well-drained, acid soil.

Landscape uses Specimen tree, screens or use as an evergreen framework for cold-climate gardens.

Growing guidelines Best planted in spring or winter. Pruning is not necessary. Fairly wind-tolerant. Mulch regularly with organic matter to keep soil moist and trees healthy. Avoid planting in hot, dry areas.

Good companions Other acid-loving plants, including dwarf conifers, azaleas and camellias.

Other varieties Dwarf varieties grow to 6 feet (1.8 m); prostrate or groundcover forms are also available.

Comments Firs are long-lived trees that maintain their attractive shape and form into old age. The Nikko fir is more tolerant of pollution than other species.

Acer spp.
ACERACEAE

MAPLE

Maples are handsome trees prized for their outstanding autumn leaf color and cool summer shade. Many have colorful autumn foliage.

Description Maples are small to tall, deciduous trees valued for their ornamental leaves and vibrant, autumn color. Many have colorful spring foliage, others have colorful bark. Flowers and winged seeds are seen in spring.

Height and spread Species vary from small trees less than 12 feet (3.6 m), to large trees to 100 feet (30 m) and as wide.

Best climate and site Varies with species but ranges from Zones 3–9; full sun to partial shade; most soils.

Landscape uses Specimen and shade trees for changing seasonal effect. *A. palmatum*, especially the weeping or dissected leaf forms, are suited to small or courtyard gardens. Useful species for a Japanese-style garden. Tall species make good street or avenue plantings.

Growing guidelines Plant bareroot, container-grown or balled-and-burlapped plants in late winter to spring. Prune in winter only to shape the young tree.

Good companions Many maples have shallow, spreading roots that make growing other plants under them difficult, but try shade-loving, spring-flowering shrubs, such as azaleas and rhododendrons.

Comments Avoid damaging bark—wounds are entry points for pests and diseases.

Albizia julibrissin
MIMOSACEAE

MIMOSA

Native to Asia, mimosa is a deciduous tree with compound leaves that give it a ferny, almost tropical effect. The fluffy, pink flowers are borne in summer.

Description This decorative, small tree has dark green, feathery foliage that turns yellow in autumn before it drops. Its broad branches form an umbrella shape. The faintly perfumed, pink flowers have many long, silky, creamy white to pink stamens and are borne in dense, terminal clusters during midsummer.

Height and spread Height to 25 feet (7.5 m) and as wide.

Best climate and site Zones 7–12; full sun; best in poor, dry soil. In cooler Zones, thrives if planted near a warm wall.

Landscape uses Use as a specimen tree and shade tree, particularly for small, warm-climate gardens.

Growing guidelines Plant in winter or spring. Withstands dry conditions but benefits from extra watering for the first year or two. Pruning is not necessary, except for shaping the tree to develop a single trunk.

Good companions Tropical and subtropical trees and shrubs, including palms, hibiscus and bananas.

Other common names Silk tree.

Comments In some warm climates, these trees suffer mimosa wilt (a soil fungus). Choose resistant cultivars and avoid wet, poorly drained soil.

Amelanchier laevis
ROSACEAE

ALLEGHENY SERVICEBERRY

Allegheny serviceberry is a pretty, multi-stemmed, deciduous tree massed in spring with white flowers. The reddish new leaves deepen to green in summer, but turn red-orange in autumn.

Description A deciduous tree with white, five-petaled flowers in spring followed by edible blue-black berries.

Height and spread Height to 30–40 feet (9–12 m) and as wide.

Best climate and site Zones 3–9; full sun to light shade; moist, acid soil.

Landscape uses Specimen or shade tree for cool, moist climates. Ideal for a woodland or glade planting. Autumn color is best in a warm, sunny spot.

Growing guidelines Plant in winter or early spring. Pruning is seldom necessary except to shape the tree when it is young. This may be carried out after flowering. Mulch, particularly while young, to keep the soil evenly moist.

Good companions Woodland bulbs, perennials; small shrubs, including mountain laurel and witch hazel. Also looks good with dogwoods.

Other varieties Look for named varieties selected for good flowering and autumn color. *A.* x *grandiflora*, apple serviceberry, is a hybrid of *A. laevis* and *A. arborea* which grows to 25 feet (7.5 m) with clusters of large, white flowers.

Comments The fruit is used by native Americans and can be cooked or preserved.

Bauhinia x *blakeana*
CAESALPINIACEAE

HONG KONG ORCHID TREE

This graceful, spreading tree is a picture in spring when covered in its deep pink, orchid-like flowers. The heart-shaped leaves also give the genus the name of butterfly tree.

Description An evergreen, single-trunked tree with pink flowers in spring up to 6 inches (15 cm) across. Some petals are marked with crimson veins. Leaves are light green and bilobed. This hybrid rarely forms seed and is thought to be sterile.

Height and spread Height to 15–24 feet (4.5–7.2 m) and as wide.

Best climate and site Zones 9–12; full sun; rich, well-drained soil.

Landscape uses Shade or specimen tree that also grows well as a street planting in a warm to tropical climate. Use the spreading canopy as a living outdoor umbrella.

Growing guidelines Plant potted specimens anytime, selecting a sheltered, well-drained spot with rich, deep soil. Shape while young to form a single trunk branching 3–6 feet (90–180 cm) above ground.

Good companions Tropical shrubs, or grow ferns, bromeliads or small, shade-loving perennials under its spreading branches.

Other species There are many species of bauhinia, some sprawling shrubs but all with distinctive, bilobed leaves that make spectacular flowering specimens in warm and tropical climates.

Comments Hong Kong orchid tree is the floral emblem of Hong Kong.

Betula papyrifera
BETULACEAE

CANOE BIRCH

Birch trees are attractive trees in cool- to cold-climate gardens. The canoe birch, which is native to northeastern North America, is grown for its white trunk and papery, peeling bark.

Description A tall, deciduous tree grown for its attractive bark and trunk. New spring leaf growth is pale green, maturing to dark green in summer and becoming butter-yellow in autumn. Catkin flowers bloom in early to midspring.

Height and spread Height to 60 feet (18 m); spread 30 feet (9 m).

Best climate and site Zones 2–8; full sun to partial shade; moist, well-drained, deep soil.

Landscape uses Specimen tree beside water and where its attractive bark can be enjoyed. Also a good choice for a woodland planting.

Growing guidelines Plant in spring. Prune to shape young trees in late summer or autumn. Keep well watered, particularly during extended dry periods, since drought stress can weaken trees, making them susceptible to pests and diseases.

Other common names White birch, paper birch.

Good companions Spring bulbs.

Other species In warmer climates, grow *B. nigra*, river birch, which tolerates swampy conditions and humidity. Zones 4–10.

Comments Can be short-lived in hot, dry areas.

Butia capitata
ARECACEAE

WINE PALM

This fast-growing palm is easy to grow in a range of climates and brings a hint of its native desert environment to any landscape.

Description A stout palm with a single trunk. The rough trunk is elephant-gray. The long, feathery fronds are gray-green. Flowers are fragrant and followed by juicy, 1-inch (2.5-cm) diameter fruit.

Height and spread Height to 20 feet (6 m); spread around 10 feet (3 m).

Best climate and site Zones 8–11 (marginally frost-tolerant); full sun; well-drained soil.

Landscape uses This distinctive, fast-growing palm grows in a wide range of situations. Use as a feature of a dry or low-maintenance garden. Young plants grow well in containers.

Growing guidelines Plant container-grown specimens anytime but best in the warmer months of the year. Tolerant of a wide range of soil types provided soil is well drained. Plant with shelter from heavy frost. Drought-tolerant when established.

Good companions Strelitzia, ornamental grasses, succulents.

Other common names Jelly palm, butia palm, pindo palm.

Other varieties Look for a compact, bushy form of wine palm.

Comments The common names of wine or jelly palm derive from the edible pulp of the fruit, which is used in making drinks.

Cercis canadensis
CAESALPINIACEA

EASTERN REDBUD

Eastern redbud is a flat-topped, broadly spreading, deciduous tree native to eastern North America with masses of pink flowers in spring.

Description This slow-growing, deciduous tree has pink flowers that light up the garden after winter. The spring flowers appear before the heart-shaped leaves that turn yellow in autumn. Young twigs are red.

Height and spread To 30 feet (9 m) tall and 20 feet (6 m) wide but slow-growing.

Best climate and site Zones 4–9; full sun to light shade; tolerant of a variety of soils.

Landscape uses Excellent small shade or specimen tree used alone or in combination with other flowering trees. Underplant with spring-flowering shrubs and bulbs.

Growing guidelines As these trees are difficult to transplant, look for container-grown plants for planting in spring. Tolerates dry summers but needs moist, well-drained soil in winter and spring.

Good companions Dogwood, evergreen azaleas; daffodils, bluebells and other spring bulbs.

Other varieties A white-flowered form and named varieties with vibrantly colored new leaf growth and good autumn color.

Other species *C. siliquastrum*, Judas tree, has purplish rose spring flowers and yellow autumn leaves. Zones 6–10.

Comments Blooms are profuse, even along the trunk.

Chamaecyparis obtusa
CUPRESSACEAE

HINOKI FALSE CYPRESS

Hinoki false cypress is a slow-growing, coniferous, evergreen tree with a broadly pyramidal form. It has given rise to many useful garden trees.

Description The species is a tall, straight tree with reddish brown bark and green, scalelike leaves with a cedar aroma. Inconspicuous, brown flowers in spring, followed by brown cones in autumn.

Height and spread To 100 feet (30 m) tall and 40 feet (12 m) wide, but many named cultivars are shorter and more compact, to 3 feet (90 cm) high and wide.

Best climate and site Zones 5–9; full sun; deep, loamy, moisture-retentive soil.

Landscape uses Specimen, background tree or windbreak planting. An excellent foil for deciduous plants and a strong, evergreen choice to bring form and structure to a cold-climate garden.

Growing guidelines Transplant container-grown or balled-and-burlapped plants in spring. Prune plants to shape in late winter or early spring.

Good companions Plant with contrasting foliage trees, such as golden, blue and burgundy conifers and spring-flowering, deciduous trees.

Other varieties Many cultivars; tall or dwarf forms with foliage colors of yellow, blue-green, reddish bronze or green with gold flecks.

Comments Avoid cutting or lopping, because plants rarely recover.

Chamaedorea elegans
ARECACEAE

PARLOR PALM

Very popular for use indoors, this palm can also be grown outdoors in shaded areas to create a raintorest look in a cool-climate garden.

Description A slender palm with a single stem. The graceful trunk is marked with closely spaced growth rings. The pinnate (feather-like) fronds are dark green. Where fruit forms (both male and female plants are needed), it is easily accessible for picking.
Height and spread Height to 10 feet (3 m); spread around 6–10 feet (1.8–3 m).
Best climate and site Zones 9–11 in frost-free areas; full sun to filtered light with afternoon shade; well-drained soil.
Landscape uses In cool or moist areas, this dwarf palm is used with other foliage plants for a rainforest look.
Growing guidelines Plant container-grown specimens anytime but best in the warmer months of the year. Tolerant of a wide range of soil types, provided soil is well drained. Keep moist and apply extra water when dry, and remove spent fronds. Protect from heavy frost and hot winds.
Good companions Combine with other foliage plants or use indoors with baskets of ferns to create a lush, tropical oasis.
Other varieties Look for attractive fine-leafed forms.
Comments This popular palm is sometimes misnamed as *Neanthe bella*.

Chamaerops humilis
ARECACEAE

EUROPEAN FAN PALM

This is the palm to choose to create the look of the subtropics in cold Zones, since European fan palm is frost-hardy and tolerant of occasional snow.

Description A handsome palm that tends to form a bushy, multi-stemmed clump. Its gray-green fronds are fan shaped and the petioles (leaf stems) carry sharp spines. Fleshy, yellow fruits develop after flowering.
Height and spread The European fan palm varies in size but is usually 6–18 feet (1.8–5.4 m) tall and wide.
Best climate and site Zones 8–10; full sun to bright light; any well-drained soil.
Landscape uses Use as a large, clump-forming specimen plant for a lawn or entrance, or include as part of a mixed foliage planting. Also suited to container growth in a well-lit area.
Growing guidelines Plant container-grown specimens anytime but best in the warmer months of the year. Provided soil is well drained, it is tolerant of a wide range of soil types. Water when dry and remove spent fronds.
Good companions Other foliage plants, including cordylines and cannas.
Other varieties One variety is grown for its tall, solitary trunk.
Comments As this plant is usually dioecious (that is, it has male and female flowers on separate plants), two plants (both male and female) are needed to produce seed.

Chionanthus virginicus
OLEACEAE

WHITE FRINGE TREE

White fringe tree is a deciduous, small tree with yellow autumn leaf color. Loose clusters of white flowers are a feature from late spring into summer.

Description A small, usually deciduous tree with a rounded crown of green leaves turning yellow in autumn before dropping. The slightly fragrant, white flowers are borne in loose clusters from late spring to early summer. There are male and female flowers found on separate trees, so fruit and seed are produced only on female trees. The fruit is blue and grapelike.
Height and spread Height to 20–30 feet (6–9 m) and as wide.
Best climate and site Zones 5–9; full sun; humus-rich, moisture-retentive, well-drained soil. Tolerant of humid and coastal climates.
Landscape uses Flowering specimen tree for late spring to summer.
Growing guidelines Plant balled-and-burlapped plants in spring or container-grown plants anytime. Prune after flowering only if shaping is required, for example to form a single trunk. Slow-growing.
Good companions Any spring-flowering shrubs, bulbs and perennials.
Other species *C. retusus*, Chinese fringe tree, is native to China, Korea and Japan and is smaller, reaching only 8 feet (2.4 m) tall with a rounded head. Zones 6–10.
Comments This tree will not be completely deciduous in warm climates.

Citrus limon
RUTACEAE

LEMON

Grown as a backyard fruit tree in warm climates, the lemon can be used in many decorative ways in small or cool-climate gardens.

Description Grows as a small, many-branching, evergreen tree with highly fragrant, white flowers in spring followed by aromatic, yellow fruit.
Height and spread Height to 15 feet (4.5 m) and as wide; some cultivars smaller.
Best climate and site Zones 8–12 (but needs winter protection in cold or frosty areas); full sun; well-drained soil.
Landscape uses A feature in a backyard orchard or vegetable garden. Can be trained as an espalier against a wall or grown in a large container.
Growing guidelines Potted lemons are planted throughout the year in warm climates. In cool Zones, grow lemons in pots to be moved for overwintering.
Good companions Vegetables, herbs and annuals.
Other varieties For a long fruiting season, choose early- and late-fruiting cultivars. For small plants, look for cultivars grown on dwarfing rootstock. Multi-grafted trees extend the number of citrus types in a small garden.
Other species Other ornamental fruiting citrus are cumquats, oranges, limes and mandarins, all great in large containers.
Comments Lemons can be stored on the tree and harvested as needed.

Cornus florida
CORNACEAE

FLOWERING DOGWOOD

Flowering dogwood is one of the finest native North American flowering trees, with showy, white blooms in spring and red berries and colored leaves in autumn.

Description The bracts rather than the flowers are showy in spring. The rather inconspicuous flowers are surrounded by four broad, rounded, white bracts followed by clustered, brilliant red fruit in autumn.
Height and spread Height to 40 feet (12 m) and as wide.
Best climate and site Zones 4–9 but best in cool microclimates; full sun to partial shade; moisture-retentive, humus-rich, well-drained soil.
Landscape uses Specimen or lawn tree, singly or in groups, or massed in a woodland.
Growing guidelines Plant in early spring. Prune trees only if necessary to shape. Keep well watered, particularly during dry times.
Good companions Japanese maples, early spring-flowering shrubs, such as azaleas.
Other varieties There are named varieties with pink or red bracts.
Other species There are many species of dogwood, native to North America (*C. alternifolia*) and to China and Japan (*C. kousa*). *C. mas*, cornelian cherry, has yellow flowers and edible fruit. Zones 6–9.
Comments Anthracnose has become a severe problem for *C. florida* in parts of North America. Plant resistant *C. kousa* or hybrids between *C. florida* and *C. kousa*.

Cotinus coggygria
ANACARDIACEAE

SMOKE TREE

Smoke tree is a rounded, bushy, deciduous tree or large shrub with glossy, green or purplish leaves that turn yellow or red in autumn.

Description This small, deciduous tree has oval, green leaves turning red or yellow in autumn. Large, feathery, pink, purple or gray plumes, which look like puffs of smoke, appear from midsummer to autumn and persist for many months.
Height and spread Height to 12 feet (3.6 m) and slightly wider.
Best climate and site Zones 5–9; full sun; well-drained soil. Tolerates infertile soils.
Landscape uses Brings autumn and summer color to shrub borders. Strongly purple leaf forms useful for foliage contrast amid green foliage shrubs.
Growing guidelines Plant in spring. Water frequently until established. Prune after flowering. Do not overfeed, since excessive nutrients produce vegetative growth at the expense of flowers.
Good companions Spring-flowering trees, shrubs, perennials or bulbs.
Other common names Venetian sumac.
Other varieties Varieties with purple foliage are available.
Other species *C. obovatus*, American smoke tree, is a small tree to 30 feet (9 m) with reddish purple young shoots and summer flowers. Zone 5–10.
Comments Heavy pruning tends to force undesirable long, thin shoots.

Cupressus sempervirens
CUPRESSACEAE

ITALIAN CYPRESS

This distinctive, column-like tree is a feature of many Mediterranean landscapes and is also widely used as a tall hedge for narrow spaces.

Description A tall, evergreen tree with a narrow shape, becoming broader with age. Dark gray-green foliage. Small nutlike cones, ripening to brown in the winter.
Height and spread Height to 15–20 feet (4.5–6 m) but may eventually reach 30–40 feet (9–12 m) in old age, spread depends on cultivar.
Best climate and site Zones 8–10 and particularly Mediterranean regions; full sun; well-drained soil.
Landscape uses Use as a focal point in gardens or to suit a Mediterranean-style design. Also useful where a narrow hedge or screen is needed.
Growing guidelines Plant container-grown plants anytime but autumn to spring ideal. Keep well watered when young but tolerant of dry conditions when established.
Good companions Other Mediterranean plants, including lavender.
Other common names Funereal cypress, Mediterranean cypress.
Other varieties The narrow, Mediterranean form is called 'Stricta'. There is also a narrow, golden cultivar.
Comments In some mature trees, side branches can flop out, spoiling the narrow, columnar shape. These should be tied back into the plant rather than pruned away.

Dypsis lutescens
ARECACEAE
(Syn. *Chrysalidocarpus lutescens*)

GOLDEN CANE PALM

The golden stems of this small, multi-trunked palm make a strong feature in a lush, tropical planting. It is one of the most widely planted ornamental palms.

Description A multi-trunked palm with golden stems, leaf stalks and leaves.
Height and spread Height to 25 feet (7.5 m); forms a clump 10 feet (3 m) across.
Best climate and site Zones 9–11; filtered sun to part shade; well-drained soil.
Landscape uses The golden cane palm is a useful accent plant in a palm or tropical foliage garden. It can also be used to disguise the bare stems of tall palms. Golden canes are also used as container plants for a well-lit position.
Growing guidelines Plant container-grown specimens anytime but best in warm parts of the year. Also grows readily from seed but may be slow to germinate. Plants may be cold sensitive when young.
Good companions Other palms and foliage plants, including crotons, acalphya, cordylines and dracaena.
Other common names Butterfly palm, cane palm.
Comments These palms have male and female flowers on separate plants. Both a male and female plant are needed for seeds. Palm fronds will have a stronger yellow color in full sun changing to light green in a shaded spot.

Eucalyptus globulus
MYRTACEAE

BLUE GUM

The young leaves of evergreen blue gum are oval and silvery blue; they mature to glossy green with a long, narrow shape. The trunk is bluish white with bark that peels off in strips.

Description A tall, evergreen tree grown for its juvenile leaves, white trunk and clusters of creamy white flowers from winter to spring.
Height and spread Height to 150 feet (45 m); spread 40 feet (12 m) but smaller in gardens. Trees are pollarded to maintain a shrubby plant and juvenile leaves.
Best climate and site Zones 8–10; full sun; adapts to a wide range of soils and tolerates drought.
Landscape uses A fast-growing shade or specimen tree used for windbreaks or street planting in warm climates. Pollarded forms can be grown in large containers.
Growing guidelines Plant smallest trees in winter or spring (tubestock is ideal). Pruning is not necessary. Can be injured by strong, cold winds.
Good companions Silver-leaved shrubs and perennials.
Other species There are many decorative eucalypts with red, pink, yellow or orange flowers in addition to the better-known cream flowers. Some have decorative, even variegated leaves, while others have stunning seedpods.
Comments A commercial timber tree in its native Australian habitat.

Fagus sylvatica
FAGACEAE

EUROPEAN BEECH

European beech is a magnificent, long-lived tree. Its interesting, colored leaf forms make the beech one of the most desirable of all deciduous trees.

Description A tall, deciduous tree with dark green, toothed leaves that turn copper-gold in autumn. Inconspicuous, greenish flowers in midspring; followed by small, triangular nuts.

Height and spread Height to 80–100 feet (24–30 m); spread varies with cultivar.

Best climate and site Zones 4–8; full sun to part shade; deep, loamy, moist, humus-rich, well-drained soil.

Landscape uses Specimen or shade tree, or train as a dense, deciduous hedge. Use varieties with colored leaves for contrast with green- or burgundy-leaved trees.

Growing guidelines Plant balled-and-burlapped or container-grown plants in spring. Prune young trees in summer to establish a straight, upright trunk or to maintain a hedge. Avoid overfeeding, which results in succulent growth that is attractive to aphids. Protect the shallow roots from disturbance.

Good companions Other tall, deciduous, cool-climate trees, conifers.

Other common names Common beech.

Other varieties Many cultivars available; some compact, others with weeping foliage and rich purple, copper, bronze and even golden foliage.

Comments Intolerant of poor drainage.

Fortunella japonica
RUTACEAE

KUMQUAT

Kumquat fruit looks like a miniature orange—about the size of a big cherry and either round or elongated. The skin is edible and sweet, and the juicy flesh ranges from tart to sweet.

Description A small, evergreen tree with ornamental and edible, orange fruit, especially in winter. The small clusters of cream, scented flowers appear in spring.

Height and spread Height 8–15 feet (2.4–4.5 m); spread 6–12 feet (1.8–3.6 m).

Best climate and site Zones 9–11; full sun; well-drained, slightly acid soil. Kumquats should be kept in warm, frost-free areas through winter, although plants can tolerate winter temperatures to 18°F (–7.7°C). Without sufficient heat in summer, fruits are few and of poor quality.

Landscape uses Kumquats make evergreen screens or decorative and long-lived container plants. In Asian or Asian-influenced gardens, they are symbols of wealth and good luck.

Growing guidelines Plant container-grown stock anytime, or set out bareroot plants in spring or autumn. Space plants 6–12 feet (1.8–3.6 m) apart. Prune only to shape or thin crowded branches.

Good companions Grow with other citrus or vegetables. Underplant potted standards with grassy or trailing perennials.

Comments Harvest fruits when they are fully colored, or leave them as decoration on the tree.

Fraxinus ornus
OLEACEAE

FLOWERING ASH

Flowering ash is a round-headed, deciduous tree with attractive, compound leaves that color in autumn. Its fragrant, white spring flowers are much more conspicuous than those of other ash species.

Description A tall, deciduous tree with green leaves turning purplish brown to coppery yellow in autumn. Panicles of white, fragrant flowers in early to late spring are followed by clusters of seeds.

Height and spread Height to 50 feet (15 m) and nearly as wide.

Best climate and site Zones 6–10; full sun; deep, humus-rich, moisture-retentive, well-drained soil. Tolerates lime.

Landscape uses Specimen or shade tree, or useful for avenue or driveway planting.

Growing guidelines Plant in spring or autumn. Prune in autumn if necessary. Keep well watered during hot or dry times. Mulch to keep soil evenly moist.

Good companions Other deciduous trees.

Other common names Manna ash.

Other species *F. americana*, white ash, is a fast-growing tree with furrowed, gray bark, growing in a rather upright form to 120 feet (36 m). Zones 4–9. *F. excelsior*, European ash, is a large tree of oval form, growing to 120 feet (36 m) tall. It has glossy, dark green leaves and deeply incised bark. Zones 5–8.

Comments Despite its common name of manna ash, it is not the Manna of Exodus, which is thought to be a tamarisk.

Ginkgo biloba
GINKGOACEAE

GINKGO

Native to China, ginkgo is a pyramidal, deciduous tree with small, fan-shaped leaves that turn bright yellow in autumn. Male and female flowers are borne on separate plants.

Description A tall, deciduous tree with yellow-green leaves changing to bright golden-yellow in autumn. Inconspicuous, greenish flowers in early spring; followed by small, orangish, unpleasant-smelling seeds on female trees.
Height and spread Height to 80 feet (24 m); spread 40 feet (12 m).
Best climate and site Zones 4–9; full sun; deep, moist, humus-rich, well-drained soil. Pollution tolerant.
Landscape uses Specimen tree, especially planted as a contrast to green foliage plants and evergreens, such as conifers. In areas where a narrow tree is needed, look for the fastigiate form, *Ginkgo* 'Fastigiata'. Since the fruit of female trees has a strong smell, plant cutting-grown male trees only.
Growing guidelines Plant in autumn or early spring. Prune in spring if necessary. Mulch with organic matter to keep the soil evenly moist, especially while plants are young.
Good companions Other plants of Asian origin, including azaleas and camellias.
Other common names Maidenhair tree.
Comments This tree is a remnant of ancient vegetation dating from the time of the dinosaurs.

Jacaranda mimosifolia
BIGNONIACEAE

JACARANDA

The clouds of mauve-blue flowers that decorate jacarandas give this tree its other common name of dream tree. It lives up to its name from late spring to early summer.

Description A spreading, deciduous tree that loses its fernlike foliage in spring, just before flowering, when clusters of mauve-blue, tubular blossoms cover the tree. Re-leafs as flowers finish. Leaves color to golden before falling.
Height and spread Height to 50 feet (15 m) and as wide.
Best climate and site Zones 9–11; full sun; fertile, well-drained soil.
Landscape uses Use its irregular outline to soften buildings. Makes a good shade or avenue tree. Fallen flowers make an attractive purple carpet over lawns. Can be grown in large containers in cooler Zones.
Growing guidelines Plant container-grown plants in spring. Protect young trees from frost. Mulch annually. Train to a single trunk when young, but avoid pruning large trees because vigorous, upright suckering growth will result. A native of desert areas of South America, the jacaranda flourishes in dry conditions.
Good companions Underplant with clumping perennials, including impatiens, clivia and bromeliads.
Other common names Dream tree.
Comments The leaf stems can be used in basket and hat making.

Koelreuteria paniculata
SAPINDACEAE

GOLDEN RAIN TREE

Golden rain tree is a deciduous tree with compound leaves that turn bright yellow in autumn. Its showy, yellow, summer flowers arrive at a time when few other trees are blooming.

Description Golden rain tree is a round-headed, deciduous tree. Its dark green leaves change to bright yellow in autumn. Yellow flowers are borne in dense, terminal racemes in midsummer, followed by decorative, papery, greenish pods that color to red during autumn.
Height and spread Height to 50 feet (15 m); spread 40 feet (12 m).
Best climate and site Zones 5–10; full sun; adapts to a variety of soil conditions and is tolerant of heat, drought and air pollution.
Landscape uses Specimen tree for autumn color. Shade or avenue tree.
Growing guidelines Plant container-grown or balled-and-burlapped plants in autumn and spring. No pruning is necessary unless to shape the tree while young; then prune in winter. Will flower poorly, or not at all, in shade.
Other varieties There are named varieties available, including a selection with a narrow (or fastigiate) habit and others that are large and later-blooming.
Good companions Shade-loving groundcovers.
Other common names Pride of China.
Comments This tree can become weedy in some warm or coastal climates.

Laburnum x watereri
FABACEAE

GOLDEN CHAIN TREE

This attractive, golden-flowered tree is planted to create stunning pleached walks in cold-climate gardens. In full flower in spring it is spectacular.

Description A small, deciduous tree with deep green, trifoliate leaves turning yellow in autumn. Golden-yellow flowers hang in long, wisteria-like clusters in late spring; followed by 2–3-inch (5–7.5-cm), pea-like pods. The commonly grown cultivar 'Vossi' has exceptionally long flower clusters.

Height and spread Height to 25 feet (7.5 m); spread 18 feet (5.4 m).

Best climate and site Zones 3–9 (but best in cool microclimates in warmer Zones); full sun; well-drained soil.

Landscape uses Particularly effective grouped against a background of evergreens or planted in a shrub border, but spectacular when trained to form an arch or arcade by the technique known as pleaching.

Growing guidelines Plant container-grown or balled-and-burlapped specimens in spring. Prune after flowering to remove crowded shoots and seeds. Train in a tree shape with a central leader, or pleach to form an arch. Protect from snails.

Good companions Mass plant.

Other common names Laburnum.

Other varieties An intergeneric hybrid between laburnum and cytisus, + *Laburnocytisus adamii*, is a curiosity.

Comments Seeds are poisonous and should be removed.

Lagerstroemia indica
LYTHRACEAE

CRAPE MYRTLE

Crape myrtle is a summer-blooming tree with silver bark that is a winter feature. As the tree re-leafs in spring, the new foliage is often bronze.

Description A small, deciduous tree with dark green leaves coloring in autumn. Curiously crinkled white, pink, red, lavender or purple flowers, which resemble crape, form terminal clusters 6–9 inches (15–23 cm) long from mid- to late summer.

Height and spread Height to 20 feet (6 m); spread 12 feet (3.6 m), but named cultivars may be smaller.

Best climate and site Zones 7–10; full sun; deep, well-drained soil.

Landscape uses A small shade or decorative tree for suburban or street plantings; use multi-trunked cultivars for screens or groundcovers.

Growing guidelines Plant container-grown or balled-and-burlapped plants in spring (potted specimens year-round in warm Zones). To train as a tree, remove lower growth when young. For a shrubby shape, prune in late winter to early spring, shortening the previous year's shoots by a half to two-thirds. Remove spent flowers.

Good companions Plant several different-colored crape myrtles together, or under-plant with autumn-flowering bulbs and perennials.

Comments Stems may die back to the ground in cold winters; new flowering shoots will grow up from the roots.

Liriodendron tulipifera
MAGNOLIACEAE

TULIP TREE

The tulip-shaped flowers that give this stately tree its common name are borne high up in the crown, and may not be readily visible.

Description A tall, straight-growing, deciduous tree with dark green, shiny leaves (each with a curiously truncated tip). The green leaves turn a rich golden-yellow in autumn. The small, yellow, tulip-shaped flowers (each with a distinctive orange blotch), which are carried from late spring to early summer, are usually well hidden in the canopy.

Height and spread Height to 100 feet (30 m); spread to 60 feet (18 m).

Best climate and site Zones 4–9 (but best in cool microclimates in hot-summer areas); full sun; deep, moist, humus-rich, well-drained soil.

Landscape uses Specimen tree or avenue planting for a large property.

Growing guidelines Plant balled-and-burlapped plants in spring, or plant barerooted stock in winter. Prune in early winter only to shape if necessary.

Good companions The butter-yellow, autumn color contrasts with red and burgundy tones of maples and liquidambars.

Other varieties In narrow or confined areas, look for cultivars with a columnar or fastigiate habit. There are also dwarf and variegated forms available.

Comments Somewhat weak-wooded. The species is too large for small gardens.

Magnolia spp.
MAGNOLIACEAE

MAGNOLIA

Magnolias are exotic, flowering trees that add style and distinction to any garden, whether the deciduous and spring-flowering or evergreen and summer-flowering species are chosen.

Description Deciduous or evergreen trees with large leaves and waxy-petaled flowers in deep cream, white, pink or rosy purple. The deciduous species carry their flowers on bare wood in late winter to spring.

Height and spread Varies with species: M. *grandiflora* to 90 feet (27 m) and 55 feet (16.5 m) wide; M. x *soulangiana* to 20 feet (6 m) and slightly wider.

Best climate and site Varies with species: evergreen species Zones 7–10; spring-flowering, deciduous species Zones 5–9; partial shade, particularly in the afternoon; moist, humus-rich, well-drained soil.

Landscape uses Specimen trees. Dwarf, evergreen cultivars are useful fence or screen plantings, or grow the species as a shade or avenue tree in warm, humid climates.

Growing guidelines Plant balled-and-burlapped or container-grown plants in late winter or spring. Prune after flowering only if necessary to shape the tree. Shelter from hot sun or wind.

Good companions Feature spring-flowering species among spring-flowering shrubs and bulbs.

Comments Select late-blooming cultivars where early-blooming flowers can be spoiled by late frosts.

Malus floribunda
ROSACEAE

CRAB APPLE

The crab apple is a round-headed, deciduous tree prized for its profuse display of pink spring flowers, followed by showy, yellow-red fruit in autumn.

Description A small, fast-growing, deciduous tree with small, green leaves turning yellow in autumn. White buds followed by pink flowers appear in spring on bare wood. Red or yellow fruit (crabs) follow flowers and ripen in summer to autumn.

Height and spread Height to 20 feet (6 m) and slightly wider.

Best climate and site Zones 4–9; full sun; deep, humus-rich, moist, slightly alkaline soil.

Landscape uses Specimen or shade tree for small gardens or to line a driveway.

Growing guidelines Plant potted specimens in early spring and barerooted trees in winter. Avoid overfeeding, because succulent growth is attractive to aphids and other insects. To reduce possibility of rust, keep at least 500 feet (150 m) from eastern red cedar *Juniperus virginiana*. Prune to keep the center of tree open and airy, to reduce disease.

Good companions Spring-flowering azaleas, spiraeas, bluebells and daffodils.

Other varieties Many named varieties and numerous species, some with large and colorful crabs, others with deep pink to red flowers. Disease-resistant cultivars.

Comments Some cultivars bloom heavily only in alternate years.

Nyssa sylvatica
NYSSACEAE

BLACK TUPELO

Its distinct, pyramidal form and vibrant colors of orange or scarlet in early autumn make the black tupelo a striking deciduous tree.

Description A tall, deciduous tree with dark green leaves turning brilliant orange or scarlet in autumn. Greenish white flowers in late spring, followed in midsummer by small, blue fruits on the female trees.

Height and spread Height to 90 feet (27 m); spread 45 feet (13.5 m), but can be smaller in gardens.

Best climate and site Zones 4–9; full sun; moist, well-drained, humus-rich soil.

Landscape uses A specimen tree or woodland planting, chiefly valued for its autumn color, but also useful in low, wet parts of large gardens. Plant where the pyramidal form and branch structure can be enjoyed in winter.

Growing guidelines Plant small, balled-and-burlapped or container-grown plants in early spring or plant barerooted trees in winter. Thrives in moist soils, particularly in hot, dry summers. To keep soil moist and roots cool, apply a layer of organic mulch around the tree in spring.

Good companions Plant with other deciduous trees. Also looks good with other moisture-loving plants.

Other common names Black gum, pepperidge sour gum.

Comments Intolerant of alkaline soil.

Olea europaea
OLEACEAE

OLIVE

Olives with their green and silver leaves lend a distinctive Mediterranean air to any garden or streetscape and have the bonus of an edible crop.

Description A small, evergreen, long-lived tree, becoming gnarled with age. The green, glossy leaves are silvery underneath. The white, fragrant, insignificant spring flowers develop green fruits that ripen to black in autumn.

Height and spread Height to 30 feet (9 m); spread to 30 feet (9 m).

Best climate and site Zones 8–10 (frost-free with low humidity and long, hot summers); full sun; well-drained soil. Can tolerate dry conditions when established.

Landscape uses Shade, avenue or orchard tree, especially in a Mediterranean garden. Good container plant for a courtyard.

Growing guidelines Plant container-grown stock anytime, or set out bareroot plants in spring or autumn (or winter in mild areas), spacing 20–80 feet (6–24 m) apart (larger spacing in dry areas). Do not plant where fallen, slippery fruit will be dangerous. Minimum pruning when young, but prune mature trees to restrict size.

Good companions Mediterranean and silver-foliage plants; surround with gravel.

Other varieties Some varieties are selected for oil production, others for fruit.

Comments Harvest fruit when green (unripe) or black (ripe) and prepare in brine for eating.

Parrotia persica
HAMAMELIDACEAE

PERSIAN PARROTIA

This spreading, small, deciduous tree is gorgeously colored in autumn, when its leaves turn orange, yellow and scarlet.

Description A small, deciduous tree with smooth, gray bark and bright green leaves that become orange, yellow, crimson and scarlet in autumn. Inconspicuous, petal-less flowers with protruding red stamens appear from late winter to early spring on bare stems. Trees may be multi-trunked with horizontal branches and mottled bark.

Height and spread Height to 40 feet (12 m); spread 45 feet (13.5 m).

Best climate and site Zones 5–9; full sun; tolerant of a variety of well-drained soils that are slightly acid for best leaf color.

Landscape uses Specimen tree of interest for its autumn foliage color, which is striking even in Zones with warm winters, and spectacular in cool Zones.

Growing guidelines Plant balled-and-burlapped or container-grown plants in early spring, or in warmer areas plant barerooted stock in winter. Prune only when young to establish a single trunk.

Good companions Other autumn-colored trees and shrubs, or plant with a background of evergreens to highlight autumn color and winter form.

Other common names Persian witch hazel, Persian ironwood.

Comments Large trees are difficult to transplant, so are best moved when small.

Paulownia tomentosa
BIGNONIACEAE

ROYAL PAULOWNIA

Paulownias are renowned as fast-growing trees. They are also admired in late winter or early spring when clusters of mauve, foxglove-like flowers appear.

Description A tall, fast-growing, deciduous tree with large, heart-shaped leaves usually with downy undersides. Fragrant, violet flowers are borne in large, pyramidal clusters in midspring.

Height and spread Height to 40 feet (12 m) and as wide.

Best climate and site Zones 5–9; full sun; any well-drained soil.

Landscape uses Specimen tree often selected for quick privacy or shade. A useful nurse tree to protect slower-growing species until they establish.

Growing guidelines Plant balled-and-burlapped or container-grown plants in early spring or plant barerooted stock in winter in warm Zones. Branches tend to be brittle, so select an area that is sheltered from strong, gusty winds. Flower buds may be killed by cold winter temperatures and young plants may die back to the roots in very cold winter Zones.

Good companions Other trees for a park-like effect, or underplant with evergreen shrubs or perennials.

Other common names Princess tree, empress tree.

Other varieties White-flowered forms.

Comments Often advertised as a "miracle" tree for its exceptional growth rates.

Picea pungens
PINACEAE

COLORADO SPRUCE

Colorado spruce is grown and admired for its evergreen blue coloring and pendulous cones. It is a beautifully structured conifer with horizontal branches and an overall pyramidal habit.

Description A tall, evergreen conifer with whorled, needle-like leaves that vary in color from green to silver-blue. Reddish brown male and female flowers are seen in late spring, followed by 5–7-inch (12.5–17.5-cm) hanging cones.
Height and spread Height to 150 feet (45 m); spread to 60 feet (18 m).
Best climate and site Zones 2–8; full sun; moist, humus-rich, well-drained soil. Grows best in cool climates.
Landscape uses Specimen tree or screen planting, particularly in cold climates where the tones of its evergreen foliage can be appreciated when all else is bare. An excellent specimen to decorate with lights in the festive season.
Growing guidelines Plant balled-and-burlapped or container-grown plants in early spring.
Good companions Other evergreens with varying foliage colors.
Other common names Blue spruce.
Other varieties There are many cultivars available of this beautiful conifer in dwarf forms, or with foliage in silver-blue, bluish white and golden colors.
Comments Intolerant of heat, drought and air pollution.

Pinus mugo
PINACEAE

SWISS MOUNTAIN PINE

Swiss mountain pine is a coniferous evergreen with stiff, needle-like leaves. The species can grow to be a small tree; many of its cultivars are more compact.

Description A small, slow-growing, evergreen conifer with bright green needles. Its insignificant, yellow male, and reddish female flowers in late spring are followed by tan or brown cones.
Height and spread Height to 20 feet (6 m) tall and slightly wider.
Best climate and site Zones 2–9; full sun; humus-rich, moist, well-drained soil.
Landscape uses Foundation plant or as a low, evergreen hedge. An excellent choice for cold, windswept sites.
Growing guidelines Plant balled-and-burlapped plants in spring. To promote compact growth, trim new shoots back by half in spring.
Good companions An evergreen shelter plant to protect cold-sensitive plants.
Other species *P. aristata*, bristle-cone pine, is a slow-growing tree with short, bluish green needles. It is very drought-tolerant. Zones 5–8. *P. strobus*, eastern white pine, is a tall tree with long needles. Plant in masses for screens or alone as a specimen tree. Zones 3–7.
Comments Plants that are described as small or dwarf may in fact be very slow growing. Plants labeled as reaching 5 feet (1.5 m) tall may grow to 15 feet (4.5 m) over time.

Plumeria rubra
APOCYNACEAE

PLUMERIA

Plumerias, or frangipanis, are fragrant, appealing small trees evocative of the subtropics. They are an excellent small tree for a warm or coastal garden.

Description A small, deciduous tree with thick, succulent, spreading branches and long leaves with a prominent midrib. The clusters of scented, propeller-shaped flowers range from pink, red, yellow and orange to white with a yellow throat.
Height and spread Height to 25 feet (7.5 m); spread to 15 feet (4.5 m).
Best climate and site Zones 9–12 (in cold-winter or frost-prone areas, plumeria needs a warm, frost-free position); full sun; well-drained soil.
Landscape uses Introduces a tropical or coastal look to a temperate garden. Position it to enjoy the floral perfume.
Growing guidelines Plant container-grown specimens year-round in tropical to subtropical Zones but in spring in districts with cold winters. Grows readily from winter cuttings, even large branches.
Good companions Tropical and subtropical foliage plants, bromeliads, bougainvillea, ixora.
Other common names Frangipani, temple tree.
Other varieties Many colored forms of plumeria are available.
Comments Flowers bruise easily when handled, but can be used in float bowls or worked into leis.

Populus spp.
SALICACEAE

POPLAR

Poplars, such as this large eastern cottonwood, are not small, garden-friendly plants but, where a fast, tall screen is needed, they have the ability to survive where few other trees can.

Description Poplars are tall, deciduous trees, often narrow when young. They are fast-growing, most with greenish catkins in spring and butter-yellow leaves in autumn that drop quickly.

Height and spread Height to 90 feet (27 m); spread to 70 feet (21 m).

Best climate and site Zones 2–10; full sun; tolerant of a variety of soil conditions, even poor, dry ones, but prefers deep, moist, well-drained soil.

Landscape uses Screens, avenues and mass plantings. An accent plant for large gardens.

Growing guidelines Plant in autumn or spring. Prune in summer or autumn, since wounds bleed if pruned at other times. Keep soil evenly moist and mulched with organic matter.

Good companions Other deciduous trees.

Other species *P. alba*, white poplar, has whitish colored bark and white undersides to the leaves. 'Richardii' has yellow upper leaf surfaces. Zones 2–10. *P. nigra* 'Italica', Lombardy poplar, has narrow, columnar growth to around 90 feet (27 m). Zones 6–10.

Comments Questing roots may spread and clog drains and sewers.

Prunus serrulata
ROSACEAE

JAPANESE FLOWERING CHERRY

The flowering cherry is a show-stopping sight in spring, when its bare branches are massed with clouds of white or pink flowers.

Description A small, deciduous tree with green, serrated leaves changing to yellow, orange and scarlet in autumn, and attractive bark. The clustered, white or pink spring flowers are single, semidouble or double.

Height and spread Height to 25 feet (7.5 m) and nearly as wide.

Best climate and site Zones 5–8 (and in cool microclimates in Zone 9); full sun; deep, humus-rich, well-drained, moist soil.

Landscape uses Specimen tree or create a spring walk.

Growing guidelines Plant container-grown or balled-and-burlapped plants in spring or barerooted plants in winter. Stake weeping forms. Prune after flowering and remove any growth that shoots below the graft. Use mulch to keep the roots cool in summer.

Good companions Underplant with spring bulbs, forget-me-nots or pastel azaleas.

Other varieties Some with bronze or copper-red foliage, others with semidouble or double flowers in white, shades of pink to purple, or with pink buds opening to white; some forms are grafted and weeping.

Comments Plants can be short-lived in warm, humid climates.

Pyrus calleryana
ROSACEAE

CALLERY PEAR

Callery pear is a pyramidal to round-headed, deciduous tree grown for its white spring flowers and striking autumn foliage colors.

Description A medium-sized, deciduous tree with glossy, dark green leaves changing to orange, scarlet and crimson in late autumn. White flowers from early to midspring, followed by roundish, green fruit.

Height and spread To 30 feet (9 m) tall or more and 18 feet (5.4 m) wide, but there are narrow-growing cultivars.

Best climate and site Zones 5–9; full sun; deep, moist, humus-rich, well-drained soil, but tolerates drier poor soils.

Landscape uses Street planting or use narrow-growing forms as specimen or driveway plants in gardens.

Growing guidelines Plant container-grown or balled-and-burlapped plants in late winter. Select a site sheltered from spring winds to prolong flowering period. Prune, if necessary, in winter or early spring to establish a single trunk.

Good companions Evergreen trees or shrubs, or spring-flowering selections.

Other common names Manchurian pear.

Other species *P. salicifolia*, willow-leaved pear, has silvery, narrow leaves but is prone to fire blight. 'Pendula' is smaller-growing with weeping branches. Zones 4–8.

Comments Can form narrow branch angles that are prone to splitting.

Quercus spp.
FAGACEAE

OAK

Oaks have a reputation for longevity and some are among the longest-lived trees. Quercus rubra has particularly fine, red autumn color.

Description There are over 400 species of oak, some evergreen, others deciduous with magnificent autumn color. Most have inconspicuous, green catkins in midspring, followed by roundish fruit (acorns).
Height and spread Varies with species but many trees reach 45–80 feet (13.5–24 m) tall with a spreading canopy 35–70 feet (10.5–21 m) wide.
Best climate and site Varies with species, but ranges from Zones 1–10; full sun; humus-rich, well-drained soil.
Landscape uses Specimen trees, particularly species with rich autumn color. All are spreading shade or avenue trees for large gardens, parks and golf courses.
Growing guidelines Plant young, balled-and-burlapped plants in autumn and spring. Prune in winter only as necessary to shape the tree.
Good companions Lawn or groundcover, or carpets of naturalized daffodils, narcissus or, for the evergreen species, clivia.
Other varieties There are named varieties selected for size and leaf color, including forms with golden new growth, strong autumn color or upright growth.
Comments The thick bark of the evergreen cork oak, *Q. suber*, is used to make corks.

Robinia pseudoacacia
FABACEAE

BLACK LOCUST

While the species is a thorny, deciduous tree, with an open, upright habit and dark green leaves, the small-growing cultivar 'Frisia' has bright yellow foliage well into summer.

Description A small to medium, deciduous tree with green leaves changing to yellow in autumn. White, pealike flowers are borne in pendulous clusters in summer; followed by long, brown pods.
Height and spread Species to 75 feet (22.5 m) tall and 45 feet (13.5 m) wide (named cultivars half this size).
Best climate and site Zones 3–10; full sun to partial shade; any soil but prefers slightly alkaline.
Landscape uses Grafted and shaped "mop top" or "lollipop" forms are useful accent trees for courtyards or small areas and can be grown in large containers. Select 'Frisia' for golden highlights and foliage contrast.
Growing guidelines Plant in winter to spring. Prune in autumn to shape the tree and form a single trunk. Use mulch, such as pebbles, to keep soil evenly moist and cool and protect root system from damage by mowing or weed control.
Good companions Low-maintenance, non-invasive groundcovers, such as liriope.
Other common names Pink wisteria tree, mop top robinia.
Cultivars Pink-flowered or golden-leafed forms are available.
Comments Suckers can be thorny.

Salix babylonica
SALICACEAE

WEEPING WILLOW

Weeping willow is an instantly recognizable tree with a gracefully weeping habit and branches that frequently touch the ground.

Description A large, deciduous tree with narrow, green leaves changing to yellow in autumn. Greenish catkins from late spring to early summer.
Height and spread Height to 40 feet (12 m) and slightly wider.
Best climate and site Zones 6–10; full sun; moist, well-drained, humus-rich soil.
Landscape uses Effective when planted near ponds, lakes or in moist ground. Useful for bank-binding soils near streams and rivers. Cut willow branches can be fashioned into fascinating living garden ornaments, arches or woven into windbreaks or hurdles.
Growing guidelines Plant in autumn and early spring. Prune in summer or autumn; may bleed if pruned in winter or spring. Weak-wooded; leaves, twigs and branches may drop. Do not plant too close to buildings, because the roots clog drains.
Good companions Arum lilies and other moisture-loving perennials.
Other species *S. caprea*, pussy willow, is used in floral arrangements. Zones 5–10. Narrow forms of *S. chilensis*, Chilean willow, are used as narrow screens and windbreaks. Zones 8–10.
Comments Some species are weeds in many parts of the world.

Sophora japonica
FABACEAE

JAPANESE PAGODA TREE

This round-headed, deciduous tree is Asian in origin and is one of the last of the large, deciduous trees to bloom when its panicles of cream flowers appear during summer.

Description A medium-sized, deciduous tree with bright green, compound leaves that hold well into winter. Profuse, creamy white and mildly fragrant flowers form large 1 x 1-foot (30 x 30-cm) pendant, terminal clusters when they appear in late summer and early autumn. The decorative flowers are followed by brown pods that persist through winter.
Height and spread Height to 30–65 feet (9–19.5 m); spread to 40 feet (12 m).
Best climate and site Zones 4–9; full sun to light shade; any soil but best in moist, well-drained soil. Tolerant of city conditions, heat and drought.
Landscape uses Late-flowering specimen tree or shady street tree.
Growing guidelines Plant young, balled-and-burlapped or container-grown plants in autumn or early spring. Prune in autumn only if necessary to shape the tree.
Good companions Other summer-flowering trees, shrubs or perennials.
Other varieties Forms are available that have a more narrow or weeping habit than the species.
Comments Bird-attracting flowers.

Sorbus aucuparia
ROSACEAE

EUROPEAN MOUNTAIN ASH

European mountain ash is a decorative, deciduous tree with compound leaves that turn red in autumn. The white spring flowers are followed by clusters of showy, orange-red fruit.

Description A medium-sized, deciduous tree with green, compound leaves changing to shades of red in autumn. Small, white flower clusters appear in late spring, followed by bright orange-red fruit.
Height and spread Height to 35 feet (10.5 m) and nearly as wide.
Best climate and site Zones 2–9 (but needing a cool-summer microclimate in warmer Zones); full sun to partial shade; well-drained, moist soil.
Landscape uses Specimen or shade tree; excellent woodland tree.
Growing guidelines Plant balled-and-burlapped or container-grown plants in autumn or spring. Prune to establish a single trunk. Keep soil moist and cool in summer with a deep organic mulch layer.
Good companions Other deciduous trees, azaleas and rhododendrons, or spring bulbs.
Other common names Rowan tree.
Other species There are many species ranging from shrubs to trees. All are decorative in autumn, especially when carrying berries, which may be red, yellow, orange or white. Best in cool to mild climates. Zones 2–9.
Comments Berries provide winter food for birds.

Thuja occidentalis
CUPRESSACEAE

AMERICAN ARBORVITAE

American arborvitae is a large, upright, pyramidal, evergreen tree more often seen in gardens as a dwarf or slow-growing evergreen in many shapes, forms and foliage colors.

Description A tall, erect, evergreen conifer with dark green or golden foliage. Inconspicuous, reddish male and yellowish brown female flowers in midspring, followed by small, dried capsules.
Height and spread Species to 60 feet (18 m) tall and 20 feet (6 m) wide, but named cultivars under 10 feet (3 m) tall and broad that are suited to gardens.
Best climate and site Zones 2–9, but best where atmospheric moisture is high; full sun; deep, moist, humus-rich loam.
Landscape uses Evergreen screens, hedges, foundation plantings or as accent plants in shrub borders or rockeries. Small or colored-leaf selections add variety and interest to a conifer garden.
Growing guidelines Plant balled-and-burlapped plants in spring or containerized plants in spring and autumn. Prune in early spring if shaping desired. Subject to sun scorch when exposed to bright afternoon winter sun and wind, so provide shelter from prevailing winter winds.
Other varieties Many dwarf, compact and slow-growing forms available.
Comments Golden forms may become deep bronze in winter.

Trachycarpus fortunei
ARECACEAE

CHINESE WINDMILL PALM

Cold-climate palms, such as the windmill palm, bring an exotic air to cool-climate gardens and provide a contrast to more commonly grown conifers or deciduous trees.

Description A handsome palm with a tall, single, fibrous trunk, topped by green, fan-shaped fronds. These persist to form a brown skirt that hangs down the trunk. Yellow flowers are produced in large, hanging clusters. Waxy fruits develop after flowering and ripen to black. Fruit production is more reliable where other windmill palms are grown nearby to aid fertilization.
Height and spread Height to 30 feet (9 m); spread to 10 feet (3 m).
Best climate and site Zones 8–10 (tolerates light snow falls); full sun to bright light; well-drained soil.
Landscape uses Use as a large specimen plant for a lawn or entrance, or as part of a mixed foliage group.
Growing guidelines Plant container-grown specimens anytime of year, but best in the warmer months. Water when plant is dry and remove spent fronds if skirt is not required.
Good companions Form a grove with clumping palms, such as European fan palm *Chamaerops humilis*.
Other common names Fan palm, chusan palm.
Comments Grows easily from seed, but can be slow growing when young.

Ulmus parvifolia
ULMACEAE

CHINESE ELM

Chinese elm is hard to categorize. It is usually deciduous in cooler climates but semi-evergreen in the warmer portions of its range. Wherever it grows, it forms a spreading, elegant tree.

Description A tall, deciduous tree, semi-evergreen in warmer climates, with small, serrated, leathery leaves which sometimes change color to yellow or other times remain into winter. Inconspicuous reddish flowers in autumn to early winter followed by persistent, small, brown seeds. Bark peels in irregular contrasting patches.
Height and spread Height to 50 feet (15 m); spread to 40 feet (12 m).
Best climate and site Zones 5–9; full sun; moist, humus-rich, well-drained soil.
Landscape uses Grown as specimen, shade and street trees. In warm climates, underprune to create a shaded, green entertaining space for summer.
Growing guidelines Plant in winter or early spring. Prune in autumn to develop a single trunk. Keep well watered when dry.
Good companions Conifers, deciduous trees, woodland plants.
Other common names Lacebark elm.
Other varieties Named varieties available, ranging from upright to broadly arching and weeping forms. Some are shrubby.
Other species For a small, weeping tree, grow pendulous varieties of *U. glabra*, the wych elm.
Comments Usually trouble-free.

Zelkova serrata
ULMACEAE

JAPANESE ZELKOVA

Japanese zelkova is a highly ornamental, deciduous tree from Japan, closely related to elms. Its habit is rounded with numerous ascending branches.

Description A tall, spreading, deciduous tree, closely resembling an elm, but with small, bright green leaves turning to shades of yellow to russet-brown in autumn. Inconspicuous, greenish flowers bloom in early spring (sometimes perfumed).
Height and spread Height to 90 feet (27 m) and nearly as wide.
Best climate and site Zones 5–9; full sun to light shade; tolerant of a variety of soil conditions but best in soils that are moist and fertile with good drainage.
Landscape uses Specimen, street trees or tall screens. An excellent substitute for deciduous elms where Dutch elm disease is a problem.
Growing guidelines Plant balled-and-burlapped or container-grown plants during autumn or spring. Prune only to shape the trees, by thinning crowded branches in late summer. Young plants are subject to frost injury, so protect in winter when in early growth.
Good companions Conifers, deciduous trees and shrubs.
Other common names Keyaki.
Other varieties There are named, fast-growing, vigorous cultivars available.
Comments Tolerant of air pollution.

Argyranthemum frutescens
ASTERACEAE
(Syn. Chrysanthemum frutescens)

MARGUERITE

Marguerites offer masses of dainty, daisy flowers over many months and are great beginner's plants. The fast growth and ferny foliage are a bonus.

Description This shallow-rooted, shrubby plant has bright green or bluish leaves and abundant, 2-inch (5-cm) daisies in white, pink or yellow with golden centers.
Height and spread To 4 feet (1.2 m) tall and as wide.
Best climate and site Zones 5–10, but only perennial in Zones 9 and 10; full sun; fertile, well-drained soil. In colder areas, protect through winter or grow as an annual when frosts have passed.
Landscape uses A fast grower to soften a new garden or for quick color in containers or window boxes. Daisies fit well in a cottage garden, perennial border or cutting garden, but suit any low-care scheme.
Growing guidelines Fertilize every 2 weeks through growing season. For best flowering, prune lightly every month or two. Use prunings as easy-to-grow cuttings.
Good companions Plant other sun-loving annuals, including zonal geraniums, verbenas and dusty millers.
Other varieties Many cultivars, including dwarf, prostrate and double-flowered forms.
Comments Leafminers tunnel through leaves, causing unsightly markings. Control by removing infested leaves and treating with insecticidal soap or petroleum spray.

Aucuba japonica
CORNACEAE

JAPANESE AUCUBA

Japanese aucuba is a plant to bring color highlights to shaded areas. The variegated cultivars are grown as houseplants but grow equally well outdoors.

Description This is a bold, glosasy-leafed, evergreen, shade-loving shrub with small, purple flowers in terminal clusters in late winter to early spring, followed by bright scarlet fruit on female plants.
Height and spread To 10 feet (3 m) tall and as wide.
Best climate and site Zones 6–10; shade; deep, moist, well-drained soil. Tolerates dense shade, air pollution and competition from tree roots.
Landscape uses Shrub borders, foundation plantings, containers, under trees.
Growing guidelines Plant in winter or spring. Male and female flowers are borne on separate plants. You'll need at least one male plant if you want the decorative red berries, which occur only on the female plants. Seldom needs pruning. Take semi-hardwood cuttings in late spring.
Good companions Shade-loving plants, including arums, ferns, azaleas, camellias.
Other common names Japanese laurel, gold dust tree.
Other varieties There are named varieties that have large leaves speckled with yellow or splashed with creamy yellow. Some cultivars are male, others female.
Comments In colder areas, aucubas may be subject to leaf browning if exposed to wind.

Berberis thunbergii
BERBERIDACEAE

JAPANESE BARBERRY

The autumn color of Japanese barberry lasts well into winter. Its dense and prickly nature makes it an excellent choice for year-round barrier planting.

Description Japanese barberry is a dense, thorny, deciduous shrub with small, rounded, green leaves that turn orange-red to purple in the autumn. The small, yellow flowers appear in late spring, and are followed by bright red fruit.
Height and spread Height to 8 feet (2.4 m); spread to 15 feet (4.5 m).
Best climate and site Zones 4–10; full sun to almost full shade; deep, moist, well-drained soil.
Landscape uses Informal hedges or barrier plantings; foundation plantings; shrub border for autumn color. Readily lends itself to pruning as a formal hedge.
Growing guidelines Plant in spring. Prune if necessary to remove overcrowded shoots after flowering or in winter after fruiting. Ensure soil is well-drained; improve drainage of heavy or wet soil before planting.
Good companions Evergreen shrubs, such as holly, euonymus and dwarf conifers.
Other varieties There are varieties with purplish brown foliage and in dwarf form. Also others with green or bronze leaves with pink splotches and marked margins.
Comments The spiny stems can trap leaves and other debris within the plant, giving it an untidy appearance.

Buddleia davidii
LOGANIACEAE

ORANGE-EYE BUTTERFLY BUSH

This is a plant that truly lives up to its common name. Butterflies flock to the flowers for nectar and bring extra color and movement to the garden.

Description This vigorous, arching, deciduous to semi-evergreen shrub has dark green, velvety leaves. Flowers are pale purple with an orange eye. They are usually fragrant and borne in upright, terminal spikes from midsummer to early autumn.
Height and spread To 15 feet (4.5 m) tall and as wide.
Best climate and site Zones 5–10; full sun; deep, moist, well-drained, humus-rich soil. Tolerates alkaline conditions.
Landscape uses Due to its size, use this plant toward the back of flower or shrub borders, as an informal hedge or in a butterfly garden.
Growing guidelines Plant in spring. Cut back severely in late winter or early spring and follow up pruning with fertilizer and a mulch of well-rotted, organic material. In the colder Zones, grow as an herbaceous perennial by pruning to ground level.
Good companions Insect-attracting flowers, such as purple coneflower and rudbeckia; also roses and perennials.
Other common names Butterfly bush.
Other varieties There are a huge number of cultivars and color variations, including white with yellow centers, also pinks, reds and purple.
Comments Tolerates urban pollution.

Buxus sempervirens
BUXACEAE

COMMON BOXWOOD

Common boxwood is most often seen as a low, clipped hedge or sculpted topiary, lending formality to any garden. It is dense and slow growing.

Description This evergreen, dense, spreading shrub has small, glossy, dark green leaves and inconspicuous, pale green, perfumed flowers in early spring.
Height and spread To 20 feet (6 m) tall and slightly wider, but usually clipped into a low hedge.
Best climate and site Zones 6–10; full sun to partial shade; deep, moist, well-drained soil.
Landscape uses Informal hedges, screens, topiary or as foundation planting. Great to prune and shape.
Growing guidelines Plant out container-grown plants in spring. Use a compost or mulch to help keep the shallow roots cool and moist. Sensitive to climate extremes with leaves browning in cold, dry winter winds. Spray foliage with an antidesiccant in autumn. Sensitive to high humidity, which can cause dieback. Use B. *microphylla*, Japanese box, in these situations.
Good companions Roses, perennials, annuals, especially white flowers.
Other common names Box, English box.
Other varieties There are variegated forms, some with contrasting margins, and a dwarf form available, which is an excellent choice for a low garden edge.
Comments Foliage can smell acrid.

Camellia sasanqua
THEACEAE

SASANQUA CAMELLIA

Add autumn or winter interest to a warm-climate garden with sasanqua camellias. The showy flowers bloom in a range of colors.

Description A tall, evergreen shrub with dense, shiny, dark green leaves and large but short-lived, pink, red, white or lavender flowers (often with showy golden stamens) from autumn to winter.
Height and spread Height to 4–15 feet (1.2–4.5 m); spread 10–15 feet (3–4.5 m).
Best climate and site Zones 7–10, but buds may be affected in colder areas; full sun to light shade; moist, well-drained, acid soil enriched with organic matter.
Landscape uses Formal or informal hedges, specimen shrub or small tree, espalier, weeping standard. Small forms can be used in containers or hanging baskets.
Growing guidelines Plant autumn to spring. In cooler Zones, plant in spring in a protected site with full sun. In hot areas, provide afternoon shade. Prune to shape after flowering or to train as a single-trunked tree when young. Mulch with compost in spring. Water when dry, particularly when buds are forming in summer and autumn.
Good companions Azaleas, hellebores, ferns, Japanese anemones, impatiens.
Other varieties Cultivars include single or semidouble flowers, some fragrant.
Other species C. *japonica*, Japanese camellia, flowers from autumn to spring.
Comments Fast growing.

Choisya ternata
RUTACEAE

MEXICAN ORANGE BLOSSOM

This fragrant, white-flowered, evergreen shrub brings perfume to cool-temperate gardens. For year-round interest, select varieties with gold foliage.

Description A medium, frost-hardy, evergreen shrub with a naturally rounded shape. The trifoliate leaflets are slightly aromatic. Heads of small, white, fragrant flowers appear in spring with a second flush in summer. They resemble orange blossom, but can be hidden among the leaves.

Height and spread To 6 feet (1.8 m) high and wide (but smaller with pruning).

Best climate and site Zones 7–10; full sun to light shade; well-drained soil.

Landscape uses Low hedge, foundation planting, shady shrub border; also widely used as a perfumed garden plant. Brighten dull areas with the golden foliage form.

Growing guidelines Plant out container-grown plants in spring. Use compost or mulch to protect roots and reduce weeding.

Good companions Other acid-loving shrubs, including azaleas and pieris, and shade-tolerant groundcovers, including *Chlorophytum comosum*.

Other varieties Golden forms and some varieties with larger flowers. Hybrid with *C. arizonica* has flowers flushed with pink.

Comments Can be slow-growing and disease-prone in hot or humid summer areas. In warm Zones, use *Murraya paniculata* as an alternative evergreen, sweetly scented planting choice.

Cistus spp.
CISTACEAE

ROCK ROSE

The large flowers of the rock rose resemble single roses. Although individual flowers are short-lived, plants are long-flowering and bring color to sunny Mediterranean gardens over many months.

Description A spreading, evergreen shrub grown for its large and attractive flowers that are white, pink or purple with crinkled petals and prominent, golden stamens. Flowers are up to 3–4 inches (7.5–10 cm) across and are prolific from summer but may flower year-round.

Height and spread Varies with species, but 2–6 feet (60–180 cm) tall and wide.

Best climate and site Zones 7–10, particularly areas with a Mediterranean-style climate; full sun; well-drained, dry soil. Rock roses will not tolerate humid summer conditions or poorly drained soils.

Landscape uses A flowering shrub for a Mediterranean garden, shrub border or rockery in a sunny situation, or in large containers with free-draining potting mix.

Growing guidelines Plant year-round (but in spring in cold Zones) in well-drained soils, rubble or rock gardens in full sun. Tolerates dry conditions and mild frosts. Tip prune after main flower flushes to develop a more compact, bushy shape.

Good companions Other Mediterraneans, such as rosemary, lavender and carnations.

Other varieties Many cultivars and a range of species.

Comments Some have aromatic foliage.

Codiaeum variegatum
EUPHORBIACEAE

CROTON

Their boldly colored leaves have made crotons hugely popular as both indoor and outdoor foliage plants for warm climates. Leaves also come in many sizes and bizarre shapes, adding to their appeal.

Description A tall to medium, evergreen shrub for a frost-free climate. The large, elliptical leaves are patterned boldly in green, yellow, orange, red or pink. Color is often concentrated around midribs and veins. Many different colors can occur on one plant. Some have ribbon-like leaves.

Height and spread To 8 feet (2.4 m) tall and as wide, but usually more compact.

Best climate and site Zones 9–12 (but only warm microclimates in Zone 9); full sun to shade; rich, well-drained soil.

Landscape uses A hedge or understory in subtropical to tropical areas. Elsewhere as potted color indoors or in courtyards.

Growing guidelines Plant year-round in warm areas (in spring to summer in cooler parts of their range). Plants may defoliate if temperatures drop below 60°F (16°C) or if plants dry out. Water well during summer.

Good companions Other subtropical and tropical foliage plants, including dracaenas, cordylines, acalyphas. Also effective with ferns and orchids.

Cultivars Many cultivars with strongly marked, shaped and colored leaves.

Comments If growing as an indoor or conservatory plant, keep away from glass or drafts during winter.

Cornus stolonifera (Syn. *C. sericea*)
CORNACEAE

RED-OSIER DOGWOOD

Red-osier dogwood is a deciduous shrub grown for its striking, red bark, which provides stunning color in winter gardens when contrasted with dark evergreens or against a snowy backdrop.

Description This clumping, deciduous shrub has red stems and white flowers in late spring that are followed by red berries. The green leaves are opposite. The plant spreads rapidly by creeping, underground stems which grow into large clumps.
Height and spread To 7 feet (2.1 m) tall and nearly as wide.
Best climate and site Zones 2–9; full sun to full shade; deep, moist, well-drained soil.
Landscape uses Shrub borders, woodland or swamp plantings. Valued for its winter color, especially when all else is bare.
Growing guidelines Plant in spring. For best stem color, prune to ground level in early spring. Remove suckers in autumn. Mulch regularly with organic matter to keep the soil evenly moist. Grows poorly in dry, alkaline soils.
Good companions Evergreens, such as ivy and conifers; early spring bulbs; forsythia.
Other varieties There are varieties with yellow or green stems and a dwarf form, which also has red stems.
Other species *C. alba* also has red stems that make a winter feature in gardens and tolerates warm climates. Zones 4–9.
Comments A native of the eastern United States.

Daphne cneorum
THYMELEACEAE

ROSE DAPHNE

Rose daphne is a low-growing, evergreen shrub with small leaves and highly fragrant, spring flowers. It is native to central and eastern Europe.

Description Evergreen, low-growing shrub with dark green leaves and dense, terminal heads of fragrant, pink flowers in late spring, sometimes repeating in autumn.
Height and spread Height to 1 foot (30 cm); spread to 3 feet (90 cm).
Best climate and site Zones 4–9; full sun; protection from winter winds; moist, well-drained, neutral or slightly alkaline soil.
Landscape uses Foundation shrubs, front of shrub borders. Grow near entrances or paths so its spring perfume can be enjoyed.
Growing guidelines Plant out container-grown plants in early autumn or early spring. Strong fertilizers are not suitable; however, a leafy mulch applied in early spring will supply adequate nutrients.
Good companions Plant under deciduous trees, or with evergreen or deciduous shrubs.
Other varieties A form with white flowers is available. Another has larger leaves and flowers.
Other species *D. odora*, winter daphne, has purple-and-white flowers and dark green, oval leaves. 'Alba' has white flowers. 'Aureo-marginata' is a hardier form, with yellow-edged leaves. Zones 7–10.
Other common names Garland flower.
Comments Plants sometimes take a long time to become established.

Euonymus alatus
CELASTRACEAE

BURNING BUSH

Outstanding in its scarlet autumn color, the burning bush is a deciduous shrub that forms a low-maintenance hedge or border plant. The mature branches develop curious, corky flanges or wings.

Description A deciduous shrub with bright to dark green leaves turning red, crimson, orange and scarlet in autumn. Inconspicuous, greeny white flowers in mid- to late spring; followed by purplish fruit. In winter, the corky flanges or wings on the branches are distinctive.
Height and spread To 10–15 feet (3–4.5 m) tall and nearly as wide.
Best climate and site Zones 3–9; full sun to partial shade; any well-drained soil.
Landscape uses Specimen shrub, shrub borders, informal hedges.
Growing guidelines Plant out balled-and-burlapped or container-grown plants in autumn or spring. Prune in winter to shape the plant; otherwise pruning is not required.
Good companions Azaleas, pieris, boxwood.
Other common names Spindle tree, winged euonymus, winged spindle tree.
Other varieties There is a low-growing, dense variety that grows to 6 feet (1.8 m).
Other species *E. fortunei* is an evergreen with waxy leaves. Many variegated cultivars. Zones 4–9. *E. japonicus* is an evergreen shrub. Zones 8–10.
Comments Cannot tolerate very wet or very dry soil.

Forsythia x *intermedia*
OLEACEAE

BORDER FORSYTHIA

Border forsythia makes a bold statement in a cold-climate garden in early spring, when its bare stems erupt in vibrant yellow to gold flowers.

Description A spreading, deciduous shrub with arching branches of bright green leaves that turn reddish purple in autumn. Bright yellow flowers are produced in early to midspring on bare branches.

Height and spread To 8 feet (2.4 m) tall and nearly as wide.

Best climate and site Zones 5–9 (flowers best where winter temperatures are below freezing); full sun; moist, well-drained soil. Tolerates lime and air pollution.

Landscape uses Specimen shrub, informal hedges, in front of evergreens.

Growing guidelines Plant in spring. Remove older, weak-growing or dead wood after flowering so plants have the whole summer to produce fresh growth. Remove suckers in autumn.

Good companions Evergreen trees and shrubs, dogwoods, early spring-flowering bulbs and annuals.

Other varieties There are varieties with various shades of yellow to gold flowers, including selections with larger flowers.

Other species *F. suspensa*, weeping forsythia, is a rambling shrub with yellow, spring flowers and three-lobed leaves. It grows to 10 feet (3 m) tall. Zones 5–9.

Comments In severe climates, late frosts can damage flowers.

Fuchsia hybrids
ONAGRACEAE

COMMON FUCHSIA

These highly decorative plants are among the most popular of all flowering shrubs. The hybrids are used in hanging baskets, or trained into standards.

Description Upright shrubs and trailing plants, deciduous or evergreen, with hanging flowers, usually with contrasting corollas. Fuchsias bloom in late spring to autumn. Leaves may be tinged purple.

Height and spread To 6 feet (1.8 m) tall and as wide, but usually more compact.

Best climate and site Zones 8–11 (overwintered in glasshouses in colder Zones; treat as spring annuals in Zones 10–11); partial shade; deep, moist, humus-rich, well-drained soil.

Landscape uses Informal hedges, standards or hanging basket plants to decorate decks, patios and pergolas.

Growing guidelines Plant late winter or spring. Prune in early spring and tip prune to promote bushy shape. Do not allow to dry out, particularly when in baskets.

Good companions Ferns and other shade-loving plants. Plant in mixed baskets with lobelia, miniature ivies and convolvulus.

Other varieties Hundreds of named varieties in white, pink, red, mauve and violet with contrasting corollas and sepals.

Comments May die to the ground in winter, but will bloom on new wood produced in spring. Mist foliage with water during hot, dry weather to discourage pests and keep plants cool.

Gardenia augusta
RUBIACEAE

COMMON GARDENIA

Gardenias are evergreen shrubs, grown for their combination of shiny, deep green foliage and creamy white, intensely fragrant, summer flowers.

Description An evergreen shrub with glossy, green leaves and very fragrant single, semidouble or double white flowers in early to midsummer (or throughout the year in warm Zones).

Height and spread To 6 feet (1.8 m) tall and as wide.

Best climate and site Zones 9–11 (grown as a greenhouse plant in cooler Zones); partial shade with protection from hot afternoon sun; peaty, humus-rich, moisture-retentive, acid soil.

Landscape uses Foundation shrubs, specimen plants or low, formal hedges. Also grows well in containers and can be trained as a standard.

Growing guidelines Plant in spring to autumn. Cut untidy plants back in early spring. Sensitive to dry soil; mulch to help retain moisture and water when dry. Use a complete fertilizer in early spring.

Good companions Hydrangeas, mondo grass, fuchsias.

Other common names Cape jasmine.

Other varieties A low-growing form with small flowers or creamy edged leaves is more cold-tolerant than the species and grows well in rockeries or to edge paths.

Comments Used as a cut flower (handle carefully, as bruised flowers turn brown).

Hamamelis mollis
HAMAMELIDACEAE

CHINESE WITCH HAZEL

Chinese witch hazel has heart-shaped leaves but its feature is the fragrant, yellow flowers that appear in winter on its bare, zigzag branches.

Description A deciduous shrub with heart-shaped, green leaves turning golden-yellow in autumn. Stems are zigzag and downy when young. The fragrant, yellow flowers with strap-shaped petals appear in winter on the bare branches.
Height and spread To 25 feet (7.5 m) tall and nearly as wide, but usually smaller.
Best climate and site Zones 5–9; full sun; light, moist, well-drained, humus-rich soil.
Landscape uses Specimen plant; shrub borders, woodland plantings, city gardens. Can be trained to grow against walls.
Growing guidelines Plant container-grown or balled-and-burlapped plants in autumn or spring. Train to a single stem by removing low-growing side branches.
Good companions Evergreen winter shrubs, early spring-flowering bulbs.
Other varieties Some forms with large flowers are available.
Other species *H.* x *intermedia* is of hybrid origin and has variously colored, fragrant, spring flowers. 'Arnold Promise' is free-flowering, with yellow flowers and reddish autumn color. 'Feuerzauber' has copper flowers. Zones 5–9. *H. virginiana*, common witch hazel, is autumn-blooming to 10 feet (3 m) tall. Zones 5–9.
Comments Intolerant of dry soils.

Hibiscus syriacus
MALVACEAE

ROSE-OF-SHARON

Rose-of-Sharon is a late-blooming, deciduous shrub with upright branches and a bushy habit. The showy, hibiscus-like flowers are single or double.

Description A deciduous shrub with dark green, glabrous leaves and trumpet-shaped flowers in white, pink, red, lavender or purple, in late summer to early autumn.
Height and spread Height to 15 feet (4.5 m); spread to 10 feet (3 m).
Best climate and site Zones 5–10; full sun; deep, moist, well-drained soil.
Landscape uses Specimen plant; borders.
Growing guidelines Plant in spring or autumn. Prune in winter to encourage larger flowers. Remove at least two-thirds of the previous season's growth. Young, vigorous plants can be winter-killed. Protect from wind and do not fertilize after midsummer.
Good companions Evergreen or deciduous shrubs.
Other common names Blue hibiscus, Syrian hibiscus.
Other varieties Many named varieties in a range of colors.
Other species *H. rosa-sinensis*, Chinese hibiscus, is a small to large, evergreen shrub with spectacular, trumpet-shaped flowers in many colors that are a feature of warm-climate gardens. Many hybrids. Zones 9–12. *H. tiliaceus*, cottonwood, is a useful coastal tree or large shrub. Zones 10–11.
Comments Self-sown seedlings can be a problem; choose cultivars with little seed.

Hydrangea macrophylla
HYDRANGEACEAE

BIGLEAF HYDRANGEA

Hydrangeas can form the main display of summer gardens as they produce large heads of blue or pink flowers that last for many months. In winter, the shrubs are leafless.

Description A deciduous shrub with broad leaves and large, flat flower clusters (blue in acid soils, pink in alkaline) up to 10 inches (25 cm) across in midsummer. Hortensia forms have sterile florets. Lacecaps have a center of fertile flowers surrounded by sterile florets.
Height and spread To 10 feet (3 m) tall and as wide.
Best climate and site Zones 6–10; partial shade with protection from hot afternoon sun; deep, moist, well-drained soil.
Landscape uses Specimen shrub, shrub borders for shaded gardens, container plants.
Growing guidelines Plant from spring to autumn. Keep well watered and mulched during summer, or plants will wilt. Cut back by half after flowering.
Good companions Fuchsias and shade-loving shrubs.
Other varieties Many named forms, including compact dwarf varieties.
Other species Many species, including *H. quercifolia*, oak-leaf hydrangea, which has large, scalloped, oaklike leaves, turning red in autumn. Zones 5–9.
Comments In cold areas, flowers are retained and develop attractive pink and green tones in late summer and autumn.

Ilex aquifolium
AQUIFOLIACEAE

ENGLISH HOLLY

Hollies are valued in cool- to cold-winter gardens for their attractive, shiny, evergreen leaves and clusters of red berries. Some forms have variegated leaves.

Description An evergreen, erect shrub with glossy, spiny foliage and small, perfumed, white flowers in late spring to early summer; followed by red or occasionally yellow fruit on female plants.
Height and spread Height to 40 feet (12 m); spread to 15 feet (4.5 m).
Best climate and site Zones 5–9; full sun to light shade; moist, well-drained soil.
Landscape uses Specimen tree or shrub, foundation plantings, hedges, wreaths.
Growing guidelines Plant container-grown or balled-and-burlapped plants in autumn or spring. Male and female flowers are borne on separate plants. At least one male is needed for every five female plants of the same species for berries. Prune in late spring to control size if desired. Leaves may turn yellow due to lack of nitrogen; fertilize regularly to keep plants green and vigorous. Mulch to keep soil moist.
Good companions An evergreen foil for deciduous shrubs.
Other varieties There are many variegated named varieties.
Other species *I. cornuta*, Chinese holly, has spiny, evergreen leaves. Some spineless varieties. Zones 6–10.
Comments Subject to pests in climates with warm or humid summers.

Lavandula angustifolia
LAMIACEAE

ENGLISH LAVENDER

Most herb growers can never have enough lavender, since this aromatic garden ornamental is also useful for crafts and cosmetics. The silvery foliage and purple blossoms are stunning in borders.

Description A compact, evergreen shrub with silver-gray, aromatic leaves and tall spires of lavender-blue flowers in summer.
Height and spread To 2–3 feet (60–90 cm) and nearly as wide.
Best climate and site Zones 6–9; full sun; light, well-drained, limey soil.
Landscape uses Shrub borders, mass plantings, low hedges; can be grown in containers and trained as a standard. Widely grown for commercial lavender.
Growing guidelines Plant in spring or autumn. Add a handful of lime to acid soils. Pinch away flowers on first-year plants to encourage vigorous growth. Shelter from winter winds. Replace old or weak plants. Prune after flowering.
Good companions Silver foliage plants, roses, perennials and annuals.
Other varieties Many varieties, including dwarf forms; white, pink to blue flowers.
Other species *L. dentata*, French lavender, has fernlike leaves; flowers from autumn to spring. Zones 8–10. *L. stoechas*, French, Italian or topped lavender, has flower spikes topped with rabbit-ear petals from spring to summer. Zones 7–10.
Comments To dry, pick flower spikes in early blossom stage during dry weather.

Mahonia aquifolium
BERBERIDACEAE

OREGON GRAPE

Oregon grape is an architectural shrub with spiny leaves that look striking in winter gardens. Yellow flower clusters precede showy, blue, grapelike fruit.

Description An evergreen shrub with erect stems and spiny, dark green leaves, often with bronze-red and purple tones in winter. Clustered, bright yellow flowers in late spring to early summer, followed by blue fruit resembling grapes.
Height and spread Height to 3–8 feet (90–240 cm); spread to 3–6 feet (90–180 cm).
Best climate and site Zones 5–9; full sun to light shade; moist, well-drained soil.
Landscape uses A plant with a strongly architectural shape to give structure as a specimen shrub, in foundation plantings, or shrub borders. Useful for foliage contrast and winter interest, particularly in shaded gardens or courtyards.
Growing guidelines Plant container-grown or balled-and-burlapped plants in spring. After flowering, cut older stems to the ground each year for compact growth.
Good companions Other shade-tolerant plants, deciduous shrubs.
Other species *M. bealei*, leatherleaf mahonia, has leathery, blue-green leaves and very fragrant flowers. It grows to 6 feet (1.8 m) tall and as wide. Zones 6–9.
Comments In colder Zones, leaves may be damaged by exposure to winter winds and afternoon sun.

Murraya paniculata
RUTACEAE

ORANGE JESSAMINE

This easy-to-grow, evergreen shrub blooms on and off year-round, but mainly in summer. Its white flowers smell delightfully of orange blossom. Provide plenty of light and water for best growth.

Description Orange jessamine is a compact shrub that bears small, bright green, glossy leaves. Waxy, white, perfumed flowers appear several times per year, followed by bright red berries.

Height and spread Height to 10 feet (3 m); spread to 6 feet (1.8 m).

Best climate and site Zones 9–12; full sun or part shade with shelter from heavy frost; deep, moist, well-drained soil with added organic matter.

Landscape uses Specimen planting, formal or informal hedges, background plantings, topiary or bonsai.

Growing guidelines Plant spring to autumn. Keep well watered, especially during summer. Fertilize in spring and early summer with an all-purpose fertilizer. Clip as desired to shape the plant.

Good companions Mass plant or grow with other white-flowered shrubs.

Other common names Mock orange.

Other varieties Look for sterile forms that do not produce berries. Dwarf forms also available for low hedges.

Comments Leaves drop and plants wilt if the soil gets too dry; otherwise, orange jessamine is fairly trouble-free. Berries are not edible but may be spread by birds.

Nandina domestica
BERBERIDACEAE

HEAVENLY BAMBOO

Heavenly bamboo is a tall and narrow, evergreen shrub, making it an ideal choice to plant along a fence or wall, or in a compact space.

Description Evergreen to semi-evergreen, bamboo-like shrub with glossy, green leaves, often pink or bronze when young, that turn shades of yellow, orange and crimson in autumn, especially in cold climates. Large panicles of white flowers in midsummer; red fruit nearly all winter.

Height and spread Height to 10 feet (3 m); spread to 6 feet (1.8 m).

Best climate and site Zones 6–10; full sun to dense shade; deep, moisture-retentive, well-drained soil.

Landscape uses Foundation plantings; hedges, narrow spaces such as fence lines and courtyards. Select dwarf forms for low border plantings.

Growing guidelines Plant container-grown or balled-and-burlapped plants in late winter or spring. Cut a few of the oldest stems to the ground each spring to encourage new growth.

Good companions Camellias, climbers, mondo grass, perennials.

Other common names Sacred bamboo.

Other varieties There is a variety with white fruit, some dwarf and compact forms and others with pink-tipped foliage.

Comments Plants may be damaged by low winter temperatures, especially in the colder parts of their range.

Nerium oleander
APOCYNACEAE

OLEANDER

Native to the Mediterranean coast, oleander is a tough, versatile shrub with masses of summer flowers. It's an ideal choice for a tall, informal hedge, or trained as a dainty standard for a pot.

Description A vigorous, evergreen shrub with shiny, dark green leaves and single or double flowers in various shades of white, apricot, pink and red, sometimes measuring up to 3 inches (7.5 cm) across, from midspring to late summer.

Height and spread Height to 20 feet (6 m); spread to 10 feet (3 m).

Best climate and site Zones 7–10; full sun; widely tolerant of heat, drought and seaside conditions, but best in good soils with regular watering through summer.

Landscape uses Informal hedges, screen plantings, shrub borders, street plantings, container plants.

Growing guidelines Plant in spring (year-round in warm Zones). Prune lightly after flowering to maintain thick, bushy growth. Prune old plants by half in winter.

Good companions Mass plant, or team with tibouchinas, hibiscus, abelia and other summer-flowering shrubs.

Other varieties Many named and unnamed cultivars with single or double flowers in colors from white, pink and red to apricot. Some have variegated foliage.

Comments All parts of the plant are toxic if eaten. Stems also exude a milky sap, which can irritate eyes.

Philadelphus coronarius
PHILADELPHACEAE

SWEET MOCK ORANGE

Sweet mock orange is a deciduous shrub that is grown for the delightful perfume of its single or double, white flowers in late spring.

Description A deciduous, sprawling shrub with bright to dark green leaves turning dull yellow in autumn before falling. The single, or occasionally double, white flowers in late spring are usually highly fragrant with prominent, yellow stamens.
Height and spread Height to 8 feet (2.4 m); spread to 6 feet (2 m).
Best climate and site Zones 4–9; full sun to partial shade; tolerant of many soil conditions, even dry soil, but best in rich, deep, moist soil.
Landscape uses Shrub borders; to add spring perfume to gardens and courtyards.
Growing guidelines Plant in spring. Prune leggy plants immediately after flowering. Cut back by one-third and cut out old canes.
Good companions Other tall shrubs, spring- and summer-flowering perennials.
Other common names Mock orange, syringia.
Other varieties Many hybrids and cultivars are available. Single or double flowers, some with pink blotches and others with bright yellow new growth or white-margined leaves.
Comments Provides little interest when not in flower, so plant toward the back of a shrub border.

Photinia serratifolia
ROSACEAE

CHINESE PHOTINIA

Chinese photinia is a large shrub or small tree widely used for hedges and screens. Its lustrous, evergreen leaves are red when they first appear in spring, or after clipping.

Description This large shrub has glossy, green leaves that are reddish at first. Mainly grown as a foliage plant, but has creamy white flowers in small clusters in late spring, followed by bright red fruit.
Height and spread Height to 30 feet (9 m); spread to 15 feet (4.5 m).
Best climate and site Zones 7–10; full sun to light shade; any well-drained soil.
Landscape uses Tall to medium hedges and windbreaks. A foliage contrast for evergreen and deciduous shrubs.
Growing guidelines Plant container-grown or balled-and-burlapped plants in spring. Prune lightly in summer to produce colorful new shoots. Water when dry and keep soil moist with organic mulch.
Good companions Evergreen or deciduous shrubs.
Other common names Chinese hawthorn, photinia.
Other varieties There are smaller-growing selections suited to low hedges.
Other species *P. villosa*, oriental photinia, is a glossy-leaved, deciduous shrub with bronzy red autumn tones. More cold-tolerant than other species. Zones 3–9.
Comments Avoid planting near pears, apples and others susceptible to fire blight.

Pieris japonica
ERICACEAE

JAPANESE PIERIS

Japanese pieris is an evergreen shrub with dark green leaves, often bronze or reddish when young. The flower bud clusters are conspicuous all winter.

Description An evergreen shrub with dark green leaves that are reddish when young. Fragrant, white flower clusters in spring resemble those of lily-of-the-valley.
Height and spread To 8 feet (2.4 m) tall and as wide.
Best climate and site Zones 4–9; full sun to light shade; moist, humus-rich, well-drained, acid soil.
Landscape uses Specimen shrub, shrub borders, foundation plantings.
Growing guidelines Plant container-grown or balled-and-burlapped plants in spring. Prune dead wood after flowering.
Good companions Azaleas, camellias, rhododendrons, aucuba, dogwood, ferns, hostas and shade-loving acid plants. Clumps of spring-flowering bulbs.
Other common names Lily-of-the-valley shrub.
Other varieties Compact forms with red buds opening to long-lasting, pink flowers, variegated foliage; cultivars with attractive pink or cream new growth.
Other species The tall-growing *P. formosa* will reach around 12 feet (3.6 m) tall and has colored, new growth. Several smaller but highly decorative cultivars. Zones 6–9.
Comments Japanese pieris cannot tolerate poorly drained soil.

Potentilla fruticosa
ROSACEAE

SHRUBBY CINQUEFOIL

Shrubby cinquefoil is a compact, deciduous shrub with compound leaves. The flowers are usually yellow, but cultivars with red, pink, orange or white flowers are also available.

Description A deciduous shrub with small, dark green leaflets and profuse, yellow, five-petaled, saucer-shaped flowers from early summer to early autumn.
Height and spread To 4 feet (1.2 m) tall and as wide.
Best climate and site Zones 2–9; full sun to very light shade; tolerant of many soil conditions, including alkaline soil, but must be well drained.
Landscape uses Informal hedges, shrub borders, edgings. Use for splashes of color.
Growing guidelines Plant in spring or autumn. Prune during winter for a thicker habit. Cut all stems back by one-third or remove a few of the oldest stems at ground level. Will not thrive in dense shade. Mulch with compost in spring.
Good companions Other small shrubs and perennials.
Other common names Bush cinquefoil.
Other varieties There are forms available with flowers in white, shades of yellow and orange. Blue-green and silvery foliage plants as well.
Comments Flower color is more intense in light shade in temperate climates. Orange selections may fade to pink.

Pyracantha coccinea
ROSACEAE

SCARLET FIRETHORN

Scarlet firethorn is grown for its masses of orange-red berries that last through autumn. This shrub is evergreen in the warmer portions of its range, deciduous in colder portions.

Description An evergreen to deciduous shrub with dark green leaves and white flowers in flat clusters from late spring to early summer, followed by persistent berries that are typically red but occasionally orange or yellow. Sharp thorns on stems.
Height and spread To 15 feet (4.5 m) tall and as wide.
Best climate and site Zones 6–9; full sun to light shade; deep, moist, humus-rich, well-drained soil.
Landscape uses Specimen shrub, foundation plantings, espalier, hedges, screens. The berries attract birds. Its thorns make it a useful barrier plant.
Growing guidelines Plant container-grown or balled-and-burlapped plants in spring. Remove suckers or excessively long shoots. Avoid overfertilizing to prevent succulent growth subject to fire blight. Plant disease-resistant cultivars. Leaves are vulnerable to cold winter temperatures.
Good companions Evergreen or deciduous shrubs.
Other varieties Yellow-fruited forms are hardier than the species. Also look for forms that are resistant to fire blight.
Comments In temperate areas, firethorns may become weedy.

Rhododendron spp. and hybrids
ERICACEAE

RHODODENDRON

The genus Rhododendron is generally divided into two groups: smaller-leaved, deciduous or evergreen types often called azalea, and larger-leaved evergreens referred to as rhododendrons.

Description Small to tall shrubs (some almost treelike) with white, pink, red, lavender, blue or yellow flowers in early spring to midsummer, varying with cultivar or species. Some forms will spot flower at other times, particularly in autumn.
Height and spread Varies with cultivar or species; range from 1–20 feet (30–600 cm) tall and as wide or slightly wider.
Best climate and site Hybrids: Zones 4–10, varying with cultivar. *R. arborescens* and *R. catawbiense*: Zones 4–8; *R. calendulaceum* and *R. carolinianum*: Zones 5–8; light shade; moist, acid soil.
Landscape uses Foundation plantings, specimen shrub, massed plantings, containers. Evergreen azaleas can be trained as standards.
Growing guidelines Plant container-grown or balled-and-burlapped plants in spring. Prune after flowering to control size or to regenerate leggy shrubs. Remove spent flower heads before new growth appears. Shallow roots need even moisture from regular deep watering. Use mulch to protect roots.
Good companions Deciduous trees and shrubs. Spring bulbs.
Other common names Azalea.

Rhododendron spp. and hybrids continued

Rosa hybrids
ROSACEAE

ROSE

Hybrid tea roses are prized for their elegant flowers and delightful fragrance. 'Peace' is a classic cultivar with large, pale yellow flowers edged in pink.

Syringa vulgaris
OLEACEAE

COMMON LILAC

Common lilac is a deciduous shrub with heart-shaped leaves that is much admired for its pastel clouds of wonderfully fragrant, spring flowers.

Other varieties Innumerable. Several groups are listed.

Evergreen azaleas perform well in temperate to subtropical Zones. There are many named cultivars with single, double or hose-in-hose flowers in white, salmon, purple, mauve, pink and red.

Exbury azaleas are deciduous: 'Berry Rose' has rose-pink flowers. 'Firefly' has red flowers. 'Gibraltar' has bright orange flowers. 'Sun Chariot' has yellow flowers. 'White Swan' has white flowers.

Gable hybrid azaleas are small-leaved and evergreen: 'David Gable' has rose pink flowers. 'Girard's Red' has red flowers. 'Purple Splendor' has purple flowers. 'Rose Greeley' has white flowers.

Ghent azaleas are deciduous, with single or double flowers: 'Bouquet de Flore' has pink flowers. 'Daviesii' has white flowers.

Other species *R. arborescens*, sweet azalea, has bright green, deciduous leaves that turn rich red in autumn. Zones 4–9.

R. catawbiense, Catawba rhododendron, has evergreen leaves. It is the parent of many hybrids. Zones 4–9.

R. minus, Carolina rhododendron, is an evergreen shrub with 3-inch (7.5-cm), dark green leaves that are brownish on the undersides. Zones 4–9.

Comments In warmer or subtropical zones, grow tropical or vireya rhododendrons.

Description A thorny bush grown for its white, pink, orange, yellow, red, lavender or multicolored single or double flowers, often fragrant, from late spring to early winter, depending on the type and cultivar.

Height and spread Range from groundcovers to tall shrubs and climbers.

Best climate and site Zones 4–10 (cold hardiness and heat tolerance vary with cultivar); full sun; humus-rich soil. Best in areas with low summer humidity.

Landscape uses Shrub or flower borders, arches, pergolas. Excellent for cutting gardens. Can be grown as standards.

Growing guidelines Plant bareroot plants in autumn or winter, and container-grown plants in autumn or spring. Dig in plenty of well-rotted organic matter before planting. Fertilize regularly in spring and again in summer to ensure many blooms. Keep well mulched with organic mulch. Prune hybrid tea and floribunda roses in late winter or early spring; prune climbers and species roses after flowering.

Good companions Iris, petunias, candytuft, and late-winter to early-spring bulbs.

Other varieties Thousands of hybrid cultivars are available.

Comments One of the world's most popular garden and cut flowers.

Description A deciduous shrub with dark green, heart-shaped leaves turning yellow in autumn. Very fragrant, lavender flowers in long clusters in mid- to late spring.

Height and spread Height to 20 feet (6 m); spread to 12 feet (3.6 m).

Best climate and site Zones 3–9; full sun to light shade; neutral or somewhat alkaline, humus-rich, well-drained soil.

Landscape uses Specimen shrub, shrub borders, screens or hedges. Excellent shrub for cut flowers.

Growing guidelines Plant in autumn or spring. Prune after flowering to remove spent flowers and to prevent seed formation. Also cut a few of the oldest stems to the ground each year. Although this shrub is extremely tolerant of neglect, it grows best with good air circulation and a dose of fertilizer in early spring.

Good companions Spring-flowering trees, shrubs, perennials and bulbs, including tulips and daffodils.

Other varieties Colors range from white, pink, mauve, lilac, blue to red; single and double flowers. Many named cultivars.

Comments Lilacs are sometimes grafted onto privet *Ligustrum* spp. rootstocks, which produce suckers. Prune off suckers as they appear.

Taxus baccata
TAXACEAE

ENGLISH YEW

English yew is a narrow-leaved, evergreen tree grown as a shrub, often clipped and trained into shapes. Its habit ranges from upright to prostrate and spreading.

Description An evergreen, slow-growing and long-lived conifer with dark green, needle-like leaves. Yellow male flowers and green female flowers appear on separate plants in early spring followed by red fruit on female plants.

Height and spread Height to 60 feet (18 m); spread to 40 feet (12 m); selected cultivars are smaller or slow growing.

Best climate and site Zones 5–9; full sun to partial shade; moist, well-drained, alkaline soil.

Landscape uses Foundation plants, hedges, topiaries.

Growing guidelines Plant container-grown or balled-and-burlapped plants in spring. Prune to shape hedges or topiaries in spring and late summer. Avoid water-logged sites.

Good companions An evergreen foil for all deciduous plants.

Other varieties Many named cultivars, including those with golden foliage colors.

Other species *T. x media*, Anglo-Japanese yew, grows in pyramidal or spreading form up to 30 feet (9 m) tall. Zones 4–9.

Comments Foliage, bark and seeds are toxic when ingested. The wood was formerly used for making longbows.

Viburnum carlesii
CAPRIFOLIACEAE

FRAGRANT VIBURNUM

Fragrant viburnum is a deciduous shrub with dark green leaves that turn purplish red in autumn. The pink flower buds open to sweetly scented, white flowers in spring.

Description A small, dense, deciduous shrub with dark green leaves turning yellow or red in autumn. Fragrant heads of white flowers tinged with pink in midspring, followed by blue-black fruit.

Height and spread To 5 feet (1.5 m) tall and nearly as wide.

Best climate and site Zones 4–9. Almost any well-drained soil. Full sun to part shade.

Landscape uses Specimen shrub; shrub borders; screens or hedges.

Growing guidelines Plant in autumn or spring. Prune to shape after flowering.

Good companions Lilac, spiraea, other spring-flowering shrubs and bulbs.

Other common names Korean viburnum, Korean spice viburnum.

Other varieties There are many named varieties with more intense flower or bud color or larger berries.

Other species Many species, all popular garden plants. *V. opulus*, European cranberry bush or snowball bush, has clusters of white flowers in midspring and red fruit that lasts into winter. Zones 3–9. *V. plicatum*, double file viburnum, has large flower clusters and markedly horizontal branching. Zones 4–9.

Comments Avoid poorly drained soils.

Weigela florida
CAPRIFOLIACEAE

OLD-FASHIONED WEIGELA

Old-fashioned weigela is a trouble-free plant that is massed with pretty, spring flowers that densely cover the long, arching canes.

Description A tall, arching, deciduous shrub with leaves that are green and opposite. Funnel-shaped, mostly rosy pink, but also white flowers in late spring.

Height and spread To 8 feet (2.4 m) tall and nearly as wide.

Best climate and site Zones 4–10; full sun to light shade; cool, deep, moist, humus-rich, well-drained soil.

Landscape uses Shrub borders, mass plantings, specimen shrub. Its arching shape and heavy flower display make it ideal for the back of a shrub border.

Growing guidelines Plant bareroot or container-grown plants in spring or autumn. Prune severely after flowering. Keep soil moist with organic mulch. Fertilize in spring and water well when dry.

Good companions Spiraea, daisies, lavender and spring-flowering shrubs.

Other common names Weigela.

Other varieties Many named varieties, including dwarf forms, flowers in pure white, pink and rosy red; variegated or dark burgundy leaves. Some named varieties have markedly larger flowers.

Other species Many species, all noted for their prolific spring flowers.

Comments Weigela may spot flower during summer and autumn.

Allamanda cathartica
APOCYNACEAE

COMMON ALLAMANDA

Native to South America, common allamanda is a vigorous, evergreen, twining vine with opposite or whorled glossy leaves, 4–6 inches (10–15 cm) long.

Description A vigorous, twining vine with glossy, green leaves and 5-inch (12.5-cm) trumpet-shaped, bright yellow flowers in summer; followed by spiny fruit.
Height and spread To 17 feet (5.1 m) with support.
Best climate and site Zones 9–12; full sun to partial shade; humus-rich, well-drained, neutral to acid soil.
Landscape uses An excellent vine to grow on fences, walls and around poles in warm climates. Elsewhere common allamanda is a good greenhouse plant. Shrubby forms grow in large containers.
Growing guidelines Plant in spring in a frost-free location. Requires frequent feeding when in active growth. Stake stems to provide support. Water freely when in active growth, less when dormant. Prune in spring. Mulch with organic matter to keep soil evenly moist. No serious diseases or pests in a garden.
Good companions Other bold, tropical and subtropical vines, trees and shrubs, including crotons and hibiscus.
Other common names Golden trumpet.
Other varieties Some cultivars have mauve or brown flowers, others have a compact, shrublike growth.
Comments Very frost-sensitive.

Ampelopsis brevipedunculata
VITACEAEA

PORCELAIN AMPELOPSIS

The main decorative feature of porcelain ampelopsis is the colorful berries, which resemble fine china. This vigorous, deciduous vine climbs using tendrils.

Description A deciduous, woody climber with hairy young stems and dark green, three- or five-lobed leaves similar to grape leaves. Its clusters of small, greenish flowers in spring are followed by amethyst-blue fruits in late summer and autumn.
Height and spread To 20 feet (6 m) with support.
Best climate and site Zones 4–9; full sun to partial shade; humus-rich, moist, well-drained soil.
Landscape uses Quick-growing cover for fences, arbors or trellises where the turquoise berries are an autumn feature.
Growing guidelines Plant in winter or spring. Cut to ground in late winter to produce new fruiting growth. Plant in medium to well-drained soil.
Good companions If mixed with spring- and summer-flowering vines, the period of interest will be extended.
Other common names Turquoise-berry vine, china berry.
Other varieties A slow-growing cultivar with white and pink variegated foliage is a good choice for planting in a container. *A. brevipedunculata* var. *maximowiczii* has deeply lobed leaves.
Comments Closely related to grapevines, but the fruit is not edible.

Bougainvillea spp.
NYCTAGINACEAE

BOUGAINVILLEA

Bougainvillea is a spectacular and vibrant, climbing plant for tropical, subtropical and warm, frost-free gardens. It is versatile in its landscape potential.

Description Several species and many cultivars of climbers, all dense and vigorous once established. Evergreen (but deciduous in cold winter areas) with smooth, bright green leaves and thorny stems. The white, inconspicuous flowers are surrounded by brilliantly colored bracts of red, yellow, purple, white or magenta all summer (and for most of the year in the tropics).
Height and spread To 20–30 feet (6–9 m) with support.
Best climate and site Zones 9–12; full sun; well-drained soil.
Landscape uses A versatile plant to cover trellises and porches or to hang over walls and banks. Clip into a dense hedge, standard or grow against a wall. Dwarf varieties suit hanging baskets. Shrubby forms can be grown in large containers.
Growing guidelines Plant year-round, but best in spring. Cut back after flowering to maintain shape and size. Mulch in spring. Plants flower well after a dry period.
Good companions Other colored varieties, plumbago.
Cultivars Many named varieties with brilliant bract colors; some with variegated foliage. Shrubby and dwarf forms.
Comments Vigorously growing plants often produce ferocious thorns.

Campsis radicans
BIGNONIACEAE

TRUMPET VINE

Trumpet vine is a summer-blooming, deciduous climber that supports itself with rootlike holdfasts. Its leaves are pinnate compounds of 7–9 leaflets.

Description A deciduous, woody vine with aerial roots, dark green, compound leaves and 2-inch (5-cm) wide orange or red, trumpet-shaped flowers, borne in terminal clusters in early to late summer, often extending into autumn.

Height and spread To 30–40 feet (9–12 m) with support.

Best climate and site Zones 4–10; full sun to semi-shade; well-drained soil.

Landscape uses Excellent flowering vines for fences, walls and trellises or to climb up trees. Vigorous and fast to establish.

Growing guidelines Plant in early spring. Prune in spring to restrain growth. Often needs additional support because of its weight. Enrich soil with organic matter to promote healthy growth.

Good companions Readily overwhelms other plants.

Other varieties A yellow-flowered variety is also available.

Other species *C. grandiflora*, Chinese trumpet creeper, is somewhat less rampant. Its leaves consist of 7–9 leaflets. Flowers are scarlet to orange. Zones 7–11.

Comments *C. radicans* can become invasive, since it tends to spread by underground runners. Remove unwanted shoots at soil level.

Clematis montana
RANUNCULACEAE

CLEMATIS

Clematis are among the most beautiful and highly desired floral climbers for gardens in cool climates. C. montana 'Rubens' has fragrant, lavender-pink flowers in early summer.

Description A deciduous, twining vine with dark green, trifoliate leaves and white or pink, perfumed flowers in late spring or early summer.

Height and spread To 8–24 feet (2.4–7.2 m) with support.

Best climate and site Zones 6–9; full sun at the tops, partial shade at the roots; moisture-retentive, humus-rich soil.

Landscape uses Outstanding flowering vines for arbors or trellises.

Growing guidelines Plant during spring or autumn. Prune after flowering to remove dead wood and to shape. Many clematis die back during winter in the colder parts of their range. Keep plants cool with mulch around the roots. Water regularly, especially during hot weather. When planting, set the crown 2–3 inches (5–7.5 cm) below the soil surface to encourage healthy growth.

Good companions All varieties of climbing rose, jasmine.

Other varieties Numerous hybrids, varying in vigor, color and flowering period.

Other species *C.* 'Jackmanii', Jackman clematis, is a popular, summer-flowering hybrid that usually reblooms in autumn.

Comments Clematis wilt can kill vines to the ground; deeply set plants may recover.

Clerodendrum thomsoniae
VERBENACEAE

BLEEDING GLORYBOWER

Native to West Africa, bleeding glorybower is a twining, evergreen vine with opposite, 5-inch (12.5-cm) leaves. The showy, red-and-white flowers bloom from summer into autumn.

Description A vigorous, evergreen, twining vine with large, oval, dark green leaves and clusters of flowers with red petals, striking white calyces and long, curving stamens in summer and autumn.

Height and spread To 10 feet (3 m) with support.

Best climate and site Zones 9–12; partial shade; rich, loamy, moisture-retentive soil.

Landscape uses Where hardy, grow on a fence or trellis. Elsewhere, makes a fine hanging basket or container plant.

Growing guidelines Plant in spring. Prune lightly after flowering if needed to control growth. Never allow to dry out, but avoid overwatering during winter when plant is not growing as quickly. Mulch with organic matter to keep soil evenly moist during spring and summer.

Good companions Rainforest plants, shade-loving shrubs, ferns.

Other common names Bag flower, bleeding heart vine, glory tree, tropical bleeding heart.

Other species There are many species of clerodendrum, ranging from climbers to shrubs and trees. All have attractive flowers and leaves and suit warm Zones.

Comments Drought-sensitive.

Gelsemium sempervirens
LOGANIACEAE

YELLOW JESSAMINE

Yellow jessamine is a real treasure—a vine that keeps its leaves and produces fragrant, yellow flowers in winter and early spring.

Description A moderately vigorous, twining vine with glossy, dark green leaves and fragrant, yellow, bell-shaped flowers in axillary clusters in winter to midspring.
Height and spread To 20 feet (6 m) with support.
Best climate and site Zones 7–10 (evergreen in warmer areas); full sun to light shade; virtually any well-drained soil.
Landscape uses Excellent flowering vine for woodland plantings or as a groundcover for banks. A non-invasive climber to plant on a fence or trellis, or in a large container on a balcony. Enjoy winter and early spring flowers and evergreen foliage.
Growing guidelines Plant container-grown plants in spring. If necessary, prune after flowering to control growth or to shape. Avoid waterlogged sites.
Good companions Spring- and summer-flowering climbers; late-winter and early-spring annuals and bulbs, such as polyanthus and jonquils.
Other common names Carolina jasmine, evening trumpet flower, woodbine.
Other varieties A double-flowering form is available.
Comments Flowers, leaves and roots are poisonous when eaten. Keep children and animals away from these plants.

Humulus lupulus
CANNABIDACEAE

HOP

The bright green or golden leaves of the hop make it a wonderful choice to contrast with foliage and flower colors. Hops are hardy, deciduous, twining vines with large, three- to five-lobed leaves.

Description A deciduous, herbaceous, twining vine with rough, almost sandpapery stems, large, lobed, green leaves and insignificant, greenish yellow flowers in late spring. On female plants, these are followed by green, conelike, papery pods, which add an extra decorative element.
Height and spread To 30 feet (9 m) with support.
Best climate and site Zones 3–9; full sun to light shade; any well-drained soil. Grows best where nights are cool and moist.
Landscape uses A fast-growing cover or screening vine for a trellis, arch or pergola. Grown for its vivid, bright foliage.
Growing guidelines Plant in spring. Prune to the ground after frost. Keep well watered during the warmer months. No serious pests or diseases.
Good companions Purple, pink and blue flowers, including lavender. Plants with contrasting (for example, burgundy) foliage.
Other varieties There is an attractive form with golden yellow leaves.
Comments Can be invasive, as the root system is prone to suckering. The female plants are the source of hops used in the commercial brewing industry. The resin in the flower gives beer its bitter flavor.

Ipomoea alba
CONVOLVULACEAE

MOON FLOWER

Before planting moon flowers, construct a support, such as vertical wires or a trellis. The plants need little care, apart from watering in dry periods.

Description The twining stems produce heart-shaped leaves and pointed buds that unfurl into funnel-shaped to flat, white blooms up to 6 inches (15 cm) across. The fragrant summer flowers open in the evening and may stay open through the next morning.
Height and spread Height to 10 feet (3 m) or more; ultimate height and spread depend on the size of the support.
Best climate and site Zones 9–12; full sun; average, well-drained soil.
Landscape uses Use as a fast-growing screen for shade or privacy. Its night-blooming habit makes it an excellent choice for planting around decks and patios where its beauty can be enjoyed on summer evenings.
Growing guidelines Plant seedlings 12 weeks after last frost. Though this plant is a perennial, it is usually grown as an annual.
Good companions Looks best with other white-flowered plants.
Other species There are many species of *Ipomoea*. *I. tricolor* is grown as an annual climber to provide colorful accents from its blue or mauve flowers. Zones 8–12.
Comments Moon flower is also sold as *Calonyction aculeatum*.

Jasminum officinale
OLEACEAE

COMMON WHITE JASMINE

The scent of jasmine lets you know spring has arrived. This vine covers itself in clusters of white flowers, and can grow quickly to provide a screen.

Description A vigorous, semi-evergreen, twining vine or loose shrub with dark green, compound leaves and clusters of pink buds opening to fragrant, white flowers in spring with spot flowering into autumn.
Height and spread To 30 feet (9 m) with support.
Best climate and site Zones 6–10; full sun to light shade; moist, humus-rich, well-drained soil.
Landscape uses Excellent for trellises, arbors or to scent a courtyard. An excellent choice for a perfumed garden.
Growing guidelines Plant during spring. Prune after flowering to keep vigorous growth under control. Keep soil moist in summer to avoid stressing the plant.
Good companions Banksia and other roses, honeysuckle.
Other varieties Pink-flowering and variegated foliage forms and a form with larger flowers.
Other species There are many jasmine species, all with fragrant flowers. *J. nitidum* has large, narrow-petaled flowers that bloom in winter. Zones 9–11. *J. polyanthum* makes a pretty pot plant or totem in mild areas. Zones 8–11.
Comments Rarely without a flower in warm climates.

Lonicera periclymenum
CAPRIFOLIACEAE

WOODBINE HONEYSUCKLE

Woodbine honeysuckle is an old-fashioned, cottage garden flower to enjoy for its wonderful fragrance and ease of growth.

Description A vigorous, deciduous vine with green leaves and fragrant flowers in varying proportions of yellow, white and red in late spring to late summer. The flowers are followed by small red berries.
Height and spread To 30 feet (9 m) with support.
Best climate and site Zones 4–10; full sun to partial shade; moist, humus-rich, well-drained soil.
Landscape uses Allow to clamber over bushes and fences, or wreath a verandah.
Growing guidelines Plant in spring. Prune after flowering to keep vigorous growth under control. Mulch with organic matter to keep soil evenly moist.
Good companions Other climbers, including roses, jasmine and nasturtium.
Other varieties There is a dark purple-flowered form with a pink center.
Other species *L. x heckrottii*, goldflame honeysuckle, is a twining vine with blue-green leaves and reddish flowers with yellow centers. Zones 5–9. *L. sempervirens*, trumpet honeysuckle, is a shrubby, evergreen to deciduous climber with non-fragrant, orange-scarlet flowers with yellow centers. Zones 4–10.
Comments The berries should not be eaten without preparation.

Mandevilla laxa
APOCYNACEAE

CHILEAN JASMINE

Chilean jasmine is a fast-growing, twining, semi-evergreen vine with heart-shaped leaves. Clusters of fragrant flowers grace the plant in summer.

Description A fast-growing, evergreen, woody vine with dark green, heart-shaped leaves and very fragrant, white to pinkish, trumpet-shaped flowers in late spring to midsummer. Deciduous in cool Zones.
Height and spread To 20 feet (6 m) with support.
Best climate and site Zones 9–11; full sun to light shade; any well-drained, humus-rich soil. Very sensitive to frost.
Landscape uses Where hardy, an excellent plant for a pillar or wall trellis. Elsewhere, a lovely greenhouse or hanging-basket plant.
Growing guidelines Plant in spring. Water freely when in full growth. Thin out and cut back in early spring. No serious problems when grown outdoors. As a greenhouse plant, whiteflies and spider mites may cause trouble. Spray with insecticidal soap.
Good companions Bougainvillea, plumbago, other colored varieties.
Other species There are many mandevillas, all an asset in warm, frost-free gardens. *M. x amoena* 'Alice de Pont' has handsome, green leaves and pink, trumpet flowers. Zones 9–11. *M. sanderi* has pink, red and white cultivars. Zones 9–11.
Comments Plants are also known as dipladenia, and are often sold as such.

Parthenocissus tricuspidata
VITACEAE

BOSTON IVY

Boston ivy is a deciduous vine that climbs by means of rootlike holdfasts. The large, maple-like leaves turn from green to brilliant scarlet in autumn.

Description A deciduous, strong-growing vine that climbs using tendrils with sucker disks. Glossy, green-lobed leaves turn brilliant shades of red and purple in autumn. Inconspicuous, white flowers in late spring are followed by purple fruit.
Height and spread To 60 feet (18 m) with support.
Best climate and site Zones 4–10; full sun to light shade; humus-rich, well-drained soil.
Landscape uses The premier foliage vine to mask a wall and create autumn interest.
Growing guidelines Plant container-grown plants in early spring. Avoid overfeeding, which provides succulent growth that is attractive to pests. Prune to keep it clear of gutters, fascias and eaves.
Good companions This dense, vigorous vine is best grown by itself as a feature. Leafy backdrop to shrubs and perennials.
Other common names Japanese ivy.
Other varieties Some purple-leaved forms are available. There is also a form with smaller leaves than the species.
Other species *P. quinquefolia*, Virginia creeper, has intense autumn color on its grapevine-like, five-lobed leaves.
Comments Boston ivy is sometimes slow to become established.

Passiflora caerulea
PASSIFLORACEAE

BLUE PASSIONFLOWER

Blue passionflower is a deciduous, summer-flowering vine with an exquisite and detailed flower, which features a distinctive "crown" of filaments.

Description A fast-growing, deciduous vine featuring blue or (rarely) white flowers in summer. These are followed by conspicuous, though inedible, orange fruit.
Height and spread To 12 feet (3.6 m) with support.
Best climate and site Zones 7–11; full sun to light shade; well-drained, humus-rich soil.
Landscape uses Grow on a trellis for the flowers and foliage. An excellent choice for a fast-growing screen or to hide a fence.
Growing guidelines Plant in spring near a warm wall for winter protection. Mulch with organic matter to keep soil evenly moist. No serious pests or diseases. Dies back to the ground annually in all but the warmest portions of its range.
Good companions Intermingle with other climbers, or give a garden a tropical feel.
Other varieties There is a white-flowered form available.
Other species *P. incarnata*, wild passion-flower, bears white flowers with blue stamens in summer; followed by edible fruit. Zones 6–9. *P. coccinea* has vibrant red flowers. Zones 9–11.
Comments Used as an understock for grafting *P. edulis*, edible passionfruit, and may sucker.

Stephanotis floribunda
ASCLEPIADACEAE

MADAGASCAR JASMINE

Stephanotis is a much-loved climber. Its waxy, white and highly fragrant, summer flowers are often used in bridal bouquets.

Description An evergreen, twining vine with dark green, glossy leaves and clusters of tubular, white flowers in midspring to autumn. Flowers are highly fragrant. In warm climates the flowers may be followed by large, woody seedpods.
Height and spread To 12 feet (3.6 m) with support.
Best climate and site Zones 9–12; filtered sun to light shade; humus-rich, moisture-retentive soil.
Landscape uses Where hardy, a compact vine to grow on a trellis. Elsewhere, a beautiful greenhouse plant to grow in a large container. Also grown for its cut flowers, used in bridal bouquets and leis.
Growing guidelines Plant in spring. Cut back long or crowded stems in autumn (early winter in the colder parts of its range). Keep soil moist with regular watering, particularly during dry periods, and an organic mulch. Avoid dry or poorly drained soil. Ensure adequate air circulation to reduce pests and diseases.
Good companions Feature amid tropical and subtropical plants.
Other common names Wax flower, bridal wreath.
Comments Plants will grow from seedpods, but may take several years to flower.

Trachelospermum jasminoides
APOCYNACEAE

STAR JASMINE

Star jasmine is fast growing and can be used as a climber, trailing plant or topiary. Its fragrant, white flowers bloom in late spring to summer.

Description A fast-growing, evergreen, twining vine with glossy, green leaves and very fragrant, 1-inch (2.5-cm) white flowers borne in small clusters in late spring to early summer. Overwhelming fragrance when in full flower.

Height and spread To 20 feet (6 m) if grown with support.

Best climate and site Zones 8–10; full sun to partial shade; moisture-retentive, humus-rich soil.

Landscape uses Excellent for screens or trellises, or as a groundcover. Train as a climber to form decorative patterns or outlines on walls or along eaves. Can also be clipped and trained into shapes as a standard, ball or topiary form.

Growing guidelines Plant in spring. Mulch to keep roots cool. Prune after flowering to control vigorous growth and to keep within its desired bounds.

Good companions Other evergreen plants, such as boxwood, mondo grass, gardenias.

Other common names Chinese jasmine, confederate jasmine.

Other varieties Variegated foliage form, one with veined leaves that turn bronze in autumn, and a yellow-flowered form.

Comments Colored foliage forms don't flower as prolifically as the species.

Vitis coignetiae
VITACEAE

CRIMSON GLORY VINE

This ornamental grapevine climbs by means of tendrils. It is an extremely rapid grower, capable of covering up to 1,000 square feet (300 sq m) of trellis in 12 months. It has brilliant autumn color.

Description A fast-growing, deciduous vine with large, green leaves that turn orange, scarlet and crimson in autumn. The clusters of inconspicuous, cream flowers in late spring are followed by black fruit which are small, poor quality and not really edible. Although it grows in warm climates, it will not color well.

Height and spread To 50 feet (15 m) if grown with support.

Best climate and site Zones 5–10; full sun; well-drained soil.

Landscape uses Valued for its autumn foliage color and as an excellent cover for trellises, arbors or to climb walls or facades.

Growing guidelines Plant in winter or spring. Prune to desired dimensions in winter. Provide stout wire or trellis support on which to climb.

Good companions Its vigorous nature makes this a good stand-alone choice.

Other species *V. amurensis*, amur grape, is a vigorous, deciduous vine with large leaves that turn crimson or purple in autumn. Zones 4–7.

Comments As a result of its enormous growth rate, crimson glory vine can exceed its desired limits. Avoid problems by choosing the site carefully.

Wisteria floribunda
FABACEAE

JAPANESE WISTERIA

The extremely long, fragrant flower clusters of Japanese wisteria make this a much sought-after climber. It is best grown where its long flowers can be enjoyed, such as on a high pergola.

Description A vigorous, twining, deciduous climber with green, compound leaves. The exceptionally long clusters of fragrant, white, pink, lavender or violet flowers appear in late spring. They may be followed by slightly hairy seedpods.

Height and spread To 50 feet (15 m) with support.

Best climate and site Zones 4–10; full sun to light shade; moist, well-drained soil, preferably with low nitrogen content. Lighter, infertile soil reduces vegetative growth and increases flowering.

Landscape uses Fine vines to climb on stout supports such as arches or pergolas. May be trained to standard form.

Growing guidelines Plant in spring. Prune after flowering during summer to remove wayward growth. Avoid poorly drained soil.

Good companions Climbing roses; spring-flowering shrubs, trees and annuals.

Other varieties Many named cultivars with single and double flowers, colors from white, pink to purple and a dwarf form.

Other species *W. sinensis*, Chinese wisteria, has mauve, perfumed flowers in early spring. Zones 5–10.

Comments Requires stout hardwood or sturdy wire support.

Acorus gramineus
ARACEAE

SWEET FLAG

This is an excellent small plant for foliage color and interest in gardens, containers or in moist places at the edge of ponds.

Description This clumping, evergreen perennial has narrow, gently curving leaves that grow in fans like an iris. Flower spikes are inconspicuous; these plants are grown for their foliage.

Height and spread Height 1 foot (30 cm); spread to about 2 feet (60 cm).

Best climate and site Zones 3–11; full sun or light shade; tolerates most soil types, but prefers moist and humus-rich.

Landscape uses A small plant, useful for accent or edging, particularly in moist situations or among pebbles or stones. Also useful to edge large containers.

Growing guidelines Plant rhizomes or potted plants in spring or summer in any moist or boggy spot, or in water up to 4 inches (10 cm) deep. Plants establish readily and can be divided in spring. Cut back if they become invasive.

Good companions Other moisture-loving plants, including water iris.

Other varieties There are several variegated forms, including silver-and-green and gold-and-green variegations. Also dwarf forms, used in aquariums.

Comments Although a member of the arum family, acorus flowers lack the spathe, or sheath.

Caltha palustris
RANUNCULACEAE

MARSH MARIGOLD

Marsh marigolds grow in moist soil and shallow wetlands and are grown in bogs or wet areas for their bold yellow, buttercup-like, spring flowers.

Description The deciduous to evergreen mounds of rounded leaves grow from a thick crown with fleshy, white roots. Butter-yellow 1½-inch (3.5-cm) flowers have five shiny petals and are carried in open clusters in early to midspring.

Height and spread Height 1–2 feet (30–60 cm); spread to 2 feet (60 cm).

Best climate and site Zones 2–8; full sun to partial shade; prefers wet, humus-rich or loamy soil.

Landscape uses Perfect for water gardens or along the low banks of streams. Early-season color from new growth is striking in spring.

Growing guidelines Plant in summer to autumn in moist soil. Grows even when covered with 1–4 inches (2.5–10 cm) of water. Once flowering is complete, moisture is less critical. Divide overgrown plants in summer.

Good companions Plant with primroses, irises and ferns in bog gardens.

Other common names Cowslip, kingcup.

Other varieties There are named varieties with fully double flowers that last for 1 week or more. There is also a white-flowered form.

Comments Also useful under deciduous trees where moisture is assured.

Cyperus involucratus
CYPERACEAE

UMBRELLA GRASS

This tall, grasslike plant grows well beside or in water and quickly forms a large clump in the right conditions. It can also be used as an indoor or container plant.

Description This clumping sedge has tall, hollow, three-cornered stalks topped with a rosette of glossy, green, narrow-ribbed leaves. Among the umbrella of leaves are the small, pale green flowers in summer.

Height and spread Height 3 feet (90 cm); spread to about 2 feet (60 cm).

Best climate and site Zones 9–12; full sun or light shade; tolerates most soil types, but prefers those that are moist to wet and humus-rich.

Landscape uses Umbrella grass is a tall accent plant for a wet spot where its light, leafy stems arch over water. It can also be grown in a pot and may be grown as an indoor plant.

Growing guidelines Because these plants can spread, consider containing them in pots in small areas. If plants are sunk into water, lift them from time to time to provide a dry period. Divide in spring. Browning leaves or lack of new growth may indicate that conditions are too dry.

Good companions Other water-loving plants, including iris.

Other species This species is sometimes sold as *C. alternifolius*.

Comments Umbrella grass may naturalize and become weedy.

Cyperus papyrus
CYPERACEAE

PAPYRUS

This tall, attractive water plant forms a large, stately clump in or beside water. It is a marvelous addition to a pond. It can also be used as a potted plant.

Description This very tall, clumping sedge has round, hollow, leafless stalks topped with a fluffy head of green "leaves," actually branchlets, that produce brown flowers in summer.

Height and spread Height 5–10 feet (1.5–3 m); spread 3 feet (90 cm) to indefinite.

Best climate and site Zones 9–12; full sun or light shade; moist to wet, humus-rich soil. Papyrus tolerates light frost but will die if water temperatures fall below around 50°F (10°C).

Landscape uses A tall accent plant for shallow water, where its airy heads on long, leafless stems arch over water. Can be grown in a large container.

Growing guidelines Plant in shallow water (up to 2 feet [60 cm] deep) or, to contain spread, grow in a large container.

Good companions Other large water-loving plants or floating water plants.

Other common names Egyptian paper reed.

Other species *C. prolifer*, dwarf papyrus, forms a smaller clump than papyrus and is only about 3 feet (90 cm) tall. It is a good choice for a small area or a pot. Zones 9–12.

Comments Used by ancient Egyptians to make paper.

Gunnera maculata
GUNNERACEAE

BRAZILIAN RHUBARB

With leaves like those of a huge rhubarb plant, Brazilian rhubarb always makes an impact. It is a great choice for a wet spot, pond or lake.

Description A water-edge plant with large, rounded and lobed, rhubarb-like leaves from spring to autumn. The leaves have prickly stems. Clublike panicles of rusty red flowers are held on stiff stalks during spring to summer.

Height and spread Height 5–12 feet (1.5–3.6 m); spread may eventually reach 10 feet (3 m) when established. Individual leaves may be 6 feet (1.8 m) or more across.

Best climate and site Zones 7–9; full sun to shade (protect from hot sun); moist, humus-rich soil. Tolerates frost and cold.

Landscape uses Grown for its huge and striking leaves, this is an accent plant for shallow water or moist soil at the edge of ponds or large water features.

Growing guidelines This herbaceous perennial dies back in winter and early spring, when it can be planted or divided. Plant in rich soil beside a pond or in a boggy spot.

Good companions Contrast with water-loving plants, such as iris, ferns and other water plants.

Other common names Chilean rhubarb, giant rhubarb, gunnera.

Comments Also good for growing under small trees at the water's edge.

Hottonia palustris
PRIMULACEAE

WATER VIOLET

Water violets appreciate still or gently moving water in which they flourish just below the water's surface. Many stems of starry flowers rise above the water in summer.

Description An aquatic perennial that forms a mat of small, leafy rosettes in shallow water or streams. Plants are submerged in shallow waters. Starry, white to lilac flowers to 1 inch (2.5 cm) across are borne on spikes that rise around 8 inches (20 cm) above the water in summer.

Height and spread Height 1 foot (30 cm); spread indefinite.

Best climate and site Zones 6–9; full sun to shade; muddy soil. Tolerates cold water but not waters that freeze solid during winter. Best in acidic water.

Landscape uses Spring and summer color before water lilies bloom. A good choice for a fish pond; fish will lay eggs among the foliage. Also useful as an oxygenator.

Growing guidelines Plant rooted pieces (stolons) in spring or summer in muddy soil in shallow water to 1½ feet (45 cm) deep. Dies back in winter to resting buds. New growth appears in spring as the water warms (and, in cold areas, when ice melts) and appears to billow below the water.

Good companions Other water-loving or floating plants, including water lilies.

Other common names Featherfoil, water feather.

Comments Can be difficult to establish.

Iris pseudacorus
IRIDACEAE

WATER IRIS

Water irises are true water plants but also adapt to water-logged soils. Enjoy the yellow iris flowers in late spring, amid the clumps of swordlike leaves.

Description An herbaceous, beardless iris that loves water. Handsome clumps of gray-green, upright, swordlike leaves produce tall spikes of flowers in spring and summer. The yellow flowers have brown or purple veining and dark patches on some petals. Plants die back in autumn.

Height and spread Height 5 feet (1.5 m); spread indefinite.

Best climate and site Zones 5–9; full sun to shade; shallow water with rich soil.

Landscape uses Grow in clumps at the edge of ponds or in a bog garden for the upright foliage and flowers. Contrast with creeping or floating plants.

Growing guidelines Grows from rhizomes planted in autumn or early spring in a shallow container that can be submerged at the water's edge. Can grow in water up to 1 foot (30 cm) deep.

Good companions Other water-loving edge plants such as papyrus, or floating plants such as water lilies.

Other common names Sweet flag, European yellow flag.

Other varieties A variegated leaf form has cream-striped golden leaves, usually fading to green in summer. The variegated form is less vigorous than the species.

Comments May spread vigorously.

Lysichiton americanus
ARACEAE

YELLOW SKUNK CABBAGE

Despite its unflattering common name, which comes from the flower's scent, yellow skunk cabbage is a dramatic plant that produces upright, yellow, arum lily-like flowers before the leaves.

Description An arum lily-like plant with a yellow spathe on a short, stout stem that appears in early spring before the leaves. Flowers have an unpleasant smell and persist as the large, crumpled leaves develop. Plants die back in autumn.

Height and spread Height 4 feet (1.2 m); spread 2½ feet (75 cm).

Best climate and site Zones 5–9; full sun; deep, rich soil. Flowers are shorter in warmer climates.

Landscape uses Grow in clumps at the edge of ponds, streams or bog gardens for striking flowers in early spring and strongly architectural leaves from spring to autumn.

Growing guidelines Grows from divisions planted in autumn or early spring. Can be lightly submerged in up to 1 inch (2.5 cm) of water.

Good companions Mass plant or combine with ferns or winter iris *Iris unguicularis*.

Other common names Bog arum, skunk lily.

Other species *L. camtschatcensis*, white skunk cabbage, has white, sweet-smelling flowers 2 feet (60 cm) tall. Zones 5–9.

Comments Yellow skunk cabbage does not like hot climates.

Marsilea mutica
MARSILEACEAE

NARDOO

This floating fern is grown for its leaves, which resemble those of clover, and float on the water's surface. As a true fern, this plant has no flowers.

Description A fern with four-leaf clover-like leaves that float on the water's surface. The leaves have four lobes and an outer edging of brown with a green center. Grows from creeping rhizomes in the mud. This plant does not produce flowers.

Height and spread Height 4–18 inches (10–45 cm); spread 2 feet (60 cm).

Best climate and site Zones 9–12; full sun to light shade; deep, rich soil in water.

Landscape uses Grow nardoo in clumps at the edges of ponds or shallow pools. Can also be grown in large containers of water and used to decorate courtyards or as a table decoration.

Growing guidelines Grows from divisions or side shoots planted during autumn or early spring.

Good companions Plant with floating flowering plants, such as water poppy *Hydrocleys nymphoides* or nymphoides *Nymphoides peltata*.

Other common names Floating fern, water clover.

Other species There are many species of nardoo native to warm-temperate areas around the world. Some tolerate cold winters to Zone 5.

Comments Can survive periods of dryness even if the fronds die back.

Myriophyllum aquaticum
HALORAGIDACEAE

MILFOIL

This is a feathery-leaved plant that grows in submerged conditions. It is valuable in ponds and streams where fish are kept; it provides shelter and oxygenates the water.

Description A perennial with tufts of fine, feathery leaves, milfoil grows in thickets submerged in still water. Leaves are blue-green to yellow-green with spikes of insignificant flowers.

Height and spread Height 6–24 inches (15–60 cm); spread indefinite.

Best climate and site Zones 9–11; full sun to light shade; sandy soil, rich in organic matter in water. This species will not tolerate cold temperatures.

Landscape uses Grow in clumps at the edges of ponds or shallow pools. Provides a soft, feathery foliage contrast to flat, floating leaves. Also provides an important environment for fish to shelter and breed.

Growing guidelines Grows from cuttings or divisions planted in spring or summer into the bottom of ponds. Remove excess as necessary.

Good companions Plant with floating flowering plants, such as water poppy *Hydrocleys nymphoides*, nymphoides *Nymphoides peltata* or water lilies.

Other common names Parrot's feather, diamond milfoil.

Comments Can become a water weed in some areas and is banned from sale in the United Kingdom.

Nelumbo nucifera
NELUMBONACEAE

LOTUS

This is one of the most elegant and dramatic of all water plants. The tall flowers rise above the large, circular leaves. After flowering, the seedpods are highly ornamental.

Description A flowering water plant that grows from a creeping rhizome. Leaves are large, circular and raised above the water. The fragrant, pink flowers rise on tall stems above the leaves. Huge, salt shaker-like seedpods follow ripening to brown.

Height and spread Height 6–36 inches (15–90 cm) depending on varieties; spread to 5 feet (1.5 m) or more.

Best climate and site Zones 6–11; full sun; soil rich in organic matter in water. Can tolerate cold winter temperatures if rhizomes are buried in the bottom of ponds, or grown in conservatories.

Landscape uses Grow in ponds, lakes or dams for dramatic flowering. Can also be grown in water containers.

Growing guidelines Divisions planted in spring or summer into the bottom of ponds or in submerged pots. Plants flower best with hot-summer conditions.

Good companions Mass plant.

Other varieties Named varieties with pink, apricot or white flowers. There are also dwarf species that are better for small ponds or containers.

Comments Seeds are edible and also highly attractive in floral arrangements (as are the dried leaves).

Nymphaea hybrids
NYMPHAEACEAE

WATER LILY

Water lilies were used to great effect by Impressionist artist Claude Monet, on the lake in his garden in Giverny, France, where they can be viewed from a Japanese-style bridge.

Description A water plant that grows from tuber-like rhizomes. Leaves are circular and float on the surface. The fragrant flowers, in tones of white, pink, blue or yellow, may float beside the leaves or be held above them on succulent stems. Flowers from spring to autumn.

Height and spread Size and spread depend on variety. Most need 1–2 feet (30–60 cm) depth of water; small varieties need a depth of 10–16 inches (25–40 cm); miniatures 6–10 inches (15–25 cm) depth.

Best climate and site Zones 5–12 depending on the variety; full sun; soil rich in organic matter in water. Hardy varieties withstand cold-winter temperatures. There are also tropical varieties.

Landscape uses Use to ornament a pond or water feature, but maintain a balance between open water and water lilies.

Growing guidelines Plant in spring, preferably in pots in a mix of soil and well-rotted manure (water lilies are heavy feeders). Cover the soil surface with gravel to stop fish disturbing the growing medium. Submerge the pots in water.

Good companions Mass plant a range of different colors.

Comments Some are perfumed.

Nymphoides peltata
MENYANTHACEAE

NYMPHOIDES

The heart-shaped leaves of these dainty little plants float on the water's surface and resemble those of miniature water lilies. The plant has small, fringed, yellow flowers.

Description A deciduous water plant that grows from tuber-like rhizomes. The small leaves are heart-shaped and float on the surface, often forming dense mats. They are bright green and mottled with brown. The dainty 1-inch (2.5-cm) flowers are yellow with fringed petals. Flowers are held above the surface from summer to autumn.

Height and spread Height 4–18 inches (10–45 cm); spread 2–6 feet (60–180 cm).

Best climate and site Zones 6–10; full sun; most soils in water.

Landscape uses Use to ornament a pond or lake, since the plants will cover large areas of water.

Growing guidelines Plant in late winter to spring, with roots in the bottom of the pond. Plants spread readily by runners.

Good companions Plant with other dainty floating plants, including nardoo.

Other common names Marshworts, water fringe, yellow floating heart.

Other species *N. indica*, water snowflake, has small, white, fringed flowers amid large leaves, but prefers warm, tropical to subtropical conditions. Zones 10–12.

Comments Not recommended for clay ponds.

Pistia stratiotes
ARACEAE

WATER LETTUCE

The large, handsome rosettes of blue-green, ribbed leaves float in clumps on the water's surface and are the feature of this water plant.

Description A floating water plant with feathery, white roots. The downy, blue-green, lettuce-like leaves are spongy, which allows them to float. The leaves have distinctive ribbing and a lustrous look. The flowers are spathes, but are inconspicuous among the leaves.

Height and spread Height 4–18 inches (10–45 cm); spread up to 2–6 feet (60–180 cm).

Best climate and site Zones 9–12; full sun to shade; most soils in water. It can be grown in cooler Zones but must be overwintered in a greenhouse.

Landscape uses Use to shade water in a pool and provide food for fish. Can also be grown in slow-moving water, but should not be allowed to enter natural waterways.

Growing guidelines Plant offsets so the roots can reach the pond bottom. They will multiply readily. Water lettuce is evergreen in warm waters but becomes deciduous in colder conditions.

Good companions Plant with contrasting, vertical foliage plants.

Other common names Shell flower.

Comments Water lettuce is considered weedy in some warm climates, where it can block waterways.

Pontederia cordata
PONTEDERIACEAE

PICKEREL WEED

This blue-flowered water plant forms imposing clumps along the water's edge, softening the sides of water features and providing height and color.

Description A deciduous, marginal aquatic plant that forms large clumps of glossy, green, lance-shaped leaves. The flower spikes are clusters of small but intensely blue blossoms that last through the summer into autumn.

Height and spread Height of plants is around 2–3 feet (60–90 cm) in a water depth of 4–18 inches (10–45 cm); spread up to 1½ feet (45 cm).

Best climate and site Zones 4–10; full sun to light shade (but fewer flowers in more shaded spots); most soils in water.

Landscape uses Adds height and foliage contrast to the sides of pools or lakes.

Growing guidelines Plant divisions in spring around the water edge. The plants will multiply. Little care is needed, other than removing spent flower spikes to encourage long flowering.

Good companions Water iris, arrowhead, thalia and floating plants, including water lilies.

Other common names Wampee.

Other varieties A white-flowered form (sold as *P. lanceolata*) grows in shallow water 4–8 inches (10–20 cm) to a height of 6–8 feet (1.8–2.4 m).

Comments Weedy in some warm climates.

Sagittaria sagittifolia
ALISMATACEAE

ARROWHEAD

Distinctive, arrow-shaped leaves on tall, thick stems and showy, white flowers make arrowhead an attractive plant for the edges of water features. The edible tubers are a bonus.

Description A deciduous, marginal, aquatic plant, which forms large clumps with pale green, variable, arrow-shaped leaves. The flower stems appear in summer with heads of single, three-petaled, white flowers, about 1 inch (2.5 cm) across, with a purple spot at the base of each petal.
Height and spread Height of plants is around 1½ feet (45 cm) in a water depth of up to 1 foot (30 cm); spread up to 1½ feet (45 cm).
Best climate and site Zones 7–12; full sun to light shade; most soils in water or wet conditions.
Landscape uses Adds height and foliage contrast to the sides of pools or lakes.
Growing guidelines Plant divisions in spring around the water edge. The plants will multiply to colonize large areas. Little care is needed, other than removing spent flower spikes to encourage long flowering. Plants die down over winter.
Good companions Water iris, pickerel weed, thalia, water lilies.
Other common names Water potato, swamp potato, swan plant.
Comments When plants die down, the small, edible tubers can be harvested to be cooked and eaten like potatoes.

Thalia dealbata
MARANTACEAE

THALIA

This water plant for the edge of pools and ponds has oval, green leaves on attractive, red stems that rise above the water. Through summer, the clumps produce stems of violet and white flowers.

Description A robust, deciduous, marginal, aquatic plant, which forms large clumps with gray-green, oval, canna-like leaves on long stems or petioles. The flower stems appear in summer with panicles of violet and white flowers.
Height and spread Height of plants is around 6 feet (1.8 m) or more in a water depth of 0–12 inches (0–30 cm) or more; spread to 2 feet (60 cm).
Best climate and site Zones 9–10 in warm water; full sun to light shade; fertile soils rich in organic matter in water or wet conditions.
Landscape uses Adds height and foliage contrast to the sides of pools or lakes.
Growing guidelines Plant divisions in spring around the water edge. The plants will multiply to colonize large areas in places where water doesn't freeze. These plants can also be grown in large pots filled with good-quality soil and water.
Good companions Water iris, pickerel weed, arrowhead, water lilies, nardoo.
Other species *T. geniculata* is smaller, growing to 4 feet (1.2 m), with columns of purple flowers. Zones 9–12.
Comments Stem color of thalia is best in warm climates.

Zantedeschia aethiopica
ARACEAE

ARUM LILY

Can be grown in moist or wet soils for its handsome clumps of green, heart-shaped leaves and showy stalks of white arum flowers during summer.

Description An evergreen to deciduous, moisture-loving plant, which forms large clumps of glossy, green, heart-shaped leaves. The pure white, arum flowers (a white spathe wrapped around a yellow spadix) rise above the leafy clump in summer (and spot-flower for much of the year).
Height and spread Height 2½–3 feet (75–90 cm) or more, in a water depth of 0–12 inches (0–30 cm); spread to 2 feet (60 cm).
Best climate and site Zones 8–12; full sun to shade; fertile soils rich in organic matter in water or wet conditions. Plants are deciduous in colder Zones.
Landscape uses Beside water or in moist, shade areas, or in containers.
Growing guidelines Plant divisions or tubers in spring. The plants multiply readily where water temperatures remain above 50°F (10°C). Compact varieties can be grown in large containers.
Good companions Other clump-forming and floating water plants, or, in moist shade spots, ferns, impatiens and hostas.
Other varieties There are dwarf, white forms and a large, green-flowered form, as well as new pink forms.
Comments Arum lily can become weedy in warm climates.

Adenium obesum
APOCYNACEAE

DESERT ROSE

At first glance, desert rose in flower resembles a plumeria or oleander. It is a striking, shrubby succulent that adds drama to a garden, especially during winter, when it flowers.

Description A shrub with dark green leaves and sparse, leafless branches growing from a swollen base. The clusters of red or pink, tubular, five-petaled flowers often have a white eye. Up to 2 inches (5 cm) across, they form clusters at branch tips.
Height and spread Height to 10 feet (3 m); spread to about 3 feet (90 cm).
Best climate and site Zones 9–12 (but requiring a warm, dry, frost-free winter in cooler Zones); full sun or light shade; well-drained soil.
Landscape uses An unusual feature in a succulent garden or other sunny situation. In cooler climates, grow in a conservatory or as a bonsai.
Growing guidelines Plant in spring or year-round in tropical Zones. Best with a distinct dry period during winter, since they come from tropical Zones with wet and dry seasons. Plants tolerate being root bound, but need good drainage.
Good companions Other succulents.
Other common names Impala lily, mock azalea, desert azalea, sabi star.
Other varieties There are subspecies with flower color variants, including white.
Comments Plants grow from cuttings but also reach flowering size quickly from seed.

Aechmea spp.
BROMELIACEAE

BROMELIAD

There are many different types of bromeliads, grown as potted or garden plants for their rosettes of often colorful leaves and long-lasting, exotic flowers, which may be followed by berries.

Description A small perennial with rosettes of stiff leaves which may be banded or variegated and are often sharp or spined. Flowers are usually a brightly colored spike with colored, petal-like bracts.
Height and spread Height depends on species but up to 3 feet (90 cm); spread to 1½ feet (45 cm) or more.
Best climate and site Zones 9–12 (but requiring temperatures above 60°F or 16°C); sun to light shade; dry, well-drained soil, or an epiphytic mix of bark chips such as is used for orchids.
Landscape uses Clumps brighten gardens with year-round leaf color and long-lasting flowers. Display on tree trunks or totems, or in pots as indoor or table decorations.
Growing guidelines Potted plants are available year-round. The rosette of leaves may form a central well that accumulates water, so flush it out regularly. Liquid feed in spring and summer.
Good companions Succulents, leafy subtropical or tropical foliage plants.
Other common names Living vase plant.
Other varieties Many named and unnamed varieties, often with colored leaves.
Comments Small offsets at the base can be detached when large enough to handle.

Aeonium arboreum
CRASSULACEAE

AEONIUM

This plant is grown for its rosettes of succulent leaves, particularly the dark, almost black, leaves of some named varieties, which are a dramatic contrast in succulent gardens or pots.

Description A small, succulent perennial with rosettes of spoon-shaped, green leaves (or dark, almost black, in some varieties). As the plants age, they develop small, trunklike stems. The yellow flowers form a pyramid-like cluster. They are usually removed from the colored-leaved forms.
Height and spread Height to 3 feet (90 cm); spread 1½ feet (45 cm) or more.
Best climate and site Zones 9–11; full sun; dry, well-drained soil.
Landscape uses Used for year-round foliage interest, particularly when dark or variegated forms are planted. Useful in succulent or seaside gardens, or in pots.
Growing guidelines Potted plants are available year-round, but plant in spring to summer in cooler Zones. Where plants are grown for leaf color, remove flowers before they bloom. Remove spent flowers and branches, which may die back after flowering. New rosettes replace those lost; aeonium also grows readily from cuttings.
Good companions Succulents; silver, gray or green foliage plants.
Comments The dark foliage form, 'Schwartzkopf', is also known as 'Zwartkop' and 'Swartzkop'.

Agave spp.
AGAVACEAE

CENTURY PLANTS

These rosette-forming succulent plants seem to take a century to bloom, hence their common name; actually, 15 years is more typical.

Description Century plants grow in rosettes of usually sharp, long, upright foliage. The blue-gray or silvery leaves are narrow, with spiny edges. *A. attenuata* has leaf tips that are not spined and is a good garden choice. It will grow into a mound up to 5 feet (1.5 m) high.

Height and spread Height and spread vary with species, but can reach 4 feet (1.2 m) across.

Best climate and site Zones 3–11; full sun; well-drained, sandy soils.

Landscape uses Small to large plants for dry gardens or modern landscapes. They are striking with pebbles or gravel, in large pots and window boxes.

Growing guidelines In pots, use a well-drained potting mix. Fertilize in spring, with an all-purpose fertilizer. Allow to dry between waterings, especially in winter. Remove dead or discolored leaves from base.

Good companions Other succulents, ice plant, gazanias, dimorphotheca, ornamental grasses, flax.

Other species *A. victoriae-reginae* (pictured) has blue-green leaves, edged and lined in white; it grows to 10 inches (25 cm) wide and is popular indoors in cool climates.

Comments Low-maintenance plants.

Aloe arborescens
ALOEACEAE

ALOE

Aloes have spires of red, bird-attracting flowers, which rise above the narrow, serrated, fleshy leaves. Flowers are seen in winter and spring.

Description A tall, many-branched shrub with a rosette of narrow, often slightly drooping, blue-gray leaves with spiny edges. In winter spires of red, tubular flowers rise above the leaves.

Height and spread Height to 6–10 feet (1.8–3 m) tall in flower; spreads to form broad mounds up to 10 feet (3 m) across.

Best climate and site Zones 9–11; full sun; well-drained, sandy soils.

Landscape uses Large, mound-forming plants for hot and dry or seaside gardens. A low-maintenance, drought-tolerant plant.

Growing guidelines Plant year-round. Fertilize in spring. Allow to dry between waterings, especially in winter. Remove dead leaves from base of stems and spent flower spikes.

Good companions Groundcovers, including other succulents, ice plant, gazanias, dimorphotheca, geraniums.

Other common names Candelabra aloe, torch plant.

Other varieties Yellow-flowered forms.

Other species Many species, including *A. plicatilis*, the fan aloe, which has fan-shaped clusters of leaves on stiff branches and red flower spikes. It grows to 5 feet (1.5 m) tall and is a dramatic accent plant. Zones 9–11.

Comments A low-maintenance plant.

Alopecurus pratensis var. *aureus*
POACEAE

YELLOW FOXTAIL GRASS

A single plant of yellow foxtail grass adds a bright splash of color to beds and borders. In a mass planting, it creates a dramatic landscape feature.

Description This low-growing, mostly evergreen, cool-season, spreading perennial grass has wide, bright yellow-green stripes on light green leaves. The cylindrical, foxtail-like flower head, soft to the touch, appears in late spring. Yellow foxtail grass is a slow spreader and non-invasive.

Height and spread Height to 1 foot (30 cm); spread 8–12 inches (20–30 cm). Flowering stems to 2 feet (60 cm) tall.

Best climate and site Zones 6–9 (best in cool climates); full sun, but partial shade in hot areas; any evenly moist soil (not dry or overly wet for long periods).

Landscape uses Use single specimens for a spot of color, or masses for an eye-catcher. Also useful in meadow gardens.

Growing guidelines Plant 1½–2 feet (45–60 cm) apart in spring or early autumn. Cut back tattered or discolored leaves in summer to neaten and to stimulate a new growth flush. Cut back browned leaves in late autumn. Fertilize if growth is poor, and water in dry weather.

Good companions A good choice for grouping with spring bulbs, summer bulbs and perennials, or other clumping ornamental grasses.

Comments Some species of foxtail grass can become weedy.

Ananas comosus
BROMELIACEAE

PINEAPPLE

Better known as a delicious fruit, the pineapple can be grown as a garden novelty. The tufty spike of leaves from the top of the fruit is all that's needed to grow a new plant.

Description Clumps of spiky, sword-shaped, gray-green leaves. The cluster of flowers fuses together to form the warty, green-and-yellow covering of the edible fruit. Inside, the flesh is yellow or almost white, with a tangy and sweet flavor.

Height and spread Height 3–6 feet (90–180 cm); spread 3–6 feet (90–180 cm).

Best climate and site Zones 9–12; full sun; well-drained, acid soil.

Landscape uses Although best known as a fruit, the pineapple is a dramatic bromeliad to grow in a container, succulent or rock garden. A talking point, novelty plant or potted decoration.

Growing guidelines Plant anytime as a potted plant, offshoot or pineapple top. In areas cooler than Zone 10, grow pineapple plants in pots, with a growing mix that contains extra sand or perlite for drainage. To produce fruit, set plants 1 foot (30 cm) apart in double rows 2 feet (60 cm) apart.

Good companions Other bromeliads.

Other varieties Named varieties with colored leaf variegations.

Comments To harvest, cut or snap the fruit from the stem when ripe (ripeness is indicated by color change, slight softening, and sweet aroma).

Arundo donax
POACEAE

GIANT REED

Giant reed may not reach flowering size in cool climates; in warm areas, long flower clusters form silky plumes in summer that last well into winter.

Description Giant reed is a warm-season, spreading perennial grass that produces wide leaves to 2 feet (60 m) long on tall, fast-growing canes. The leaves are evergreen in frost-free areas but die down in winter in cooler areas. Plants spread by short, creeping rhizomes.

Height and spread Height 6–20 feet (1.8–6 m); spread unlimited.

Best climate and site Zones 7–10; full sun; well-drained soil.

Landscape uses Giant reeds are striking as specimens or as background plants for flower borders or tropically-inspired gardens. They are also useful as screens and windbreaks, especially in seaside gardens. Giant reed can be invasive in warm climates, so choose its location carefully.

Growing guidelines Set plants 5 feet (1.5 m) apart in spring. Propagate by dividing clumps in spring. In areas where the plant turns brown in winter, cut the dead stems to the ground in winter.

Other varieties Named varieties with showy yellow- to white-variegated or striped leaves.

Comments Fast-growing giant reed can be used as a building material for fences and roof thatching; it is still used for reeds in musical instruments.

Bambusa spp.
POACEAE

BAMBOO

True bamboo is a tall, fast-growing grass that can be used to create a fast screen or hedge, or to bring character to an Asian-inspired garden. It can also be grown in large pots.

Description A tall, fast-growing grass with many woody stems and clusters of narrow, grasslike leaves from the nodes. Stems are segmented and often arch gracefully. Spreads via underground rhizomes. Flowers are insignificant and rarely seen.

Height and spread Height varies with species but may grow to 6–10 feet (1.8–3 m) tall; can spread to form broad mounds up to 10 feet (3 m) across.

Best climate and site Zones 9–12; full sun to light shade; well-drained, humus-rich soils.

Landscape uses Large, clump-forming plants for screens, accents or to add character, sound and movement to oriental gardens.

Growing guidelines Plant year-round. Fertilize in spring. Water when dry.

Good companions Mass plant or combine with low shrubs, such as azaleas, hebes and other clumping grasses. Combines well with gravel or pebbles and rocks.

Other species Many species, including *B. multiplex*, hedge bamboo, with arching stems and good cold tolerance. It grows to 10–30 feet (3–9 m) tall. Zones 9–12.

Comments *Bambusa* spp. are usually less invasive than other types of bamboo.

Billbergia nutans
BROMELIACEAE

QUEEN'S TEARS

These delightful plants can be an attractive feature in a garden or container. In cooler areas they are also grown as indoor plants.

Description Clumps of light green, coarse leaves with pendulous, arching flower stems in spring. Beneath the bright pink bracts are drooping, bell-shaped, dark blue and green flowers with prominent stamens.
Height and spread Height to 2 feet (60 cm); can spread to large clumps.
Best climate and site Zones 9–12; full sun to light shade; well-drained, humus-rich soil.
Landscape uses Mass plant as an understory in foliage gardens or among rocks. An elegant feature in a pot or urn.
Growing guidelines Plant potted plants year-round in a warm spot, since plants can be damaged by temperatures below 50°F (10°C). Feed occasionally with diluted liquid fertilizer. Mist to maintain humidity. Separate offshoots to form new plants. If growing in containers, use a coarse, free-draining potting mix.
Good companions Shade-loving plants, such as tradescantia, foliage plants.
Other common names Friendship plant.
Other species *B. amoena*, with rosettes of broad, dramatically colored and striped leaves and colorful spikes of flowers that may reach 3 feet (90 cm). Zones 9–12.
Comments One of the easiest of all bromeliads to grow.

Briza media
POACEAE

QUAKING GRASS

The flowers, or florets, of quaking grass tremble in the slightest breeze, adding movement to flower borders and rock gardens.

Description Quaking grass is an easy-to-grow, cool-season, clumping perennial grass. The tiny, heart-shaped, green florets shake in the breeze in late spring. They turn purple, then golden-yellow in summer. The leaves are green in spring but straw-colored by summer.
Height and spread Height 1–2 feet (30–60 cm); clumps to about 1 foot (30 cm) wide. Flowers bloom on 2–3-foot (60–90-cm) tall stems.
Best climate and site Zones 4–10; full sun to light shade; moist, humus-rich soil.
Landscape uses Edgings, rock gardens, meadows and flower borders or as a low-maintenance groundcover. Position where plants will be ruffled by the breeze.
Growing guidelines Set plants 1–2 feet (30–60 cm) apart in spring or autumn. Don't fertilize. Cut back old flower heads and unsightly foliage to a few inches above the crown in midsummer, to encourage fresh basal growth. Cut back again in late autumn and divide if necessary.
Good companions Other grasses, perennials and rockery plants.
Other species *B. maxima*, big quaking grass, is an annual that grows 1–2 feet (30–60 cm) tall.
Comments Can become weedy.

Calamagrostis x acutiflora
POACEAE

FEATHER REED GRASS

One of the most spectacular grasses, feather reed grass is evergreen in warm climates and deciduous in cold regions.

Description This cool-season, clumping perennial grass has flowers from late spring or early summer. These are held on erect, tall spikes and consist of 1-foot (30-cm) long, pinkish green clusters that later become beige. Seed clusters form in summer and last into winter.
Height and spread Height 1½–2 feet (45–60 cm); spread to about 2 feet (60 cm). Flowering stems to 6 feet (1.8 m) tall.
Best climate and site Zones 5–9; full sun to light shade; tolerates most soil types, but prefers those that are moist and humus-rich.
Landscape uses Feather reed grass is a tall accent plant. Its rich, golden, late-summer colors make spectacular screens or masses in backgrounds. Its flowering stems sway in the slightest breeze, adding movement to the garden.
Growing guidelines Set plants 2–3 feet (60–90 cm) apart in spring or autumn. Divide in spring or autumn and cut back by late winter.
Good companions Late summer- to autumn-flowering perennials.
Other varieties Select named varieties of feather reed grass for earlier and larger blooms and good winter effect.
Comments May not bloom well in hot climates.

Carex elata
CYPERACEAE

TUFTED SEDGE

*Grow tufted sedge as an accent plant near a pond,
water garden or quiet stream that reflects the bright
color. 'Bowles Golden' is a striking cultivar.*

Description This outstanding foliage
plant is a clump-forming sedge with bright,
semi-evergreen leaves. Some forms have
golden leaves edged with green. Brownish
flowers appear in late spring.
Height and spread Height to 2 feet
(60 cm); spread 2–5 feet (60–150 cm).
Best climate and site Zones 5–9;
morning sun or light shade; moist, acid soil
(or in very shallow water).
Landscape uses Foliage contrast and
accents in bog gardens or beside water.
Growing guidelines Set plants 2–3 feet
(60–90 cm) apart in spring in wet spots
or in shallow water up to 4 inches (10 cm)
deep. Remove brown leaves as needed.
Good companions Grow with other
moisture-loving plants.
Other varieties Golden foliage forms.
Other species Many garden-worthy
carex with interesting and attractively
colored leaves. C. *comans* 'Bronze',
bronze New Zealand hair sedge, has fine,
brownish-white foliage. Height 1–6 feet
(30–180 cm). Zones 7–9. C. *glauca*, blue
sedge, is a blue-toned groundcover that
forms a low-growing, 6-inch (15-cm) tall
mat. Zones 5–9.
Comments Plants prefer acid soil, so avoid
using lime or wood ashes around them.

Carnegiea gigantea
CACTACEAE

GIANT SAGUARO

*The giant saguaro is one of the most impressive
of all cacti and is spectacular when included in
a dry-landscape planting.*

Description A treelike, slow-growing
cactus, branching with age into a
candelabra shape. The ribbed trunk and
stems have clusters of long, sharp spines.
White flowers are produced near the top of
the cactus when plants are several feet high.
Height and spread Height to 30 feet
(16 m); spread 20 feet (7 m) or more. Large
plants are extremely heavy. Mature
specimens are very old, probably as much
as 200–300 years old.
Best climate and site Zones 9–11; full
sun; well-drained soil. In colder climates,
grow in a heated greenhouse.
Landscape uses Mature specimens
are striking plants for arid gardens and are
impressive silhouetted against the skyline.
The flowers attract nectar-feeding birds,
such as hummingbirds.
Growing guidelines Plant in a well-
drained soil enriched with organic matter.
Mature specimens have large, well-
developed root systems. Seedlings take
many decades to reach flowering size.
Keep dry from mid-autumn to early spring.
In a pot, use a cactus mix.
Good companions Shrubby succulents,
cacti and sun-loving groundcover plants.
Comments Avoid purchasing plants that
have been taken illegally from the wild.

Coix lacryma-jobi
POACEAE

JOB'S TEARS

*Job's tears is grown for its hard, beadlike seeds.
It is perennial in very warm climates, but it will grow
as an annual in cooler areas.*

Description A warm-season, clumping,
tender perennial grass, often grown as an
annual. It has coarse, shiny, upright leaves
to 1 foot (30 cm) long that surround the
stems. Flowers are short, gray tassels in
midsummer. The ¼-inch (6-mm), light
green seeds turn white or black and drop
when ripe.
Height and spread Height to 6 feet
(1.8 m); clumps to 2 feet (60 cm) wide.
Best climate and site Zones 9–10 (but
an annual in colder climates); full sun;
moist to wet, rich soil.
Landscape uses A living screen in warm
climates. In most areas, it is grown as an
accent plant for its ornamental seeds.
Growing guidelines Plant in spring.
Job's tears is extremely sensitive to cold,
so wait until after the last frost date to set
out seedlings about 2 feet (60 cm) apart.
Water during dry spells to keep the soil
evenly moist. Seeds should be soaked
before planting.
Good companions Vegetables, other
flowering plants.
Comments Job's tears was one of the first
grasses ever grown as an ornamental.
Its hard seeds were once used as beads
in necklaces and rosaries.

Cordyline australis
AGAVACEAE

NEW ZEALAND CABBAGE TREE

In areas that are too cold for palms and tropical foliage plants, the New Zealand cabbage tree adds height and a lush, leafy effect, particularly around swimming pools and ponds.

Description The palmlike New Zealand cabbage tree has straplike leaves up to 3 feet (90 cm) in length. The leaves form rosettes around the tall, central stem. The fragrant, white flowers are borne on large panicles in spring and summer and these are followed by white berries. Flower stems can be 3 feet (90 cm) long.

Height and spread Height 16–33 feet (5–10 m); clumps to about 5 feet (1.5 m) wide with age. Slow growing.

Best climate and site Zones 8–12; full sun or semi-shade; most soil types.

Landscape uses An accent plant or for color contrast in a foliage garden, around swimming pools, in seaside gardens or in containers. Lends a tropical look to a cold-climate garden.

Growing guidelines Plant anytime, but spring is best in cool climates. Feed with compost and mulch with leaf mold annually. Water when dry.

Good companions Palms, ferns, colorful shrubs, agapanthus.

Other varieties Named forms are available with variegated, bronze, purple or pink-flushed leaves.

Comments This species is moderately frost- and salt-tolerant.

Cordyline fruticosa
AGAVACEAE

TI

The colored leaf and variegated forms of this tall, straight, tropical foliage plant are striking in warm-climate gardens.

Description The palmlike ti tree forms a strongly branching trunk with lancelike leaves up to 2½ feet (75 cm) long and 6 inches (15 cm) wide. The leaves form rosettes around the tall, central stem. The fragrant, white to mauve flowers are borne on large panicles in summer and followed by red berries. Flower stems can be 1 foot (30 cm) long.

Height and spread Height to 10 feet (3 m); clumps to about 5 feet (1.5 m) wide with age. Slow growing.

Best climate and site Zones 10–12; semi-shade; most soil types. In colder Zones, ti can be grown in warm, frost-free microclimates.

Landscape uses An accent plant, or grow for color contrast in a tropical to sub-tropical foliage garden. Excellent around swimming pools or in containers.

Growing guidelines Plant anytime. Feed regularly with compost and mulch with leaf mold. Water when dry.

Good companions Palms, ferns, colorful shrubs, including hibiscus, ixora, acalypha.

Other varieties Named forms with variegated, bronze, purple or pink-flushed or striped leaves. Leaf size and shape varies.

Comments This plant is also sold as *C. terminalis*.

Cortaderia selloana
POACEAE

PAMPAS GRASS

Pampas grass is a showy and popular ornamental grass where it is hardy. It forms large, grassy clumps and many spikes of white or sometimes pink, plumelike flowers.

Description A warm-season, clumping perennial grass that forms large clumps of sharp-edged leaves that are deciduous in autumn in cool climates but perennial elsewhere. Spectacular, plumelike, 3-foot (90-cm) flower heads, either white or pink, rise on tall spikes in midsummer and until late autumn.

Height and spread Height 5–12 feet (1.5–3.6 m); spread to 12 feet (3.6 m). Flowering stems may be 8–15 feet (2.4–4.5 m) tall.

Best climate and site Zones 8–10; full sun to light shade; any soil.

Landscape uses Dramatic screens, background clumps or elegant specimens amid lawns or mixed plantings.

Growing guidelines Set plants 5–8 feet (1.5–2.4 m) apart in spring to avoid overcrowding. Water when dry. Cut foliage back every second year in early spring. Divide in spring.

Good companions Lawns, other ornamental grasses, perennials.

Other species Some plants sold as *C. selloana* may be weedy relatives (such as *C. jubata*), which spread aggressively.

Comments Wear long sleeves, pants and gloves when working with the sharp leaves.

Cycas revoluta
CYCADACEAE

SAGO PALM

The sago palm is often mistaken for a true palm. It is, however, a type of cycad, a plant group that has existed since the time of the dinosaurs.

Description A palmlike plant, with a large rosette of fronds on a short, stout trunk. Fronds can be 3–5 feet (90–150 cm) long and have spines. Male and female "flowers" are borne on separate plants. Plants form large, underground, tuberous roots.

Height and spread Height 10 feet (3 m); spread to 10 feet (3 m). This size is only achieved after many years of slow growth.

Best climate and site Zones 9–12; full sun to light shade; any well-drained soil.

Landscape uses Dramatic focal point or massed to create a low, palmlike effect. Useful around the base of buildings, under trees or in gardens that are viewed from above. Sago palms can also be grown in large containers.

Growing guidelines Plants are very slow-growing, but mature plants are available and transplant well. Water when dry and fertilize once a year. Remove untidy fronds, taking care to avoid handling the spiny base without protection.

Good companions Lawns, rainforest or foliage plants, understory beneath trees and palms.

Other common names Cycad, Japanese sago palm.

Comments The starchy fruit is poisonous unless well-prepared by leaching toxins.

Dicksonia antarctica
DICKSONIACEAE

SOFT TREE FERN

This tall fern is a stately addition to any shade garden, or where it can overhang a pool. Nestle shade-loving groundcovers beneath its broad fronds.

Description A tall fern that can reach tree-like size, with long, spreading, lacy fronds. A soft, downy, brown trunk (actually fibrous roots) supports the fronds. Fronds uncurl and reach 5–10 feet (1.5–3 m) long.

Height and spread Height 10 feet (3 m) but can be taller; spread to 10 feet (3 m).

Best climate and site Zones 9–12; light shade; moist but well-drained, humus-rich soil. Plants will tolerate some direct sun.

Landscape uses Mass plant in a shaded area under a light tree canopy or around a water feature. Use to bring an exotic element to a shaded, moist or fern garden.

Growing guidelines Plant anytime. These tree ferns are usually sold as cut trunks. Keep plants moist by watering over the top of fronds. Remove old or brown fronds. Mist fronds when dry. Plants reproduce by spores that form as brown lumps under the fronds. Spore is released in dusty clouds.

Good companions Rainforest or foliage plants, other palms, shade-loving groundcover plants. Epiphytic orchids can be attached to or surround the fibrous trunk of the tree fern.

Comments In cold Zones, can be grown in a conservatory.

Dracaena marginata
AGAVACEAE

DRACAENA

A popular indoor foliage plant and also a useful and colorful accent plant for warm-climate gardens and shady corners.

Description A tall, leafy and slow-growing tree or shrub. The rosettes of narrow leaves have colored margins. Usually grown for its colored leaf and variegated forms.

Height and spread Height 5 feet (1.5 m), taller in tropical gardens but smaller indoors; spread to 3 feet (90 cm).

Best climate and site Zones 9–12; light shade; moist but well-drained, humus-rich soil. Plants will not tolerate frost.

Landscape uses Mass in shaded areas such as under trees or in courtyards. Also grown as indoor pot plants.

Growing guidelines Plant anytime, but best in spring to summer in cooler Zones.

Good companions Rainforest or foliage plants, palms.

Other varieties Named varieties with striped leaves in cream and pink.

Other species *D. draco*, dragon's blood tree, is a striking, broad-spreading tree that grows to 30 feet (9 m) with rosettes of stiff leaves, a stout trunk and gnarled branches. Zones 10–11. The popular indoor foliage plant, *D. fragrans* 'Massangeana', known as happy plant or corn plant, has variegated leaves and occasional clusters of fragrant, creamy flowers. Zones 10–12 (elsewhere an indoor plant).

Comments Tolerant of low light levels.

Echeveria elegans
CRASSULACEAE

HEN AND CHICKENS

Small, tight rosettes of blue-green succulent leaves make hen and chickens a popular groundcover in a dry garden or with other succulents.

Description A low, spreading succulent with rosettes of blue-green leaves with red margins. Bell-shaped, pink flowers on long stems rise above the foliage.
Height and spread Height 2 inches (5 cm); spread to 18 inches (45 cm).
Best climate and site Zones 8–11; full sun; dry, well-drained soils.
Landscape uses Mass in sunny areas, such as rockeries, or to edge paths. Also grown in pots.
Growing guidelines Plant anytime, but best in spring to summer in cooler Zones. Water well during spring and summer but keep drier during winter. Avoid feeding, because this may produce week, lanky growth. Use a very free-draining mix in a pot. Mulch with gravel. Plants are easy to propagate by division or leaf cutting.
Good companions Other succulents and sun-loving groundcover plants including Livingstone daisies, ice plants and blue chalk sticks *Senecio serpens*.
Other species There are many species of *Echeveria* which form decorative rosettes, often with colorful leaf margins. Some such as *E.* x *imbricata* have fancy and frilled, succulent leaves. Zones 8–11.
Comments Excellent as an ornament in quirky containers.

Echinocactus grusonii
CACTACEAE

GOLDEN BARREL CACTUS

The round, ball-like shape of this spiny cactus makes it popular in dry-climate and arid gardens. Group several to form a striking feature.

Description A round, ribbed cactus with clusters of golden spines. A ring of bright yellow flowers appears like a crown at the top of the cactus ball in summer. Flowers are produced mainly on older plants.
Height and spread Height and spread to 3 feet (90 cm).
Best climate and site Zones 9–12; full sun; dry, well-drained soils.
Landscape uses Useful in arid gardens. Mass in hot and sunny, dry areas such as rockeries or succulent gardens. Also grows well in pots. Keep away from paths or areas where the spines may injure passersby.
Growing guidelines Plant anytime, but best in spring to summer in cooler Zones. Protect from frost and low winter temperatures. Keep watered during spring and summer, but allow soil to dry out during winter. In containers, use a very free-draining mix. Mulch with gravel.
Good companions Other cacti, especially tall and narrow-growing forms to contrast with the rounded, barrel shape; succulents and sun-loving groundcover plants.
Other common names Mother-in-law's seat.
Comments Handle plants carefully using tongs or wadding to avoid injury from the many sharp spines.

Elymus magellanicus
POACEAE
(Syn. *Agropyron magellanicum*)

BLUE WHEAT GRASS

Blue wheat grass produces handsome clumps of narrow, blue leaves. The summer flower spikes are attractive in arrangements.

Description Blue wheat grass is one of the bluest grasses. This cool-season, clumping perennial grass forms dense clumps of foliage that are dormant in cold climates and evergreen in warm regions. The mid-summer flower spikes turn from blue-green to straw-colored.
Height and spread Height 6–18 inches (15–45 cm); similar spread.
Best climate and site Zones 5–10; full sun; moist, well-drained soil. Blue wheat grass does well on coastal slopes but not in hot, dry areas or wet soil.
Landscape uses Foliage contrast, edging or foundation plant.
Growing guidelines Set plants 2 feet (60 cm) apart in spring or autumn. Cut brown foliage back to about 4 inches (10 cm) in late autumn or early spring (foliage color is less intense in winter). Propagate by seed in spring or by division in autumn or early spring. May be short-lived.
Good companions Low-growing shrubs or perennials. Blue wheat grass is also a good companion for low-growing evergreens in a foundation planting.
Comments Blue wheat grass is also sold as *Agropyron magellanicum*.

Festuca cinerea
POACEAE

BLUE FESCUE

The leaf color of blue fescue can range from dark green to bright blue, depending on the cultivar. Most plants produce spiky clumps of blue-gray foliage.

Description A cool-season, clumping perennial grass, blue fescue is noted for its rounded mounds of beautiful, silver-blue, spiky, evergreen foliage. The gray-green flowers are not especially noteworthy.
Height and spread Height 8–12 inches (20–30 cm); spread to 2 feet (60 cm).
Best climate and site Zones 4–10; full sun to light shade in hot climates; moist, well-drained soil. Plants are drought-resistant but grow poorly in hot, humid areas.
Landscape uses The showy foliage color and interesting texture make blue fescues attractive accent plants for borders, rock gardens and seaside plantings, or use for edging, groundcover or containers.
Growing guidelines Set plants 1–2 feet (30–60 cm) apart in spring or autumn. Cut back in early spring or autumn for new growth. Individual plants are short-lived; divide and replant every 2–3 years. May self-sow readily; seedlings range in color from blue to green; clipping off the flower spikes prevents reseeding.
Good companions Achillea, geranium, lavenders.
Comments Blue fescue is also sold as *F. glauca, F. ovina* and *F. ovina* var. *glauca*, which are very similar, and often confused in cultivation.

Hakonechloa macra 'Aureola'
POACEAE

VARIEGATED HAKONE GRASS

Variegated hakone grass forms slow-spreading clumps of elegant, bamboo-like leaves. The yellow-striped foliage takes on pinkish tints in autumn.

Description A warm-season, slow-spreading perennial grass, variegated hakone grass is a well-behaved, low-growing, arching, deciduous grass. Its star feature is its soft, bright yellow, bamboo-like leaves that are striped with green in summer and reddish in autumn. Clumps get larger with age but are not invasive. Inconspicuous flowers bloom in late summer. The species *H. macra* has light green leaves and is more heat-tolerant than the variegated form.
Height and spread Height 1½–2 feet (45–60 cm); spread 2 feet (60 cm) or more.
Best climate and site Zones 5–11; light shade; moist, well-drained, fertile soil.
Landscape uses Lovely as a single specimen plant or massed in shade or as an edging. Also grows in containers. It is a favorite for oriental gardens because of its bamboo-like appearance.
Growing guidelines Set plants 2 feet (60 cm) or more apart in spring or early autumn. Protect from full sun, and water to keep the soil evenly moist. Propagate by division in spring.
Good companions Asters, oriental-style plants such as bamboo.
Comments Hakone grass is one of the best groundcover grasses.

Hordeum jubatum
POACEAE

FOXTAIL BARLEY

Foxtail barley is a very attractive grass when in flower and seed. Clumps are excellent contrasts with flowering plants.

Description Foxtail barley is a perennial grass usually grown as an annual. In summer and autumn it produces arching stems with long, tufted and very attractive seed heads 2–3 inches (5–7.5 cm) long. These are green tinged with red when young, but dry to golden before dispersing.
Height and spread Height 1–1½ feet (30–45 cm); spread to 1 foot (30 cm).
Best climate and site Zones 5–9; light shade; moist, well-drained soil.
Landscape uses This handsome clumping grass is effective among flowers in beds and borders. Plant where its feathery seed heads can be seen backlit, especially in autumn.
Growing guidelines Sow seed or plant in situ (where plants are desired) in spring. Water to keep the soil evenly moist. Cut back or remove in autumn when plants die down. Plants may self-seed.
Good companions Purple and blue summer- to autumn-flowering perennials, such as balloon flower *Platycodon grandiflorus*, or hot-colored flowers, such as marmalade daisies *Rudbeckia* spp. or goldenrods *Solidago* spp.
Other common names Squirrel grass.
Comments For a cut flower, seed heads should be picked before they fully ripen.

Imperata cylindrica 'Red Baron'
POACEAE

JAPANESE BLOOD GRASS

If possible, position Japanese blood grass where the morning or late afternoon sun can shine through it; backlighting will really make the red color glow.

Description This Japanese grass is a warm-season, slow-spreading perennial. Its spectacular foliage starts green with red tips in spring. Gradually the red color spreads, so by summer's end it is blood red. The leaves turn copper in autumn and this endures throughout winter. Unlike the species, the cultivar 'Red Baron' does not flower, so it does not set seed and is not invasive.
Height and spread Height 1–1½ feet (30–45 cm); spread to 2 feet (60 cm).
Best climate and site Zones 6–9; full sun to partial shade in hot climates; fertile, moist, well-drained soil.
Landscape uses Dramatic as a mass planting or for a colorful touch in flower borders, near swimming pools or in pots.
Growing guidelines Set plants 1–2 feet (30–60 cm) apart in spring or early autumn. Red color is best in full sun, except in hot climates, where plants need partial shade during the heat of the day. Blood grass tolerates drought, but watering during dry spells will prevent leaf tips from turning brown.
Good companions Other grasses, soft-colored flowers.
Comments Also sold as 'Rubra'.

Liriope muscari
CONVALLARIACEAE

LILY TURF

This grassy lily is massed for a low, soft edging to beds and borders, or to form a dark green or variegated ribbon effect among other plants.

Description This evergreen, grasslike perennial forms a soft clump of narrow, dark green or variegated leaves. It has spires of blue to mauve flowers in autumn that may be hidden among the leaves.
Height and spread Height 1–2 feet (30–60 cm); spread to 1½ feet (45 cm).
Best climate and site Zones 6–10; full sun to partial shade; fertile, moist, well-drained soil.
Landscape uses Lily turf is dramatic as a mass planting for an edging along a path or garden bed. Can also be used as a low groundcover or planted in a container. Use the variegated forms to brighten dark corners of the garden.
Growing guidelines Set plants 6 inches (15 cm) apart in spring or early autumn (or year-round in warmer climates). Remove old or brown leaves in early spring as new growth appears.
Good companions Shrubs, ferns, foliage plants, ornamental grasses.
Other varieties There are many named varieties with variegated leaves (green and cream striped). Some varieties have wider leaves, taller growth or large flower spikes.
Comments This plant is very similar to and may be confused with mondo grasses *Ophiopogon* spp.

Milium effusum 'Aureum'
POACEAE

GOLDEN WOOD MILLET

Golden wood millet is a shade-loving perennial grass grown for its yellow flowers and yellow leaves. It is especially eye-catching in large masses.

Description A cool-season, clumping perennial grass. In spring, open, airy clusters of golden-yellow flowers bloom above loose clumps of arching, evergreen leaves. The leaves are bright yellow in spring and later fade to greenish yellow.
Best climate and site Zones 6–9; light shade; moist, fertile soil.
Height and spread Height 6–18 inches (15–45 cm) in leaf; spread to 2 feet (60 cm). Flowers on stems to 2 feet (60 cm) tall.
Landscape uses Golden foliage and blooms make this plant a captivating accent in the shady border or to brighten dull corners. It is also good for rock gardens or in shady spots. The flowers are excellent in both fresh and dried arrangements.
Growing guidelines Set plants 1–1½ feet (30–45 cm) apart in spring or late summer. Golden wood millet enjoys cool spots, so provide additional shade and moisture in hot climates. Cut off flower heads before seeds form so they won't produce seedlings. Propagate by division in spring.
Good companions Ferns, hostas and other shade-loving perennials.
Other common names Bowles golden grass, Bowles golden sedge.
Comments The species is pale green.

Miscanthus sinensis
POACEAE

JAPANESE SILVER GRASS

Japanese silver grass, also commonly called eulalia grass, is one of the best large ornamental grasses. It is especially attractive near streams and ponds.

Description Warm-season perennial grass that forms large clumps of long, pointed, sharp-edged leaves. The silvery color of early summer develops into autumn tones of red, yellow and brown. Decorative flower plumes from silver to reddish purple rise above the foliage from midsummer through early autumn and hold into winter.

Height and spread Height 3–5 feet (90–150 cm) for foliage; spread to 3 feet (90 cm) or more. Flowering stems can grow 6–10 feet (1.8–3 m) tall.

Best climate and site Zones 5–9; full sun; light, moist, humus-rich soil.

Landscape uses Large cultivars form screens, hedges and background plantings, especially in large gardens. Choose compact cultivars for accenting flower beds.

Growing guidelines Many cultivars with differing cultural needs, so check catalog descriptions or labels for details. In general, set plants 2–4 feet (60–120 cm) apart in spring (closer for small varieties). Provide light shade and extra water in hot climates. Stake if necessary, and divide in spring.

Good companions Asters, goldenrods *Solidago* spp., and other autumn-blooming perennials.

Comments A good winter silhouette.

Musa spp.
MUSACEAE

BANANA

Bananas are large perennials of treelike proportions. There are many ornamental forms, such as Japanese banana M. ornata, with large leaves and decorative flowers and fruit.

Description A tall, clump-forming perennial which grows from a rhizome to produce stems with many large, paddle-shaped, green leaves. Some have colored edges or midribs. Clusters of flowers form upright or hanging spikes depending on the species. Fruit follows.

Height and spread Height 8–30 feet (2.4–9 m); spread 8–20 feet (2.4–6 m).

Best climate and site Zones 10–12; full sun to part shade; well-drained, slightly acid soil.

Landscape uses Brings a bold, leafy look to foliage gardens. Some are grown for fruit.

Growing guidelines Plant anytime, spacing plants 10–20 feet (3–6 m) apart. Bananas do not need cross-pollination, so fruit is produced from just one plant. The "stem" is really a pseudo-stem, a tightly wound sheath of leaves that dies to the ground after fruiting, but is replaced by others. Bananas are heavy feeders, so fertilize regularly and provide abundant water. Cut down the fruiting pseudo-stem after harvest.

Good companions Palms, strelitzias, tropical and subtropical foliage plants.

Comments To harvest edible bananas, cut off the entire stalk when some fruits just begin to turn color.

Ophiopogon japonicus
LILIACEAE

MONDO GRASS

Mondo grass is a sod-forming, grasslike perennial from Asia that is excellent for groundcovers and borders. There are many varieties, from dwarf tufts to those that form soft clumps.

Description The dark green, coarse-textured leaves are 15 inches (37.5 cm) long and ⅛ inch (3 mm) wide. Lavender to white, ¼-inch (6-mm) flowers in summer are often hidden by leaves. Flowers are followed by blue, pea-sized fruits. Plants spread by rhizomes.

Height and spread Height to 8 inches (20 cm); spread unlimited.

Best climate and site Zones 7–11; full sun to shade; well-drained, humus-rich, acid to neutral soil.

Landscape uses A groundcover under trees or beside paths. Use dwarf forms between paving or to edge containers. A fine choice for seaside planting or an oriental garden.

Growing guidelines Set plants 8 inches (20 cm) apart in spring (year-round in warm climates). Remove damaged or brown growth in spring. Keep well watered, especially if exposed to strong summer sun.

Good companions Azaleas, flowering shrubs and perennials.

Other species *O. planiscapus* is similar in growth habit, but its green leaves become purple-black when mature. Zones 6–10.

Comments Sometimes confused with lily turf *Liriope muscari*, which it resembles.

Pennisetum alopecuroides
POACEAE

FOUNTAIN GRASS

Fountain grass is one of the most beautiful and adaptable of all ornamental grasses. The showy seed heads cascade like a fountain over mounds of glossy, green leaves.

Description A warm-season, clumping perennial grass that blooms in midsummer, with spikes of creamy white to pinkish flowers in 4–10-inch (10–25-cm) long clusters shaped like little foxtails. The seed heads later turn reddish brown and remain until autumn.

Height and spread Height of foliage to 3 feet (90 cm); similar spread. Flowering stems to 4 feet (1.2 m) tall.

Landscape uses Excellent accents in borders, foundation plantings or drifts. A good choice for coastal plantings, too, since they tolerate wind.

Best climate and site Zones 5–9; full sun (tolerates light shade); prefers fertile, moist, well-drained soil, but adapts to most soils.

Growing guidelines Set plants 2–3 feet (60–90 cm) apart in spring. Keep watered in dry weather. Cut back dead leaves by early spring.

Good companions Flowering perennials and shrubs.

Other varieties Compact forms that grow only 2–3 feet (60–90 cm) tall are ideal for small gardens. Zones 6–8.

Other common names Swamp foxtail.

Comments Fountain grass can become weedy in warm climates.

Phalaris arundinacea var. picta
POACEAE

WHITE-STRIPED RIBBON GRASS

Grow white-striped ribbon grass for the white-striped foliage that grabs attention and gives it its other common name, gardener's garters.

Description A warm-season, perennial grass that spreads rapidly by rhizomes. The leaves are narrow and pale green with white stripes. The flowers are white spikes in early summer. In autumn, leaves turn buff-colored.

Height and spread Height 2–3 feet (60–90 cm); spread unlimited. Flowering stems to 4 feet (1.2 m). It will grow in shallow water up to 4 inches (10 cm) deep.

Best climate and site Zones 4–9; light shade; wide range of soil types, but does best in moist, fertile soil.

Landscape uses A spreading groundcover also helpful for erosion control or to edge ponds. Great in containers.

Growing guidelines For groundcover, set plants 1–2 feet (30–60 cm) apart in spring. Leaves may brown in hot sun. Cut back sprawling plants in summer for dense, new growth. Can be invasive; grow where its creeping habit is not a problem, or control the spread by planting it in a bottomless bucket sunk into the soil.

Good companions Water- or moisture-loving plants.

Other varieties Forms with white-striped foliage touched with pink are less invasive.

Comments To maintain variegated form, remove all-green shoots.

Phormium tenax
AGAVACEAE

FLAX

There are many handsome cultivars of flax, with leaf tones ranging from green to red and copper and some with variegated gold and cream forms.

Description A tough, clump-forming, evergreen, grasslike succulent with olive-green, straplike leaves. The flowers are tall, cream to red spikes that rise above foliage.

Height and spread Height 6–10 feet (1.8–3 m); spread to 6 feet (1.8 m). There are some dwarf cultivars.

Best climate and site Zones 8–11; full sun to light shade; wide range of soil types, but does best in moist, fertile soil.

Landscape uses A dramatic clump for bold foliage contrast among mound-forming or groundcover plants. Colored forms make striking accent plants. Also use for a subtropical feel in cool-climate gardens. Good near the sea or in large pots.

Growing guidelines Set plants 3 feet (90 cm) apart in spring (year-round in warm climates). Remove brown or discolored leaves from time to time.

Good companions Ornamental grasses, daylilies, subtropical foliage plants.

Other varieties Many named forms, including some dwarf and many highly colored forms, often striped with one or more colors. Some are hybrids with *P. cookianum*.

Other common names New Zealand flax.

Comments Native to New Zealand, where it is used for fiber for traditional crafts.

Phyllostachys spp.
POACEAE

BAMBOO

Bamboos introduce a delightful rustling sound to gardens and are well-suited to large containers, courtyards and gardens with an oriental theme.

Description A tall, clump-forming grass with canelike stems that spreads by rhizomes known as runners. Some have variegated leaves and colored stems.

Height and spread Varies in its mature height and may spread indefinitely.

Best climate and site Zones 6–11; full sun; fertile, moist, well-drained soil.

Landscape uses Fast-growing screens, hedges or ornaments for oriental gardens, courtyards or containers. Species with colored stems add year-round highlights.

Growing guidelines Plant potted plants or divisions in early spring (or year-round in warm climates). Keep watered until well established and during dry periods. Control spread of running types with root barriers.

Good companions Mass plant.

Other species *P. aurea*, fishpole or golden bamboo, grows to about 20 feet (6 m) tall at maturity. *P. bambusoides*, timber bamboo, can grow to 72 feet (22 m) tall and 6 inches (15 cm) in diameter. *P. nigra*, black bamboo, reaches 30 feet (9 m) and has striking black stems. Zones 6–11.

Comments Where climate and space allow, some species provide edible shoots.

Pleioblastus auricoma
POACEAE

BAMBOO

This brightly colored, grassy bamboo is surprisingly frost-tolerant and brings a bright tropical feel to a cool-climate garden.

Description A clump-forming grass that spreads by underground rhizomes known as runners. Several jointed stems with small, papery, golden leaves from each node.

Height and spread Height to 5 feet (1.5 m) or taller; spread indefinite.

Best climate and site Zones 7–10; full sun to light shade; fertile, moist, well-drained soil.

Landscape uses Fast-growing screens, hedges or ornaments for oriental gardens and courtyards. Suits containers.

Growing guidelines Plant potted plants or divisions in early spring (or year-round in warm climates). Keep well watered. Cut down existing stems in early spring for vibrant, golden new growth. Surround with gravel or pebbles.

Good companions Mass plant one species.

Other species Several dwarf and variegated species. *P. pygmaeus* only reaches 1½ feet (45 cm) in height but spreads indefinitely. Seen as a variegated form with fernlike leaves. Zones 6–10.

Other common names Kamuro-zasa.

Comments "Running" bamboos spread by underground rhizomes and must be contained by a strong underground barrier at least 3 feet (90 cm) deep into the ground, or a large container.

Sansevieria trifasciata
AGAVACEAE

MOTHER-IN-LAW'S TONGUE

Mother-in-law's tongue is best known as an indoor plant, but in warm-climate Zones it is a striking, tall groundcover and accent plant.

Description Plants grow from a short, stout rhizome. The rigid, tonguelike, green leaves are banded or edged with yellow or cream. Spires of greenish white flowers appear in warm climates. Flowers are highly fragrant at night.

Height and spread Height to 2–4 feet (60–120 cm); spread 2 feet (60 cm).

Best climate and site Zones 9–12 (elsewhere as an indoor potted plant); sun to light shade; well-drained soil. Tolerates dry, shaded conditions.

Landscape uses Mass plant for a striking, tall groundcover or accent plant in hot, dry positions, especially when planted in clumps among rocks or pebbles. Suits containers, courtyards and modern gardens.

Growing guidelines Plant potted plants year-round. Keep well watered. In areas where winter temperatures fall below 50°F (10°C), grow as an indoor plant in an area with high light. In warm-climate gardens, it has a reputation for being indestructible.

Good companions Evergreen trees, other succulents.

Other varieties Colored and patterned leaf forms.

Other common names Snake plant.

Comments Plants readily form sports (new color variations).

Stipa gigantea
POACEAE

GIANT FEATHER GRASS

Giant feather grass is especially stunning where its handsome flower plumes are backlit by the morning or late afternoon sun.

Description Giant feather grass is a cool-season perennial grass that forms dramatic clumps of arching, rolled, evergreen leaves. Spectacular, oatlike, golden flowers hang from tall stems that rise 2–3 feet (60–90 cm) above the gray-green foliage in late spring.
Height and spread Height of foliage to 2 feet (60 cm); clumps spread to 2 feet (60 cm) or more. Flowering stems grow to 5 feet (1.5 m).
Best climate and site Zones 7–10; full sun; well-drained, fertile soil. Established plants are somewhat drought-tolerant; must have excellent drainage wherever rainfall is heavy.
Landscape uses Masses as a screen or singly as a dramatic, tall specimen. Good seaside plant. Attractive in breezy sites.
Growing guidelines Space 2–3 feet (60–90 cm) apart in spring or autumn. Cut back the foliage to about 6 inches (15 cm) by early spring.
Good companions Other grasses, shrubs and perennials.
Other species *S. capillata*, height to 2 feet (60 cm) with feathery blooms. Zones 6–9.
Other common names Golden oats.
Comments Useful in fresh or dried flower arrangements.

Strelitzia nicolai
STRELITZIACEAE

BIRD OF PARADISE

This giant, palmlike plant adds dramatic, tall foliage and striking blue and white flowers to gardens. Use it as a substitute for palms in cooler climates.

Description Clumps of woody stems produce fans of large, green, banana-like leaves to 5 feet (1.5 m) long. Spectacular, exotic, white and blue flowers, which are birdlike in appearance, are produced in summer from the top of the plant.
Height and spread Height to 20–30 feet (6–9 m) in flower; clumps spread to 12 feet (3.6 m) or more. Flowering stems grow to 5 feet (1.5 m).
Best climate and site Zones 10–12; full sun to part shade; well-drained, fertile soil. Established plants are drought-tolerant.
Landscape uses Mass as a tall screen or use singly as a dramatic specimen plant. Create a subtropical look by mass planting.
Growing guidelines Plant year-round, allowing space for the plant to spread as it matures. Remove dead foliage. Water when dry but leave drier through winter. Fertilize in spring.
Good companions Palms, cycads, bromeliads, tree ferns, cordylines.
Other species *S. reginae* forms a leafy clump to 3 feet (90 cm) high and wide, with striking orange and purple flowers on long slender stems. Highly bird-attractant. Zones 9–12.
Other common names Wild banana.
Comments Highly bird-attractant.

Yucca gloriosa
AGAVACEAE

ADAM'S NEEDLE

This tall succulent is magnificent in flower through summer and autumn, when it makes a dramatic statement with its tall spires of cream flowers.

Description Stemless when young, Adam's needle develops stout, gray, multi-branched stems with age. Its green leaves are stiff and swordlike with sharp tips. In summer, erect flowering stems arise from the clump, with panicles of cream, bell-shaped flowers that freely form seeds.
Height and spread Height to 6 feet (1.8 m); spread to 10 feet (3 m). Flowering stems to 8 feet (2.4 m).
Best climate and site Zones 7–10; full sun; well-drained soil. Established plants are drought-tolerant.
Landscape uses Use as a focal point in a succulent or dry garden, or a living sculpture in a modern landscape.
Growing guidelines Plant year-round or in spring in cool Zones. Remove aged leaves and cut down spent flower stalks to prevent seeding.
Good companions Other succulents, including agaves and aloes, and heat-loving groundcover plants such as treasure flowers *Gazania rigens* and hybrids.
Other species *Y. elephantipes* is a sculptural plant that lacks the sharp leaf tips of some yuccas. Zones 10–12.
Other common names Spanish dagger, Roman candle, palm lily.
Comments Bird-attractant flowers.

Ajuga reptans
LAMIACEAE

AJUGA

The short, spinach-like leaves of this low-growing groundcover spread rapidly to form a solid carpet. Many colorful cultivars of ajuga are available.

Description Dark green, but cultivars are available with purple, bronze or variegated foliage. Ajuga is evergreen in warm areas but tends to turn brown by midwinter in cold climates. Long spikes of ¼-inch (6-mm) blue or purple flowers bloom in spring or early summer.

Height and spread Height of foliage to 3 inches (7.5 cm); spread unlimited. Flower height to about 6 inches (15 cm).

Best climate and site Zones 3–10; full sun to partial shade (shade in hot climates); well-drained, moist garden soil.

Landscape uses A flowering groundcover under trees and shrubs and on slopes or as a strong-growing edge to a path or shrubbery.

Growing guidelines Set the plants 1–1¼ feet (30–37.5 cm) apart anytime during growing season. Propagate by division. Ajuga can invade lawns, creating a maintenance headache. Keep them separate with an edging strip.

Good companions All woodland plants.

Other common names European bugle, blue bugle, common bugle.

Other varieties Varieties with bronze or burgundy foliage and others with large heads of flowers.

Comments Ajuga can also be grown in a container.

Arabis caucasica
BRASSICACEAE

WALL ROCK CRESS

The spreading, evergreen mounds of wall rock cress are accented with masses of sweetly scented, pink or white flowers in spring. Cut plants back after bloom to promote compact growth.

Description Wall rock cress forms spreading mounds of grayish green, 1-inch (2.5-cm), toothed leaves. In spring, the mounds are smothered in clusters of small, fragrant, pink or white, four-petaled flowers.

Height and spread Height of foliage 4–6 inches (10–15 cm); spread to 1½ feet (45 cm). Flower height to 1 foot (30 cm).

Best climate and site Zones 3–9; full sun; fertile, well-drained soil.

Landscape uses An ornamental for rock gardens or planting in crevices in a stone wall. Also a good edging choice for the front of a flower border.

Growing guidelines Set plants 1 foot (30 cm) apart. Cut back by half after bloom to remove the spent flowers and to promote compact new growth.

Good companions Spring-flowering bulbs, early perennials.

Other varieties Named varieties with pink or double flowers.

Other species *A. procurrens* grows in sun or light shade. Clusters of tiny white flowers in spring rise 1 foot (30 cm) above mats of shiny, green leaves. Needs excellent drainage and tends to rot in humid areas. Zones 5–9.

Comments Easy to grow from seed.

Asarum europaeum
ARISTOLOCHIACEAE

EUROPEAN WILD GINGER

European wild ginger is one of the best evergreen groundcovers for partial shade. The glossy, leathery leaves and creeping roots are aromatic if crushed.

Description European wild ginger forms spreading colonies of kidney-shaped, evergreen leaves up to 3 inches (7.5 cm) wide. In late spring, small, purplish brown flowers bloom beneath the foliage.

Height and spread Height 5–7 inches (12.5–17.5 cm); spread to 1 foot (30 cm).

Best climate and site Zones 4–9; partial shade; moisture-retentive, humus-rich, somewhat acid soil.

Landscape uses Grows quickly into a weed-suppressing clump. Plant along a garden path or shaded area.

Growing guidelines Set the plants 8–12 inches (20–30 cm) apart in early spring. Don't plant too deep; set the crowns just at the soil surface. Keep them evenly moist the first season after planting; water established plantings in dry weather. Fertilize in early spring with a topdressing of compost or leaf mold.

Good companions Ferns, wildflowers, hostas and crested iris *Iris cristata*.

Other common names Asarabacca.

Other species *A. canadense*, Canada wild ginger, grows 6–8 inches (15–20 cm) tall and has large, heart-shaped, deciduous leaves. Zones 3–8.

Comments This plant was once used in snuff powders.

Campanula portenschlagiana
CAMPANULACEAE

DALMATIAN BELLFLOWER

The trailing stems of Dalmatian bellflower creep over the ground or sprawl over stone walls. This pretty plant is also attractive along the front of flower borders or in pots.

Description This low-growing *Campanula* has small, heart-shaped, toothed leaves. It is covered with large numbers of bell-shaped, lavender-blue, 1-inch (2.5-cm) flowers from late spring to midsummer.

Height and spread Height 6–8 inches (15–20 cm); spread to 2 feet (60 cm).

Best climate and site Zones 4–10; full sun to light shade in hot climates; well-drained, sandy soil.

Landscape uses Ideal as a groundcover in rock gardens, on rocky slopes, and in nooks and crannies in stone walls. Can also be grown in hanging baskets or window boxes, to spill over the edge.

Growing guidelines Set the plants 1–1½ feet (30–45 cm) apart in spring. Plants need no special care. Propagate by division in early spring.

Good companions Cottage garden plants.

Other varieties There is a deep violet-colored variety with flowers that are larger than the species.

Other species *C. carpatica*, Carpathian harebell, has upward-facing, purple to white flowers. Height 6–12 inches (15–30 cm). Zones 3–8.

Comments Color is more vivid in light shade during summer.

Cerastium tomentosum
CARYOPHYLLACEAE

SNOW-IN-SUMMER

Snow-in-summer carpets the ground with mats of woolly, gray leaves. The white flowers that give it its common name appear in late spring and continue through summer.

Description This fast-growing evergreen with light gray, woolly foliage forms large mats with its creeping stems. Abundant, small, white flowers with star-shaped petals cover the foliage for weeks from late spring.

Height and spread Height 6–10 inches (15–25 cm); spread to 3 feet (90 cm).

Best climate and site Zones 2–10; full sun; dry, well-drained, poor soil or sand.

Landscape uses Snow-in-summer forms a good groundcover for dry, sunny spots, especially in difficult areas such as dry, rocky slopes. Plant it where the spread won't be a problem, or surround the planting with an edging strip.

Growing guidelines Set plants about 1–1½ feet (30–45 cm) apart in spring. Once they are established, cut the stems back after flowering to prevent seeding. Propagate by division or seed in spring or autumn. Poorly drained soil will cause plants to rot and die.

Good companions Silver or gray foliage plants, including dianthus; also daisies.

Comments Snow-in-summer can become invasive. Divide plants every few years as they get out of bounds, or cut them back hard in early spring to control the spread.

Chamaemelum nobile
ASTERACEAE

ROMAN CHAMOMILE

Roman chamomile is a delightful, low-growing herb with feathery, green leaves with a sweet, apple-like scent, and is widely used as a lawn substitute. The daisy-like flowers make a soothing tea.

Description Small, daisy-like, white flowers with yellow centers appear above the spreading mat of foliage in mid- to late summer.

Height and spread Height to 2 inches (5 cm); spread to 3 feet (90 cm). Flower stems 6–12 inches (15–30 cm) tall.

Best climate and site Zones 3–9 (but not in areas with high summer humidity); full sun, but tolerates partial shade; sandy, poor soil; good drainage is a must.

Landscape uses A lawn alternative which, when mowed, becomes compact and lawnlike in a mild climate. Also charming between paving.

Growing guidelines Set plants 6 inches (15 cm) apart in spring. Water new plants regularly. Remove spent flowers to prevent invasive reseeding. The plant can take some foot traffic, so mow established plants several times a season to prevent flowering.

Good companions Herbs, cottage garden flowers.

Other varieties There is a non-flowering form that is better suited as a lawn.

Comments For groundcover use, do not confuse with annual *Matricaria recutita*, German chamomile which grows to 2 feet (60 cm) tall.

Cotoneaster horizontalis
ROSACEAE

ROCKSPRAY COTONEASTER

The dense, branching habit and horizontal growth of rockspray cotoneaster make it an excellent groundcover. It spreads as the branch tips touch the ground and take root.

Description This popular, low-growing, woody shrub bears round, ½-inch (12-mm) wide, shiny, dark green leaves on horizontally spreading branches. The deciduous leaves turn orange-red in autumn. (In warmer climates it is not completely deciduous.) Small, pinkish flowers bloom along the stems in spring, followed by ornamental, red berries in autumn.
Height and spread Height 2–3 feet (60–90 cm); spread normally to 6 feet (1.8 m) but unlimited where branches can touch the soil and form roots.
Best climate and site Zones 5–10; full sun is best but can tolerate light shade; light, well-drained, neutral to slightly acid soil containing plenty of humus.
Landscape uses An excellent groundcover for mass plantings, borders, foundation plantings and rock gardens. It can also be trained against a wall or rockwork as an espalier.
Growing guidelines Set plants 2–4 feet (60–120 cm) apart in spring or autumn.
Cultivars Named varieties with white-edged leaves, or leaves that turn purplish in autumn.
Comments The tangled stems can trap leaves and debris.

Delosperma cooperi
AIZOACEAE

HARDY ICE PLANT

Long-blooming hardy ice plant offers a colorful show of purple flowers from summer through to the first frost. It looks wonderful cascading down slopes and over stones in rock gardens.

Description This low-growing succulent is becoming increasingly popular for its small, rosy purple, daisy-like flowers, which bloom in mid- to late summer, above mats of narrow, curving leaves.
Height and spread Height 4 inches (10 cm); spread to 1 foot (30 cm).
Best climate and site Zones 7–11; full sun; any well-drained to dry soil.
Landscape uses Hardy ice plant is a tough, beautiful, long-blooming groundcover for rock gardens or sunny banks. The electric color of the flowers makes it a feature while it is in flower. It can also be grown to cascade from urns.
Growing guidelines Set plants 1 foot (30 cm) apart in spring. They like dry soil in winter and do best when temperatures don't go below 50°F (10°C). In warm climates, the plants bloom all year but grow mostly in the summer. Established plants need little care.
Other species *D. nubigenum* grows to 2 inches (5 cm) tall and 8–10 inches (20–25 cm) wide. This fast-growing, tough plant has bright yellow flowers in late spring and yellow-green leaves that turn red in winter. Zones 5–11.
Comments An excellent seaside choice.

Doodia aspera
BLECHNACEAE

PRICKLY RASP FERN

Ferns are wonderfully versatile in the garden; however, most need moist, shaded conditions to do well. The prickly rasp fern will grow well in areas that receive both sun and shade.

Description An evergreen, low-growing fern with upright, rough fronds that forms a mat by means of a black, wiry, creeping rhizome. In spring the new growth is an attractive pink or red and becomes deep green with age.
Height and spread Height 1 foot (30 cm); spread unlimited.
Best climate and site Zones 9–11; full sun to shade; moist, well-drained, acidic soil with added organic matter.
Landscape uses Plant closely in clumps under trees, in rockeries or in containers. Great choice in courtyards and at the edge of a shade garden where it will receive periods of full sun.
Growing guidelines Set plants close together in clumps. Keep plants in sunny situations well watered. Plant in slightly acid soil that has been enriched with organic matter. Surround with an organic mulch. For container-grown plants, select an extremely well-drained potting mix. Only use fertilizers at half strength.
Good companions Other ferns, shade- and acid-loving plants such as azaleas, pieris and aucuba.
Other common names Hare's foot fern.
Comments Frost-tolerant.

Euonymus fortunei
CELASTRACEAE

WINTERCREEPER

This evergreen produces long stems that take root as they travel over the ground. The clinging stems will climb up trees, walls and buildings.

Description The oval, waxy, green, 2-inch (5-cm) leaves become deep red in autumn when grown in full sun. Inconspicuous, white flowers bloom on mature stems in summer, followed by pink fruits in autumn.
Height and spread Height 1–2 feet (30–60 cm); stems spread to 30 feet (9 m).
Best climate and site Zones 5–9; full sun to partial shade; well-drained, slightly acid, fertile, humus-rich soil. Protect plants from cold winds.
Landscape uses Wintercreeper is useful as a low-growing evergreen for erosion control on banks. It grows relatively slowly in shade, but it is one of the best groundcovers for dry, shady spots. Excellent choice for foliage contrast.
Growing guidelines Set plants 1 foot (30 cm) or more apart in spring or autumn. Trim and shape established plants as needed in early spring.
Good companions Other acid-loving shrubs and trees.
Other varieties Named varieties with variegated foliage of green and gold, green and white, or pink-tinged that turns purplish in autumn. Look for compact forms if its spread is likely to be a problem.
Comments Once established, this plant needs little care.

Gazania rigens
ASTERACEAE

TREASURE FLOWER

Treasure flowers usually bloom in red, orange or yellow but can also be pink, purplish or white. Flowers close at night and during cloudy weather.

Description This perennial is grown as a half-hardy annual. Plants form low mats of narrow-lobed, green leaves that are silvery underneath. From midsummer until frost, plants are topped with brilliantly colored, daisy-like flowers to 3 inches (7.5 cm) wide.
Height and spread Height 8–12 inches (20–30 cm); spread to 1 foot (30 cm).
Best climate and site Zones 9–11; full sun; average, well-drained soil.
Landscape uses Treasure flower adds an explosion of color to beds and borders. Use it as an edging plant, for example, along a driveway, or mass plant.
Growing guidelines Sow seed directly into the garden 12 weeks after the last frost for late-summer bloom. Thin seedlings or place plants 8 inches (20 cm) apart. In cold areas, dig up a few plants before frost and bring them indoors for winter bloom.
Good companions Any sun-loving shrubs or groundcovers, including Californian poppy, gaura, or plants with silver foliage.
Other varieties There are many cultivars and strains with contrasting patterns, and narrow or curved petals. Colors range from yellow to reddish orange. Seed-raised plants may be highly variable.
Comments Where it self-seeds it may become weedy and invasive.

Hedera helix
ARALIACEAE

ENGLISH IVY

English ivy is available in a range of leaf colors and patterns, including gold and cream. The plain green ivies tend to be most cold-tolerant, but many of the variegated ones are surprisingly hardy.

Description This evergreen vine has lobed leaves that are 2–5 inches (5–12.5 cm) long on woody stems. The stems creep over the ground, sending down roots as they travel. When they meet an upright surface, they climb with clinging rootlets.
Height and spread Height to 6 inches (15 cm); spread limitless.
Best climate and site Zones 5–10; partial to full shade; any soil.
Landscape uses A dependable, fast-spreading groundcover. Use on slopes for erosion control or as a groundcover beneath deciduous trees where lawn is hard to establish. Use small-leaved and decorative forms in mixed containers.
Growing guidelines Set plants about 2 feet (60 cm) apart in spring or autumn. Prune as needed to control and direct the growth (which can be highly invasive).
Good companions Use alone or combine leaf patterns and colors.
Other varieties Many named varieties with variegated foliage in green and gold, green and white, or leaves that turn reddish purple in autumn.
Comments The upright stems mature to produce unlobed leaves, green flowers and black berries.

Juniperus horizontalis
CUPRESSACEAE

CREEPING JUNIPER

Plant creeping junipers for erosion control on slopes or for an evergreen accent in rock gardens and foundation plantings. They prefer full sun and well-drained soil.

Description Creeping junipers are low-growing, evergreen shrubs with spreading branches carrying scaly or needle-like, blue-green leaves. Dark-colored fruits form on short stems in late summer.
Height and spread Height 6–18 inches (15–45 cm); spread to 8 feet (2.4 m).
Best climate and site Zones 3–10; full sun; prefers well-drained, sandy soil, but tolerates any soil, even clay.
Landscape uses Ideal for covering slopes, including steep slopes where other plants won't thrive.
Growing guidelines Plant in spring or autumn. Spacing varies according to size of cultivar. Set out bareroot plants in spring and potted or balled-and-burlapped plants anytime during growing season. Prune in summer only to control size. Don't just shear off shoot tips; cut unwanted stems back to another stem or to the ground.
Good companions Mass plant for a uniform effect or intersperse with tuft-forming grasses and perennials.
Other varieties Many, including compact varieties and those with excellent blue or blue-green foliage.
Comments There are many other prostrate juniper species.

Lysimachia nummularia
PRIMULACEAE

CREEPING JENNY

Creeping Jenny is an attractive groundcover for moist-soil areas where its spread isn't a problem, The yellow-leafed cultivar 'Aurea' is less invasive than the species.

Description This creeping perennial has shiny, round, ¾-inch (18-mm) leaves that resemble coins. The trailing stems bear bright, 1-inch (2.5-cm), yellow flowers throughout the summer. The stems root rapidly as they creep over the soil.
Height and spread Height 2–4 inches (5–10 cm); spread to 3 feet (90 cm).
Best climate and site Zones 3–10; full sun (in cool climates) to full shade (in warm climates); moist, fertile soil.
Landscape uses Creeping Jenny is a good groundcover around ponds and streams. It will also grow in rockeries or containers.
Growing guidelines Set plants 8 inches (20 cm) apart in spring or autumn. It can be invasive, and it rapidly becomes a weed problem when it spreads into lawn areas. Propagate by division in spring or autumn.
Good companions A groundcover under shady trees such as Japanese maple.
Other common names Moneywort.
Other varieties There is a variety with golden yellow foliage that turns lime-green in summer and is not as invasive.
Comments Creeping Jenny has been used since medieval times for the treatment of wounds and sores.

Myosotis sylvatica
BORAGINACEAE

FORGET-ME-NOT

Forget-me-not blooms are often sky-blue with white or yellow centers, but there are also pink- and white-flowered varieties. They are ideal companions for spring bulbs and other annuals.

Description These short-lived perennials are usually grown as hardy biennials or annuals. Plants form dense clumps of narrow, lance-shaped, hairy leaves. Sprays of many ⅓-inch (8-mm) wide, blue flowers bloom over the leaves from midspring through early summer.
Height and spread Height usually 1–1½ feet (30–45 cm); spread 8–10 inches (20–25 cm).
Best climate and site Zones 5–10; partial shade; average to moist, well-drained soil.
Landscape uses Invaluable for spring color in shady gardens, as an early-season groundcover under shrubs or deciduous trees, or grow them in beds and borders.
Growing guidelines For bloom the same year, buy plants in early spring, or start seed indoors 4–6 weeks before your last frost date. Set plants out 12 weeks before the last frost date. Space plants or thin seedlings to stand 6 inches (15 cm) apart.
Good companions Tulips, daffodils, other spring bulbs and spring-flowering annuals.
Other varieties Many named varieties; pink or white flowers or compact growth.
Comments Remove the finished plants and seeds promptly, as seeds stick to clothes and pet hair.

Stachys byzantina
LAMIACEAE

LAMB'S EARS

Lamb's ears spread quickly to form dense, broad clumps of tightly packed leaves. They are an excellent edging plant.

Description Lamb's ears are appealing groundcovers with felted, silvery leaves forming dense rosettes from a creeping, fibrous-rooted rhizome. The small, two-lipped, rose-pink flowers are carried in whorls on woolly stems in early summer; they are secondary to the foliage.
Height and spread To 1–2 feet (30–60 cm) high.
Best climate and site Zones 4–10; full sun or light shade; light, sandy or loamy, well-drained soil.
Landscape uses Plant lamb's ears at the front of formal and informal gardens, along paths, in rock gardens or atop rock walls.
Growing guidelines Divide in spring or autumn to control spread or for propagation. Take cuttings in summer. In wet, humid weather or poorly drained soils, rot may occur. Remove the affected portions and improve air circulation.
Good companions Bearded irises, ornamental onions, grasses, yuccas, sedums and cranesbills *Geranium* spp.
Other common names Lamb's tails, lamb's tongues.
Other varieties Compact and yellow-green foliage varieties.
Comments Hot, humid weather causes leaves to brown, droop and decay.

Thymus serpyllum
LAMIACEAE

MOTHER OF THYME

Mother of thyme is an easy-to-grow, fast-spreading groundcover for sunny, well-drained sites. Clusters of tiny flowers top the aromatic, evergreen leaves in late spring.

Description This creeping, woody-stemmed groundcover has aromatic, bright green leaves and clusters of small, rose-purple flowers in late spring and summer.
Height and spread Height 2–4 inches (5–10 cm); spread unlimited.
Best climate and site Zones 4–10; full sun; well-drained, slightly alkaline, sandy soil.
Landscape uses Set loose on dry slopes or stone walls. Spread between stones in a walk or patio. A fragrant addition to a Mediterranean-style garden or to form a low, decorative hedge in an ornamental vegetable garden. Can be grown in pots.
Growing guidelines Space the plants 8–12 inches (20–30 cm) apart in spring. Fertilize or mulch with organic matter sparingly, if at all, or plant will get spindly and floppy. Pull weeds as they appear.
Good companions Other herbs, silver foliage plants.
Other common names Wild thyme, creeping thyme.
Other varieties Varieties are available with white, pink, crimson-pink and bronze-pink flowers.
Comments Prevent root rot by only planting in well-drained soil.

Viola odorata
VIOLACEAE

SWEET VIOLET

Sweet violet, also called English violet, is the common violet used by florists and fashioned into fragrant posies. It spreads by runners that take root and produce new plants.

Description Fragrant, five-petaled, deep violet blooms come up in late winter to early spring from clumps of heart-shaped leaves that are 3 inches (7.5 cm) long.
Height and spread Height 5–8 inches (12.5–20 cm); spread to 2 feet (60 cm).
Best climate and site Zones 6–10; full sun to partial shade, but tolerates full shade in hot climates; well-drained, moist, fertile, cool soil.
Landscape uses Sweet violet makes a fragrant groundcover in wild gardens and rock gardens and under trees and shrubs or beside a path.
Growing guidelines Set plants 1 foot (30 cm) apart in spring. Start a new patch when older plants become overgrown and weak. Prune in autumn to remove old leaves and to make way for flowers.
Good companions Bulbs, wildflowers, hostas, early perennials, cottage garden flowers.
Other varieties Many named varieties in shades of white, blue, pink and purple; double flowers.
Comments Sprinkle water over picked flowers to keep them fresh for longer.

Plant Hardiness Zone Maps

These maps of the United States, Canada and Europe are divided into ten zones. Each zone is based on a 10°F (5.6°C) difference in average annual minimum temperature. Some areas are considered too high in elevation for plant cultivation and so are not assigned to any zone. There are also island zones that are warmer or cooler than surrounding areas because of differences in elevation; they have been given a zone different from the surrounding areas. Many large urban areas, for example, are in a warmer zone than the surrounding land. Plants grow best within an optimum range of temperatures. The range may be wide for some species and narrow for others. Plants also differ in their ability to survive frost and in their sun or shade requirements.

The zone ratings indicate conditions where designated plants will grow well and not merely survive. Many plants may survive in zones warmer or colder than their recommended zone range. Remember that other factors, including wind, soil type, soil moisture, humidity, snow and winter sunshine, may have a great effect on growth.

Some nursery plants have been grown in greenhouses and they might not survive in your garden, so it's a waste of money, and a cause of heartache, to buy plants that aren't right for your climate zone.

Average annual minimum temperature °F (°C)

Zone 1		Below -50°F (Below -45°C)
Zone 2		-50° to -40°F (-45° to -40°C)
Zone 3		-40° to -30°F (-40° to -34°C)
Zone 4		-30° to -20°F (-34° to -29°C)
Zone 5		-20° to -10°F (-29° to -23°C)

Zone 6		-10° to 0°F (-23° to -18°C)
Zone 7		0° to 10°F (-18° to -12°C)
Zone 8		10° to 20°F (-12° to -7°C)
Zone 9		20° to 30°F (-7° to -1°C)
Zone 10		30° to 40°F (-1° to 4°C)

Australia and New Zealand

These maps divide Australia and New Zealand into seven climate zones which, as near as possible, correspond to the USDA climate zones used in the United States, Britain and Europe and in this book. The zones are based on the minimum temperatures usually, or possibly, experienced within each zone. Over the year, air temperatures heat then cool the soil and this is important to plants. Some cannot tolerate cold or even cool temperatures, while others require a period of low temperatures to grow properly. Although this book is designed primarily for cool-climate gardens, the information in it can be adapted for gardens in hotter climates.

In this book, the ideal zones in which to grow particular plants are indicated and when you read that a plant is suitable for any of the zones 7 through to 13, you will know that it should grow successfully in those zones in Australia and New Zealand. There are other factors that affect plant growth, but temperature is one of the most important.

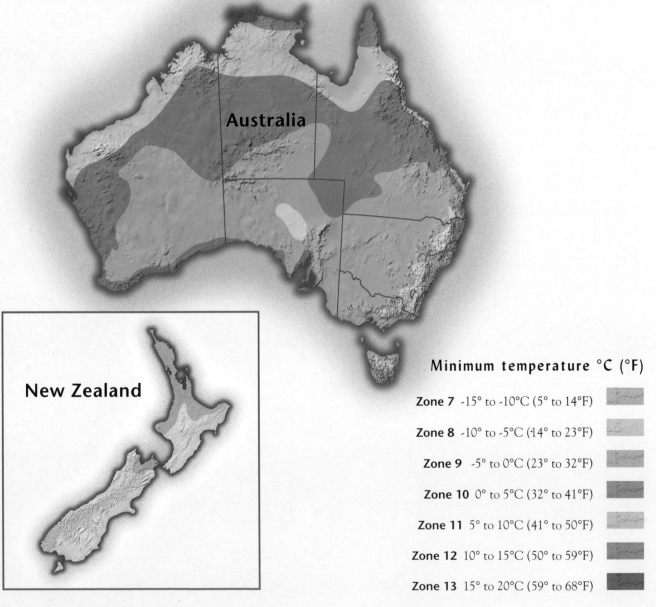

Australia

New Zealand

Minimum temperature °C (°F)

Zone 7 -15° to -10°C (5° to 14°F)

Zone 8 -10° to -5°C (14° to 23°F)

Zone 9 -5° to 0°C (23° to 32°F)

Zone 10 0° to 5°C (32° to 41°F)

Zone 11 5° to 10°C (41° to 50°F)

Zone 12 10° to 15°C (50° to 59°F)

Zone 13 15° to 20°C (59° to 68°F)

Index

Page references in *italics* indicate photos and illustrations.

Acknowledgments

KEY l=left, r=right, c=center, t=top, b=bottom, f=far

AZ=A–Z Botanical Collection; BCL=Bruce Coleman Ltd; CN=Clive Nichols; DF=Derek Fell; GB=Gillian Beckett; GPL=Garden Picture Library; HSC=Harry Smith Collection; IH=Ivy Hansen; JC= John Callanan; JY=James Young; JP=Jerry Pavia; LC=Leigh Clapp; LR=Lorna Rose; PD=PhotoDisc; PH=Photos Horticultural; SM= Stirling Macoboy; SOM=S. & O. Mathews; TE=Thomas Eltzroth; TR=Tony Rodd; WO=Weldon Owen; WR=Weldon Russell

Endpapers LC 1l GPL/J. S. Sira; c GPL/Mayer/Le Scanff; r GPL/ A. Lord 2c GPL/Steven Wooster 4c GPL/Ron Sutherland 6c GPL/ Mark Bolton 10c IH 12tr CN; bl LC/Queenstown Gardens, New Zealand 13tr IH; bl LC; br CN 14tl LC; br GPL/Brigitte Thomas 15tl PH; br JP 16tr WO; bl WR 17b LC 18tr JP; bl LC 19t GPL/ J. S. Sira 20c LC 22tr BCL/Jules Cowan; bl GPL/CN 23tr GPL/ John Glover 24tr GPL/CN; bl WO 25br GPL/Mayer/Le Scanff 27tl CN; br GPL/Ron Sutherland 28t WO; bl GPL/Rex Butcher; br JP 29br GPL/ Rex Butcher 30tl IH 31tr GPL/John Glover; bl WO 32tl GPL/Linda Burgess 33br IH; all others GPL/Jon Bouchier 34c GPL/Howard Rice 36t APL/Corbis; bl IH; br JP 37b IH 38tr LC; bl GPL/John Glover 39tl WO; tr JP; bl GPL 40tr Photo Essentials; bl CN br LC 41t LC/ Faulkner and Chapman, Vic; br CN 42tl LC; br Photo Essentials 43br LC/Ronni Nettleton; tl, tc CN 44bl WO/JY; br CN; all others PD 45t CN; b LC 46tc SOM; tr CN; bl IH 47t LC; bl TE; br SOM 48tl WO/JY; tr PD; bl GPL/Nigel Francis 49tc LC; bl GPL/Howard Rice; all others PD 50tr PH; all others CN 51tr WO/JY; br CN 52bl LC; br SOM 53c CN 54 bl LC; br GPL 55b JP; all others GPL 56c GPL/Eric Crichton 58 all images CN 59t IH; bl LR; br LC 60t SOM; b CN 61tr GPL/John Glover; bl GPL/J. S. Sira; tr GPL/Mayer/Le Scanff; bl GPL/ Steven Wooster 63tr WO/JY; bl SOM 64tr LR; bl LC 65tr GPL; bl LC/InsideOut Urban Garden Living 66tr GPL/Neil Holmes; bl Andrew Lawson 67tr TE; bl WO/John Hollingshead; br PH 68c GPL/CN 70tr GPL/John Glover; bl GPL/ J. S. Sira; br GPL/Brigitte Thomas 71t GPL/Mark Bolton; br GPL/John

Glover 72tl WO; bc GPL/Jacqui Hurst 73tl GPL; tr GPL/Howard Rice; b EWA Photo Library 74t GPL/ Howard Rice; bl TE 75bl GPL/ J. S. Sira 76tr GPL/Neil Holmes; bl CN 77bl JY 78tr GPL/Howard Rice; bl GPL/Steven Wooster 79tr GPL/ Alan Bedding; br GPL/David Cavagnaro 80tr GPL/Howard Rice; bl GPL/Neil Holmes 81br GPL/ Michael Howes 82tc GPL/John Glover; tr GPL/Mayer/Le Scanff; bl GPL/Mark Bolton; bc GPL/John Glover 83 all images PH 84c LR 86b WO 87tl IH; tr WO/Leo Meier; b SOM 88t WO/Leo Meier; b SOM 89bl IH 90tl PD; br WO/JY 91tc WO/JY; bl GPL/Jacqui Hurst 92bl IH; br SOM 93tl HSC; tc GPL/John Glover; tr PH 94t JP; cr LC; bl PH 95bl LC/Heronswood; br PH 96tr IH; bl GPL/Howard Rice 97tr LC; bl PH 98tc DF; cr IH 99tl JP; br Gary Rogers 100tc GPL/Steven Wooster; tr GPL/Brigitte Thomas 101tr CN; br COR 102bl APL/Corbis/Christian Sarramon 103tr LC/Heronswood; bl GPL/Alan Bedding; br WO/JY 104tl GPL/Mayer/Le Scanff; tr PH 105tr CN; bl APL/Corbis/Eric Crichton 106c JP; bl WO/JY 107tl IH; tc GPL/\JP; br IH 118c GPL/Ron Sutherland 120tr GPL/J. S. Sira; bl GPL/Ron Sutherland 121tr GPL/ Juliette Wade; bl WO 122tl GPL/ Jacqui Hurst; br GPL/Marianne Majerus 123tl GPL/John Glover; br GPL/Claire Davies 124tc GPL/ Sunniva Harte; bl GPL/Steven Wooster; br GPL/Christi Carter 125tl GPL/John Glover; br GPL/ Juliet Greene 126tr GPL/Howard Rice; bl GPL/Neil Holmes 127tr GPL/ John Neubauer; bl GPL/ Christi Carter 128tr GPL/Brigitte Thomas; bl GPL/Ron Sutherland 130tl GPL/Lamontagne; br SOM 131tl GPL/Friedrich Strauss; br CN 132tr GPL/Neil Holmes; bl GPL/ Lynne Brotchie 133tr GPL/Juliette Wade; bl GPL/Lamontagne 134tr GPL; bl GPL/Ron Sutherland 135tr GPL/John Glover; bl TE 136tr WO; bl GPL/Michael Paul br LC 138tr BCL/Hans Reinhard; bl GPL/Lynne Brotchie 139tr SOM; bl GPL/ Lamontagne 140tl DF; tr GPL/John Glover; bc GPL/Neil Holmes 141tc GPL/John Glover; bl GPL/Alan Bedding; br WO/JY 142 all images CN 143tl GPL/John Ferro Sims; tr GPL/Rex Butcher; bl GPL/Marijke Heuff 144tl GPL/Rachel White; br GPL/Sunniva Harte 145tl GPL/Ron Sutherland; tr PD; br GPL/John Glover 146c IH 148tr GPL/Ron Sutherland; bl GPL/Clay Perry

149tr LC; bl IH 150 all images CN 151 all images LC 152tr GPL/Brian Carter; bl IH 153tr GPL/John Neubauer; bl WO 154tr GPL/Kathy Collins; bl IH 155tr JP; bl GPL/ Ellen Rooney 156tr GPL/John Glover; bl GPL/Howard Rice 157tr GPL/Marianne Majerus; br GPL/ Kathy Collins 158tc GPL/Steven Wooster; bl GPL/John Glover; br LC 159tl PH; br PD 160tr GPL/Howard Rice; bl LC 161tr COR; bl LC 162bl CN 163tl GPL/CN; br GPL/ Ron Sutherland 165tr GPL/Steven Wooster; bl GPL/Juliet Greene 166tr CN; bl GPL/Juliet Greene 167tl GPL/Ron Sutherland; bl IH; br LR 168tr WO/JY; c PD; bl GPL/ Linda Burgess 169tl WO/JY; br CN 170 all images CN 171tr WO; bl PD; br GPL/Howard Rice 172tr GPL/Tommy Candler; bl GPL/John Glover 173tr GPL/Ron Sutherland; bc PH 174–5 all images CN 176c LR 178tl SOM; tc WO/JY; tr GB 179tl HSC; tc WO/JY; tr PH 180tl JP; tc WO/JY; tr TE 181tl JP; tc JP; tr GPL/Lamontagne 182tl WO/JY; tc JY; tr WO 183tl GB; tc WO/JY; tr TE 184tl TE; tc TE; tr WO/JY 185 all images TE 186tl WO/JY; tc WO/ JY; tr TE 187tl GPL/Jacqui Hurst; tc WO/JY; tr WO/JY 188tl TE; tc TE; tr GB 189tl TE; tc TE; tr PH 190tl WO/JY; tc SOM; tr TE 191tl WO; tc JP; tr WO/JY 192tl HSC; tc GPL/ Lamontagne; tr HSC 193tl CN; tc SOM; tr GB 194tl JP; tc APL/ Corbis/Eric Crichton; tr WO/JY 195tl GPL/Brian Carter; tc SOM; tr WO/JY 196tl WO; tc WO/JY; tr DF 197tl SOM; tc SOM; tr JP 198tl JC; tc SOM; tr PH 199tl Photo Essentials; tc CN; tr JC 200tl GB; tc TE; tr TE 201tl HSC; tc SOM; tr JP 202tl GB; tc TE; tr WO/JY 203tl HA; tc DF; tr JP 204tl JP; tc PH; tr JP 205tl WO/JY; tc WO/JY; tr AZ/Anthony Cooper 206tl JC; tc GB; tr SOM 207tl WO; tc TE; tr SOM 208tl Holt Studios Inter-national/Primrose Peacock; tc TR; tr TE 209tl HSC; tc GPL/Brian Carter; tr WO/JY 210tl HSC; tc JP; tr WO 211tl HSC; tc SOM; tr SOM 212tl SOM; tc GB; tr WO/JY 213tl CN; tc AZ/Geoff Kidd; tr WO/JY 214tl WO/JY; tc WO/JY; tr CN 215tl HSC; tc TE; tr GB 216tl SM; tc WO/JY; tr TE 217tl SM; tc LR; tr PH 218tl LR; tc SM; tr DW 219tl GPL/Howard Rice; tc JY; tr JY 220tl WO/JY; tc DF; tr TE 221tl GPL/ Lamontagne; tc LR; tr Pam Pierce 222tl DW; tc TE; tr JC 223tl JC; tc TR; tr DF 224tl TE; tc TE; tr JC 225tl TE; tc JC; tr PH 226tl TE;

tc Michael Dirr; tr SM 227tl JC; tc GPL/Ron Sutherland; tr Photo Essentials 228tl DW; tc TR; tl Michael Dirr 229tl WO/JY; tc JC; tr JC 230tl John J. Smith; tc TE; tr PH 231tl LR; tc TE; tr PH 232tl JP; tc TR; tr WO/JY 233 all images TR 234tl APL/Corbis/Tania Midgley; tc GPL/Brian Carter; tr WO/JY 235tl Michael Dirr; tc PH; tr PH 236tl TR; tc Anita Sabarese; tl Rodale Stock Images 237tl TR; tc TE; tr WO/JY 238tl PH; tc CN; tr TR 239tl SM; tc JC; tr TE 240tl TR; tc PH; tr WO/JY 241tl TR; tc PH; tr WO/JY 242tl WO/JY; tc SM; tr JC 243tl TR; tc BCL/Eric Crichton; tr WO 244tl TR; tc TE; tr JC 245tl PH; tc WO/JY; tl PH 246tl TE; tc TE; tr DF 247tl GPL/Janet Sorrell; tc PH; tr WO/JY 248tl TE; tc WO/ JY; tr TE 249tl TE; tc PH; tr JC 250tl JY; tc PH; tr TE 251tl LR; tc LR; tr APL/Corbis/Roger Tidman 252tl APL/Corbis/Eric and David Hosking; tc GPL/Didier Willery; tr LR; 253tl GPL/Howard Rice; tc GPL/JP; tr WO 254tl LR; tc GPL/ Mel Watson; tr APL/Corbis/Eric Crichton 255tl PH; tc TR; tr LR 256tl LR; tc GPL/Howard Rice; tr JY 257tl GB; tc JY; tr HSC 258tl Holt Studios International/Nigel Cattlin; tc TE; tr LR 259tl GPL/ Howard Rice; tc DF; tr TE 260tl HSC; tc APL/Corbis/Dave Houser; tr TE 261tl GPL/Christopher Gallagher; tc APL/Corbis/Douglas Peebles; tr GB 262tl LR; tc GPL/ Christi Carter; tr LR 263tl GPL/ Christi Carter; tc GPL; tr HSC 264tl GB; tc GB; tr GPL/J. S. Sira 265tl HSC; tc APL/Corbis/Michael Boys; tr PH 266tl GB; tc HSC; tr TE 267tl TE; tc JP/Joanne Pavia; tr LR 268tl BCL/Eric Crichton; tc PH; tr LR 269tl HSC; tc GPL/Lamontagne; tr GPL/Ron Evans 270tl TE; tc WO/ JY; tr DF 271tl HSC; tc TE; tr HSC 272tl WO; tc GB; tr LR 273tl TE; tc GB; tr WO/JY 274tl HSC; tc Holt Studios International/Nigel Cattlin; tr PH 275tl CN; tc WO/JY; tr TE.

Illustrations by Artville, Anne Bowman, Tony Britt-Lewis, Helen Halliday, Angela Lober (pages xxx, xx), David Mackay, Stuart McVicar, Oliver Rennert, Edwina Riddell, Barbara Rodanska, Jan Smith, Kathie Smith, Sharif Tarabay.

The publishers wish to thank Dean Jennings, for editorial assistance; Bronwyn Sweeney, for proofreading; and Tonia Johanson, for indexing.